Reflecting God's Presence

A Companion on the Journey

Edited by Bill Firman FSC

*'Make it a habit
to think often
of the holy presence
of God.'*

Saint John Baptist de La Salle

**Lasallian
District of Australia, New Zealand
and Papua New Guinea**

Published in 2008/2017 by

David Lovell Publishing

PO Box 44 Kew East VIC 3102

tel +61 3 9859 0000

publisher@davidlovellpublishing.com

in association with

The Lasallian District of Australia

New Zealand & Papua New Guinea

26 Meredith St Bankstown NSW 2200 Australia

tel +61 32 9795 6400 fax +61 2 9795 6499

www.delasalle.org.au

© copyright this collection Bill Firman fsc 2008

© copyright individual authors for their contributions 2008

This book is copyright. Apart from any fair dealing or the purpose of private study, research, criticism or review, as permitted under the Copyright Act, no part may be reproduced by any person without written permission. Inquiries should be addressed to the publisher.

Design and production by David Lovell Publishing
Cover photo: Andrejs Zemdega
Typeset in 10/14 Hoefler Text
This edition printed through Ingram Spark

National Library of Australia card number
& ISBN 978 1 86355 170 0

Foreword

Br Ambrose Payne FSC AM AO

The final days that lead up to the conclusion of 'schooling' – as we tend to think about pre-primary, primary and secondary education – tend to be jammed full of final bits and pieces of wisdom. Most have neither the time nor certainly the opportunity to reflect quietly, on one's own, about all that is being said. *Reflecting God's Presence* addresses that fact.

Among the many 'last words', it is almost certain that there will be some expression of the hope and the encouragement to reach one's potential. Departing from that point provides the opportunity to address the challenges of developing further on the school experience. Spiritual, intellectual, physical, aspirational, attitudinal and values-oriented avenues of gaining a sense of fulfilment, happiness and self-worth are among the dimensions that those who worry about us most wish for us as we begin the next phase of our journey. They pray that we achieve our potential – that's all that they expect and dream for us.

To achieve one's potential calls for creativity. *Reflecting God's Presence* demonstrates the achievement of potential in the way we learn best.

Here is a series of stories about people. There is one for every day of the year. There is an historical account that links the day with real people in real time who have done what no one expected of them. There is a 'thought for each day' that challenges the status quo of our everyday ordinariness or sometimes lets us simply relax in the knowledge that the best effort is the essential one for our lives. There is what most of us like most – a story. Sometimes it is historical. More often it is allegorical, just like those favourite fables of tortoises and hares about which we now smile. And there is a daily prayer free of any coercion and geared to who and what we are.

And what does this have to do with creativity? Creativity unlocks our potential. Some of us remember Edward de Bono and coloured hats as a way of unlocking what seemed ordinary and unavoidable. Others can recall PMI – plusses, minuses and interesting. All these 'methods' are tools. Tools are what we need to gear creativity into action. *Reflecting God's Presence* is such a tool. The textbooks on creativity list many ways to release the genie from the bottle: reward curiosity, build motivation, encourage confidence and a willingness to take risks, focus on mastery and self competition, provide balance, teach by example. In *Reflecting God's Presence* there is a simple, unpressured, timely opportunity to do just that. Once a day, in the quiet of one's own time, it's possible to allow the world of ordinary people like ourselves to be brightened by what has been shown can be.

Those who care most about you want to make this volume available as a small gift just for you. Take it with you as a continuing reminder that you matter and that someone really cares. Our hopes go with you for the very best of futures.

Introduction

This book was originally produced as a gift to graduating students coming to the end of their schooling. When students graduate from school, good teachers do not stand back and say, 'That is another group finished, educated and on their way.' No, there is something profoundly moving in educating young people to be ready for what lies ahead after schooling. Graduating students may physically leave their school but the values learned at school go with them for the rest of their lives.

In that sense, I like to use the words of Horace, the classic Roman poet who died just before Jesus was born, who wrote: *'Exegi monumentum aere perennius'* ('I have built a monument more lasting than bronze'). Graduated students do not pass through the school gates again as growing boys or girls, but, to their school, they are *Monumentum aere perennius*, more precious than bronze, individual persons who are living monuments or witnesses to the education they received.

Whoever receives this book is invited to use it to reflect quietly each day on its content and to continue the journey of life with an increasing awareness of the presence of God. For some it may even help them discover that they are more 'religious' than they think, not in the sense of being pious but by being a good person trying to lead a decent life, ready to help one's neighbour when the need arises. Perhaps this book may also be a useful resource book for educators looking for ideas, quotations and reflections to be used as a starting point for a lesson or homily.

There are some blank pages at the back with the heading *Mirabile dictu*. This Latin phrase translates as 'Wonderful to say'. It is a space for readers to write in their own thoughts, or passages they come across, that they wish to remember.

Reflecting God's Presence has been produced by the principal and staff of De La Salle College, Malvern, one of the oldest schools of the De La Salle Brothers in the District of Australia, New Zealand and Papua New Guinea. William M. Thackeray wrote that 'The world is a looking glass and gives back to every person the reflection of one's face'. We are pleased to share our reflections with all fellow travellers on life's journey.

In offering you this reflective book, we would hope you might find some empathy with Anna Quindlen who said:

> *I read and walked for miles at night along the beach, writing bad verse and searching endlessly for someone wonderful who would step out of the darkness and change my life. It never crossed my mind that that person could be me.*

God is present with us. Now that really should give us confidence for our personal journeys.

Br Bill Firman FSC
Editor

Reflecting
God's
Presence

Reflecting God's Presence

Some significant events on this day

Year	Event
45 BC	New Year's Day is celebrated for the first time in history as the Julian calendar is implemented.
1808	The importation of slaves into the USA is banned. Illegal trade continued.
1934	A Law for the *Prevention of Genetically Diseased Offspring* is passed in Nazi Germany, allowing for forced sterilisation.
1999	A single currency, the Euro, is introduced for 11 European countries. On 1 January 2002, Euro banknotes and coins entered circulation.

Key thought for today

'Those who neglect the present moment, throw away all they have.'
— Johann von Schiller

Reflection

By Gemma Austin. I offer you these thoughts for the beginning of this New Year.

Welcoming a New Year

A new year stands on my doorstep,
ready to enter my life's journey.
Something in me welcomes this visitor:
the hope of bountiful blessings,
the joy of a new beginning,
the freshness of unclaimed surprises.

Something in me rebuffs this visitor:
the unnamed events of future days,
the wisdom needed to walk love well,
the demands of giving away and growing.

A new year stands on my doorstep,

with fragile caution I move
to open the door for its entrance.
My heart leaps with surprise,
joy jumps in my eyes,
for there beside this brand new year
stands my God with outstretched hand!

God smiles and gently asks of me:
Can we walk this year together?
And I, so overwhelmed with goodness,
can barely whisper my reply:

Welcome in!

Prayer

Lord, help me to welcome you more into my life during this coming year.

Some significant events on this day

Year   Event

1860   At the Academy of Sciences in Paris, scientists claim to have discovered a new planet called Vulcan. The claim was never substantiated but the name was utilised in the world of science fiction in productions such as *Star Trek*.

1959   The Russian spacecraft *Luna 1*, launched by the USSR towards the moon, becomes the first artificial object to escape the gravitational pull of the earth.

1969   South African surgeon Christian Barnard performs the second successful heart transplant operation. The first patient had lived only 18 days but this second lived a further 19 months. Heart transplants became standard surgery from this time.

Key thought for today

Do not walk through time without leaving worthy evidence of your passage.
— Pope John XXIII

Reflection

By Gemma Austin

Our life is a journey. We are always 'on the road'. Each time January greets us, we have an opportunity to pause, to see where we have been, to notice how far we have come, and to ponder how that journey has been for us. Each year is also a time to rethink our vision, to take stock of our resources, and to refresh our dreams as we set out once more on the journey that is ours.

No two Januarys are ever the same: the New Year is always unique. The beginning of the New Year is a good time to reflect on one's life. We gain wisdom by looking at the places of our hearts where we have travelled during the past year. As we look back over the journey, it is helpful to identify the places that blessed us, affirmed us, enlivened us and enriched us. We also need to reflect on the situations that challenged us and tested us.

When we have looked over our past travels, it is a good time to take stock of our present situation. What are our inner resources? Do we need to refuel, to restore our energies? Are we prepared to continue on the road? Have our spiritual suitcases worn thin with all the clutter we've stuffed into them along the way? What kind of nourishment will we provide for ourselves as we travel?

Prayer

God of this New Year, we are walking into mystery. We face the future, not knowing what the days and months will bring to us or how we will respond. Be love in us as we journey. May we welcome all who come our way. Deepen our faith to see all of life through your eyes. Fill us with hope and an abiding trust that you dwell in us amidst all our joys and sorrows. Thank you for the gift of being able to rise each day with the assurance of you walking through the day with us. God of this New Year, we praise you. Amen.

Reflecting God's Presence

Some significant events on this day

Year   Event

1924   English explorer Howard Carter discovers the sarcophagus of the ancient Egyptian ruler, Tutankhamun, in the Valley of the Kings near Luxor.

1969   Michael Schumacher, who later became a record-breaking world champion car race driver, is born.

1988   Margaret Thatcher, the first female prime minister in European history, becomes the longest serving British prime minister of the twentieth century.

2000   The last daily *Peanuts* comic strip, which began on 2 October 1950, is published on this day, the day after the death of its creator Charles Schultz.

Key thought for today

The greatest tragedy to befall a person is to have sight but lack vision.
— Helen Keller

Reflection

By Br Bill Firman

H.G. Wells wrote a novel called *The Country of the Blind*. In it he poignantly describes the experiences of a traveller with ordinary vision who finds himself in a land where all the inhabitants are blind. It is hard to grasp what must be the feeling of deprivation of people who are blind, who cannot see the world around them. Helen Keller said it is a greater tragedy to have sight but not real vision.

Do we look around us to see the needs of others or do we suffer from a selfish passivity, a myopic unconcern for what can be done to help others? If we do not see the needs of others, we have still a lot to learn about becoming unselfish. Of course we can see need and think the problem is too big for us to do anything about it.

It is true we cannot solve the great problems of the world on our own, but we can unite our efforts to those of others. I like the words of Cardinal Newman:

    You are right, we cannot do everything at once but we can do something at once.

We need to have clear vision – or at least to dream dreams of what we want to achieve. Malcolm S. Forbes said:

    When you cease to dream you cease to live.

If we lose our vision for the future, if we lose hope of achieving a goal, then life loses meaning. When we cease to be fired up with hopes and dreams, we are entering the valley of the blind.

Prayer

Lord, help me to see, to dream and to do.

Reflecting God's Presence

Some significant events on this day

Year   Event

1643   Birthday of Sir Isaac Newton, scientist and philosopher.

1809   Birthday of Louis Braille, teacher of the blind, inventor of Braille.

1959   The Russian *Luna 1* becomes the first spacecraft to reach the vicinity of the moon.

Key thought for today

Genius is one per cent inspiration and ninety-nine per cent perspiration.
— Thomas Edison

Reflection

By Murray Enniss

One Day at a Time

There are two days in every week about which we should not worry; two days which should be kept free from fear and apprehension.

One of these days is Yesterday, with its mistakes and cares, its faults and blunders, its aches and pains. Yesterday has passed forever beyond our control. All the money in the world cannot bring back yesterday. We cannot undo a single act we performed, we cannot erase a single word – Yesterday is gone

The other day we should not worry about is Tomorrow, with its possible burdens, its large promise and poor performance. Tomorrow is also beyond our immediate control. Tomorrow's sun will rise, either in splendour or behind a mask of clouds – but it will rise. Until it does, we have no stake in Tomorrow, for it is yet unborn.

This leaves only one day – Today! Anyone can fight the battle of just one day. It is only when you and I have the burden of those two awful eternities – Yesterday and Tomorrow – that we break down.

It is not the experiences of Today that drives people mad. It is the remorse or bitterness for something which happened Yesterday or the dread of what Tomorrow may bring.

Let us, therefore, live but one day at a time.

(Author unknown)

Prayer

God, help me to greet each day cheerfully and to live this day as well as I can. I give thanks for what has passed and look forward with faith and hope to what is to come. God, I desire to live this day with love for you, my family and my friends. Help me to live one day at a time. Amen.

Reflecting God's Presence

Some significant events on this day

Year   Event

1896   The discovery of X-ray radiation by Wilhelm Roentgen is announced.

1948   The first colour newsreel is shown by Warner Brothers.

1993   The oil-tanker *MV Braer* runs aground on the coast of the Shetland Islands, north of Scotland, spilling 84,700 tons of oil.

Key thought for today

Aspire not to have more but to be more.
— Archbishop Oscar Romero

Reflection

By Br Bill Firman

I still recall clearly, as a senior student at De La Salle College, reflecting on the parable of the talents. It led me to resolve that I should give God some return on the talents I had received. Sobering gospel words, I thought:

'To whom much is given, much is expected.'

I knew I had been given much in life. Was I really 'called' to the celibate life of a Brother? Girls were very attractive; but so was the ideal of making a life by being a brother to all whom I would meet. Even more important was my love for home and family, but the message of that parable was powerful. So it was that I began the journey as a De La Salle Brother with the aspiration to give my talents in vowing 'to go wherever I may be sent or to do whatever may be required of me' (from the vow formula of the De La Salle Brothers).

About that time, I also read a small book which began with a sentence that I have never forgotten: 'The road that stretches before a man tests the strength of his heart long before it tests the strength of his legs.' That sentence seemed to me to be profound then and the passing of time has not lessened its significance.

Where that road would lead me, I did not really know. Very early I learned that happiness was not the same as a life of ease and comfort. There is so much in life that is really a test of our inner strength, of the determination of our minds, of the resolution of our wills, of the faith and hope in our hearts. In the era of my childhood, when more stress was placed on the value of asceticism, on the place of penance and sacrifice in the Christian way of life, I think we were perhaps more aware of the need to develop strength of mind and heart.

My mother, not sure that I knew what I was doing when I decided to be a Brother, said to me: 'Promise me if you are not happy you will come home.' It has never come to that. As a Brother, it has been my special opportunity to use my talents, as well as I can, to help many young people learn to aspire to *be* more rather than to have more. I regard my life as a genuine privilege.

Prayer

God, help me to be more rather than have more, to use my talents well rather than just use them for my own pleasure. Amen.

Some significant events on this day

Year   Event

        The Epiphany, the twelfth day of Christmas, is commemorated as the day of the visit of the Magi (the three wise men) to the infant Jesus.

1838   The first electric telegraph is successfully tested by Samuel Morse.

1942   Pan American Airlines becomes the first commercial airline to have a flight around the world.

Key thought for today

The person who is wise is not the one who is wise in words but the one who is wise in deeds.
   — Pope Saint Gregory I

Reflection

By Br Bill Firman: I invite you to reflect on these words by Bishop Geoffrey Robinson on healthy love.

> *There are three conditions for healthy love. First, the love must give people and things the freedom to grow. It must not be possessive love that suffocates, the conditional love that manipulates, the selfish love that seeks only its own good, or the mistaken love that denies one's deepest good. Love is not an ability but a capacity, for it consists in creating space in which people and things are free to grow. If love does not create the freedom to grow, it is not true love.*

> *Second, if it is to give meaning and energy, the love must in some manner be returned. Flowers return our love just be being beautiful, even though they will wither and die ... Persons are by far the most satisfying, for no object or activity can return love in the way they can, but they are also the most dangerous, for no object or activity can hurt in the way they can.*

> *Third, there must be some balance and proportion among the things we love. If the young person ... spent so much time practising the violin that there was no time left over for people, the love would have become an obsession that would suffocate rather than allow love to grow.*

> *There are many paradoxes in love. If we want to see our love returned, we should always give without thought of return. Love is not bought or sold; it is always gift. It is fallen into rather than planned. The more we love a person, or even a thing, the more we must make ourselves vulnerable to be hurt by that person or thing. And yet, despite these paradoxes, it is love alone that gives meaning to our lives.*

Jesus gave us the commandment to love God and to love our neighbour. Love is our deepest longing. Satisfy that longing and life has meaning.

Prayer

The wisdom of the Christian is to love both in heart and in deed. Help me to love unselfishly so that my love creates the freedom to grow. Amen.

Reflecting God's Presence

Some significant events on this day

Year   Event

1953   US President Harry Truman announces the development of a hydrogen bomb one thousand times more powerful than the existing atom bombs.

1980   Indira Gandhi is re-elected Prime Minister of India in a landslide victory three years after she had been voted out of office.

1999   The impeachment trial of US President Bill Clinton begins.

Key thought for today

When one door closes, another door opens; but we often look so long and so regretfully upon the closed door that we do not see the ones which open for us.

— Alexander Graham Bell

Reflection

By Br Bill Firman

My father believed strongly in the attitude expressed in the 17th century Jesuit dictum:

The education of youth is the renewal of the world.

Having received little formal education himself, my father was determined that his children would receive a 'good education' and the opportunities that he believed would follow from that. A kindred sentiment was expressed more graphically just a few years ago by Dr Jonathon Sacks, Chief Rabbi of the Hebrew Congregations of the Commonwealth, when speaking about the importance of religious education in schools. He said: 'You defend a country by armies. But you defend a civilisation by schools.' When President George W. Bush took the USA to war in Iraq for the second time, many people asked the question: 'Can you attack another country without direct provocation and still be civilised?'

A good upbringing teaches us to think clearly about what we are doing and why. In recent years, the debate over the use of drugs in sport has reached new levels. The all too frequent examples of sportspersons failing to act honourably is very disappointing. Where is their vision of who they are as role models and heroes? Anyone privileged to be an elite athlete should not want to win by using drugs: better to lose honourably than to 'win' by cheating. If we cheat, we only appear to have won. We may even gain the material rewards of winning - but if we have lost our integrity, we have lost part of ourselves.

An honourable person acts with consideration and determination to preserve his or her integrity. Every good person is armed with a strong sense of justice. As St Paul reminds us: 'Nothing can harm a person of justice.' Further, a good education teaches us to be generous and giving. Teilhard de Chardin wrote:

The most satisfying thing in life is to have been able to give a large part of oneself to others.

Prayer

Let me never hesitate to close the door on cheating but rather to open the door to a life of integrity and generous service of others. Amen.

Some significant events on this day

Year   Event

1935   Birthday of Elvis Presley.
1958   Bobby Fischer, aged 14, wins the US Chess Championship.
1961   The French people vote to give Algeria its independence.
1994   Russian cosmonaut Valeri Polyakov begins his record-breaking time in space on the *Mir* space station. He stayed 437 days to 22 March 1995.

Key thought for today

Your vision will become clear only when you look into your heart. Who looks outside, dreams. Who looks inside, awakens.
— Carl Jung

Reflection

By Maria Zanelli: I came across this short story, called 'A Vision for the Future', which I would like to offer for reflection.

The old Indian chief was dying. His face was lined with life lived, his eyes filled with peace and patient waiting. Summoning his three sons, he spoke of his final wish.

'When I die, one of you must succeed me as the leader of our tribe. I want each of you to climb our holy mountain and bring back something of beauty. The one whose gift is the most outstanding will succeed me.'

The sons departed, following the path deep into the forest, travelling with the height of tall trees, and finally climbing the mountain, old and stone-solid. After some days, they returned from their travels. The first brought his father a flower from the summit, rare, beautiful and delicate, with a preciousness that called for great care. The second son brought a stone, colourful, smooth and round, polished by rain and sandy winds. The third son's hand was empty.

He said, 'Father, I have brought nothing back to show you. As I stood at the peak of our holy mountain, I saw on the other side, through the cleft and out into sunlight, a beautiful land filled with green pastures and a crystal lake. I breathed the mist and caught in my eyes the glisten of the coming sun. And I had a vision of where our tribe could go for a better life. I was so overwhelmed by what I saw and by what I was thinking that I returned with nothing.'

And the father replied, 'You shall be our tribe's new leader, for you have brought back the most precious gift of all – the gift of vision for a better future.'

(From Stories and Parables for Preachers and Teachers by P. Wharton)

Prayer

Lord, give us your gift of hope that we may see in the adventure of living, not only the reality of the present, but also the future to which you call us. Amen.

Reflecting God's Presence

9 JANUARY

Some significant events on this day

Year	Event
1349	The Jewish population of Basel, Switzerland, believed to be the cause of Bubonic plague, is rounded up and incinerated on an island.
1768	Philip Astley stages the first modern circus in London, with shows of acrobatic riding in a round ring, utilising centrifugal force for balance.
1901	A patent is submitted by Frank Hornby of Liverpool for his invention 'Mechanics made Easy', soon to be called Meccano.

Key thought for today

Everything is funny as long as it happens to somebody else.
— Will Rogers

Reflection

By Br Bill Firman: I like this story by Bruce Barton which I have modified a little.

There are two seas in the Holy Land. One is fresh, and fish are in it. Trees spread their branches over it, and stretch out their thirsty roots to sip its healing waters. Along the shores the children play, as children played when Christ was there. He loved it. He could look across its silver surface when he spoke his parables. And on a rolling plain, not far away, he fed five thousand people.

The River Jordan makes this sea, with the sparkling water from the hills. People build their houses near it and birds build their nests, and every kind of life is happier, because the sea is there.

The River Jordan also flows into another sea. Here there is no splash of fish, no children's laughter, no song of birds. Travellers choose another road unless they are on urgent business. The air hangs heavily over its waters, and neither people nor animals will drink from it.

What makes the difference in these neighbouring seas? Not the River Jordan. It empties its water into both. Not the soil in which they lie, not the country about them.

This is the difference. The Sea of Galilee receives but does not keep the water from the Jordan. For every drop that flows into it another drop flows out. The other sea is shrewder, hoarding its income jealously. It will not be tempted into any generous giving. Every drop it gets it keeps.

The Sea of Galilee gives and lives. The other gives nothing. It is named the Dead Sea. There are two seas in the Holy Land – and there are two kinds of people in the world!

Prayer

Let me be alive and giving, rather than dead and unforgiving. Amen.

Some significant events on this day

Year	Event
1863	The initial section of the world's first underground passenger railway is opened in London.
1946	Fifty-one nations are represented at the first General Assembly of the United Nations, held in London.
1969	After 147 years of production, the last edition of the US magazine *The Saturday Evening Post* is published.

Key thought for today

The final heartbeat for the Christian is not the mysterious conclusion to a meaningless existence. It is rather the grand beginning to a life that will never end.
— James Dobson

Reflection

By Br Bill Firman

Almost every year on this date, I am enjoying a holiday at a place called Crowdy Head, about four hours north of Sydney on the NSW coast. It is an annual event for several De La Salle Brothers and two Jesuit priests to form a temporary community at this beautiful location surrounded by the unspoiled beaches of a national park.

Each evening one of the Jesuits, Peter or Chris, celebrates the Eucharist in the house. On this date it is always Chris who is principal celebrant as we remember his mother, Doreen, who died on this day in 1994. Doreen lived a long and full life, a very good woman whose natural passing is described well by the pithy, Italian proverb:

> *A good death does honour to a whole life.*

Chris also offers Mass for the intentions of two people close to me who also died on this day: my niece Jane and her mother Pat. Jane had just finished Year 12 at Sacré Coeur when she was killed in a car accident along with another 18-year-old, Gerard. Poignantly, we buried Jane, a really vibrant, sparky kid, very popular with her peers, quick-witted and not intimidated by adults, from St Roch's on the Saturday before her Year 12 results came out. The two who were killed were passengers in a car carrying four young people who had been to a coffee shop. A woman doctor, well above the .05 blood-alcohol limit, had ploughed into the side of the young people's car, knocking them into a ditch. Pat, Jane's mother, died seven year's later, a 'victim' of breast cancer yet still full of courage, dignity and a great love of her family, a teacher to the very last.

The deaths of those near to us are never easy to accept. We grieve for those who died and also for ourselves in our loss. We pray at anniversaries for those who died – and again for ourselves that we may be as ready as we can be when our time comes.

Prayer

Lord, I know that I must one day face death myself. Let me live this gift of life as well as I can, for as long as I have it, and be ready to pass to the next life when my time comes. Amen.

Reflecting God's Presence

Some significant events on this day

Year   Event

1908   A prominent young lawyer, Mohandas Gandhi (later called Mahatma), is jailed in South Africa for refusing to register as an Asian.

1922   Frederick Banting and Charles Best use insulin for the first time to treat diabetes in a human patient.

1935   Amelia Earhart becomes the first woman to fly solo from Hawaii to California.

Key thought for today

There is sufficiency in the world for human need but not for human greed.
— Mahatma Gandhi

Reflection

By Br Quentin O'Halloran

When we have really done our best and something happens to mar our effort, we know the feeling of discouragement that occurs. I find that I spark up if I remember an incident in the life of Bertel Thorvaldsen, the famous Danish sculptor.

Having just finished a clay figure of Christ with arms extended and face looking upwards to heaven, he was delighted with his triumphant, conquering creation. Over the next 24 hours, fog and mist seeped into his waterside studio, causing the clay to slacken. He was disappointed and frustrated to see how the head and arms had dropped until he realised his Christ figure now looked down with love and compassion. The statue, 'Come Unto Me', has become world famous.

Sometimes, seeming failure in our lives may mean improvement, even success.

Prayer

(By Margaret McPhee)

Creativity

Regardless of what our occupation is,
We are all creative beings.
We often associate creativity with the arts:
Music, theatre, visual arts and literature.
We need to be mindful that we all create
Every day,
Whether it is creating a meal,
Creating an occasion for friends or family to meet,
Creating a lesson plan,
Creating a piece of art,
Creating a relationship,
Creating business opportunities.
May we continue to enjoy our own creations
And appreciate and value the creations of others.

12 JANUARY

Reflecting God's Presence

Some significant events on this day

Year   Event

1915   The US House of Representatives rejects a proposal to give women the right to vote.

1965   In an experiment, scientists burn up a nuclear rocket in Nevada, causing a radioactive cloud over Los Angeles.

1991   An Act of the US Congress is passed authorising the use of military force to drive Iraq out of Kuwait.

Key thought for today

The Lord does not look at the things we look at. We look at the outward appearance, but the Lord looks at the heart.
    —1 Samuel 16:7

Reflection

By Paul Maxted

> Neo: 'This ... this isn't real?'
>
> Morpheus: 'What is real? How do you define real? If you're talking about what you can feel, what you can smell, what you can taste and see, then real is simply electrical signals interpreted by your brain.'

The 1999 film *The Matrix* depicts a world that is orchestrated in minute detail by an artificial intelligence computer program. What appears real is not. It seems that the writers of the film had Descartes' First Meditation in mind, the hypothesis that what we perceive as the world might be a comprehensive illusion, perhaps created by a 'malicious demon'. The senses have been known to lie, since when we are dreaming we often do not realise that we are dreaming.

Like Neo's artificial dream world, it's easy to have all the appearances of being a godly person, but be far from God. You can surround yourself with 'Christian' things – fish emblems on your car, perhaps a Christian book or Bible on the coffee table. You might belong to the local parish church, surround yourself with Christian friends and play Christian music. It all looks very Christian. But only God and you know the truth. Sometimes it's all a disguise; it looks good on the outside but it's artificial.

God doesn't care how good we look on the outside. He cares what's in our hearts. When God sent Samuel to David's family to anoint a new king, Samuel checked out David's tall, strong and handsome brothers, but rejected them all for the youngest, David. When God looks into your heart, will he find a real desire to please him – a true love for God and your neighbour?

Prayer

Lord, I want to be real: a genuine Christ-follower. I want to be a son who has an intimate relationship with his heavenly Father and real love for others, not just someone who looks good. Don't let me be content with simply letting the world think I'm doing okay. Help me walk the walk, living my life before you in truth. Amen. (Janet Ruben)

Reflecting God's Presence

Some significant events on this day

Year	Event
1930	The *Mickey Mouse* comic strip makes its first appearance.
1992	Japan apologises for having forced up to 200,000 Korean women, some as young as 11, into sexual slavery as 'comfort women' during World War II.
2001	An earthquake in El Salvador kills more than 800 people.

Key thought for today

Grown up, and that is a terribly hard thing to do. It is much easier to skip it and go from one childhood to another.

— F. Scott Fitzgerald

Reflection

By Br Bill Firman

Every young person rightly aspires to become an independent, responsible adult, free to make their own decisions. With freedom comes responsibility. Young people will demand freedom but may not be ready to accept the corresponding responsibility. Parents understandably may have many fears and be reluctant to loosen control.

Parents may worry that their child may meet unscrupulous people who will try to lead the child, as a potential client, into drug use. Parents may fear that their child could be picked up by a paedophile. What loving father does not worry that his beautiful daughter may be romantically attracted to some young 'stud' who is not really seeking a responsible relationship but sexual activity. So there is often some conflict in finding the right balance between wise, parental concern and emerging, youthful independence.

Diana Hutchinson once wrote in an excellent article called 'These Pilate Parents Days':

> *Nobody washed their hands from a discreet distance over our behaviour. Nobody left us quietly to work it out in our own way and in our own time. I am not saying that parents are right. Parents are never one hundred per cent right. We fulminated against their unfairness, their lack of understanding. And in bouncing against the immutable rock of parental authority we saw clearly the value and strength of our own opinion. Often they were shoddy and badly calculated. But at least we knew where we stood.*

It is important that young adult children learn what their parents think and feel. Young adults will be annoyed at times by parental restraint but ultimately will be aided in making their own decisions by knowing their parents' values and attitudes. If parents can trust their child, it is easier for them to lessen restraint. But if a deceitful young person, who says one thing and then does another, argues from the basis of being trusted, it is a farce. Deceit does not lead to trust, and without trust there will be no genuine co-responsibility.

Prayer

God, make me totally trustworthy so that it is easy for my parents to give me responsibility.

Some significant events on this day

Year   Event

1794   Elizabeth Bennett successfully gives birth by Caesarian section, the first US woman to do so. Her husband, a doctor, performed the operation without an anaesthetic.

1875   Birth of Albert Schweitzer, physician, missionary and musician.

1943   By flying from Miami to Morocco to meet Winston Churchill, Franklin D. Roosevelt becomes the first US President to travel by airplane while in office.

1990   *The Simpsons* first airs on television.

Key thought for today

A heavy guilt rests upon us for what the whites of all nations have done to the coloured peoples. When we do good to them, it is not benevolence – it is atonement.

— Albert Schweitzer

Reflection

By Br Bill Firman

In 1963, Pope John XXIII addressed the encyclical *Pacem in Terris* (Peace on Earth), not just to Catholics, but to 'all people of good will'. He discussed civil disobedience, responsibility to the poor and the protection of rights. He advocated the obligations to provide aid to developing countries and the rights of refugees. He deplored the stockpiling of armaments and demanded the arms race cease.

By 1963, after two world wars and the Korean War, the world was caught up in the tensions of the Cold War. The Cuban missile crisis in 1962 had brought the world to the brink of catastrophic confrontation. The Berlin Wall, a great symbol of division, had been erected, and spiralling defence budgets and a multi-billion dollar arms trade were major concerns. Colonialism had declined rapidly – a good thing as nations were granted self-determination – but the downside was often disorder and civil unrest in the countries that were granted independence. Racism in the USA and apartheid in South Africa had emerged as major sources of unrest, civil disobedience and even riots.

Each of these major problems has been addressed to varying degrees. Unfortunately, new problems such as terrorism have emerged. Clearly change is possible, thanks to the courage and vision of strong leaders such as Pope John XXIII, Martin Luther King Jr, Nelson Mandela and Mikhail Gorbachev.

Edmund Burke once said, 'For evil to triumph it is only necessary for good people to do nothing' – but great good can be achieved when good people do something!

Prayer

Let me live in accord with the truth stated by Pope John XXIII: 'It is not true that some human beings are by nature superior and others inferior. All people are equal in their natural dignity.'

Reflecting God's Presence

Some significant events on this day

Year   Event

1842   Birth of Mary MacKillop, the first Australian saint, in Brunswick Street, Fitzroy, less than seven years after William Faulkner sailed up the Yarra.

1929   Birth of Martin Luther King Jr in Atlanta, Georgia.

2001   The multi-lingual, free content website Wikipedia goes public. Written collaboratively, it now has over a million registered contributors.

Key thought for today

There where you are, you will find hope.
— Mary MacKillop

Reflection

By Karen Tillotson, Jacqueline Irwin, Mary Thomas, Carolyn Hamilton (De La Salle Mary MacKillop Enrichment Centre aides)

Mary MacKillop was born in Melbourne in 1842. She left home to work when she was 14, giving all the money she earned to her family. In 1860, Mary became a governess in Penola, SA, where she met Father Julian Tenison Woods who became her spiritual director. Together they opened Australia's first free Catholic school. Pupils were accepted whether their parents could afford to pay or not. Mary was a great teacher, and soon became very popular in the community. Several years later they founded a new congregation, the Josephite Sisters, whose mission was to found schools and orphanages. In 1869, Mary professed her final vows.

The Bishop of Adelaide attempted to control the congregation. He excommunicated Mary on the charge of disobedience but he later apologised for his actions and absolved Mary from excommunication. In 1873, Mary travelled to Europe, where she was well received in Rome. The Holy Father permitted the congregation to have a superior-general, who could move the sisters from house to house within the congregation and across diocesan borders. Mary MacKillop was elected to the office of superior-general in 1875. The congregation flourished even in the face of internal dissensions. Mary suffered from rheumatism for many years, but finally died from a stroke on 25 May 1909.

Pope John Paul II visited Australia in 1995 for the formal beatification of Mary – the first step towards her canonisation. Now her role in a second miracle must be proved for her to become Australia's first saint. We would like to share the story of Mary MacKillop, especially with graduating students. We hope that Mary's life will inspire others to live the Gospel and face life's challenges with faith, courage and determination. It is remarkable the impact that one good person can have on the lives of others.

Prayer

Most loving God, we thank you for the example of Blessed Mary MacKillop, who, in her living of the Gospel, witnessed to the human dignity of each person. She faced life's challenges with faith and courage. We pray, through her intercession, for our needs. May her holiness be acknowledged by the universal church. We make this prayer through Jesus, our Lord. Amen.

Some significant events on this day

Year   Event

1581   The English parliament outlaws Roman Catholicism

1969   In protest against the Soviet invasion of his country in 1968, Jan Palach, a Czech student, sets fire to himself, attracting world attention. He died three days later.

2003   The space shuttle *Columbia* takes off on a standard mission. Sixteen days later it disintegrated on re-entry.

Key thought for today

Non-violence is the answer to the crucial political and moral question of our time; the need for mankind to overcome oppression and violence without resorting to oppression and violence. Mankind must evolve for all human conflict a method that rejects revenge, aggression and retaliation. The foundation of such a method is love.

— Martin Luther King Jr

Reflection

By Patrick Jurd

Martin Luther King Day is celebrated in the United States of America close to his birthday on 15 January. What an extraordinary man! And he achieved all he did before he had reached the age of 40. As you read this, 40 will sound ancient, but believe me, it's not – once you've gone past that age!

There are plenty of people whose names are barely recorded in history that were the victims of racism. Martin Luther King's distinction is that he came along and led *at the right time*. His words and actions have inspired countless people, all around the world, including artists like Stevie Wonder, U2 and Ben Harper.

Here is a quote from his most famous speech delivered on 28 August 1963, which has come to be known by its frequent phrase 'I have a dream' (The words and an audio of the speech are available at http://www.americanrhetoric.com/speeches/mlkihaveadream.htm):

> *With this faith, we will be able to work together, to pray together, to struggle together, to go to jail together, to stand up for freedom together, knowing that we will be free one day.*

Our faith, our strength, are not tested when everything is going right. They are tested when things are going poorly.

Prayer

Dear Lord, may I have the grace and strength to use my gifts to help others, especially when the going gets tough, knowing that 'We must learn together as brothers or perish together as fools' (Martin Luther King Jr).

Reflecting God's Presence

Some significant events on this day

Year   Event

1773   Captain James Cook becomes the first explorer to cross the Antarctic circle.

1945   Soviet forces liberate the Polish city of Warsaw from the Nazis.

1991   The first Gulf War begins as Operation Desert Storm is launched.

Key thought for today

Little children ... I give you a new commandment. Love one another as I have loved you. By this everyone will know that you are my disciples.
     — Jesus in the Gospel of John, 13:33-35

Reflection

By Bernice Manuell

In his memoir of his life as a young man newly immigrated to New York City, the Irish-American writer Frank McCourt tells the story of his landlady Agnes Klein.

Agnes is a Catholic widow of a Jewish man she lost to the Nazis, and the mother of a boy named Michael who never grew up after what he saw in the concentration camps. In the book, Agnes follows her tenant around with her vodka and orange juice while she tells the sad story of her life and its many betrayals. Every couple of weeks, two nuns come in to help Agnes, Sister Mary Thomas and Sister Beatrice. Their job is to bathe Michael, wash his sheets, clean the apartment and watch over Agnes. Sister Mary Thomas spends most of her time pursuing the young McCourt, reminding him to go to Mass, telling him to leave New York University where he is in danger of losing his faith, and making plans secretly to baptise Michael. Sister Beatrice, on the other hand, 'is always so busy she rarely speaks'. Here is how McCourt describes this nun:

> *While Sister Mary Thomas tries to save my soul from atheistic communism, Sister Beatrice is giving Mrs Klein a bath or cleaning Michael. Sometimes when Sister Beatrice opens Michael's door the smell that drifts up the hall is enough to make you sick but that doesn't stop her from going in. She still washes him and changes him and changes his bedclothes and you can hear her humming hymns. If Mrs Klein has drunk too much and gets cranky over having to take a bath Sister Beatrice holds her, hums her hymns and strokes the little brown tufts on her skull until Mrs Klein is a child in her arms.*

This kind of love goes way beyond being a good neighbour. It is far more than honouring a neighbour's rights, respecting their space and doing a good deed now and then. Keeping Jesus' commandment to love is the tangible sign of abiding in Jesus and of his abiding in us.

Prayer

God, may an unpleasant exterior never prevent me from understanding and loving the precious person inside. Amen.

Some significant events on this day

Year	Event
1788	The first 736 convicts, transported from England, land in Botany Bay, establish the first Australian penal colony
1943	In the Warsaw Ghetto, the first uprising of the Jews against the Nazis takes place.
1977	Australia's worst rail disaster occurs at Granville, Sydney, killing 83 passengers and injuring 213.
2003	In Canberra, a firestorm destroys 491 homes, resulting in four deaths.

Key thought for today

The martyrs were bound, imprisoned, scourged, racked, burnt, rent, butchered – and they multiplied.
— Saint Augustine

Reflection

By Br Bill Firman

Today is the feast day of Brother Jaime Hilario. He was one of 97 De La Salle Brothers killed in Catalonia during the Spanish Civil War and the first to be recognised as martyr. But faced with martyrdom, the Brothers grew stronger. The description which follows is based on the summary on the website of the De La Salle Brothers Institute.

Manuel Barbal Cosan was born on 2 January 1898 in Enviny, a small town at the foot of the Pyrenees in northern Spain. Known for his serious nature, he was only 12 years old when, with the blessing of his devout and hardworking parents, he entered the minor seminary of the diocese of Urgel. He soon developed hearing problems and was advised to return home. Convinced that God was calling him, he was overjoyed in 1917 to learn that the Institute of the Brothers would accept him in the novitiate at Irun, where he was given the name, Jaime Hilario. After 16 years in various teaching assignments, his hearing problems forced him to abandon the classroom to work in the garden at the house of formation at San José, in Tarragona.

In July of 1936 he was at Mollerosa on his way to visit his family at Enviny when the civil war broke out. Recognised as a Brother, he was arrested and jailed. In December he was transferred to Tarragona and confined in a prison ship with several other Brothers. On 15 January 1937 he was given a summary trial. Though he could have been freed by claiming to be only a gardener, he insisted on his identity as a religious brother and thereby sealed his doom. He was brought to the cemetery known as the Mount of Olives on 18 January to face execution. His last words to his assailants were, 'To die for Christ, my young friends, is to live.' When two volleys failed to meet their mark, the soldiers dropped their rifles and fled in panic. The commander, shouting a gross insult, fired five shots at close range and the victim fell at his feet. He was beatified on April 29, 1990 and canonised on 21 November 1999.

Prayer

God, grant me the courage to stick to my convictions, as did Br Jaime, and so reach eternal life.

Reflecting God's Presence

Some significant events on this day

Year   Event

1966   Indira Gandhi is elected Prime Minister of India.

1995   Mary MacKillop is beatified by Pope John Paul II at Randwick Racecourse in Sydney, NSW.

2001   American twin girls, at the centre of an internet adoption scandal, are seized from a hotel in North Wales and taken into care.

Key thought for today

You cannot shake hands with a clenched fist.
— Indira Gandhi

Reflection

By Br Bill Firman

A disturbing incident of trading in babies occurred in 2001.

A California couple, Richard and Vickie Allen, paid an adoption agency US$8000 for the twin baby girls and had been caring for them for two months when the birth mother, Tranda Wecher, showed up and asked for a final farewell visit. Wecher then kidnapped her own babies and sold them again, this time to a Welsh couple, Ian and Judith Kilshaw, for $16,400 using the same adoption brokers. The Kilshaws knew that the twins, Belinda and Kimberly, were already adopted but were persuaded by Wecher that they were the preferred parents. The Kilshaws took them back to England. In a chaotic situation, local social services and the police eventually confronted the Kilshaws while a US television crew filmed the bizarre procedures. Eventually the legal judgement required the babies to be returned to the USA where they are now cared for by foster parents.

Foster care never offers the same possibility for stability as does adoption. So the baby twins were the real losers in this real-life manipulated scenario. Most people feel a justifiable revulsion to the notion of buying and selling babies. There are overtones of slavery in such human commerce – just as there is when girls from poor countries are 'imported' into developed countries to act as sex workers.

Human exploitation is an insult to the dignity of people. The greed of television networks trying to boost ratings by publicising such exploitation is also a concern. The fact that technology facilitates such exploitation is a modern problem which challenges us to take a stand on values and standards. There are some who promote the attitude that to exploit others is okay, but exploitation always leaves someone else hurting or even psychologically scarred.

Buying or selling human beings, no matter their age or circumstances, is a failure to respect their full human dignity. A just society is built on principles of respect for all.

Prayer

May I never exploit others but treat all people with profound respect.

20 JANUARY

Reflecting God's Presence

Some significant events on this day

Year   Event

1945   US President Franklin D. Roosevelt is inaugurated for an unprecedented fourth term; he died three months later.

1981   Minutes after Ronald Reagan is installed as US President, in place of President Jimmy Carter, Iran releases 52 American hostages.

1991   Islamic law is imposed nationwide by Sudan's government, worsening the civil war between the country's Muslim north and Christian south.

Key thought for today

The service we render for others is really the rent we pay for our room on this earth.
— Wilfred Grenfell

Reflection

By Br Denis Loft

I was in India with a group of Australian student 'Coolies' working on housing at 'Reaching the Unreached' (RTU). Our task was mostly digging foundations and carrying house blocks. Of the 12 families selected for housing, one caught our interest. A deserted mother, Lakshmi, had been left with two sons aged about ten and 14. The elder, Surab, was sent by her to work as a table cleaner in a restaurant at Madurai. He received 500 rupees a month. Two hundred was taken out for his food and keep, and the remaining 300 he sent home for the support of his mother and brother (300 rupees is about A$10.00). RTU, as well as organising the building of a house, also arranged that if Surab went to school Lakshmi would receive 300 rupees per month.

When we came to build the house we found out that the size of their parcel of land was not even enough for the regular size home of 5 metres by 5 metres. We attempted to purchase more land for them, but this was impractical, so we ended by adapting the house to be just two rooms, one for the boys and the other for the mother, which incorporated the kitchen and bathroom!

Their house was high up a hill, so it meant carrying block after block up this hill, and it seemed an unending task as all except Mitch Smith, could manage only one block at a time. We'd work for an hour making about seven or eight trips, then take a break with fluids and a rest. Lakshmi would just keep slowly plodding away. When we finished in the afternoon, she would keep going. We would notice another 20 or so blocks piled up the next morning when we arrived and she would already be there with another perched on her head.

Her persistence, calmness, and gratefulness won our hearts. She had little or nothing, but always remained gracious. We spent part of Christmas day sharing our joy with her and her boys.

Prayer

God, make us grateful for what we have, knowing many people are far more grateful for far less.

Reflecting God's Presence

Some significant events on this day

Year   Event

1911   The first Monte Carlo car rally takes place.
1976   Concorde, the first supersonic commercial jetliner, begins its service.
1977   Nearly all Vietnam War draft dodgers are pardoned by President Jimmy Carter.

Key thought for today

A true Christian may be almost defined as one who has a ruling sense of God's presence within him.
— John Henry Newman

Reflection

By Br Bill Firman: Cardinal John Henry Newman wrote these inspiring words, expressing his determination to be of service.

> *God has created me for some definite service.*
> *He has committed some work to me that he has not committed to another.*
> *I have my mission, which I may not even know in this life.*
> *I am a link in a chain, a bond of connection between persons.*
> *He has not created me for naught.*
> *I shall do this destined work.*
> *I shall be an angel of peace, a preacher of truth in my own place,*
> *using only myself as example.*
> *I will therefore trust him, whatever, wherever I am …*
> *I can never be thrown away –*
> *If I am in sickness, my sickness serves.*
> *If I am in sorrow, this is my task.*
> *God does nothing in vain.*
> *He knows what he is about.*
> *He may take away my friends;*
> *He may throw me among strangers;*
> *He may make me feel desolate, and my spirits sink;*
> *He may hide my future from me.*
> *Still, he knows what he is about.*
> *He has committed to me some work which he has not committed to another*
> *– I have my mission!*

Prayer

Cardinal Newman said that 'Nothing would be done at all, if a man waited until he could do it so well that no one could find fault with it.' Let me go ahead and simply do my best, without worrying what others may say or think. Amen.

Some significant events on this day

Year Event

1840 The first British colonists arrive in New Zealand.

1901 Queen Victoria of Great Britain dies at the age of 82 after a reign of 64 years.

1905 The Russian Revolution is ignited by 'Bloody Sunday'. When Russian workers marched to the Winter Palace in peaceful protest, Czarist troops massacred a hundred people.

Key thought for today

To love our neighbour in charity is to love God in other people.
— Saint Francis De Sales

Reflection

By Br Bill Firman

The gospels of Matthew and Luke tell us to do unto others what we would have them to do to us. All Christian denominations hold that as an important value. Some other great world religions do not express it quite so positively but do teach essentially the same message. The Buddhists say:

Hurt not others in ways that you yourself would find harmful.

The Confucian equivalent is:

What you do not like when done to yourself, do not do to others.

In Hinduism we read:

Do not do to another what is disagreeable to yourself.

The Judaic statement is similar:

What is hateful to you, you do not do to your fellow human being.

This unanimity is not surprising when we consider that the ancient Greek philosophers also asserted similar convictions. Socrates stated:

Do not do unto others that which angers you when they do it to you.

Aristotle said:

How should we behave to our friends? As we should wish our friends to behave to us.

The challenge of Jesus was even stronger in that he told us to do good not only to our friends but also to our enemies, to those who hate and persecute us. Caring for other people is one of the clearest universal principles. What brings people together in support of helping others is always stronger than what divides. Indeed, when we focus on doing good to others, differences of creed seem pretty shallow.

Prayer

Lord, help me to treat others the way I would like them to treat me. Let me focus on the needs of others rather than on my own desires. Amen.

Reflecting God's Presence

Some significant events on this day

Year   Event

1911   Nobel Prize winner Marie Curie is refused acceptance into the all-male membership of the French Academy of Sciences.

1968   North Korea captures the USS *Pueblo* and takes her crew hostage.

1999   Christian Australian missionary Graham Staines, and his two sons aged eight and ten, are burned alive in their car by radical Hindus in eastern India who opposed Christianity.

Key thought for today

We must fear God through love, not love God through fear.
— Jean-Pierre Camus

Reflection

By Br Bill Firman

On 23 January 1968, the USS *Pueblo*, a navy intelligence vessel, was intercepted by North Korean patrol boats. According to US reports, the *Pueblo* was in international waters almost 16 miles from shore, but the North Koreans turned their guns on the lightly armed vessel and demanded its surrender. The North Koreans opened fire, wounding the commander and two others. Several more crew members were shot before the *Pueblo* was boarded and taken to Wonson Harbour. The 83-man crew was bound and blindfolded and transported to Pyongyang, where they were charged with spying within North Korea's 12-mile territorial limit and imprisoned. It was the biggest crisis in two years of increased tension and minor skirmishes between the United States and North Korea.

The United States then began a military build-up in the area. North Korean authorities, meanwhile, coerced a confession and apology out of the *Pueblo* commander and the rest of the crew also signed a confession under threat of torture. In August, the North Koreans staged a news conference in which the prisoners were to praise their humane treatment, but the Americans thwarted the Koreans by inserting innuendoes and sarcastic language into their statements. Some also rebelled in photo shoots by sticking out their middle finger, a gesture their captors didn't understand. Later, the North Koreans caught on and beat the Americans for a week.

On 23 December, exactly 11 months after the *Pueblo*'s capture, negotiators reached a settlement to resolve the crisis. That day, the surviving 82 crewmen walked across the 'Bridge of No Return' at Panmunjon to freedom in South Korea. They were hailed as heroes and returned home to the US in time for Christmas. This kind of brinkmanship, occurring periodically between the end of World War II in 1945 and the fall of the Berlin Wall in 1989, was typical of the Cold War era, causing people to fear that such an incident could lead to a global conflict of catastrophic proportions. Lasting peace is to be cherished and nourished but never taken for granted.

Prayer

May our world grow in peace, love and understanding rather than hatred and fear. Amen.

Some significant events on this day

Year   Event

1848   The Californian gold rush begins when gold is found near Sacramento.

1908   The world's first Boy Scout organisation is formed in England by Sir Baden Powell.

1924   Following the Russian Revolution, St Petersberg is renamed Leningrad.

1972   Japanese soldier Shoichi Yokoi is found in a Guam jungle where he had been hiding for 28 years in adherence to the Imperial Army's non-surrender code. He was hailed as a hero and eventually died of a heart attack in 1997 aged 82.

1989   American serial killer Ted Bundy is executed in Florida. Just before he died, he confessed to killing another 19 women.

Key thought for today

We get no deeper into Christ than we allow him to get into us.
    —John Henry Jowett

Reflection

By Brian Long

We often interpret the prayer 'Live Jesus in our hearts' as a call for Jesus to come and dwell within us. Maybe we can look at it differently – as a proclamation, an affirmation that Jesus is already there in the heart of each of us, that in fact Jesus does not live anywhere else. In Jesus, God became absolutely and utterly immersed in creation, and especially in humanity. Jesus lives in my heart – the place of my angels and demons, the source of my passion, joys and loving; the place too of my doubts, fears, wrong turnings and big mess-ups. Yet Jesus is happy to dwell amongst the mess, willing to help me do a bit of spring-cleaning when I'm ready and able.

The necessity of allowing Jesus to shine from my heart is summed up in the words of St Teresa of Avila:

> *I have no hands but yours*
> *to embrace my wounded children.*
> *I have no eyes now but yours*
> *to look with compassion on my suffering ones.*
> *I have no tongue now but yours*
> *to speak healing words to my hopeless children.*
> *I have no feet now but yours*
> *to bring the good news of freedom to my oppressed little ones.*
> *I have no ears now but yours*
> *to listen with love to my voiceless victims of injustice.*

Prayer

Jesus, may you shine always from my heart so that I may be your blessing and your face to those you place in my path today. Amen.

Reflecting God's Presence

Some significant events on this day

Year	Event
1949	In the first election in Israel, David Ben-Gurion becomes Prime Minister.
1959	The Second Vatican Council, called by Pope John XXIII, begins.
1971	Charles Manson and three female 'Family' members are found guilty of murder.
1971	Idi Amin leads a coup deposing Milton Obote as President of Uganda.
2005	At least 250 people are killed in a stampede during a Hindu pilgrimage in India.

Key thought for today

I learned early that success didn't build character but rather character built success.
— Gaylene Clews

Reflection

By Br Bill Firman

Businessman Keith Ready was invited to a function to celebrate the 25th anniversary of a business owned by a good friend. Keith was running 20 minutes late, so the friend held the start of the function until he arrived. The friend began the speech by thanking individually all who were there. Ready then described what his friend said in these words:

> *During the course of the speech, he referred to a saying that reflected his overall approach to both his business and personal life: 'Always dance with the person you took to the dance'. He went on to talk about the importance of remaining loyal to those people who had supported him from the beginning of his business and through all the highs and lows of the last 25 years. He also mentioned that during this time many people had offered their services and even sometimes provided a very tempting and perhaps better business arrangement, however, he had no issue in saying 'thank you but no thank you'. What was and still is important to him is always to remember what people have done and continue to do, and this is always paramount in all of his business and personal decisions.*
>
> *His warm and genuine acknowledgements were to those people who had offered more than just their services, support and loyalty, it was about a deeper level of professional and personal friendship which in the end makes our lives all that much more enjoyable and rewarding.*
>
> *As I drove away that afternoon, I reflected on how lucky we are to have people in our lives that stick by us through all the highs and lows and most importantly are good friends.*
>
> *High levels of integrity, loyalty and appreciation bring their reward personally but also in business. No matter who else you might dance with, never neglect the person you take to the dance!*

Prayer

Long ago, Seneca said that 'Loyalty is the holiest good in the human heart.' Help me to hold my friends loyally in my heart. Amen.

Some significant events on this day

Year	Event
1340	The English monarch King Edward III is proclaimed King of France.
1788	Captain Arthur Phillip founds the colony of Australia. A public holiday commemorates this event.
1926	Television is first demonstrated in London by John Logie Baird.
1994	In Sydney, David Kang fires two blank shots from a starting pistol at Prince Charles.

Key thought for today

A person who has not made a mistake has not done anything.
— Melvin Chapman

Reflection

By Br Bill Firman

We celebrate 26 January as Australia Day. Initially, this was viewed as the day the white man came proudly to *terra nullius*, a supposedly empty land, but we now know it was the beginning of a process of driving the Aboriginal people from their traditional country. Perhaps it was a massive mistake, based on ignorance, or maybe it reflected that a different attitude prevailed in 1788. Certainly there was an underlying racial prejudice that viewed black people as inferior and less than fully human. It is not a step that can simply be undone, as more than twenty million people today would have nowhere to go, but more just attitudes now prevail.

On this day in 1994, David Kang startled everyone by firing blank shots at Prince Charles. David's intention was to highlight the plight of the Cambodian boat people but it was a silly thing to do which could have brought him a criminal conviction. Fortunately, the court treated him relatively leniently and he was given 500 hours of community service. Today, he is a barrister specialising in criminal and medical law.

Mistakes are a part of everyone's lives and every nation's history. Some can have enormous consequences and some can be fixed with compassionate consideration. We cannot afford to be bitter about past mistakes. Further, we should not expect we can avoid making mistakes. Even the church, with centuries of accumulated wisdom, has made some huge mistakes. Children are especially prone to making mistakes. Bishop Geoffrey Robinson has this to say on how to react to the mistakes children make:

> *As children grow up, their parents must gradually stand back and allow them to make their own mistakes and learn from these mistakes. If the children abuse their freedom, the parents can only hope that the day will come when they see that their actions are not contributing to their growth, health or happiness, and will want to change. Through all of this process, however long it takes, the most important thing for the parents is to keep their relationship with their children and continually show them that they love them, so that the children will want to turn to them when they experience the need. A church should act in the same way.*

Prayer

God, may I never be bitter about the mistakes of others, and be honest about my own.

Reflecting God's Presence

Some significant events on this day

Year   Event

1606   The trial of Guy Fawkes and other English Catholics accused of attempting to assassinate the Protestant King opens on this day. Four days later, they were found guilty and hung, drawn and quartered.

1945   Soviet forces liberate Auschwitz, the Nazi killing camp in which more than one million Jews were murdered.

1967   US astronauts Gus Grissom, Edward White and Roger Chaffee are killed in a fire during a test of the *Apollo 1* spacecraft

1983   The world's longest tunnel under water (53.9 kms) is opened in Japan, connecting the islands of Honshu and Hokkaido.

Key thought for today

Too few people have experienced the divine image as the innermost possession of their own souls.
— Carl Jung

Reflection

By Patrick Jurd: I invite reflection on this following passage which contains an important message. It comes from the video program, *Free To Be Me*.

> *Do you really love yourself? Could I ask you to make a little test with yourself? It has to be done in the bathroom tonight. Be sure to lock the door. Any witnesses will certainly wonder.*
>
> *Go to the mirror and say, 'Hey, I love you!'*
>
> *Now, that is not the test. I presume that you will do that. The test is: How did you feel when you did that? Can you say those words and really mean them? Or would you rather feel that such an act of loving one's self is silly and ridiculous?*
>
> *Carl Jung, the great psychiatrist, once reflected that we are all familiar with the words of Jesus: 'Whatever you do to the least of my brethren, you do unto me.'*
>
> *Then Jung asks a very probing question: 'What if you discovered that the least of the brethren of Jesus, the one who needs your love the most, the one you can help the most by loving, the one to whom your love will be most meaningful – what if you discovered that this least of the brethren of Jesus ... is you?'*

Prayer

In you we live and move; in you we have our being. We are enfolded in your love, enfolded in your peace, surrounded by your might. Open our eyes, Lord: enlarge our vision. Open our hearts, Lord: increase our faith (From The Open Gate by David Adam).

Some significant events on this day

Year   Event
1935   Iceland becomes the first country to legalise abortion.
1986   The space shuttle *Challenger* explodes 73 seconds after lift-off, killing all seven astronauts on board.
1999   The Ford car company announces it is buying the Volvo company for US $6.45 billion.
2002   An Ecuadorian Airlines Boeing 727 crashes in the Andes in Southern Columbia, killing 92 people.

Key thought for today

Science without religion is lame; religion without science is blind.
— Albert Einstein

Reflection

By Br Bill Firman

Human beings are not just another life form. Every human being is made in the image and likeness of God, persons called to love God and one another, mirroring the Trinitarian love of God. That is our fundamental belief based on Christian revelation.

There is much that we do not fully understand. Science, which strives for certainty, has many more mysteries than does religion which demands faith but leaves room for doubt.

Science tries to give us predictability; religion gives us hope. Science gives us incomplete knowledge; religion gives us incomplete faith. Science can only describe the act of loving; religion requires us to strive to love.

In both science and religion there are gaps and mysteries that we are not even close to answering. But we have a destiny with God, expressed so well by St Augustine 1600 years ago in the *City of God*:

> *There we shall rest and we shall see.*
> *We shall see and we shall love.*
> *We shall love and we shall praise.*
> *Such will be the end without end,*
> *When we possess the kingdom*
> *that will have no end.*

It is indeed good to be a Christian. It is a gift to me personally from my parents and all my teachers. Gilbert Brenken said:

> *Others see only a hopeless end, but the Christian rejoices in an endless hope.*

Prayer

G.K. Chesterton said, 'Let your religion be less of a theory and more of a love affair.' Let us be filled with endless faith, hope and love. Amen.

Reflecting God's Presence

Some significant events on this day

Year	Event
	Feast day of Saint Francis de Sales (1567–1622).
1886	Karl Benz, in Germany, patents the first successful gasoline-driven automobile.
1933	Adolf Hitler is appointed Chancellor of Germany.
1996	After widespread criticism over several years, the French President finally announces an end to his country's nuclear testing.

Key thought for today

Have patience with all things, but chiefly have patience with yourself. Do not lose courage in considering your own imperfections, but instantly set about remedying them – every day begins the task anew. Do not wish to be anything but what you are, and try to be that perfectly.
— Saint Francis de Sales

Reflection

By St John Baptist de La Salle

It was the gentleness and tenderness for his neighbour that made it possible for St Francis de Sales to convert so many people to God. It has been estimated that as many as seventy-two thousand heretics were won back by him from their errors. In fact, this virtue won the hearts of all those with whom he dealt, and the affection they felt for him was a means he used to bring them to God. One apostate even confessed that it was the saint's gentleness and patience that made him come back to the bosom of the church.

Do you have these sentiments of charity and tenderness toward the poor children whom you have to educate? Do you take advantage of their affection for you to bring them to God? If you have for them the firmness of a father to restrain and withdraw them from misbehaviour, you must also have for them the tenderness of a mother to draw them to you, and to do for them all the good that depends on you (Meditation on St Francis de Sales)

Prayer

The poet Henry Wordsworth Longfellow wrote:

> *Each morning sees some task begun,*
> *Each evening sees it close.*
> *Something attempted, something done,*
> *Has earned a night's repose.*

Help me to live each day well with patience, gentleness and kindness, knowing that others will forgive my faults while I am willing to forgive theirs. None of us is perfect.

Reflecting God's Presence

Some significant events on this day

Year   Event

        Today is the feast day of De La Salle Brother Saint Mutien-Marie.

1595   The first performance takes place of Shakespeare's play *Romeo and Juliet*.

1847   Yerba Buena, California, is re-named San Francisco.

1945   In the deadliest maritime disaster in recorded history, the *Wilhelm Gustaff* sinks in the Baltic Sea, killing approximately 8000 people.

1948   Hindu extremist Nathuram Godse assassinates the Indian independence leader and pacifist, Mahatma Gandhi.

Key thought for today

At the end of life we will not be judged by how many diplomas we have received, how much money we have made, how many great things we have done. We will be judged by 'I was hungry and you gave me to eat, I was naked and you clothed me, I was homeless and you took me in.' Hungry not only for bread – but hungry for love. Naked not only for clothing – but naked for human dignity and respect. Homeless not only for want of a room of bricks – but homeless because of rejection.

— Mother Teresa

Reflection

By Patrick Jurd from the De La Salle Brothers' website

Louis Wiaux, the third of six children, was born, in 1841, in Mellet, a small village in French-speaking Belgium where almost everyone was a devout practising Catholic. No sooner had he met the De La Salle Brothers in a nearby school than he determined to enter the novitiate at Namur where he was given the name Mutien-Marie. After two years of teaching elementary classes, Brother Mutien was assigned to the boarding school at Malonne where he would spend the next 58 years.

He had difficulties at first coping with the demands of both teaching and prefecting. He was rescued by the Brother in charge of the courses in music and art, at the time an important feature of the curriculum. From then on Brother Mutien was not only an effective teacher of those subjects, a vigilant prefect in the school yard and a catechist in the nearby parish, but a tremendous influence on the students by his patience and evident piety. Among the Brothers, it was said that he had never been seen violating even the smallest points of their Rule.

Brother Mutien died at Malonne on 30 January 1917. He was beatified by Pope Paul VI in 1977 and canonised by Pope John Paul II in 1989. Br Bill was privileged to have a front row seat in St Peter's for this ceremony.

Prayer

Brother Mutien overcame initial difficulties to become an effective teacher. May the life of St Mutien inspire me to deal with life's difficulties and persevere with humility and fidelity in my search for God.

Reflecting God's Presence

Some significant events on this day

Year	Event
1876	The US government orders all Native Americans to move onto reservations.
1953	The combination of a high spring tide and a fierce storm causes a breach of the dikes and flooding of low-lying areas of northern Belgium and southern Netherlands. More than 1800 people died in the surge of water.
1990	The first McDonald's in Russia opens in Moscow.

Key thought for today

The strongest tree of the forest is not the one protected from the storms and hidden from the sun. It's the one that stands in the open where it is compelled to struggle for its existence against the wind and the rain and the scorching sun.
— Napoleon Hill

Reflection

By Br Bill Firman

We cannot transmit our own experience to our children: experience is something they must gain for themselves. Most of us, however, can identify with the father who said, 'I am only trying to keep him from making the same mistakes I made.' To which his son replied, 'It would be better fun making my own mistakes.'

Hopefully, it is more than fun. We learn from the things we do wrong. We become stronger through having to cope with our mistakes and, in fact, any difficulties that come our way. Ultimately, parents are trying to raise adults, not children, and much of adult life is concerned with being able to face and resolve difficulties.

It is a mistake for parents to be over-protective for too long. It is necessary to let children make decisions and develop their own character and independent strength. There is much that children gain in experiencing things they do that go wrong – albeit a painful episode at the time. Yes, parents have a great role in trying to make sure the things that go wrong aren't too major. Parents also have a significant part to play in helping children 'pick up the pieces' after things fall apart. Nonetheless, parents should keep in mind the metaphor that the young tree that will grow to be the strongest is not the one most protected.

It is good to challenge oneself with difficult but realistic attainments. To climb Mt Stapleton in Victoria's Grampians would be challenging but realistic for a fit young person, but to climb Mt Everest would be unrealistic except for very few well-trained and experienced climbers. There is a wonderful sense of satisfaction in working towards a clear goal and achieving it.

Prayer

Lord, help me to be as sturdy as a tree. Amen.

1 FEBRUARY

Reflecting God's Presence

Some significant events on this day

Year   Event

1884   The first edition of the Oxford English Dictionary is published.

1981   Trevor Chappell bowls his infamous 'underarm ball' to Brian McKechnie to prevent New Zealand scoring a six and tying the game, on the last ball of the third match in the final of the World Series Cup. It led directly to the banning of underarm bowling by the International Cricket Council as not within the spirit of the game.

2003   The space shuttle Columbia disintegrates during re-entry into the earth's atmosphere, killing all seven astronauts aboard.

2004   Two hundred and fifty-one people are trampled to death and 244 injured in a stampede at the Hajj pilgrimage at Mecca in Saudi Arabia.

Key thought for today

What doesn't kill me makes me stronger.
— Albert Camus

Reflection

By Br Denis Loft

Before coming to De La Salle, I had ten years running Hohola Youth Centre in Papua New Guinea. The centre's motto was: 'Be like the spider'. The centre was for students who had not scored high marks in the end of primary school exams. At that time there was only room for 50 per cent of students to proceed to secondary school. Our students were labelled as school drop-outs.

King Robert I of Scotland (1274–1329), better known as Robert The Bruce, led Scotland during the Wars of Scottish Independence against the Kingdom of England. According to legend, at some point while he was on the run during the winter of 1305-6, Bruce hid in a cave on the east coast of Rathlin Island, where he observed a spider trying to spin a web. Each time the spider failed, it started all over again. Inspired by this, Bruce returned to inflict a series of defeats on the English, thus winning him more supporters and eventual victory. The story serves to explain the maxim: 'If at first you don't succeed, try, try again.' Other versions have Bruce defeated for the seventh time by the English, then let him watch the spider spin seven webs, fail, then spin an eighth and succeed.

The students at Hohola were inspired by this simple motto. They did not have the resources available to their peers, but they did have an amazing capacity to attempt all sorts of tasks, and, often with flair and creativity, achieve goals that parents, previous teachers and others thought way beyond their capabilities. The simple rule, 'Be like the spider', was their motivation.

Prayer

Lord, inspire us with resilience, patience and tenacity. Don't let us accept mediocrity, but give us the strength to strive to achieve the goals we set ourselves.

Reflecting God's Presence

2 FEBRUARY

Some significant events on this day

Year   Event

1899   The Australian Premiers' Conference, meeting in Melbourne, takes the historic decision to locate the Australian capital (now Canberra) between Sydney and Melbourne.

1933   Adolf Hitler, only two days after becoming Chancellor of Germany, dissolves the German parliament.

1971   Army officer Idi Amin replaces President Milton Obote as leader of Uganda and unleashes a reign of terror that lasted until 1979.

1990   South African President F.W. de Klerk permits the African National Congress to function again and promised to free human rights activist Nelson Mandella.

Key thought for today

The worst part of imprisonment is being locked up by yourself. You come face to face with time and there is nothing more terrifying than to be alone with sheer time. Then the ghosts come crowding in.
— Nelson Mandela

Reflection

By Br Bill Firman

Several times in my life I have been close to bushfires but mostly at a safe distance. It was far from safe, however, when I was caught in the Ash Wednesday Bushfires of 1983, at Gembrook in the Dandenong Ranges out of Melbourne, in charge of 80 Year 9 students. We were staying in a scout camp surrounded by bush when the sky turned dark but with an eerie red glow.

In my mind I began to establish priorities. The first would be to keep everybody calm and to create at least the reassuring appearance of being in control. So we gathered the boys and I spoke quietly to them about moving to open ground. The only problem was an over-anxious teacher shouting excitedly, 'Listen to Brother, listen to him!' We did not need the panic in his voice!

We broke out fire hoses, moved to the open and eventually, after very confused input from those who were trying to advise us, crowded aboard over-loaded vehicles, leaving our tents and personal items behind, and evacuated to the Gembrook sports ground. I managed, in that era before mobile phones, to get one important, reassuring phone call back to the school which was being besieged by anxious parents seeking information. The students were lamenting the presumed loss of their belongings but I still recall meeting people crying: 'I can't find my wife, my kids'. Somehow the loss of clothing or other belongings took on a lesser significance by comparison. Eventually it rained down ash and water and the terror abated!

Another teacher said to me later, 'I was glad you were there.' In retrospect, I was glad I was there too. I was proud of the boys who responded so well. We all faced ghosts of fear and uncertainly that night and we knew, with confidence in one another, we had overcome the danger.

Prayer

Lord, help me to face unexpected challenges, be it alone or with others, knowing that you will be there with me. Amen.

Some significant events on this day

Year   Event

1931   The Napier earthquake in New Zealand kills 258 people. A substantial area of land, now utilised, was lifted above sea level.

1959   Buddy Holly, Ritchie Valens and the Big Bopper are killed in a plane crash in Iowa, USA, after a concert the night before. Their deaths have become known as 'The Day the Music Died'.

1967   The last person to be executed in Australia, Ronald Ryan, is hanged in Pentridge Prison, Melbourne.

Key thought for today

Children have more need of models than of critics.
— Joseph Joubert

Reflection

By Br Bill Firman

Every good parent experiences the paradox of guiding and directing a child while taking the necessary steps back to let the child learn to make his or her own decisions. The instinct of parents is to hang on to their children, to protect them and to enjoy the bonds of dependency. Yet they know they must nourish independence and prepare their children for responsible adulthood. Children must grow to make their own choices and decisions, to establish integrity and love of others, to learn the value of unselfishness and generosity, of kindness and morality. This is highlighted by an author, whose name I can't recall, who wrote a poignant statement entitled 'From Parent to Child'. I quote from this below.

> *I gave you life, but cannot live it for you;*
> *I can take you to church, but cannot make you believe;*
> *I can teach you right from wrong, but I cannot always decide for you;*
> *I can teach you, of course, to share, but I cannot make you unselfish;*
> *I can teach you respect, but I cannot force you to show honour;*
> *I can advise you about your friends, but I cannot choose them for you;*
> *I can tell you about drugs, but I cannot say no for you;*
> *I can tell you about lofty goals, but I cannot achieve them for you;*
> *I can teach you about kindness, but I cannot force you to be gracious.*

Each child will become a man or woman. It is the hope of every parent that their child will become a man or woman of honour and strength who values the freedom to choose, who makes right decisions, and respects the rights of others to make their personal choices.

Prayer

Today I recall the words of Robert Ingersoll that 'one laugh of a child will make the holiest day more sacred still'. Teach me to cherish children, in their innocent optimism, and make each day with them more sacred.

Reflecting God's Presence

Some significant events on this day

Year   Event

1789   George Washington is elected the first US President. Three years later on this day he was re-elected to a second term.

1948   Ceylon, later re-named Sri Lanka, becomes independent within the British Commonwealth.

1974   The Symbionese Liberation Army kidnaps US newspaper heiress Patty Hearst.

Key thought for today

It is one thing to show a man that he is in error, and another to put him in possession of the truth.
— John Locke

Reflection

By Br Bill Firman

'Stockholm Syndrome' describes the behaviour of kidnap victims who, over time, become sympathetic to and establish an emotional bond with their captors. The name derives from a 1973 hostage incident in Stockholm, Sweden. At the end of six days of captivity in a bank, several kidnap victims actually resisted rescue attempts, and afterwards refused to testify against their captors.

One of the most documented cases is that of Patty Hearst in the United States. On 4 February 1974, Patty Hearst, the 19-year-old daughter of newspaper publisher Randolph Hearst, was kidnapped from her apartment in Berkeley, California. Three days later, the Symbionese Liberation Army (SLA), a small US leftist group, announced in a letter to a Berkeley radio station that it was holding Hearst as a 'prisoner of war'. The apparent leader, Donald DeFreeze, wanted to start a revolution by declaring war on those with status and money. By her account, Patty was kept blindfolded for two months in a closet at the group's headquarters, unable even to use the bathroom in privacy. DeFreeze worked to turn her into an angry revolutionary, using harsh techniques such as isolation, physical and sexual abuse, death threats and lies about how the gang was oppressed by the establishment.

By early April, she was deemed ready to accompany the gang on their next activity. A surveillance camera took a photo of Hearst participating in an armed robbery of a San Francisco bank, and she was also spotted during a robbery of a Los Angeles store. She later declared, in a tape sent to authorities, that she had joined the SLA of her own free will. Finally, on 18 September 1975, after criss-crossing the country with her captors – or co-conspirators – for more than a year, Hearst, or 'Tania' as she called herself, was captured in a San Francisco apartment and arrested for armed robbery. Despite her claim that she had been brainwashed by the SLA, she was convicted and sentenced to seven years in prison. She served 21 months before her sentence was commuted by President Carter. She was pardoned by President Clinton in January 2001. The power people can exercise over others by psychological manipulation is quite alarming.

Prayer

Let me treasure my freedom and that of others. God, make me open and honest but never manipulative of those whom I meet. Amen.

5 FEBRUARY

Reflecting God's Presence

Some significant events on this day

Year   Event

1885   King Leopold of Belgium establishes the Congo as his personal possession.

1936   Charlie Chaplin releases his last-ever silent movie *Modern Times*.

1997   The 'big three' banks in Switzerland announce the creation of a $71 million fund to aid Holocaust survivors and their families.

Key thoughts for today

The paradox of courage is that a man must be a little careless of his life even in order to keep it.
— G.K. Chesterton

The courage we desire and prize is not the courage to die decently, but to live manfully.
— Thomas Carlyle

Reflection

By Br Bill Firman

One of the most inspirational stories I have read was about a young man called Bart Bunting. Although blind, Bart had a very clear vision of what he wanted to achieve. Bart is a former student of Oakhill College in Sydney. I reprint his story here:

> *In an interview with the* Sydney Morning Herald *after winning his first Gold medal at the Winter Paralympics, Bart Bunting (Class of 1993) said, 'It's a little scary, not being able to see anything and going so fast'. Our belief is that, as well as being a world-class athlete, Bart is a master of understatement!*
>
> *Bart, who has been blind since birth, won two Gold (Downhill and Super-G) and one Silver (Giant Slalom) medals at the Winter Paralympics. Bart's best previous performance was two Gold medals at the 2000 World Championships in Anzere, Switzerland. An incredible accomplishment and all the more so when one considers Bart has been skiing for less than five years.*
>
> *Bart is guided on the slopes by his long-time friend, Nathan Chivers. Nathan has a microphone in his helmet and a loudspeaker attached to his bum bag; verbal directions from Nathan are all Bart has to guide him as he skis downhill at speeds of up to 80 kilometres per hour ... Bart's achievements have been recognised in many ways, including the issue of a special set of stamps by Australia Post.*

The capacity of the human spirit to overcome disadvantage and achieve the impossible is extraordinary. I enjoy skiing but it takes every bit of my concentration to stay on my feet and not let those inevitable bumps in the terrain throw me off balance. Imagine trying to do that with no vision. For a career path, Bart chose to study computer science. Another huge challenge.

Prayer

There is a French proverb that says, 'To a brave heart nothing is impossible.' Grant me, God, a brave heart to face the future, so that I may be ready to rise to heights beyond my expectations.

Reflecting God's Presence

Some significant events on this day

Year   Event

1840   The British and the Maori nation sign the Treaty of Waitangi, the founding charter of New Zealand.

1952   Elizabeth II, on holiday in Kenya, becomes Queen on the death of her father King George VI in England.

1959   Jack Kilby of Texas Instruments files the first patent for an integrated circuit, initiating the digital revolution.

Key thought for today

When I give food to the poor, they call me a saint. When I ask why the poor have no food, they call me a communist.
— Dom Helder Camera

Reflection

By Betty Rudin

Brazilian, Dom Helder Camera, Archbishop of Olinda and Recife, is widely considered one of the great Catholic figures of the 20th century. He had an uncompromising commitment to assisting the many poor people in Brazil. In the book, *Through the Gospel with Dom Helder Camera,* I came across the following passage which struck a chord with me. I offer it for your reflection:

> *I love hearing the apostles ask, 'Lord, teach us how to pray.'*
>
> *We may sometimes think we've learnt how to pray already. All the same, knowing the Lord's Prayer off by heart isn't enough. The important thing is to learn to live the prayer the Lord has taught us, beginning with 'Our Father'. Are we really convinced that God is the Father of us all? Not merely 'my Father', but 'our' Father. If he is 'ours', then we are all brothers and sisters. People with the same father are brothers and sisters.*
>
> *It is very easy at Mass to say 'Peace be with you' to the person standing next to you, but after that we each go home and the other person is forgotten. If the other people were really our brothers and sisters and we knew they were ill, in misery, perhaps even dying of hunger, we would do all we possibly could for them, and more ...*

Prayer

Lord, my God, help me to see you as a loving Father to me, my family, friends and colleagues.
We ask you to create life anew. Give us
    — *faith, the confidence to bear,*
    — *hope, continuously expectant,*
    — *love, the true beginning.*
We ask this through Christ our Lord and our Brother. Amen.

Reflecting God's Presence

Some significant events on this day

Year   Event

1909   Birthday of Dom Helder Camera in Brazil.
1971   Women gain the right to vote in Switzerland.
1990   Led by Mikhail Gorbachev, the Soviet Communist Party gives up its monopoly of power.
1992   The European Union is formed.

Key thought for today

There is no single definition of holiness: there are dozens, hundreds. But there is one I am particularly fond of: being holy means getting up immediately every time you fall, with humility and joy. It doesn't mean never falling into sin. It means being able to say, 'Yes, Lord, I have fallen a thousand times. But thanks to you I have got up again a thousand and one times.' That's all. I like thinking about that.

— Dom Helder Camera

Reflection

By Betty Rudin: One of my favourite passages is written by Dom Helder Camera.

Then again, when we say, 'Thy will be done', it's easy enough to accept God's will when it coincides with our own. We know exactly how to ask the Lord for things, but the Lord had better look out and agree with what we want. And on no account should the Lord think or want anything different.

And yet, very often, what we ask for isn't what is good for us. We are like little children as far as the Lord is concerned. A father knows better than to give his child the knife it wants to play with, or to let it go down the stairs on its own.

You know the prayer I love to say? 'Lord, may your grace help me to want what you want, to prefer what you prefer.' Want what you want, prefer what you prefer ... For, honestly, what do we know? We ought to do everything as though all depended on us, at the same time putting ourselves into the Lord's hands, knowing that our own strength lies in offering him our weaknesses.

We really need to learn to live Christ's prayer.

Prayer

Help me to be holy in the way Helder Camera talks of holiness, of having the courage to rise again immediately when I fall, with humility and joy. Let me never be so arrogant that I cannot admit I was wrong. When I need to, let me apologise joyfully for my mistakes. Let me say consistently: 'Thy will be done.'

Reflecting God's Presence

Some significant events on this day

Year   Event

        Today is the Parinirvana (or Nirvana Day), the celebration of Buddha's death, when he is alleged to have reached total Nirvana at the age of 80.

1969   A large meteorite, aged 4.5 billion years, scatters several tons of material over a large area of Mexico.

1983   Champion racehorse Shergar is kidnapped in Ireland and never recovered. Lloyd's of London paid out insurance of £10.6 million.

Key thought for today

Cowards die many times before their deaths. The valiant never taste of death but once.
— William Shakespeare (*Julius Caesar*)

Reflection

By James Walton

Many have seen the film *Dead Poets Society* starring Robin Williams as an English teacher who encourages his pupils to change their life of conformity for a life of absolute passion, living by the motto *Carpe diem* – 'Seize the day'. One memorable scene depicts Williams' character showing the boys black and white photographs of previous pupils of the school, whispering,

> *They're not that different from you, are they? Same haircuts. Full of hormones, just like you. Invincible, just like you feel. The world is their oyster. They believe they're destined for great things, just like many of you. Their eyes are full of hope, just like you. Did they wait until it was too late to make from their lives even one iota of what they were capable? Because, you see, gentlemen, these boys are now fertilising daffodils.*

The message he is trying to instil in his pupils is that time is fleeting. If you do not seize your opportunities, it will not be long before life has passed you by. As John Lennon said,

> *Life is what happens while you are busy making plans.*

While it is important to spend time reflecting on your life, it is also important that you seize the opportunities that appear before you and make the most of every moment; before long, time will have passed you by. We only have one life on this earth and it is important that we make the most of it.

A life lived in fear is a life half lived. *Carpe diem*.

Prayer

God, help me realise that I need to take each day and make the most of it, being the best that I can be and giving the best that I can give. Grant me the courage to try new things and never be afraid that I may fail, knowing you will always be there with me. Amen.

Some significant events on this day

Year   Event

        Feast day of Saint Miguel Febres Cordero, De La Salle Brother.
1965   The first US combat troops are sent to Vietnam.
1969   The Boeing 747 airplane undergoes its first test flight.
2001   The American submarine, USS *Greenville*, accidentally collides, in Pearl Harbour, with the Ehime-Maru, a Japanese training ship operated by the Uwajima Fisheries High School.

Key thought for today

If there is light in the soul, there will be beauty in the person.
If there is beauty in the person, there will be harmony in the house.
If there is harmony in the house, there will be order in the nation.
If there is order in the nation, there will be peace in the world.
    — Chinese proverb

Reflection

By Patrick Jurd from the De La Salle Brothers' website

Francisco Febres Cordero was born in 1854 in Cuenca, Ecuador, into a family that had always been prominent in Ecuadorian politics. He received the name Brother Miguel when given the religious habit of the De La Salle Brothers in March 1868. Brother Miguel was a gifted teacher from the start and a diligent student. When he was not quite twenty years old, he published the first of his many books, a Spanish grammar that soon became a standard text. He wrote many textbooks as well as works on literature and the natural sciences. The Academy of Ecuador named him as one of its members.

Despite high academic honours, teaching remained his first priority, especially his classes in religion and for the young men he prepared for first communion. His students admired his simplicity, his directness, his concern for them, and the intensity of his devotion to the Sacred Heart and the Virgin Mary. Outstanding as a scholar and a saint, he was also the epitome of kindness and approachability.

He moved to Spain and was supervising novices when he contracted pneumonia and died on 9 February 1910. Pope Paul VI beatified him in 1977 and he was canonised by Pope John Paul II in 1984, the first Ecuadorian saint and a venerated national hero.

Prayer

Brother Miguel once wrote: 'I must engage in all the works that I undertake with a spirit of love, of gratitude for the divine goodness which has been gracious enough to employ me for his glory and the salvation of souls.' Like Miguel, dear Lord, may I always aspire for excellence in all parts of my life, while never forgetting to put my gifts at the service of those around me.

Reflecting God's Presence

Some significant events on this day

Year	Event
1763	The Seven Years War ends with the signing of the Treaty of Paris and the ceding, by France, of Canada to Great Britain.
1898	The German author and playwright Bertolt Brecht is born.
1931	New Delhi becomes the capital of India.
1964	The aircraft carrier, HMAS *Melbourne*, in a collision off the south coast of NSW, sinks the destroyer HMAS *Voyager* with the loss of 82 lives.

Key thought for today

Do not fear death so much, but rather an inadequate life.
— Bertolt Brecht

Reflection

By Br Bill Firman

There is an old Semitic saying, which I think has its origin in one of the translations of the Bible, that says:

As you live so shall you die.

If we live our lives with honesty, compassion and a strong sense of justice and love in our dealings with others, in a word, with 'integrity', then that is how we shall approach our death when it comes.

'Integrity' relates to the word 'integer' which means a whole number. Integrity describes a person feeling whole or complete. The psychologist Erik Erikson, described life in terms of the passage through eight 'psycho-social crises'. The last of these is described as the crisis of 'integrity versus hopelessness or despair'.

If we stick to our principles, if we practise what we believe in, if we value honour and truth more than opportunism and injustice, if we try to assist others rather than capitalise on their inadequacies or weakness, then we become rich in Gospel values, then we are living with integrity. It will not matter if we do not have much money or material success. We will feel the wholesomeness that only good people know.

We shall know that our lives have been more than adequate and have made a difference for the better. Death is no more than the inevitable transition every person must make – sooner or later. It holds no fears for those who live well.

Prayer

Benjamin Franklin once said, 'Death takes no bribes.' Lord, I ask for the strength to avoid trying to bribe, cheat and connive my way through life but rather to face it head on. Help me to value my personal integrity and reputation more than any perceived short-term benefit. Help me to live well so that I may die well. Amen.

Some significant events on this day

Year   Event

1858   The Blessed Virgin Mary appears to Bernadette Soubirous in a grotto in Lourdes, France.
1978   China lifts a ban on reading the works by Aristotle, Shakespeare and Dickens.
1979   Ayatollah Khomeini seizes power in Iran.
1990   After 27 years, Nelson Mandela is freed from prison in South Africa.

Key thought for today

Humanity is essentially a freedom-event. As established by God, and in its very nature, it is unfinished. Humanity freely determines its own everlasting nature and bears ultimate responsibility for it.
— Karl Rahner

Reflection

By Brian Long: I offer for your reflection the following beautiful poem by Mary Oliver in which she observes beauty on a summer's day.

The Summer Day

Who made the world?
Who made the swan, and the black bear?
Who made the grasshopper?
This grasshopper, I mean,
the one who has flung herself out of the grass,
the one who is eating sugar out of my hand,
who is moving her jaws back and forth instead of up and down,
who is gazing around with her enormous and complicated eyes.
Now she lifts her pale forearms and thoroughly washes her face.
Now she snaps her wings open, and floats away.
I don't know exactly what a prayer is.
I do know how to pay attention, how to fall down
into the grass, how to kneel down in the grass,
how to be idle and blessed, how to stroll through the fields,
which is what I have been doing all day.
Tell me, what else should I have done?
Doesn't everything die at last, and too soon?
Tell me, what is it you plan to do
with your one wild and precious life?

Prayer

My Creator God, who holds me and sustains me, help me to live each day to the full my one wild and precious life. Amen.

Reflecting God's Presence

Some significant events on this day

Year   Event

1912   China adopts the Gregorian calendar.
1999   President Bill Clinton is acquitted by the US Senate in his impeachment trial.
2001   *Shoemaker*, the first spacecraft to touch down on an asteroid, lands on the 'saddle' region of 433 Eros.
2002   The trial of former President of Yugoslavia Slobodan Milosevic begins at the UN war crimes tribunal in The Hague, Holland.

Key thought for today

All children wear the sign: I want to be important NOW. Many of our juvenile delinquency problems arise because nobody reads the sign.
— Dan Pursuit

Reflection

By Br Bill Firman:

American author Don Marquis (1878–1937) once wrote:

Ours is a world where people don't know what they want and are willing to go through hell to get it.

Those words resonate with me when I think about the attitude of some people today to children's rights. Recently I met a smiling, blond-haired boy, aged four, who was enjoying the company of his grandparents. I'll call him 'Tom' (not his real name). Grandparents are a wonderful invention, who can bring much support and love in abundance to a child. The need of every child for nurture, security, feelings of love and belonging can be provided in many ways, most obviously by good parents. Yet we know many children grow to be fine adults when other adults, such as grandparents, step in to provide care. There is no single right way to bring up a child – no guaranteed path to success or failure. Tom, this little blond boy with large hopeful eyes and a warm smile, in fact was born to a single mother, fathered by an anonymous donor in the In Vitro Fertilisation (IVF) program.

I have no doubt Tom is much loved but, leaving aside considerations of the ethical arguments about his conception, I found myself wondering how he will feel as he becomes older. Inevitably, he will wonder who his dad was, or is. Most people want to know their roots, their personal history. Such children raise the question – should science be used this way? No doubt at all that Tom's mother asserted her 'right' to a baby, but should not the new person, the baby, also have rights? At the other end of the scale, aborted foetuses are also attributed no right to life. It is argued that the mother has a right not to have a baby; but surely babies are not just convenient items to possess or dispose of? It is a sad reflection on our society when we accord no rights to young children simply because they are powerless. I am sure Tom is much loved, but it is a strange way to begin the lifelong task of affirming that he is important.

Prayer

My creator God, I ask to stand with you in affirming the sacredness of all human life. Amen.

Some significant events on this day

Year   Event

1633   Galileo Galilei arrives in Rome to be tried by the Inquisition for his belief that the earth revolves around the sun.

1668   Spain recognises Portugal as an independent nation.

1990   An agreement is reached for a two-stage plan to reunite East and West Germany.

Key thoughts for today

I do not feel obliged to believe that the same God who has endowed us with sense, reason and intellect intends us to forgo their use.
— Galileo Galilei

Past the seeker as he prayed came the crippled and the beggar and the beaten. And, seeing them, he cried, 'Great God, how is it that a loving creator can see such things and yet do nothing about them?' God said, 'I did do something. I made you.'
— Sufi teaching

Reflection

By Patrick Jurd

On this day in 2008, the Australian Prime Minister Kevin Rudd issued an apology to the Aboriginal people for their treatment by previous federal governments, especially for the taking of their children, in what has come to be known as the 'Stolen Generations'. In his speech, Rudd said,

> *We apologise especially for the removal of Aboriginal and Torres Strait Islander children from their families, their communities and their country.*
>
> *For the pain, suffering and hurt of these Stolen Generations, their descendants and for their families left behind, we say sorry.*
>
> *To the mothers and the fathers, the brothers and the sisters, for the breaking up of families and communities, we say sorry.*
>
> *And for the indignity and degradation thus inflicted on a proud people and a proud culture, we say sorry.'*

The indigenous 'Father of Reconciliation' Pat Dodson described the apology as a 'seminal moment in the nation's history'.

Prayer

Dear Lord, may we respect the first people of Australia, traditional custodians of these lands. May we also have the courage to acknowledge the mistakes in our lives, apologise for them and do what we can to right our wrongs. We ask God's blessing on the Wurujndjeri people of the Kulin nation, the first carers of the land on which De La Salle College now stands.

Reflecting God's Presence

14 FEBRUARY

Some significant events on this day

Year   Event

1779   Captain James Cook is killed by the natives of the Sandwich Islands.

1876   Alexander Graham Bell and Elisha Gray separately apply for a patent for the telephone. The US Supreme Court ruled in favour of Bell.

1918   The Soviet Union adopts the Gregorian Calendar.

1989   Iranian leader Ayatollah Khomeini issues a *fatwa*, encouraging Muslims to kill Salman Rushdie, author of *The Satanic Verses*. Some bookstores were firebombed for selling the book. Rushdie came out of hiding in 1998 when the Iranian government declared it would not carry out the *fatwa*.

Key thought for today

One word frees us from all the weight and pain of life: that word is love.
    — Sophocles

Reflection

By Peter Riordan

I have always enjoyed my work as a teacher and love my work at De La Salle, but, without doubt, the most important part of my life is my wife and my family. I count myself blessed by the great love of my family who give me strength and support me in my work as a teacher.

Families create fascinating interactions which make each new day exciting, each new event a challenge in which to share our love. The bond of family love is not something we have to express but we do enjoy sharing special celebrations when the occasion arises. Inevitably there must be give and take between family members, and trust, with some risk-taking by parents and acceptance by the children of some limits. The essential safety net, which my children understand implicitly, is the willingness of parents to offer unqualified support if something goes wrong. I cherish my family time. In one way, I am sad to see my children growing to be independent young adults as I love to be with them. On the other hand, my pride in seeing them grow and develop to mature young persons capable of giving and finding love in the wider community, increasingly independent of our nuclear family, far outweighs any regrets. With my family I am rich beyond measure and everything else becomes insignificant. Our love, nonetheless, is a gift to be shared.

With my wife, I rejoice in the successes of our children. We encourage and support them in their growing independence and especially in any times of disappointment. We shall love them always, no matter what eventuates, as we watch the ripples of our love spread out.

Prayer

Jesuit priest Teilhard de Chardin wrote: 'Only love can bring individual beings to their perfect completion as individuals because only love can take possession of them and unite them by what lies deepest within them.' Lord, grant us the fullness of such love. Amen.

Some significant events on this day

Year   Event

399 BCE The Greek philosopher Socrates is tried and sentenced to death.
1936   Adolph Hitler announces to the German people the building of the Volkswagon.
1965   The red-and-white maple leaf design is adopted as the flag of Canada.

Key thought for today

One isn't necessarily born with courage, but one is born with potential. Without courage, we cannot practise any other virtue with consistency. We can't be kind, true, merciful, generous or honest.
— Maya Angelou

Reflection

By Br Denis: Irena Sendler (1910–2008) is credited with saving over 2500 children during World War II. Hers is an inspiring story.

During the World War II German occupation of Poland, Irena Sendler lived in Warsaw while working for the city's Social Welfare Department. She started helping Jews a long time before the Warsaw Ghetto was established. Helping Jews was very risky in German-occupied Poland – all household members were punished by death if a Jew was found hidden in their house.

In 1942, as a worker of the Social Welfare Department, she had a special permit to enter the Warsaw Ghetto, to check for signs of typhus, something the Nazis feared would spread beyond the ghetto. During the visits, she wore a Star of David as a sign of solidarity with the Jewish people and so as not to call attention to herself.

She organised the smuggling of Jewish children from the ghetto, carrying them out, and placing them with Polish families, the Warsaw orphanage of the Sisters of the Family of Mary or Roman Catholic convents. She kept lists of the names, hidden in jars, in order to keep track of original and new identities.

Arrested in 1943 by the Gestapo, she was severely tortured and sentenced to death. The underground saved her by bribing the German guards on the way to her execution. Officially, she was listed on public bulletin boards as among those executed. Even in hiding, she continued her work for Jewish children.

Prayer

May I seek opportunities to work actively for justice for those who are persecuted. May I not sit impassively by and allow others to oppress those who are not able to speak up for themselves. I ask you, Lord, to give me the strength to act responsibly when I need to. Amen.

Reflecting God's Presence

Some significant events on this day

Year   Event

600   Pope Gregory I declares 'God bless you' is the correct response to a sneeze.

1973   Birthday of athlete Cathy Freeman.

1983   Seventy people die in the Ash Wednesday bushfires in Victoria and South Australia.

Key thought for today

A day without laughter is a day wasted.
    — Charlie Chaplin

Reflection

By Br Bill Firman

One of the most prolific of modern English writers Hilaire Belloc (1870–1953) once wrote:

> *From quiet homes and first beginning,*
> *Out to the undiscovered ends,*
> *There's nothing worth the wear of winning*
> *But laughter and the love of friends.*

Laughter and the love of friends are the things that sustain us, that create quality in our lives day by day. Laughter and the love of friends support families in times of grief. Life must go on with laughter and the love of friends. Even in times of grief we should agree with Nicholas Chamfort who wrote:

> *The most wasted of all days is that on which one has not laughed.*

Teachers and parents can improve relationships with children dramatically, and thereby promote the freedom to love and share at school or in the home, if laughter is never far away. Most people enjoy the image evoked by the words of George and Weedon Grossmith, authors of *The Diary of a Nobody* who wrote: 'I left the room with silent dignity and caught my foot in the mat.'

It is sometimes most opportune to catch one's foot in the mat! Laughter breaks tension. Fun is needed more than dignity.

Prayer

God, help me when I feel down to laugh my way back up, knowing that most events do have a funny side if we are humble enough not to worry that we made a mistake. Grant me laughter, and the love of friends, today. Amen.

Some significant events on this day

Year   Event

1867   The first ship passes through the Suez Canal.
1933   The Blaine Act ends prohibition in the USA, allowing the sale of alcohol.
1938   The first public demonstration of Baird colour television is transmitted in London.
1963   The basketball player Michael Jordan is born.
1996   World champion Garry Kasparov defeats the Deep Blue supercomputer in a chess match.

Key thoughts for today

The easiest way to deal with poor people is to close our eyes and pretend they are not there.
— Weary Fletcher

You learn about equality in history and civics, but you find out that life is not really like that.
— Arthur Ashe

Reflection

By Larry Evans

I've had the opportunity to travel a little and have visited some very poor countries. I have been struck, time and time again, by the good-natured acceptance of these people of their lot in life. And their lot is little. I visited the 11-year-old girl I sponsor through Plan and found it the most humbling experience. Lila lives in rural Nepal, is one of five siblings, and one of the nine who share her single-roomed house. Yet, we were made to feel special by a very proud family who have very little worldly means.

I pray that we truly appreciate our lot, and that we can have a part in tipping the balance more toward the Lilas of this world.

Prayer

A prayer to end poverty

May God bless us with discomfort at easy answers, half truths, and superficial relationships, so that we may live deep within our hearts.

May God bless us with anger at injustice, oppression, and exploitation of people, so that we may work for economic justice for all people.

May God bless us with tears to shed for those who suffer from pain, hunger, homelessness and rejection, so that we may reach out our hand to comfort them and to turn their pain into joy.

And may God bless us with enough foolishness to believe that we can make a difference in the world so that we can do what others claim cannot be done.

Reflecting God's Presence

Some significant events on this day

Year Event

1885 Mark Twain's *Huckleberry Finn* is published.

1930 Clyde Tombaugh, studying photographs of the night sky, discovers Pluto.

1991 The IRA explodes bombs in the early morning at both Paddington Station and Victoria Station in London.

Key thought for today

When I was a boy of 14 my father was so ignorant I could scarcely stand to have the old man around, but when I got to be 21 I was astonished at how much the old man had learned in seven years.
— Mark Twain (in the words of his character, Huckleberry Finn)

Reflection

By Br Bill Firman

Parents invest a lot in their children when they send them to Catholic or Independent schools for their education. It is an act of love from the heart. Pope John XXIII could well have had parents and their children in mind when he said:

I have looked in your eyes with my eyes. I have put my heart near your heart.

Family members have eyes that look deeply into the eyes of other family members. Parents and their children put their hearts close together. The school years represent quite a journey of parents and children together. It usually begins with Mum holding the hand of her apprehensive child as the child ventures to school for the first time; and it often ends with assertive, over-confident youth, technologically more skilled than their parents, launching into cyberspace.

It is not the sense in which the poet, W.B. Yeats, penned the following beautiful words but they can appropriately be applied to God's hopes for each of us and to parents' hopes for their children stepping forth from school:

I have spread my dreams under your feet;
Tread softly because you tread on my dreams.

As young men come to the end of their schooling, I invite them to accept this advice from Pope John XXIII:

Consult not your fears but your hopes and your dreams. Think not about your frustrations, but your unfulfilled potential. Concern yourself not with what you tried and failed in, but with what it is still possible for you to do.

Prayer

May we always respect the dreams of those who are near and dear to us, putting failures and mistakes behind us and concerning ourselves with what we intend to achieve.

Reflecting God's Presence

Some significant events on this day

Year   Event

1878   The phonograph is patented by Thomas Edison.
1915   The Battle of Gallipoli begins, with French and British ships shelling Turkish fortifications in the Dardanelles.
1942   Darwin is attacked by nearly 250 Japanese planes, killing almost 1100 people.

Key thought for today

The presence of a superior reasoning power, revealed in the incomprehensible universe, forms my idea of God.

— Albert Einstein

Reflection

By Br Bill Firman

Every person in a Lasallian school becomes very familiar with the simple prayer

Let us remember we are in the holy presence of God.

A sense of God's abiding presence is very important. Remembering God's presence can have a great effect on our lives. Jesus told us: 'Whatever you do to the least of my children, you do also to me', and 'Where two or three are gathered together in my name, there am I in the midst of them.'

Of course it is not easy. Parent, Kathy Smith, once wrote: 'It is a whole lot easier to see Christ in a Cambodian refugee than in someone who leaves traces of peanut butter all over the kitchen I just cleaned.' This same mother, in an article entitled 'Blessed are the family peacemakers', talks of finding Christ in the family. She says: 'I think it is a kind of spiritual Murphy's Law that the ability to see Christ in another person is in inverse proportion to how closely you rub shoulders with that person ... Looking for Christ-like qualities in your spouse and children can be a real eye-opener.' What a wonderful thought – to look for Christ in the people we love. If we cultivate an abiding sense of God in our family – the God whom Jesus told us to regard very personally as 'Our Father' – if we regard the people with whom we live as God's gifts to us, then the Gospel values will be obvious in our families. There will be respect and love: everyone will feel valued.

'Let us remember we are in the holy presence of God.' It is a simple prayer we can use on any family occasion. It does not require us to be sanctimonious: it is an act of faith that God is never far away. God is always with us if we open our hearts to him. God is always in our family when family members relate to one another with love. God touches us in a mother's tender love, a father's robust care or a child's trusting response. There is no need to look for Christ outside of the family – have a good look within. Loving family members bring God to one another.

Prayer

Be with me, God, on my journey, holding me up when I tend to fall. Give me the faith, if I stray, always to return to your loving presence. Amen.

Reflecting God's Presence

20 FEBRUARY

Some significant events on this day

Year   Event

1962   Aboard *Friendship 7*, John Glenn becomes the first American to orbit the earth.

1987   In Salt Lake City, the 'Unabomber' explodes a bomb in a computer store.

1991   A gigantic statue of Enver Hoxha, Albanian dictator from 1944 to 1985, is pulled down in the capital Tirana, by mobs of protesters.

Key thought for today

Those who are not capable of enduring poverty are not capable of being free.
— Victor Hugo

Reflection

By Br Bill Firman

When the Hoxha regime in Albania crumbled with the collapse of communism, the world discovered a backward country with little industry, barely any telecommunications technology and farming techniques from the previous century. The bizarre legacy of Hoxha's 41-year regime was 600,000 concrete bunkers built across Albania to repel potential attacks – one for every five people! The people were living in poverty imposed on them from above by a repressive regime. Yet the Albanian people had shown some of the strongest courage in World War II. Albanian nationalist groups fought against the Italians and subsequently the Germans. By October 1944 they had thrown the Germans out, the only East European nation to do so without the assistance of Soviet troops. Albania is unique in that it is the only European country occupied by the Axis powers that ended World War II with a larger Jewish population than before the war. Only one Jewish family out of six was deported during the Nazi occupation there. Not only did the Albanians protect their own Jews, they provided refuge for Jews from neighbouring countries. The Albanians refused to hand over lists of Jews. Instead they provided Jewish families with forged documents and helped them disperse among the Albanian population.

Poverty, imposed on such good and courageous people by a repressive ruler, is an unjust evil. Yet there is a kind of poverty, an attitude to material goods, that can be liberating and uplifting for the human spirit. Christopher Shorrock explains, in speaking of St Francis:

> *To most people, poverty is essentially a negative thing. To be poor means to be without the things which most people see as vital – money, the necessities of life, security, respectability, and so on. To accept poverty cheerfully might be regarded as virtuous; to desire poverty might be thought abnormal and eccentric; while to make poverty an ideal to be fought for with all your strength would be considered unintelligible ... Francis saw poverty as providing him with the freedom to enjoy what God gave him. To Francis, then, poverty was not only an ideal but a source of joy. Poverty brought one into union with God in a special way.*

Prayer

May I always keep perspective with respect to the things that enrich me and those things in which I am poor. Help me to recognise that 'all things are passing, except God alone'.

21 FEBRUARY

Reflecting God's Presence

Some significant events on this day

Year   Event

1801   Birth of John Henry Newman in London, the eldest of six children in an Anglican family.
1848   Karl Marx, aged 29, publishes *The Communist Manifesto* in England.
1875   Jeanne Calment is born in France. She went on to live for 122 years and 164 days, the longest confirmed life span in human history.
1953   Francis Crick and James Watson discover the structure of the DNA molecule.
1965   The African-American civil rights leader Malcolm X is assassinated in New York city.

Key thought for today

Fear not that your life shall come to an end, but rather fear that it shall never have a beginning.
— John Henry Newman

Reflection

By Br Quentin O'Halloran:

In the everyday struggles of life, we can sometimes feel quite alone.

This is a very human situation experienced by the famous and lowly alike. One who experienced many disappointments in his long life of ninety years was Cardinal John Henry Newman, but he had the wisdom to see through appearances. Newman was an Anglican priest who converted to Catholicism and became a Catholic priest. He was, later in life, made a cardinal and in 1991, just over 100 years after his death, was proclaimed 'Venerable' and may eventually be proclaimed a saint.

His quite famous personal manifesto can help us to be courageous too:

> *Let us put ourselves in God's hands and not be startled though he leads us by a strange way. Let us be sure he will lead us right, that he will lead us to that which is, not indeed what we think best, not what is best for another, but what is best for us. We are all created for his glory. We are all created to do his will.*
>
> *I am created to do something or be something for which no one else is created; I have a place in God's counsels, in God's world, which no one else has. Whether I be sick or poor, despised or esteemed, God knows me and calls me by name.*

Prayer

Let me never forget that the same God who made me, made the whole world and all animals that are in it. Give me the grace to love all God's works for God's sake, and all people for the sake of my Lord and saviour who has redeemed me on the cross (from John Henry Newman's prayer to St Philip Neri).

Reflecting God's Presence

Some significant events on this day

Year   Event

1956   Elvis Presley appears on the music charts for the first time with *Heartbreak Hotel*.

1997   In Scotland, Dolly, a Finn Dorset sheep, is successfully cloned from a specialised adult cell from the udder of a six-year-old sheep. Dolly lived for six years, about half the life-span of a normal sheep of that breed.

2006   In the UK's biggest robbery, at least six men stole 53 million pounds from a bank in Tonbridge, Kent.

Key thought for today

The difficulties of life are intended to make us better – not bitter.
— Mandy Ellingson

Reflection

By Br Bill Firman

In the novel *The Great Gatsby*, author Scott Fitzgerald describes a scene on an oppressively hot summer's day when one of the principal, self-indulgent characters, Daisy, asks the question: 'What shall we do today, tomorrow and the next thirty years?'

Daisy is very rich, very bored and has a pervading sense of futility about her. Wealth and self-indulgence have not brought her happiness. There are many people who pursue the myth that more money will bring greater happiness. In this era of incredible comforts and entertainments, we all run the risk of developing an undesirable softness and a pleasure-orientated lifestyle where we think having more will make life better. We should not forget the value of some voluntary self-restraint and even asceticism. We need to develop strength of character to be able to cope with good times as well as bad. Even rich people can become very depressed!

What we *do* with our life is more important that what we have. Part of that doing is striving to become better. 'The moral man', says John Dewey, 'is the man who is moving to become better', not the person just staying in the same place. To become a better high jumper, we don't just keep comfortably clearing the same height. No, we constantly strive to jump higher. To become a better golfer we don't just try to play to our handicap; we try to lower our handicap. To become a better doctor, we can never say we know all there is; we know there is more we can and should learn to improve our diagnostic and prescriptive skills.

Striving to become better, at anything, is a great way of avoiding self-indulgence and boredom. Depressed people seem to lose the energy to strive. On the contrary, people can fire up with enthusiasm when they have something they wish to achieve. Doing nothing does not bring happiness. Achieving something worthwhile, and becoming a better person in some way, does.

Prayer

Lord help me to measure up to these words of Martin Luther King Jr: 'The ultimate measure of a man is not where he stands in moments of comfort ... but where he stands at times of challenge and controversy.' Amen.

Some significant events on this day

Year Event

1455 This is the traditional date for the publication of the first Western book printed with moveable type, the Gutenberg Bible.

1689 The Dutch Prince William III is proclaimed King of England.

1821 The death of poet John Keats.

1874 Walter Winfield patents a game called 'sphairistike', now more commonly known as lawn tennis.

1954 The first mass vaccination of children against polio, using the Salk vaccine, begins in Pittsburgh, USA. Dr Jonas Salk never patented his vaccine but distributed the formula freely, thereby saving millions from death or lives spent in wheelchairs.

Key thought for today

It would scarcely be necessary to expound doctrine if our lives were radiant enough. If we behaved like true Christians, there would be no pagans.
— Pope John XXIII

Reflection

By Patrick Jurd: Much loved Pope John XXIII lived out the message expressed in this passage below from John Powell's book, Why Am I Afraid To Love? Doctor Jonas Salk also put the message into practical effect, caring more for his fellow human beings than for profit. I offer it for your reflection.

> *There is a story about the evangelist St John, the one who wrote: 'God is love ... if any man tells me that he loves God, whom he does not see, but does not love his brother whom he does see, he is simply a liar.'*
>
> *It is of this John that the story is told that in the evening of his long life he would sit for hours with his younger disciples gathered at his feet. One day, as it is related in this well-established tradition, one of his disciples complained, 'John, you always talk about love, about God's love for us and about our love for one another. Why don't you tell us about something else besides love?'*
>
> *The disciple, who once, as a youth, had laid his head over the heart of God-made-man, is said to have replied, 'Because there is nothing else, just love ... love ... love.'*
>
> *Love is the only way to our human destiny and to the feet of God, who is love.*

Prayer

We pray with Dietrich Bonhoeffer: 'Give me such love for God and people as will blot out all hatred and bitterness.' Amen.

Reflecting God's Presence

Some significant events on this day

Year   Event

1938   The first toothbrushes made with nylon bristles rather than animal hair go on sale.

1989   A United Airlines Boeing 747 plane, bound for Sydney from Honolulu, is ripped open just above 22,000 feet, with nine passengers sucked out to their deaths. The pilot lands the plane safely at Honolulu airport with no further loss of life.

1999   English singer Elton John is knighted.

Key thought for today

Far better is it to dare mighty things, to win glorious triumphs, even though checkered by failure … than to rank with those poor spirits who neither enjoy much nor suffer much, because they live in a grey twilight that knows not victory nor defeat.
—Theodore Roosevelt

Reflection

By Br Bill Firman

Jesuit Fr Tom O'Donovan, writing when the Cold War still cast a division through Europe, said:

> *All suffering is a growth point: properly accepted it can become for any person a loving principle of renewal. As a result the people of Eastern Europe have become much stronger spiritually than their Western brothers. Suffering has strengthened their character. It has drawn them together, making them more concerned for one another, more compassionate, more ready to serve one another.*

All of human life is a gift from God, including suffering. Most people do not seek suffering but when it comes, as O'Donovan says, it should strengthen our character. Jesus came to fill suffering with his presence. The tender love one person shows to another who is suffering is a great gift, and the opposite is also true. Deliberately inflicting pain on another and succumbing to hatred is one of the greatest sins. Caring for others in need, on the other hand, is central to the Beatitudes, and draws the greatest blessings.

Suffering is not something we seek but it is something we may have to accept, something that can require us to grow beyond our own comfortable limits and become closer to our God who suffered and died on the cross. Paul Claudel summed this up succinctly when he wrote:

> *Jesus did not come to explain away suffering or remove it. He came to fill it with his presence.*

Most of us tend to recoil from suffering, as did Jesus in his full humanity when he prayed in the Garden of Gethsemane: 'If it is possible let this pass me by.' Yet, just as Jesus did, ordinary people can cope with suffering and can find incredible, interior strength when it is needed.

Prayer

Milo Chapman wrote that 'The strangest truth of the Gospel is that redemption comes through suffering.' Lord, help me to embrace redemption and be ready to suffer when it comes. Amen.

Some significant events on this day

Year Event

1932 Austrian immigrant Adolf Hitler receives German citizenship.
1964 Cassius Clay (who later changed his name to Muhammed Ali) defeats Sonny Liston to win the world heavyweight boxing championship for the first time.
1968 In a single ceremony in Korea, 430 Unification Church (Moonies) couples marry.

Key thought for today

Enter this day into sentiments of true humility and confusion at the thought that you seek to avoid occasions of suffering, whereas Jesus Christ submitted to all such through love of us.
— Saint John Baptist de La Salle

Reflection

By St John Baptist de La Salle

Make it a habit to think often of the holy presence of God, for this is the chief fruit of mental prayer (Letter to Br Denis).

When you feel inclined to impatience in class, wait some time before acting or speaking until this feeling has passed. Always be serious in class for good order in the school depends to a large extent on this (Letter to Br Hubert).

Always have God in view in your actions. This is important in order to perform them in a Christian manner. (Letter to Br Hubert).

If you are a true lover of Christ, you will take every possible means to instil his holy love in the hearts of your children whom you train to be his disciples (Meditation on St Ignatius, Martyr).

That your words may produce their full effect on your pupils, preach by example before their eyes what you wish them to accept (Meditation on St John Chrysostom).

If you desire to remain pure, as your calling requires, watch carefully over your senses so as not to lose control over them on a single occasion, if possible (Meditation on St Francis de Sales).

Prayer

De La Salle was concerned to prepare Brothers for their mission. Henry Martin wrote that 'the Spirit of Christ is the spirit of mission, and the nearer we get to him the more intensely missionary we must become.' Fill me with your Spirit, Lord Jesus, and inspire me with zeal to further your mission. Amen.

Reflecting God's Presence

Some significant events on this day

Year   Event

1952   Winston Churchill announces that Britain had developed its own atomic bomb, making it the third nuclear power after the USA and the USSR.

1991   Tim Berner-Lee introduces the World Wide Web, the first internet browser.

1995   Barings Bank, the oldest investment bank in the UK, collapses after securities broker Nick Leeson lost US$1.4 billion by speculating on the Singapore International Monetary Exchange using futures contracts.

Key thought for today

Don't try to reach God with your understanding: that is impossible. Reach him in love: that is possible.
— Carlo Carretto

Reflection

By Br Bill Firman

In 2006, the accepted description of our solar system changed. After several years of debate, Pluto was officially 'downgraded'. The solar system now has eight recognised planets rather than nine. Of course the universe has not changed. Pluto is still there. It is our scientific understanding and conventional description that have changed as we have learned more. Pluto was only discovered in 1930 as telescopes and photography were improved. Until 1978, it was thought to be larger than it is because scientists had not realised it had a nearby moon with a diameter over half that of Pluto. Pluto's moon, Charon, was discovered in 1978. Some scientists consider the two bodies to be, effectively, a double planet. Unlike a normal planet where the centre of gravity lies within, the centre of gravity of Pluto and Charon lies between them.

No doubt many people have taken little interest in Pluto. Yet the debate and the change of status is a reminder that the Bible was written in the light of the scientific knowledge of the time. It was not written as a science text book. The writers of the books of the Bible never even knew Pluto existed. Neither the universe nor Pluto changed in the recent past. Our knowledge has changed.

C.S. Lewis (1898–1963), one of the literary and theological giants of the last century, wrote:

> *All that is not eternal is eternally out of date.*

Lewis, a very intelligent man, strove early in life to be an atheist yet found he could not be true to himself and also be an atheist. In seeking the truth, he found God. It is a pity about Pluto and all those science books now out of date. But it is a reminder that we all must keep on learning and seeking the One Eternal Being.

Prayer

Give us the gift of understanding and the wisdom to use our knowledge well in the faithful service of our neighbour and our God.

27 FEBRUARY

Reflecting God's Presence

Some significant events on this day

Year   Event

1997   Following a 1995 referendum, the Irish Family Law Act, legalising divorce, is enacted.
2002   More than 50 Hindu pilgrims are killed when a train catches fire after it leaves Godhra railway station in India. This triggers riots that led to the deaths of thousands of people, mostly Muslims.
2004   Terrorists bomb a large ferry in the Philippines, killing 116 passengers.

Key thought for today

The commonest fallacy among women is that simply having children makes one a mother – which is as absurd as believing that having a piano makes one a musician.
— Sydney Harris, journalist

Reflection

By Br Bill Firman: Here is a beautiful poem by Donna Gargis entitled 'A Wish for You, My Child'. It sums up the hopes of most loving parents for their children.

If there could be only one thing in life for me to teach you, I would teach you to love ...
To respect others so that you may find respect in yourself;
To learn the value of giving, so that if there ever comes a time in your life
    that some one really needs you, you will give;
To act in a manner that you would wish to be treated; to be proud of yourself;
To laugh and smile as much as you can, in order to bring joy back into this world;
To have faith in others; to be understanding;
To stand tall in this world and to learn to depend on yourself;
To take only from this earth those things which you really need so there will be enough for others;
To not depend on money or material things for your happiness but to learn
    to appreciate the people who love you,
    the simple beauty that God gave you
    and to find peace and security within yourself.
To you, my child, I hope I have taught all of these things, for they are love.

Prayer

May I learn to live up to my parents' expectations, and perhaps even exceed them. Amen.

Reflecting God's Presence

Some significant events on this day

Year   Event

1947   In Taiwan, 30,000 people are killed when a civilian protest is put down.

1993   US law enforcement agents raid the Branch Davidian compound in Waco, Texas, leading to 86 deaths and a 51 day siege.

2004   Over one million Taiwanese form a 500 kilometre hand-in-hand human chain to commemorate the 1947 massacre of 30,000 civilians by the communist administrators.

Key thought for today

The voice of the Lord is the voice of common sense, which is shared by all that is.
— Samuel Butler

Reflection

By Br Bill Firman

David Koresh, the leader of the Branch Davidians in Waco, Texas, claimed to be an agent of God. The Branch Davidians came from a schism in the Seventh Day Adventist Church. After Koresh took control of the group, he annulled the marriages of his followers, claiming that only he could be married. He 'normalised' the notion that girls in the cult, as young as 12, should have sexual intercourse with him. Former followers told authorities that Koresh would beat the children.

A showdown with the cult began on Sunday 28 February 1993. Agents with the Bureau of Alcohol, Tobacco and Firearms attempted to arrest Koresh. It has not been determined who fired first, but gunfire erupted. Four ATF agents and six cult members were killed and another 16 wounded. The FBI took control of the situation, and President Clinton endorsed a negotiated settlement. Koresh made a tape of his teachings and promised to surrender if the recording was broadcast nationally. It was broadcast but Koresh said that God had told him to wait. He made rambling religious statements interspersed with threats of violence. The FBI became concerned that the Davidians would commit mass suicide. Over the next 51 days, negotiations went back and forth. The Davidians held children up in the windows of a tower on the compound and a sign saying: 'Flames Await'.

On Monday 19 April, the FBI notified the Davidians of an imminent tear gas assault. The Davidians begin shooting after the attack began shortly after 6 am. The FBI continues to maintain that members of the cult started fires. Fire-fighting efforts began, but the wooden structures quickly became engulfed. Koresh and 76 followers, including 20 children, died. It is disturbing that one man could gain such control over other people. In common with many cults, an excessive focus on the leader, bizarre sexual practices, a disdain for normal society and an abandonment of common sense were evident among the Branch Davidians.

Prayer

God preserve us from religious extremism that assaults our common sense. Jesus taught the love of little children, not their abuse. Help me to live with balance and respect for all other people.

Some significant events on this day

(*A leap year day only*)

Year   Event

- 1504   Christopher Columbus uses his knowledge of a lunar eclipse this night to convince Native Americans to provide him with supplies.
- 1960   An earthquake in Morocco kills over 3000 people and nearly totally destroys Agadir in the southern part of the country in just 15 seconds.
- 1964   In Sydney, Dawn Fraser sets a new world record in the 100 metres freestyle swimming competition (58.9 seconds).

Key thought for today

This is the day the Lord has made; let us be glad and rejoice in it.
  — Psalm 118

Reflection

By Paul Marshall

Leap Years come about because a year consists of approximately 365 days and 6 hours. Therefore, every four years, an extra day is added to account for the extra 24 hours which have accumulated.

How am I going to experience this 'extra' day? What am I going to do with this day? Time and the passage of time can be such a mystery: some days speed by in a flash, while others seem to drag on. Sadly, some days come and go without my having reflected on the learning and meanings contained therein.

So, to whom will I reach out today? How will I extend myself and be aware of others? Whom will I build up; to whom will I give an extra cheery smile. How will I be generous and compassionate? And how will I express my gratitude for the extraordinary gift that is today and all that it offers.

(*Note for the mathematically inclined: Technically the length of a year is actually 365.2422 days per year, not 365.25. This small difference of .0078 of one day means the average length of every year is actually 11 minutes 15 seconds too long – which amounts to one whole day in 128 years. To counterbalance this, every 100 years the leap year is omitted. However, every 100 years is actually an over-compensation. So every fourth 100 years, the leap year goes ahead. The consequent arrangement is that no century year is a leap year unless it is exactly divisible by 400. Hence 2000 and 2400 have been scheduled as leap years but 2100, 2200, 2300, 2500 will not be leap years.*)

Prayer

I thank you, God, for all that today promises. Help me to live this day intentionally, unselfishly, and joyfully.

Reflecting God's Presence

Some significant events on this day

Year	Event
1872	The US Congress authorises the creation of the world's first national park, Yellowstone National Park.
1912	In a London demonstration, suffragettes smash shop front windows.
1954	The US detonates its second H-bomb on Bikini Atoll, an explosion three times larger than expected and 1000 times more powerful than the bomb dropped on Hiroshima to end World War II.
1966	Soviet probe *Venera* crashes into Venus, making it the first unmanned craft to land on another planet.

Key thought for today

If only there were evil people somewhere, insidiously committing evil deeds, and it were necessary only to separate them from the rest of us and destroy them. But the line dividing good and evil cuts through the heart of every human being. And who is willing to destroy a piece of his own heart?
— Alexander Solzhenitzyn

Reflection

By Br Bill Firman

Afro-American poet, Dr Maya Angelou wrote:

I have found that among its other benefits, giving liberates the soul of the giver.

The nineteenth century author, poet and art critic, John Ruskin, warned us of the opposite when he wrote:

When a man is wrapped up in himself, he makes a pretty small package.

Giving is one of the great paradoxes. There is as much, or more, joy for the one who gives as for the one who receives. Somewhere, deep inside, we find that to give is to liberate the soul. To be unselfish and loving towards others is the key to genuine happiness. There is no greater gift to a hungry person than to appease that hunger. There is no greater gift to a cold and homeless person than the gift of shelter. There is no greater gift to the unemployed than the dignity that comes with a job and the capacity to earn a living. There is no greater gift to a child than security and love. When we give to help others we do in fact enrich our own lives. Twentieth century army general Peyton Conway March calls it the 'law of nature'. He wrote:

There is a wonderful mythical law of nature that the three things we crave most in life – happiness, freedom and peace of mind – are always attained by giving them to someone else.

'Small package' people never discover this wonderful fact. One of the world's wealthiest men in the first half of the twentieth century, the philanthropist John D. Rockefeller Jr wrote:

Think of giving not as a duty but as a privilege.

Prayer

Let me unwrap this small package of myself and always be ready to share what I have with others.

2 MARCH

Reflecting God's Presence

Some significant events on this day

Year	Event
1807	The US Congress abolishes the slave trade, effective from 1 January 1808.
1931	Birthday of Mikhail Gorbachev, last president of the United Soviet Socialist Republic (USSR).
1969	In France, the supersonic airliner Concorde makes its maiden flight.
2002	Operation Anaconda, code name for the US-led invasion of Afghanistan, begins.

Key thought for today

It is a very beautiful work, but there are already too many walls between people.
— Mikhail Gorbachev on the Great Wall of China

Reflection

By Br Bill Firman

The prophet Micah, writing many hundreds of years before the birth of Christ, penned the following beautiful words:

> *Hear what our God ask of us:*
> *To live justly,*
> *To love tenderly*
> *And to walk humbly with our God.*
>
> *(Micah 11:13)*

This is a succinct summary of what is required if we are to live life with full human dignity. This passage is from a part of the Bible jointly venerated by Christians, Jews and Muslims. The notion is one of fair and caring people, accepting that what they have are ultimately gifts from God.

Humankind is ascribed the dignity of walking with God. It is fundamental that we accept all other people as deserving the same dignity and respect. It is also a basic truth that we are made by God and God has given us a variety of gifts to use. So if we are successful in any enterprise, we need to avoid the arrogance of self-praise and recognise that we are simply using our God-given talents. We are expected to act with integrity, treating others justly and loving them tenderly.

Justice, love and humility – Micah's words, God's expectations, and good advice to us.

Prayer

Let me live in accord with the words of St Ambrose: 'The rule of justice is plain, namely, that good people ought not to swerve from the truth, nor inflict any unjust loss on anyone, nor act in any way deceitfully or fraudulently.'

Reflecting God's Presence

Some significant events on this day

Year   Event

1847   Birthday of Alexander Graham Bell, inventor of the telephone.

1931   *The Star Spangled Banner* is declared the national anthem of the USA.

1991   The beating of Rodney King, caught speeding by Los Angeles police, is recorded on video and telecast to a world-wide audience.

Key thought for today

The heights by great men reached and kept
Were not attained by sudden flight,
But they, while their companions slept,
Were toiling upwards in the night.
    — H.W. Longfellow

Reflection

By Brian Coulthard

As you move on from school to university or to the wider world, you will be searching for success in all areas of your life, including social, financial, family and home life.

It is important to learn the secret of success. Is it hard work? Not on the basis of evidence. Many people work hard at menial jobs and don't make it. Some people work hard and succeed financially but don't find happiness in their family life.

This question was considered deeply by Albert Gray, who was involved in life insurance in America and who wrote his findings in a pamphlet called 'The Common Denominator of Success'. He studied the lives of successful men through the ages and discovered what they had in common. He boiled his findings down to one short statement:

> *The common denominator of success – the secret of success of every man who has ever been successful – lies in the fact that he formed the habit of doing things that failures don't like to do.*

In other words people can't be successful by simply doing the things they enjoy. They have to develop the habit of doing the things they don't enjoy.

So, set some big life goals for yourself and make them happen. Remember, the enemy of a great life is a good life.

Prayer

Lord, send your Spirit to live in my heart. Give me the strength to make right and sensible decisions and lead me on to a successful life in all areas, in your name. Amen.

Some significant events on this day

Year   Event
1787   The US Congress meets for the first time and the Constitution comes into effect.
1877   Tchaikovsky's ballet *Swan Lake* is performed for the first time at the Bolshoi Theatre in Moscow.
1980   In a national election, Robert Mugabe becomes the first black president of Zimbabwe (formerly Rhodesia).

Key thought for today

God does not refuse grace to those who do what they can.
   — Latin proverb

Reflection

By Joy Bew. I found the following story quite moving and I invite you to reflect on it.

A young and successful executive was travelling down a neighbourhood street, going a bit too fast in his new Jaguar. He was watching for kids darting out from between parked cars and slowed down when he thought he saw something. As his car passed, no children appeared. Instead a brick smashed into the Jag's side door! He slammed on the brakes and backed the car back to the spot where the brick had been thrown. The angry driver jumped out, grabbed the nearest kid and pushed him up against a parked car shouting, 'What was that all about and who are you? Just what the heck are you doing? That's a new car and that brick you threw is going to cost a lot of money. Why did you do it?'

The young boy was apologetic. 'Please, mister ... please. I'm sorry but I didn't know what else to do', he pleaded. 'I threw the brick because no one else would stop ...' With tears dripping down his face and off his chin, the youth pointed to a spot just around a parked car. 'It's my brother', he said. 'He rolled off the curb and fell out of his wheelchair and I can't lift him up.' Now sobbing, the boy asked the stunned executive, 'Would you please help me get him back into his wheelchair? He's hurt and he's too heavy for me.'

Moved beyond words, the driver tried to swallow the rapidly swelling lump in his throat. He hurriedly lifted the handicapped boy back into the wheelchair, then took out a linen handkerchief and dabbed at the fresh scrapes and cuts. A quick look told him everything was going to be okay. 'Thank you and may God bless you', the grateful child told the stranger. Too shook up for words, the man simply watched the boy push his wheelchair-bound brother down the sidewalk towards their home.

It was a long, slow walk back to the Jaguar. The damage was very noticeable, but the driver never bothered to repair the dented side door. He kept the dent there to remind him of this message: Don't go through life so fast that someone has to throw a brick at you to get your attention!

Prayer

God whispers in our souls and speaks to our hearts. Sometimes, when we don't have time to listen, he has to throw a brick at us. It's our choice to listen or not. Lord, help me to listen and respond as I should. Amen.

Reflecting God's Presence

Some significant events on this day

Year	Event
1956	The US Supreme Court upholds the ban on segregation between black and white students in schools, colleges and universities.
1990	Aged 13.9 years, Jennifer Capriati becomes the youngest tennis player to reach a professional tennis final. She lost 6-4, 7-5 to Gabriela Sabatini.
1997	For the first time in 25 years, North and South Korea meet for peace talks.

Key thought for today

Whatever women do, they must do twice as well as men to be thought half as good. Luckily, this is not difficult.
— Charlotte Whitton

Reflection

By Br Bill Firman

I think one of the more patronising utterances of a saint are these words of St Basil from the fourth century:

Ready service, according to our ability, even in very small things and even if rendered by women, is acceptable to God.

Basil was right to affirm serving others but the telling words 'even if rendered by women' reveal an underlying inappropriate attitude that endured into the 20th century, that women are less important or less able to serve than men. I like the irony expressed by the novelist Joseph Conrad (1857–1924) who penned these words:

Being a woman is a terribly difficult trade, since it consists principally of dealing with men.

Although there is ongoing need for affirmative action, considerable progress in women's rights has been made in recent years and women have reached the top in many professions. I personally regret that the church has not done more to accept the rightful equality of women. Fortunately, there are many men and women in relationships based on wholesome respect and equality but, nonetheless, abuse and domination of some women by their male partners is still a terrible problem in Australian society.

A woman seeking to leave a violent situation, if she has school-age children or younger, almost always finds it very hard to obtain a job which will leave her with sufficient time to care for her children. So, month after month, year after year, some valiant women put up with emotional and physical abuse by their partners because they have no other way of supporting their children and simply cannot afford to go elsewhere. Women in domestic violence situations are one of the most disadvantaged classes of people in Australian society. They are to be admired, not criticised, and helped in any way we can.

Prayer

Lord, I pray always to respect women: never to swear in their presence; never to denigrate them by my talk nor abuse them by my actions; always to see them as my equal partners in living. Amen.

Some significant events on this day

Year   Event

1836   The 12-day siege of the Alamo ends, with only six of the 155 men still alive.

1869   Dimitri Mendeleev, the Russian chemist, presents the first Periodic Table of the elements to the Russian Chemical Society.

1987   The English Channel car ferry, the *Herald of Free Enterprise*, capsizes near the Belgian port of Zeebrugge.

1990   Following seventy years of communism, the Russian Parliament passes a law that permits the ownership of private property.

Key thought for today

Darkness cannot drive out darkness; only light can do that. Hate cannot drive out hate; only love can do that.

— Martin Luther King Jr

Reflection

By Euan Walmsley

What might we have eyes to see?

Jesus resisted those who were tempted to make hostile and absolute judgements about the sins or failings of others. He healed Gentiles, called on the adulterous woman to be forgiven and called on us to forgive, 'Not seven times, I tell you, but seventy-seven times'.

Do we have the eyes to notice those among us who need special consideration at school, in our clubs, at social gatherings? Who seems lonely? Who needs encouragement? Who is cruising rather than demanding more of themselves? What needs do we tend to pass by so often?

Some suffer from their own inertia, others from inadequate assurance or resolution. Many of us tend to avoid intervening or taking initiatives to assist or ignite those near us. For Australians, who have relished easy or comfortable lives, we not only need eyes to notice but language to intervene diplomatically when our friends are 'floating' through life rather than challenging themselves.

Jesus' call for tolerant understanding of those unlike ourselves is also a call for us to challenge our friends when they need it and to make demands on ourselves.

Prayer

G.K. Chesterton once wrote that 'Christ did not love humanity. He never said that he loved humanity. He loved people.' In other words, Christ does not love in the abstract but he loves each person. We are called to do the same. We are not called vaguely to be loving, but we pray that we may see the real needs of each person we meet and do something about them.

Reflecting God's Presence

Some significant events on this day

Year　Event

1936　German troops invade the Rhineland in violation of the Locarno Pact and the Treaty of Versailles.

1942　Japanese troops, headed for Australia, land in New Guinea.

1965　During a march from Selma to Montgomery, Alabama, demonstrators, demanding better voting rights for African-Americans, are attacked by US state troopers.

Key thought for today

In modern warfare there are no victors; there are only survivors.
— Lyndon B. Johnson

Reflection

By Br Bill Firman

My father fought in the First World War. I was born during the Second World War, which followed only 21 years later. In spite of all of the carnage of the so-called 'Great War', nations of the world had learned little and plunged into another mass slaughter that lasted more than five years.

When I began school, Australian males still faced the prospect of compulsory military training: De La Salle College had a very active Army Cadet Corps and National Service was the destiny of all 18-year-old males. My eldest brother Ron was only briefly a cadet but did his National Service in the Royal Australian Air Force. By the time my brother Jack was 18, three years later, the National Service scheme was no longer compulsory. I think I had the distinction of becoming the first College Captain who had not joined the cadets.

Attitudes have gradually changed as generations have changed. Young people no longer grow up with the anxiety that they may be forced to fight in a war. Further, school-age young people today have no first-hand recollection of the pre-1989 Cold War tensions. The generations of Australians who were ever grateful for US support in World War II are being supplanted by increasingly disenchanted younger Australians who regret our involvement in the conflict in Iraq. It is one of the supreme ironies that old people send countries to war and young people are expected to risk their lives doing the fighting.

Sadly, our new fear today is terrorism. It would seem to me that never has it been more important to be able to view our modern society with our minds well-informed by the events of recent history and with developed skills in thinking and acting with clear moral purpose.

Prayer

William Temple said that Christians at war 'are called to the hardest of all tasks: to fight without hatred, to resist without bitterness, and in the end, if God grant it so, to triumph without vindictiveness'. Lord, this would not be easy. Please grant us to live, instead, in peace.

Some significant events on this day

Year   Event

1917   The February Revolution (so-called because this was the month of the Russian calendar in which it occurred) begins with riots for food in Petrograd (later called Leningrad).

1965   The first 3500 US troops land in South Vietnam at Da Nang, beginning the US involvement in the Vietnam War.

1971   In the boxing match advertised as 'The Fight of the Century', Joe Frazier defeats Muhammed Ali. Ali won two later re-matches.

Key thought for today

Courage is resistance to fear, mastery of fear, not absence of fear.
— Mark Twain

Reflection

By Br Bill Firman:

Mark Inglis likes to ski. He is a double amputee who won a cycling silver medal in the 2000 Paralympics in Sydney. He lost his legs in 1982 from frostbite after he and a mountaineering mate Phil Doole survived 14 days trapped in an ice cave near the top of Mt Cook, New Zealand's highest peak. Mark was only 22 when he lost his legs. He had no tertiary education but went back to study, gaining a science degree in engineering and microbiology. He now has everyday legs plus special legs for climbing, cycling and skiing. He works as a winemaker. On 7 January 2002, Inglis again climbed Mt Cook. On 27 September 2004, his 45th birthday, he climbed to the top of Choy Oyu, the sixth highest peak in the Himalayas at 8201 metres. His next aim is to climb Mt Everest. Mark, who is also a motivational speaker, says success is 20 per cent aptitude and 80 per cent attitude.

At a reunion of my class from school, I met up with Les Boeckly, whom I had first met in 1958 as a boy. It is only now that I can grasp the full significance of his story. When he was 14, just before the Hungarian revolution in 1956, Les' family escaped across the border. After a year in a refugee camp, the family migrated to Australia. I can imagine how hard it must have been for Les' parents to make that decision to try to escape. What a risk to take. What a blessing that it turned out well, with all the family well established in Australia.

Some time ago I saw on television a bike rider take off from a ramp and do a reverse double somersault on his push-bike. He missed the first time but landed it the second. The commentator said it was the first time it had been done in competition. I found myself thinking: How would you ever practise that? If you don't quite make it the consequences could be dreadful.

Mark, Les, the bike rider and those like them, possess incredible courage and determination. They remind us that the most serious disadvantages and losses in life or the biggest challenges, are there to be overcome.

Prayer

In the words attributed to Reinhold Niebuhr: 'God grant to me the serenity to accept the things I cannot change, the courage to change the things that should be changed, and the wisdom to know the difference.'

Reflecting God's Presence

Some significant events on this day

Year   Event

1945   The firebombing of Tokyo by US forces begins. Japanese homes were made of timber and paper and packed tightly together – more than 250,000 homes were destroyed and 85,000 people killed.

1959   The first Barbie Doll goes on display at an international toy fair in New York.

1967   The daughter of Josef Stalin, Svetlana Alliluyeva, defects to the west by seeking asylum in the US Embassy in India.

Key thoughts for today

The only disability in life is a bad attitude.
    — Scott Hamilton

A story is told of a man who, resisting the cost of oats he fed his mule, decided to gradually substitute sawdust in its diet. Everything went fine for a while – but by the time the mule was satisfied with sawdust, he died. What do you feed on? Is it possible that you are mentally digesting junk? Beware! Before you know it, through lack of nourishment, you may become mentally, emotionally and spiritually dead.
    — Grant M. Bright

Reflection

By Patrick Jurd

I'd like to share a story of a young man called Mark who attended St Bede's College about 20 years ago. He had spina bifida, but this did not seem to affect his mood at all. He was one of the most cheerful and considerate young men with whom I have ever had dealings. On athletics day there were a number of reluctant participants who needed to be 'press ganged' into events. One event specifically designed for this was the 'one lap race' (at the time the track wasn't 400 metres). Mark put up his hand to be part of this event. All the able-bodied young men ran their race, even the unwilling, leaving Mark alone, shuffling along as best he could.

He eventually came to the top of the back straight, alone, in front of where the whole school was sitting in their house groups. I still get chills thinking of how the whole school stood as one, cheering Mark on, as he eventually finished his race. It is a moment in time I would love to bottle! At that moment, I believe Mark was the whole school's teacher about grace, courage and determination. It was a day when you were proud to be there and proud to be a part of the College community. I never had Mark in any classes – but he was my teacher!

Prayer

Let me not pray to be sheltered from dangers, but to be fearless in facing them.
Let me not beg for the stilling of my pain, but for the heart to conquer it.
Let me not look for allies in life's battlefield, but to my own strength.
Let me not crave in anxious fear to be saved, but hope for the patience to win my freedom.
Grant me that I may not be a coward, feeling your mercy in my success alone, but let me find the grasp of your hand in my failure (Rabindranath Tagore).

Some significant events on this day

Year   Event

49 BCE   Julius Caesar and his army cross the Rubicon, a small river in Northern Italy, from Gaul. The modern identity of the Rubicon is uncertain.

1876   Alexander Graham Bell speaks on the telephone for the first time.

1997   The Taliban, in Afghanistan, ignoring all protests, announce the destruction of two colossal 6th century statues of Buddha carved into the Bamiyan Hills.

Key thought for today

We are shaped and fashioned by what we love.
   — Johann von Goethe

Reflection

By Brother Bill Firman

One of the richest passages in the Bible is to be found in St Paul's letter to the Ephesians:

If we live by the truth and in love, we shall grow in all ways into Christ.

This brief sentence brings into focus what it is to be truly Christian: to be seekers of truth and givers of love. Youth, who lack experience, can be very awkward in a relationship as can we all. It was Judith Wright who wrote poetically:

Yet I go on from day to day, betraying the core of light, the depth of darkness – my speech inexact, the note not right, never quite sure what I am saying – on the periphery of truth.

We don't have to be right all the time. Sometimes we can be on the periphery of truth, uncertain of the truth, but always we can be seekers of the truth. There is no more pathetic image in the gospels than Pontius Pilate washing his hands of the death sentence for Jesus and saying, 'What is truth?'

Of course the second injunction is even more important – to live by love. Remember the injunction of love on the early Christians:

By this shall everyone know you that you love one another.

Our family and friendship groups should be remarkable because we care about one another. We respect the feelings of others and try to help others always. This is what it means to be Christ-like. Ignore the truth and you destroy trust. Without trust there is no love. But with truth and love we are at the heart of Christianity.

Prayer

God, assist me to be a genuine person who seeks after truth, who looks for the good in others and tries to meet them with a loving attitude as a brother or sister who is precious to God – and to me. Amen.

Reflecting God's Presence

Some significant events on this day

Year   Event

1811   The Luddite riots begin in Nottingham, England, with poor workers destroying stocking and lace-making machines that they feared would replace them in factories.

1942   General Douglas MacArthur famously states, 'I shall return', as he pulls American forces out of the Philippines.

1985   After the death of Konstantin Chernenko, Mikhail Gorbachev becomes leader of the Soviet Union.

Key thought for today

Life is action and passion; therefore, it is required of a man that he should share the passion and action of the time, at peril of being judged not to have lived.
— Oliver Wendell Holmes

Reflection

By Brother Bill Firman

Boys at De La Salle know Br Denis Loft as a very good Maths teacher. But that is only part truth. In fact, Br Denis worked in PNG for 20 years where his rapport with the local people is legendary. Now he is passionate about helping impoverished people in India – as well as teaching Maths!

Each year, Brother Denis leads a group of students who have just completed Year 12 to India. They raise the finance to build houses for impoverished families in the Tamil Nadu province and then go there to do the building. It is an extraordinary step by ordinary young men who overcome their trepidation and discover that there are many things they really can do – even regular, hard, physical, unpaid labour in the heat. So they become 'Coolies' while others indulge in 'Schoolies' week. One year a generous parent arranged a donation of work boots and other goods. I heard someone ask Br Denis the next year where his boots were from last year. 'I needed a new pair', he said. 'The ones I had last year eventually fell apart after I wore them so often.' I have to admit it: I can't remember when I last wore out a pair of work boots!

In India and PNG it becomes obvious that you don't have to own a lot to be happy. There are many smiling faces. Our young men come to appreciate the importance of companionship and friends, of courage in adverse circumstances, of making the most of a situation rather than pleasure-seeking. The Brothers, along with others who have been inspired and imbued with this Lasallian ethos, endeavour to bring care and hope to people in developing regions and countries. There is nothing more fulfilling than using the gifts God gave us to help others, to be people for others, to be ordinary people doing extraordinary things.

Prayer

Lord, I pray that there will be many more ordinary young men who will respond to the challenge to do extraordinary things – like the men we call 'Brother'.

12 MARCH

Reflecting God's Presence

Some significant events on this day

Year   Event

      Feast day of the Benedictine monk Pope St Gregory the Great (540–604 CE).

1894   Bottled Coca-Cola is sold for the first time. Dr John Pemberton created the drink in 1886 and patented it in 1893.

1938   German troops enter Austria and Hitler declares it as now part of Germany.

1994   Thirty-three women become the first female priests ordained in the Church of England in a ceremony in Bristol Cathedral.

Key thought for today

God is within all things but not included; outside all things, but not excluded; above all things but not beyond their reach.

— Pope Saint Gregory I

Reflection

By St John Baptist de La Salle

Saint Gregory was destined by his father to succeed him in his position as a senator in a Rome, but this saint, while still young and following the death of his father, built several monasteries and retired to one of them, leaving the world and all his wealth ...

Saint Gregory suffered throughout his life with extreme patience. First he practised excessive severity as a monk. Second, the pains of gout made his body so emaciated that it was difficult to recognise him. Third, he suffered from persecution ... The only remedy he used in all this suffering was recourse to prayer.

When this saint was elected Pope, he immediately took to flight, but finally, despite his feelings, accepted responsibility of head of the church ... After he became Pope, he sent out evangelical labourers to preach the faith to infidels and to instruct them in our religion. By such conduct this saint showed it was only his humility that made him flee the papacy, because once he had accepted it, his zeal led him to accomplish great things for the cause of religion.

You do not have infidels to convert, it is true. Yet you are obliged by your state to teach your children the mysteries of religion and to give them the spirit of Christianity. This is a task of no less importance than the conversion of infidels. So apply yourself to it with all possible care and attention (Meditation on Pope St Gregory the Great)

Prayer

Pope St Gregory said: 'The word of God, that you receive by ear, hold fast in your heart. For the word of God is the food of the soul.' Help me to hold fast to the word of God so that what I do is consistent with what I believe. Amen.

Reflecting God's Presence

Some significant events on this day

Year   Event

1781   The planet Uranus is discovered by William Herschel.

1881   Tsar Alexander II is assassinated in St Petersberg, Russia.

1930   Clyde Tombaugh discovers the ninth planet in our solar system. It was named Pluto, a name suggested by 11-year-old Venetia Burney from Oxford, on 24 March 1930.

1996   Sixteen children and a teacher are killed when a gunman opens fire at Dunblane Primary School in Scotland.

Key thought for today

When we have learned to offer up every duty connected with our situation in life as a sacrifice to God, a settled employment becomes just a settled habit of prayer.

— Thomas Erskine

Reflection

By Brian Long: *I found the following in a book I'm reading and I want to share it with you.*

In Los Angeles, at the Catholic Worker soup kitchen, the work begins with this prayer:

'Make us worthy, Lord, to serve our brothers and sisters who live and die in poverty and hunger. Give to them through our hands this day their daily bread and, by our understanding love, give peace and joy.'

One volunteer reports that often this initial prayer does not suffice:

'No sooner are these words out of our mouths than the vigorous chopping of vegetables for the soup and salad begins, as we prepare for the thousand-plus meals we will serve in a few hours. As a result, sometimes I get all caught up in the heavy responsibilities of our task, and I have to take a step back to repeat the words of the prayer again. And then I remember, "Oh yes, I'm not in charge. God is. Somehow, there will be enough food; somehow, there will be enough time to prepare it; and, somehow, there will be enough volunteers to serve it. Somehow, we will get through this day".'

During the food preparation, one person volunteers to go off and pray for an hour. The crew insists on this practice even though the extra pair of hands could be chopping vegetables or making coffee. They want it to be God's work, not theirs. And by eliminating the time for prayer they would be yielding to the workaholism of our culture. In addition, one morning a week the entire community gathers for a half-hour of meditative prayer. For activists on the front lines, prayer serves as part oasis and part emergency room' (Philip Yancey, Prayer*).*

Prayer

God, it is your work I am called to do. May I step aside and allow you to work through me. May I do my best and leave the rest to you. Amen.

14 MARCH

Reflecting God's Presence

Some significant events on this day

Year   Event

1757   British Admiral John Bing, accused of neglect of duty after losing Menorca to French forces, is tried and executed by firing squad on board his ship *The Monarch*.

1945   The British RAF drops the first grand slam 'dam buster' bombs on Germany.

1991   The so-called 'Birmingham Six' are freed after wrongful imprisonment for terrorism.

Key thought for today

In times when the government imprisons and unjustly, the true place for a just man is also the prison.
— Henry D. Thoreau

Reflection

By Br Bill Firman

Being imprisoned would be bad enough. Being imprisoned and knowing you were innocent would be far worse. In teaching boys, I have often marvelled at their strong innate sense of justice. If they are caught out for a misdemeanour, most will accept a sanction or penalty quite readily. But accuse a boy unjustly and, in normal circumstances, that boy will react most vigorously to protest his innocence.

On 21 November 1974, the Irish Republican Army (IRA) killed 21 people by exploding bombs in two Birmingham hotels. Earlier that evening six men had left Birmingham to attend a funeral of an IRA member and were boarding a ferry bound for Ireland when news of the bombing came through. They were arrested as suspicious, subsequently assaulted and beaten by the police in order to extract confessions. Although obviously bruised, they were convicted when the case came to court the following August and they were sentenced to life in prison. They appealed the conviction unsuccessfully. It was not until 1991, after six years of publicity stirred up by journalist Chris Mullins, that a further appeal was held. The fabrication of evidence by police was demonstrated and after 16 years in gaol the Birmingham Six had their convictions overturned. After a further ten years, they received some compensation. What an ordeal to suffer: to set out to perform one of the so-called 'corporal acts of mercy', to bury the dead, and finish up imprisoned for life.

It is impossible to compensate someone adequately for such deprivation of freedom and such an abuse of justice. We don't know how often unjust verdicts are carried by courts but the advent of DNA testing has certainly revealed many wrongful imprisonments. The actions of the police in fabricating evidence were seriously wrong. The incorrect decisions of juries is not usually culpable but no doubt, even with honestly presented evidence, before them, juries make wrong decisions. I believe we should be very careful to respect the sense of justice of others and never be party to fabricating evidence, no matter what our personal convictions may be.

Prayer

God, grant me a strong sense of justice and the courage to live always by my convictions; but make me very slow to judge others. I'll leave that task to you. Amen.

Reflecting God's Presence

Some significant events on this day

Year   Event

44 BCE   'Beware the Ides (15th day) of March' Caesar was warned. On this day, Julius Caesar is murdered on the steps of the Roman Senate.

1887   England and Australia begin their first test cricket match at the Melbourne Cricket Ground. Eventually the match was won by Australia.

1939   Hitler breaks the Munich Pact, signed only six months earlier, by invading Czechoslovakia.

Key thought for today

My mother taught me the importance of self-reliance, self-respect and self-discipline. She believed, as I do, that having these characteristic traits there was nothing I couldn't accomplish in life. She inspired me to be a great human being and to treat people as I would want them to treat me. She instilled in me to never take anything for granted, because life is a precious gift, and the gift of life shouldn't be misused but treasured. I hope that through my existence the world sees how my mother truly inspired me to be a great person.

— Jackie Joyner-Kersey

Reflection

By Br Bill Firman: Teachers are professional instructors of others, but parents are the most important teachers of their children. To teach is a privilege and an awesome responsibility. In this beautiful passage, Pearl Buck sums up the awesome trust of anyone who is called to teach.

Only the brave should teach – the men and women whose integrity cannot be shaken, whose minds are enlightened enough to understand the high calling of the teacher, whose hearts are unshakeably loyal to the young, whatever the interests of those who are in power.

There is no hope for our world unless we can educate a different kind of man and woman. I put the teacher higher than any other person today in world society, in responsibility and in opportunity. Only those who love the young should teach. Teaching's not a way to make a livelihood; the livelihood is incidental. Teaching is a vocation. It is as sacred as priesthood, as innate as a desire, as inseparable as the genius that compels a great artist.

If a teacher has not the concern of humanity, the love for living creatures, the vision of the priest and of the artist, that person must not teach. Teachers who hate to teach can only have pupils who hate to learn. Great and true teachers think of the child, dream of the child, see visions not of themselves but of the flowering of the child into adulthood. They think of the child first and always not of themselves. It takes courage to be a teacher and it takes unalterable love for the child; only the brave should teach (Pearl S. Buck).

Prayer

May we have the courage to be good teachers and to live up to our responsibilities. Amen.

16 MARCH

Reflecting God's Presence

Some significant events on this day

Year   Event

1521   The Spanish explorer Ferdinand Magellan reaches islands in the Pacific, which he names The Philippines in honour of the Spanish king.

1976   In his eighth year as Prime Minister of Britain, Harold Wilson resigns.

1978   The former Prime Minister of Italy, Aldo Moro, is kidnapped in Rome by the Red Brigade. His bullet-ridden body was found on 10 May.

Key thought for today

If a free society cannot help the many who are poor, it cannot save the few who are rich.
—John F. Kennedy

Reflection

By Brother Bill Firman

Helping the poor and oppressed is a key dimension of the Christian faith. The gospels recount many stories of Jesus, the embodiment of God's love, reaching out to those in need, even to the point of intervening miraculously to help them. Jesus clearly proclaims, by his actions, and in the following passage, the importance of social action. The Evangelist Luke describes Jesus getting up to read in the synagogue on the Sabbath. Jesus selected scripture from the prophet Isaiah (Luke 4:18-19):

> *'The Spirit of the Lord is upon me,*
> *because he has sent me to bring the good news to the poor,*
> *to proclaim liberty to the captives,*
> *and to the blind new sight,*
> *to set the downtrodden free*
> *and to proclaim the Lord's year of favour.'*

The US Catholic bishops, in their summary of the strong tradition of the Catholic Church of helping the poor and needy, state: 'We are our brothers' and sisters' keepers, wherever they live. We are one human family, whatever our national, racial, ethnic, economic and ideological differences'.

In the early church, care for the needy was clearly understood to be a priority. In the letter of James we read how the early Christians were urged to care for the widow and orphan (James 1:27). In Acts, seven deacons were chosen to look after the widows and to meet the social justice needs of the community (Acts 6:1-7). As centuries passed, many religious orders were established on the principle of sharing the goods of the earth with the poor and of recognising people's essential dignity, without regard to their economic or social status.

Prayer

A Latin proverb says: 'Not those who have little, but those who wish for more, are poor.' Help me to be content with what I have and to be willing to share unselfishly with those who have less.

Reflecting God's Presence

Some significant events on this day

Year Event

Feast day of Saint Patrick, patron saint of Ireland (c.389-461)
1912 On Captain Robert Scott's South Pole expedition, Lawrence Oates walks into blizzard to die, sacrificing himself so that the rest of the party will not be slowed and might survive.
2000 More than 500 die by fire in a mass suicide by a doomsday cult in Uganda.

Key thought for today

In a single day I have prayed as many as a hundred times, and in the night almost as often.
— Saint Patrick

Reflection

By Br Bill Firman

The Catholic faith was first brought to Melbourne by Irish immigrants who experienced sectarian resentment. Irish-Australian Catholics reacted by celebrating St Patrick's Day with much spirit. Until 1969, many secondary schools used to march in the St Patrick's Day Parade. Melbourne's cathedral is named after St Patrick. Melbourne Archbishop Denis Hart speaks of St Patrick's in these terms.

> *Saint Patrick's is a place of God, an oasis of peace and beauty. A small immigrant community built it with courage, vision and love. It is a lasting reminder of God's constant presence among the people of Melbourne. As a small boy I remember my father bringing me in for a visit. Later, as a seminarian, I saw that it was the focus of the church and I attended ordinations there. Forty years ago this year I myself was ordained a priest. Later, as a priest at the cathedral, I came to know the many moods our cathedral has: the peace of early morning, the prayerfulness of those who come for a visit, the comfort of reconciliation offered at lunchtime as the cathedral becomes light and the day is splendid. On Good Friday afternoon, often everything is bathed in golden light coming from the west, which gradually subsides as the quiet of evening descends.*
>
> *In word and song our great celebrations make it resound in praise of God. The beauty of our liturgies enhances the beauty of the place and draws us to remember the wonder of God. The cry of a baptised infant, the joy of confirmation, the life-giving hope of ordinations and marriage are matched by the peace of the sacrament of reconciliation of drawing people back to God. Whenever I stand at the altar celebrating Mass in the cathedral, I am always humbled and amazed at what we have – a treasured place to praise God and meet with him, constant focus of teaching life-giving truth, a never-ending sign of his mercy and consolation.*
>
> *Saint Patrick's has been the centre of so much of my priestly life and work and now as a bishop I am deeply grateful for what our Catholics of today hold and pass on to others. May Saint Patrick's long remain a place of wonder. 'How awesome is the place. This is a house of God and gate of heaven' (Genesis 28:17).*

Prayer

Thank you for the heritage of my Catholic faith and the challenge it presents to me. Amen.

Some significant events on this day

Year   Event

1962   After seven years of war, the French sign a peace treaty with Algerian rebels, so ending 130 years of French rule in Algeria.

1965   Soviet Cosmonaut Alexei Leonov becomes the first man to walk in space when he leaves *Voshkod 2* for 12 minutes. His space suit ballooned and he had to let some air out to get back in.

1992   White South Africans vote in a referendum to end apartheid, the system of laws introduced in 1948 that segregated South Africans according to race. The referendum also gives all South Africans the right to vote.

Key thought for today

Our main task in life is to give birth to ourselves, to become what we potentially are. The most important product of our own effort is our own personality.
— Erich Fromm

Reflection

By Clare Kennedy-Curtis

My mother used to love bragging about the fact that when I graduated from FCJ College in Benalla, I was dux of the school. My family and I always had a quiet chuckle when we overheard her because she invariably neglected to include one very important detail – my Year 12 cohort consisted of four students! Finishing school was an exciting time and a frightening time because it also meant I was leaving home. My parents were brave parents, firmly believing they had done a good job if they had given their six children the 'wings to fly away'. The sacrifices they made only impacted on me much later in life when I became a teacher and a parent.

Also, much later in life, I read a speech given by John Lewis, former headmaster of Geelong Grammar School and then of Eton College in the UK, and it reminded me very much of the lessons taught within our home. When Lewis was speaking to students who were graduating, leaving college, he wished that these were the attributes that they took away with them:

> *That they had minds of their own, for instance; to do their own thinking and not allow others to do it for them; to distinguish sense from nonsense; and (the ultimate test of an independent mind) a readiness to change it, as circumstances change or evidence compels. And an eye for others: in significant ways, of course, but also in social situations where others are being ignored or left out. And lastly, a backbone: 'No, it's wrong, it's not on; I won't do it, I won't have any part of it.'*

Prayer

Lord, help me to become the person I want to be, able to think and decide for myself, able to make good judgements of what is right and what is nonsense, able to notice and respond to the needs of others and able to act with backbone when faced with moral decisions. Help me to be a person of integrity.

Reflecting God's Presence

Some significant events on this day

Year   Event

1932   After eight years of construction, the Sydney Harbour Bridge is opened. At the time it was the world's largest single-span bridge.

1967   The oil tanker *Torrey Canyon* runs aground, badly contaminating 125 km of the French coastline.

1982   The Argentine flag is raised on South Georgia Island, resulting in Prime Minister Margaret Thatcher leading Britain into the Falklands War against Argentina.

Key thought for today

You must be holy in the way God asks you to be holy. God does not ask you to be a Trappist monk or a hermit. He wills that you sanctify the world and your everyday life.
— Vincent Pallotti

Reflection

By St John Baptist de La Salle

Because St Joseph was made responsible by God for the care and external guidance of Jesus, it was important that he had the qualities and virtues necessary to fulfil worthily so holy and exalted a ministry. The gospels tell us about three, all very fitting for the responsibility entrusted to him ...

The first quality that the gospels attribute to St Joseph is that he was just ... The gospels say of him that he was just before God, that is, holy in every way ... Take St Joseph as your model and strive to make yourself worthy of your ministry and to excel in virtue like this great saint.

The second virtue the gospels point out to us in St Joseph is his holy and entire submission to God's orders ... He does not hesitate a single instant to carry out what God desired of him. Do you have as much at heart to do God's will as this saint?

The gospels also make us admire in St Joseph the care he had for the holy Child Jesus ... Two things inspired this great solicitude St Joseph felt for Jesus: the commission the eternal Father had given him and the tender love he had for Jesus ... You must have a similar great attention and affection for preserving or procuring the innocence of the children entrusted to your guidance, and to keep them away from whatever might interfere with their education or prevent them from acquiring a religious spirit ... You have been made responsible for these children just as St Joseph was made responsible by God for the Saviour of the World (Meditation on St Joseph)

Prayer

Thomas Fuller wrote: 'There is no true holiness without humility.' Joseph was just such a humble working class man who was always just and caring. Help me to live with similar dedication to and care for those precious to me that characterised St Joseph. Amen.

Some significant events on this day

Year   Event

1916   Albert Einstein's *General Theory of Relativity* is published in German.

1995   Sarin gas is released in the Tokyo subway by the Aum Shinrikyo religious cult, killing 12 people and causing 5500 people to seek hospital treatment.

2003   Under President George W. Bush, American missiles are fired on Baghdad beginning the US-led campaign to oust Saddam Hussein from power.

Key thought for today

Frequently give yourself to the Spirit of our Lord to act only under his influence and not through any self-seeking.

— Saint John Baptist de La Salle

Reflection

By Brother Bill Firman

The ultimate test for a Christian is to be able to make sacrifices and to cope with suffering when it comes our way. Real strength is in the heart, not in the legs. Such strength, like physical strength, just doesn't happen. It has to be cultivated over time.

My mother had such strength. When my father died it was she who had the most to grieve about, but it was also she who held us all together and helped us all to cope. She had known profound grief before, learned from it, dealt with it and got on with life. Mum had such strength, as many mothers do.

Such strength is cultivated in a family when parents insist the children learn to be unselfish, to give up things for others and to share with others. Good parents place demands on their children and insist they live up to them. We grow in strength every time we make a commitment and live up to that commitment.

Some people shy away from visiting the sick or the bereaved. Certainly it can be a challenge to visit when we know words will be hard to find, but we show who we are by how we respond at such times.

The mature faith of a Christian is demonstrated by his or her ability to accept suffering simply as part of the human condition that we are privileged to share with Jesus. The Christian strives to become more Christlike, to follow Christ not just down the pleasant path of fulfilment in love, but to walk with Christ along the road of suffering when such is demanded.

Prayer

Lord, grant me your peace in joy and in suffering, in peace and in conflict. Give me the heart to face whatever may come.

Reflecting God's Presence

Some significant events on this day

Year   Event

1857   Approximately 107,000 people die when an earthquake hits Tokyo.

1960   In the Sharpeville massacre in South Africa, Afrikaner police open fire on peaceful black demonstrators killing 50 and wounding 169.

1963   Alcatraz Penitentiary for men in San Francisco Bay closes as a prison.

1980   President Carter announces a US boycott of the Moscow Olympics.

Key thought for today

Sport is one area where no participant is worried about another's race, religion or wealth: and where the only concern is 'Have you come to play?'
— Henry Roxborough

Reflection

By Br Bill Firman

After the Soviet Union intervened in Afghanistan in December 1979 to prop up an unstable pro-Soviet government, the United States reacted by suspending arms negotiations with the Soviets and threatening to boycott the Olympics to be held in Moscow in 1980. The Soviets refused to withdraw their troops. On 21 March 1980, President Jimmy Carter met with 150 US athletes and coaches to explain his decision. Carter defended his action, stating, 'What we are doing is preserving the principles and the quality of the Olympics, not destroying it.'

Most US athletes only reluctantly supported the decision. More than 45 nations supported the US-led boycott. Australia did compete, though many athletes chose – or were pressured – not to attend. At the opening and closing ceremonies, athletes from a number of countries marched under the Olympic flag, instead of their national flags. In the end, 80 nations – a third less than in Munich eight years earlier – competed. Not surprisingly, the USSR won 87 gold medals. In fact, excluding the East Germans who won 47 gold medals, the USSR won more gold medals than the combined totals of the other 78 teams competing.

The 1984 Summer Olympics were held in Los Angeles, USA. On 8 May 1984, the Soviet Union issued a statement that the USSR would boycott them because of 'chauvinistic sentiments and an anti-Soviet hysteria being whipped up in the United States'. Thirteen Soviet allies joined the boycott. Iran was the only country which did not participate in either Moscow or Los Angeles. The US decision to boycott the 1980 Olympic Games had no impact on Soviet policy in Afghanistan (Russian troops did not withdraw until nearly a decade later), but it did tarnish the prestige of the games in Moscow. Even sporting arenas were not immune from Cold War tensions. At the time it seemed unthinkable that only five years after the LA Games the Berlin Wall, symbol of the East-West divide, would come tumbling down.

Prayer

Let us use sport and all other meetings of people in fun, to unify countries rather than create divisions. Amen.

Reflecting God's Presence

Some significant events on this day

Year	Event
1457	The first printed book is published, the Gutenberg Bible, named after the inventor of the printing press, Johannes Gutenberg
1979	Sir Richard Sykes, British ambassador to the Netherlands, is assassinated by the IRA.
1979	The Israeli government approves a peace treaty with Egypt.
1984	Seven teachers in the McMartin Preschool are indicted for child abuse.

Key thought for today

If we believe absurdities, we shall commit atrocities.
— François Marie Voltaire

Reflection

By Br Bill Firman

As Director of BoysTown, I once found myself dealing with an increasingly hysterical situation generated by an emotional mother whose two-year-old son had said something to her about a naked man in the BoysTown chapel. Bizarrely, I found myself defending the position that neither the Brothers nor the chaplain would be naked in the chapel. Thankfully, after a few days, someone realised the two-year-old was talking about the bronze statue of a street kid in shorts on a bench outside the chapel. Misinterpretation, and manipulation, of answers of young children can occur and children themselves have vivid imaginations.

In a well-documented case, seven teachers at the McMartin Preschool in Manhattan Beach, California, were indicted by the Los Angeles County grand jury after hearing testimony from 18 children. Seven years and millions of dollars later, the case against the teachers came to a close with no evidence of wrongdoing and no convictions. This began on 12 August 1983 when Judy Johnson reported to the police that she believed her son had been molested at the McMartin Preschool. On 8 September, the Manhattan Beach Police Department sent out a form letter to more than 200 families, alerting them of an investigation into the allegations of child molestation. The letter set off a wave of hysteria in the community.

Compounding the problem, virtually every child who attended the school was sent to an organisation that claimed it could get children to reveal abuse even when they didn't want to talk about it. The allegations that were produced grew more bizarre every day. The children reported that they had been taken to a cemetery where dead bodies were dug up and hacked to pieces. There was no corroboration of these wild allegations but their truth or falsity mattered little to the community at large. More recent research has demonstrated that questioning techniques of children can easily be manipulated so that the child will give the answer the questioner desires. We should be alert to abuse but also be careful not to create innocent victims.

Prayer

Let me be calm and rational, especially in passing judgement in emotional situations. Amen.

Reflecting God's Presence

Some significant events on this day

Year	Event
1956	Pakistan declares itself an Islamic republic with an Islamic constitution, the first in the world.
1999	NATO gives a 24-hour ultimatum to Yugoslavia's President Slobodan Milosevic to withdraw Serbian troops from Kosovo. When he failed to comply, NATO made its first attack against a sovereign European nation on 24 March.
2001	After 15 years in orbit, the Russian *Mir* space station is brought down over the ocean between Chile and New Zealand.

Key thought for today

At times our own light goes out and is re-kindled by a spark from another person. Each of us has cause to think with deep gratitude of those who have lit the flame within us.
— Albert Schweitzer

Reflection

By Brother Bill Firman

I was surprised to read in a newspaper report that 41 per cent of all people at some stage or other are subject to feeling seriously depressed. I have no idea what criteria were used to reach this conclusion but the notion of so many people feeling depressed, no matter what the niceties of the definitions, is disturbing.

There are some young people, not a large percentage, who suffer from depression or related illnesses, but every school day I meet hundreds of students who are mostly very cheerful, energetic and optimistic. What goes wrong, as they grow older, if so many become victims of depression? There are many possible causes, as the reality of post-school life tempers natural optimism – unstable relationships, money problems, lack of achievement and so on. Psychologists use all kinds of terms but I want to make only one suggestion here.

Filled with energy, young people seek lots of fun and activity. Life becomes a search after pleasure in its various forms. As we age and energy levels settle down, our focus shifts more to thinking about the life we are carving out and career becomes more important than social activity. Endless partying is no longer satisfying. We are happier when we get a job we like and a job that is better paid. We want to feel we are going somewhere, achieving, progressing, not just being a 'good time guy'.

This phase also, however, does not last. We come to realise we are looking for something more. Our deepest longing is for meaning and that meaning is found in love. For a time 'love' of a particular activity or sport may provide that meaning but ultimately we need to give and feel the genuine love of other people. Other persons light our flame within. One really caring partner or friend can be enough to lift us above depression.

Prayer

May I, with all my failings, know that I am loved by God and may I cherish, and be cherished by, other people. Amen.

Reflecting God's Presence

Some significant events on this day

Year   Event

1603   On the death of Queen Elizabeth I, King James VI of Scotland succeeds to the English throne, uniting the two countries and becoming James I

1989   The *Exxon Valdez* runs aground in Prince William Sound, Alaska, spilling oil that affected 2900 kms of coastline and killed 250,000 birds.

1997   The Australian federal government overturns the Northern Territory Act, passed two years earlier, which permitted euthanasia.

Key thought for today

We know we only preach the subversive witness of the Beatitudes, which have turned everything upside down.

— Oscar Romero

Reflection

By Patrick Jurd

On this day in 1980, Archbishop Oscar Romero was shot and killed while celebrating Mass in a hospital chapel. Despite death threats, he had continued to speak against the repressive regime in El Salvador. He gave his last homily on 24 March. Moments before a sharpshooter felled him, reflecting on scripture, he said, 'One must not love oneself so much as to avoid getting involved in the risks of life that history demands of us, and those that fend off danger will lose their lives.' The homily that sealed his fate took place the day before when he took the terrifying step of publicly confronting the military. On 23 March, he metaphorically walked into the fire. He openly challenged an army of peasants, whose high command feared and hated his reputation. Ending a long homily broadcast throughout the country, his voice rose to breaking:

> *Brothers, you are from the same people: you kill your fellow peasant ... No soldier is obliged to obey an order that is contrary to the will of God.*

There was thunderous applause. Then his voice burst, 'In the name of God, then, in the name of this suffering people I ask you, I beg you, I command you in the name of God: stop the repression.' Romero was a surprise in history. The poor never expected him to take their side and the elites of church and state felt betrayed. He was a compromise candidate elected to head the Bishops' Conference by conservative fellow bishops. He was predictable, an orthodox, pious bookworm. But he lived by real convictions that he expressed boldly:

> *A civilisation where the trust of one for another is lost, where there is so much lying and no truth, has no foundation of love. There can't be love where there is falsehood. Our environment lacks truth. And when the truth is spoken, it gives offence, and the voices that speak the truth are put to silence.*

Prayer

Lord, may I be a person of truth who is inspired by the strength of others to live a good life. Amen.

Reflecting God's Presence

Some significant events on this day

Year   Event

1807   The Abolition of the Slave Trade Act is passed by the British Parliament, thereby banning trade in human beings throughout the British Empire.

1947   Elton John, singer and songwriter, is born.

1957   The European Economic Community is initiated when France, West Germany, the Netherlands, Belgium, Italy and Luxembourg sign the Treaty of Rome. The Common Market, as it was also known, became a reality in January 1958.

1967   Martin Luther King Jr leads a march of 5000 anti-war protestors in Chicago, arguing against the Vietnam War.

Key thought for today

Whatever God's dream about a person may be, it seems certain it cannot come true unless the person cooperates.
— Stella Terrill Mann

Reflection

By Br Quentin O'Halloran

This is the traditional date for remembering the Annunciation, the announcement by the Angel Gabriel to Mary that she had been chosen to bear a son conceived by the Holy Spirit. Mary said 'Yes' and Jesus was conceived. We are challenged to respond to situations in our everyday life with faith and courage similar to Mary's.

> *There are many ways of saying 'Yes'.*
> *There is a muttered 'Guess I have to' type of Yes.*
> *There is a merely adequate Yes.*
> *There is a terse unwilling Yes.*
> *There is a questioning, challenging Yes.*
> *And there is a positive, determined Yes, spoken with joy, in a spirit of cooperation and vibrantly alive.*
> *Thus did Mary say Yes to God.*

Prayer

Here we stand before you, Mary, to entrust to your maternal care ourselves, the church, the entire world. Plead for us with your beloved Son that he may give us in abundance the Holy Spirit, the Spirit of truth which is the fountain of life. We entrust to you all people, beginning with the weakest: the babies yet unborn, and those born into poverty and suffering, the young in search of meaning, the unemployed, and those suffering hunger and disease. We entrust to you all troubled families, the elderly with no one to help them, and all who are alone and without hope (Pope John Paul II, 2000).

Reflecting God's Presence

Some significant events on this day

Year	Event
1973	The London Stock Exchange admits women for the first time in its 200-year history.
1997	In San Diego, 39 members of the Heaven's Gate cult are found dead in a mansion. They died believing they would leave their bodies and be taken aboard an alien spacecraft that, according to their leader, was hidden behind the Hale-Bopp comet.
1999	The Melissa computer virus infects more than one million personal computers causing damage estimated at US$80 million.

Key thought for today

Speaking without thinking is shooting without aiming.
— William Benham

Reflection

By Br Bill Firman

Some give and take is an inevitable part of growing up with even the very best parent-child relationships. There will need to be the trust of integrity on both sides – some risk-taking by parents and a willingness to offer unqualified support if something goes wrong. It is especially hard for parents to protect their daughter from an exploitative relationship. Sometimes parents may have to distinguish between trusting their child's honesty, integrity and good intentions and not yet trusting the judgement of the child who still lacks experience in life. So it is hardly wisdom to 'throw a child to the wolves' when the child first begins to experience life outside of the parents' protective cloak. Judgement improves with experience.

One US woman, Mary Molloy, a Catholic mother of seven girls, expressed it this way when one of her daughters fell pregnant out of marriage: 'The ramifications of this particular sorrow cannot be imagined by those who have not had to face it.' She speaks of the young unmarried couple, Mary and Bob:

> *For me the turning point of that experience occurred within the first 48 hours of their breaking the news. I had been crying almost without ceasing for two days. We had talked to our pastor, a compassionate and understanding priest. He began by pointing out what an easy sin this was to commit and yet how lifelong the consequences inevitably were. 'Go home', he said, 'and give her a wedding, the best you can afford.' But still I wept until I did indeed go home and took a long look at my lovely, stricken daughter. All I could think of was how I loved her. In that moment I discovered something of what God's love for us must be. No matter how we disappoint or fail him, he simply loves us.*

Mary was writing some twenty years ago. Attitudes have changed a lot since then and there is less stigma attached to falling pregnant outside of marriage. But when a parent looks at a child and says, 'All I could think of was how I loved her', that parent is indeed offering the same kind of unqualified love and support that God offers to us. The genuine Christian family is one that shares a bond of love no matter what the upsets and storms of life.

Prayer

God, help me and my family to weather all storms sensitively, compassionately, lovingly. Amen.

Reflecting God's Presence

Some significant events on this day

Year   Event

1905   Fingerprint evidence is used for the first time in Britain to solve a murder case.

1977   In the worst aircraft accident ever, two planes collide on a foggy runway in Tenerife, killing 583 people.

1980   A North Sea platform, housing men who work on a nearby oil rig, collapses and capsizes in a gale, drowning 123 workers.

Key thought for today

When I approach children, they inspire in me two sentiments: tenderness for what they are, and respect for what they may become.
— Louis Pasteur

Reflection

By Br Bill Firman

Most young men coming to the end of their schooling are ready and even eager to move on, yet there is also the regret of letting go of a place where most have felt at home. They can understand the message of Hilaire Belloc who said: 'Always keep a-hold of nurse for fear of finding something worse.'

Yet young men leaving school must now let go and step forth to a more independent and self-reliant lifestyle where the capacity to say 'Yes' must be marked by an equal resolution to say 'No' when the occasion demands it. This is the real light of learning to which we have endeavoured to lead young men – the ability to think clearly, act resolutely and live with integrity.

The ancient philosopher Socrates said:

Nothing can harm a good person, either in life or in death.'

If each young man can live with the integrity of being true to his own dignity as a human being, loved by God and called to love others, he can be confident that he will overcome the inevitable trials and troubles that are part of life's journey.

Teachers say a respectful farewell at the end of Year 12 but the role of parents does not cease. Parents and children now begin the walk together as adult friends. Each young man will always be his parents' child. The challenge is now to move to a new equality in the relationship as an adult friend.

Ralph Waldo Emerson says:

A friend is someone with whom I can be sincere. With him or her I may think aloud.

The lifestyle of parents and children may increasingly diverge as the young man heads to university or employment, but the sharing, the thinking aloud, the touching of minds should not.

Prayer

May my closest friends be my parents and siblings; may nothing come between us. May we be united in our ability to think aloud openly and honestly together.

Some significant events on this day

Year   Event
1854   The Crimean War begins when France and Britain declare war on Russia.
1979   A nuclear accident occurs at the Three Mile Island nuclear reactor in Pennsylvania, USA.
2001   In a much criticised decision, US President George W. Bush announces the withdrawal of his nation's signature from the Kyoto Protocol.

Key thought for today

In nature there are neither rewards nor punishments – there are consequences.
— Robert G. Ingersoll

Reflection

By Br Bill Firman

The Three Mile Island nuclear power plant was built in 1974 on a sandbar on Pennsylvania's Susquehanna River, ten miles downstream from the state capital Harrisburg. In 1978, a second state-of-the-art reactor began operating. On 28 March 1979, the worst accident in the history of the US nuclear power industry began when a pressure valve in the Unit-2 reactor failed to close. Cooling water, contaminated with radiation, drained from the open valve into adjoining buildings, and the core began to overheat dangerously. Left alone, safety devices would have prevented the development of a larger crisis. However, human operators in the control room misread confusing and contradictory readings and the core heated to over 4000 degrees, just 1000 degrees short of meltdown. Plant operators realised they needed to get water moving through the core again and restarted the pumps. The reactor had come to within less than an hour of a complete meltdown.

No one outside Three Mile Island had their health adversely affected by the accident. Nonetheless, the incident greatly eroded the public's faith in nuclear power. Since that accident, not a single new nuclear power plant was ordered in the US, though two new nuclear reactors are being planned for a Texas field just a few miles from the Gulf of Mexico. The existing 103 nuclear reactors already provide 20 per cent of America's electricity needs. The nuclear industry says almost two thirds of Americans support new reactors. With demand expected to soar 40 per cent by 2030, the Department of Energy estimates 35 new nuclear plants could be built. There are still many scientists who say nuclear is the wrong direction to go. Radioactivity is incredibly dangerous and radioactive waste very hard to store safely. We do not know how to dispose of it effectively.

While Australia hesitates about whether to embark on a nuclear path, in South Texas there are fewer doubts. I don't like global warming but I am also convinced we must find better options than nuclear power if we are to look after the beautiful planet earth which is our home. Opinion will shift if there is another Chernobyl or a more disastrous Three Mile Island. It is hard to eliminate the possibility of human error.

Prayer

Lord, may we cherish the planet you have given us and build a sustainable future. Amen.

Reflecting God's Presence

Some significant events on this day

Year   Event

1901   The first federal elections are held in Australia, resulting in the election of Edmund Barton as Prime Minister.

1912   Antarctic explorer Captain Robert Scott makes the last entry in his journal before perishing with his starving party only a few kilometres from a food depot.

1974   NASA's spacecraft *Mariner 10* lands on Mercury, taking the first close-up photos.

2004   The Republic of Ireland becomes the first nation to ban smoking in all enclosed public spaces.

Key thought for today

Our most basic common link is that we all inhabit this small planet, we all breathe the same air, we all cherish our children's futures, and we are all mortal.
— John F. Kennedy

Reflection

By Larry Evans

I really like the 'Prayer of Acceptance and Love' below, as it points to the heart of many of our problems, problems created by ourselves, based on differences between one another.

The time has come for us to transcend this shallow perspective and think at a higher level, on a human level, and appreciate and respect our sameness as human beings. The consequent understanding and compassion that will flow from this attitude will prove a revelation for many.

Prayer

O God, we have so many ways of drawing lines between us – gender and sexual preference, race and nationality, political party and philosophy, social status and economic class, gifted and challenged. Not to mention school, neighbourhood, company, family, club, vocation and religion.

It quickly becomes easy to see the lines that divide, instead of the ones that connect, to allow identifying marks to become labels, until all that we see are the differences between us, instead of the common threads that tie us all together.

Help us, O God, to see one another through your eyes. To remember that there is room for everyone at the foot of the cross. To show one another that there are no ticket-takers at the doors of your kingdom, no entrance exam, no qualifying match.

May we become mirrors of your love – a love that transcends lines and labels and differences – to each and every person we encounter today. Amen.

30 MARCH

Reflecting God's Presence

Some significant events on this day

Year Event

1867 William Seward, US Secretary of State, purchases Alaska from Russia for $7,.2 million. The deal was dubbed 'Seaward's Folly' by the press.

1870 The Fifteenth Amendment to the US Constitution is passed, granting African-American men the right to vote.

1981 US President Ronald Regan is shot in the chest by John Hinckley Jr.

1987 Vincent van Gogh's painting 'Sunflower' sells at a Christie's auction for a record US$39,921,759.

Key thoughts for today

The one who forgives ends the quarrel.
— African proverb

The noblest vengeance is to forgive.
— English proverb

Reflection

By Br Bill Firman

Wise parents do not get too uptight when children are self-centred or self-willed. Ultimately, parents are trying to raise adults, not children, who, in turn, will raise their own children – aided principally by the modelling behaviour of their own parents!

One of the most important skills we each need is that of knowing how to forgive. There will be moments of upset in every family that require forgiving and forgetting.

Every family needs a good dose of 'f' words – not the swearing variety but forgiveness, forgetting annoyances, friendship, fun and the freedom for children to make mistakes, knowing that they will be supported and their feelings respected.

Jean Paul Richter wrote:

Humanity is never so beautiful as when praying for forgiveness or else forgiving another.

The poet, William Blake, put it this way:

Mutual forgiveness of each vice;
Such are the gates of paradise.

Prayer

'Forgive us our trespasses as we forgive those who trespass against us.' Help me to forgive others so that they might forgive me.

Reflecting God's Presence

Some significant events on this day

Year   Event

1889   The Eiffel Tower is officially opened, with Gustav Eiffel, its designer, climbing the 1710 stairs and unfurling the French flag from the third level.

1991   The Soviet-led Warsaw Pact ends after 36 years.

2005   Brain-damaged patient Terri Schiavo dies after having had her feeding tube removed on 19 March.

Key thoughts for today

Life is filled with meaning as soon as Jesus Christ enters into it.
— Stephen Neill

A blessed life may be defined as consisting simply and solely in the possession of goodness and truth.
— Saint Ambrose

Reflection

By Br Bill Firman

Anglican priest Grant Bullen, then the Vicar of Mount Waverly parish in Melbourne, wrote in his July 2005 parish newsletter:

> *What matters is the 'straining forward' (epektasis) of love and longing that permeates the whole of a human life – the journey. What matters is that each and everyday choice to choose life in the arena of moral struggle, temptation and uncertainty. It is the journey, the living driven by the desire for goodness, the longing for God, that matters.*
>
> *I look back over my life and it's not a great picture of achievement, triumph or success. But the desire has been there. I've done a good job of wanting more. And now, as I enter the latter chapters of life, I'm going to take Gregory of Nyssa's advice on the journey. I'm simply going to keep on going, not looking back at my stumblings and failures, but rather keeping my eyes fixed forward on Jesus, on that beauty and goodness that calls me.*
>
> *I'm going to 'strain forward'. Even as my body slows my heart can keep journeying, through to the very last breath I draw.*
>
> *We are on a journey into God – a journey into infinite goodness.'*

These are powerful words, urging us forward on the journey into God, to 'strain forward', to rejoice in an endless hope over the coming years. We all face inevitable moments of grief as loved ones die, as well as the personal grieving for our own declining skills and faculties as we age.

We need to be ready to accept with confident and prayerful hope, whatever happens to us. If we lead a good life, we are on the 'journey into God'. The alternative has nothing to recommend it.

Prayer

Donald Nicholl asserted that 'Holiness is not an optional extra to the process of creation but rather the whole point of it.' Let me not fear to be holy and to grow in holiness year by year.

1 APRIL

Reflecting God's Presence

Some significant events on this day

Year   Event

1918   The Royal Air Force is founded in Britain.
1982   Steve Wozniak and Steve Jobs form the Apple Computer Company, working from a garage building computers. By 2005, they employed 14,800 people.
1997   The Hale-Bopp comet reaches its perihelion – the point of its orbit where it is closest to the sun.

Key thought for today

All of us can attain to Christian virtue and holiness, no matter in what condition of life we live and no matter what our life-work may be.
— Saint Francis de Sales

Reflection

By St John Baptist de La Salle

How good it is to give oneself to God. The Lord rewards us even in this life and fills with sweet consolation the soul that consecrates itself to him (Meditation for the Feast of the Purification of Mary).

It is a good thing to apply yourself to your spiritual reading. It will be very profitable to you, particularly in helping you to make mental prayer (Letter to Br Denis).

It usually happens that after we have abandoned ourselves to God, he manifests extraordinary marks of his goodness and providence (Meditation for the Fourth Sunday in Lent).

In union with the entire church, let us today proclaim the sublime honour that is conferred on the most Blessed Virgin of becoming the Mother of God, which is the greatest favour that could possibly be bestowed upon a created being (Meditation for Annunciation).

Do not complain when you experience trials whether interior or exterior. Rest assured, on the contrary, that the more you suffer, the easier it will be for you to give yourself entirely to God (Meditation for the Fourth Sunday after Easter).

Prayer

Cardinal Suenens stated: 'I am a man of hope, not for human reasons nor from any natural optimism, but because I believe the Holy Spirit is at work in the church and in the world, even when his name remains unheard.' Lord, give me confidence in the workings of the Holy Spirit so that I may be a person of hope. Amen.

Reflecting God's Presence

Some significant events on this day

Year   Event

1917   Jeanette Pickering Rankin becomes the first female member of the US Congress.

1982   Argentina invades the Falkland Islands.

2005   Polish-born Pope John Paul II (Karol Jozef Wojtyla) dies at 9.37 pm after almost 27 years as leader of the Roman Catholic Church.

2008   A covenant of close relationship is signed between the Anglican diocese of Newcastle and the Catholic dioceses of Maitland-Newcastle and Broken Bay.

Key thought for today

Tonight our Covenant invites us into relationship – with our God and with each other – beyond the signatures on the page of those chosen to sign this significant document. The Covenant must take on flesh and bones, and we the people of God are those flesh and bones.

— Sr Jenny Gerathy OP

Reflection

By Brother Bill Firman: What unites Christians is always more important than what divides. So the signing of a covenant of close relationship was a very positive move for the Catholic and Anglican churches. Dominican Sister Jenny Gerathy had this to say:

Why do we choose to enter into this covenantal relationship? We come responding to the stirrings of the Spirit at the core of our beings with a desire that others may come to know the God who calls us in love, and for love. We come not for ourselves, rather for the kingdom! And if we should be anxious as to how we might fulfil this covenantal relationship, we have a blueprint in our first reading from the Acts of the Apostles: 'The whole group who believed were of one heart and soul ...' There is not one of us here who has not been graced by our loving God. We have all received grace upon grace. That being the case, the challenge is before us to be more daring together; to take risks for the kingdom together; to be a presence that disturbs together. This moment is a graced moment. Let us seize this moment through, with and in our God ... In the gospels we are reminded, 'The wind blows where it pleases' – the Spirit moves where the Spirit pleases. The Spirit has moved and will continue to move among the communities of people gathered here tonight, drawing us into covenantal relationship.

Tonight is the night to let go of the wounds of the past, whatever they be, because of earlier divisions between our churches. Let go of the hurt that might have come as a result of a mixed marriage; of not being able to attend a family member's wedding or funeral because their faith denomination was different to ours. What a gift we are being offered tonight! Tonight is the night to transfer all that is fearful into boldness of heart – for the kingdom. Tonight, the signing of the covenant symbolises the fact that together, in a common cause, individuals can make a difference, for the kingdom, God's kingdom. Tonight, it's time to switch on together for the reign of God. Earth Hour! – Church Hour! Now is the hour!

Prayer

God grant us the good will, and the flexibility, to establish lasting Christian unity. Amen.

Some significant events on this day

Year	Event
1885	Gottlieb Daimler patents the first water-cooled engine.
1922	Josef Stalin becomes the leader of the Soviet Union in place of Vladimir Lenin.
1972	The first mobile phone call is made in New York.
1986	IBM launches its first laptop computer.

Key thought for today

Is it progress if a cannibal uses a knife and fork?
— Stanislaw Lec

Reflection

By Brother Bill Firman

I completed secondary school in 1961, studying mainly science and maths. There were no calculators – only log tables for all and slide rules for a few. We had heard there were some universities and research laboratories that had several rooms occupied by large 'powerful computers', but by the time I had completed a Bachelor of Science degree in 1968, I still had not seen a computer or calculator.

The 20th century was a time of remarkable technological change, made possible by one very important event – the discovery of electricity. An extraordinary range of devices has been invented that depend on electricity and associated electronic knowledge. I grew up with radio and telephone and in 1956 witnessed the introduction of black and white television just before the Melbourne Olympics. I remember the first long-playing records in the mid-50s replacing the old 78s and was proud of the new stereo my dad bought. Cassette players were not yet invented in the early 60s but rapidly gained popularity in the latter part of the next decade. Lasers had not yet been discovered, so there were no CDs or DVDs or fibre optic cables. Nintendos, Play Stations or any other virtual reality game equipment did not exist. But we played plenty of cricket, football, tennis and other outdoor sports.

The first two, and only, atomic bombs used in combat were dropped two years after I was born. Since then people have lived with the fear of a nuclear holocaust which peaked in the early 60s but there has been no further global war and the Cold War has ended. This would be a major plus were it not for the rise of terrorism and the fear that terrorists will one day unleash a nuclear device. Global warming is an emerging fear. We are living in the most incredible period of technological development this planet has seen to date. Are we better off? Aldous Huxley once remarked with a typical touch of cynicism: 'Technological progress has merely provided us with more efficient means for going backwards.'

Backwards? Only if we fail to keep a correct perspective! What is essential is that we remember that technology must never control us. The human heart and spirit have been around much longer. We need to reassert respect for all peoples and our planet.

Prayer

God, help me to use the gift of technology well and not to abuse others or this planet. Amen.

Reflecting God's Presence

Some significant events on this day

Year   Event

1581   Sir Francis Drake becomes the first sea-captain to circumnavigate the earth.

1818   The US Congress introduces the American flag, with 13 red and white stripes and one star for each state of the Union (at that time 20).

1968   Civil Rights campaigner and Nobel Peace Prize winner (1964) Martin Luther King Jr, aged 39, is assassinated in Memphis Tennessee by James Earl Ray.

Key thought for today

Our lives begin to end the day we become silent about things that matter.
— Martin Luther King Jr

Reflection

By Patrick Jurd: I invite you to recall these inspiring words of Martin Luther King Jr.

I have a dream that one day this nation will rise up and live out the true meaning of its creed: 'We hold these truths to be self-evident that all men are created equal.'

I have a dream that one day on the red hills of Georgia, the sons of former slaves and the sons of former slave owners will be able to sit down together at the table of brotherhood.

I have a dream that one day even the state of Mississippi, a state sweltering with the heat of injustice, sweltering with the heat of oppression, will be transformed into an oasis of freedom and justice.

I have a dream that my four little children will one day live in a nation where they will not be judged by the colour of their skin but by the content of their character ...

And this will be the day, this will be the day when all of God's children will be able to sing with new meaning, 'My country 'tis of thee, sweet land of liberty, of thee I sing ...'

And so let freedom ring from the prodigious hilltops of New Hampshire. Let freedom ring from the mighty mountains of New York. Let freedom ring from the heightening Alleghenies of Pennsylvania. Let freedom ring from the snow-capped Rockies of Colorado. But not only that. Let freedom ring from Stone Mountain of Georgia. Let freedom ring from Lookout Mountain of Tennessee. Let freedom ring from every hill and molehill of Mississippi, from every mountainside, let freedom ring!

And when this happens, when we allow freedom to ring, when we let it ring from every village and every hamlet, from every state and every city, we will be able to speed up that day when all of God's children, black and white, Jews and Gentiles, Protestants and Catholics, will be able to join hands and sing in the words of the old Negro spiritual: 'Free at last! Free at last! Thank God Almighty, we are free at last!'

Prayer

Lord, may I be a person of justice in my life, especially in small ways. May I remember that 'just as you did it to one of the least of these who are members of my family, you did it to me'. Amen.

Some significant events on this day

Year	Event
1986	Two people are killed and over 100 injured in a terrorist bomb attack on a West German disco.
1992	Serb paramilitaries murder peace protester Suada Dilberovic, initiating the Siege of Sarajevo, the longest modern siege, lasting until 29 February 1996.
1998	With a main span of 2.1 km and after 10 years of construction, the largest suspension bridge in the world is opened to link the Japanese islands of Honshu and Shikoku.

Key thought for today

Faith always shows itself in the whole personality.
— Martin Lloyd-Jones

Reflection

By Br Bill Firman

I have come across many impressive people in my life and some remarkable ones. Remarkable people are easy to remember because they do something startling and/or achieve something extraordinary. So Cathy Freeman, Tiger Woods and Kevin Rudd are in my remarkable category though I don't know them well enough to classify them as impressive people or not. Impressive people to me are those who have a clear system of beliefs and act in accord with those convictions, not choosing the easy pathways but the right ones. They are people of moral strength, with integrity that emanates from inner faith. I have been very fortunate to live with such men as Brother Quentin and Brother Julian who model for me different individual personalities through which faith shines.

The great spiritual writer, Thomas Merton, wrote:

> *Ultimately, faith is the only key to the universe. The final meaning of human existence, and the answers to the questions on which our happiness depends cannot be found in any other way.*

Faith is the only key. Why? John Henry Newman said that

> *Faith is illuminative, not operative; it does not force obedience, though it increases responsibility; it heightens guilt, it does not prevent sin; the will is the source of the action.*

The faith-filled person is a truly free person who makes right decisions, not based on pleasure-seeking or a thirst for power or to win the esteem of others, but in accord with a well-formed conscience, grounded in the extraordinary conviction that God loves us and has made all people lovable. Such impressive persons do not seek the limelight, although others may well esteem them if they get to know them. Again, it is Thomas Merton who expresses so well the inner strength of the person of faith:

> *The deep secret of the mystery of faith lies in the fact that it is a 'baptism' in the death and sacrifice of Christ. We can only give ourselves to God when Christ, by his grace, dies and rises again spiritually within us.*

Prayer

Lord, help me to seek after truth, to try to enrich my faith rather than neglect this gift which is 'the only key'.

Reflecting God's Presence

6 APRIL

Some significant events on this day

Year	Event
1896	After a 1500-year break, the Olympic Games are re-born in Athens. Only men competed on that first occasion.
1917	The US enters World War I with a declaration of war on Germany.
1974	Swedish band ABBA wins the Eurovision song contest with their song 'Waterloo'.

Key thought for today

Work is not a curse. It is a blessing from God who calls us to rule the earth and transform it so that the divine work of creation may continue with human intelligence and effort.
— Pope John Paul II

Reflection

By Brother Bill Firman

Surely one of the modern heresies, promoted by the incessant advertising with which we are now bombarded, is the belief in comfort and pleasure as pre-eminent values. The continual pursuit of the comfortable life, of those practices that give pleasure and of the multiplicity of gadgets designed to make life easier, is not wrong per se, but it does become a problem if not tempered by moderation and if there is no recognition that we must still learn to bear with hardship when unavoidable.

Sunita Singhi had this to say:

> *If you want to accomplish something, there are two kinds of pain you might encounter: the pain of discipline and the pain of regret. Whenever you take that first step toward a new goal, you often experience the pain of discipline, the pain of hard work, the pain of sacrifice, as you single-mindedly pursue your dream. On the other hand, if you don't go after your dreams, you might experience an even greater type of pain: the pain of staying stuck, which eventually turns into the pain of regret ... The great thing about discipline is if you discipline yourself on a daily basis, eventually something 'magical' will happen to you, almost without your realising it – one day the discipline will turn into desire. A runner who 'makes' himself/herself run on a daily basis, one day gets up 'wanting' to run.*

This is true of study. It is taking the first steps towards being a good student which is difficult. There is a discipline in giving time regularly to study. But one day you wake up and you realise that you want to study. If we discipline ourselves regularly, one day we will discover that discipline has become a desire.

Young people must be schooled in interior resolve, in doing without. Real strength is in the heart, not in the legs. Such strength, like physical strength, does not just happen. It has to be cultivated over time.

Prayer

God, give me strength of heart and the courage to take the first step. Help me to find discipline and then desire. Amen.

Some significant events on this day

Year   Event

1719   The death on Good Friday, at St Yon, near Rouen in France, of John Baptist de La Salle.

1795   France adopts the metric system of measurement.

1964   Birthday of Russell Crowe, actor, who lives in Australia.

1983   Don Peterson and Story Musgrave become the first people to walk in space, that is, to undertake EVA – extravehicular activity – from a space shuttle.

Key thought for today

The spirit of this Institute is first a spirit of faith, which should induce those who compose it not to look upon anything but with the eyes of faith, not to do anything but in view of God, and to attribute all to God.

— Saint John Baptist de La Salle

Reflection

By Tom McIlroy

John Baptist de La Salle's life was one marked by unexpected turning points. His life changed dramatically as he, guided by his trust in God's providence, made the transition from a wealthy young man and a leading prelate in his community to that of innovative educator of poor children and patron saint of teachers.

Sometimes it is hard for us to compare ourselves to great men and women. We are not all saints, but we can learn a great deal from John Baptist de La Salle. He lived the message of Christ by believing in the providence of God and was fully open and accepting of God's plan for him.

Instead of the recognition he deserved, De La Salle, in 17th century France, met with opposition and strong criticism from many. He believed in his mission so much that he gave up his wealth and status, brought his fellow teachers into his home and persisted in establishing schools even when the work seemed hopeless. What better example for us when we have to make tough decisions in our lives?

De La Salle knew that nothing in life happened by chance – he listened for the message of Christ and was not afraid to answer the call. As Lasallians, we have been blessed to receive the example of the Founder of the Brothers of the Christian Schools. May we find direction in his wisdom, emulate the example of his humility and gain motivation to work for the good of others by the witness of his zeal.

We have entered the Lasallian family to learn. We go forth ready to serve.

Prayer

God, you inspired St John Baptist de La Salle to take practical action so that young people, especially the poor, received a Christian education. Inspire us to walk as brothers or sisters to those in need and share our gifts with those who have not been so blessed. Amen.

Reflecting God's Presence

8 APRIL

Some significant events on this day

Year   Event

1820   The statue of Venus de Milo is discovered on an Aegean Island, Melos. This ancient Greek statue, made of marble and 203 cm tall, dates back to 130 BCE.

1945   The courageous Lutheran pastor Dietrich Bonhoeffer is hanged for plotting against the Nazi dictatorship in Germany. Some would argue he should be canonised as a saint for all Christian denominations.

   Kim Malthe-Brunn is executed the same day (see below).

2005   Pope John Paul II's funeral takes place in St Peter's Basilica, Rome.

Key thought for today

His life was what it was. Because children grow up, we think the child's purpose is to be grown up. But a child's purpose is to be a child. Nature does not disdain what lives only for a day. It pours the whole of itself into each moment. We don't value the lily less for not being made of flint and built to last. Life's bounty is in its flow, later is too late. Was the child happy while he lived? That is the proper question.

— Tom Stoppard in *Shipwreck*

Reflection

By Br Bill Firman

Kim Malthe-Brunn, aged 22, was executed on 8 April 1945. Just before he died he wrote to his young sweetheart words that express the beautiful unselfish love we have when we really care for another. Kim wrote:

> *What do I possess that I can give you in farewell, that you may live on and become an adult, in sorrow and yet with a happy smile? We sailed upon the wild sea, we met each other in the trustful way of playing children, and we loved each other. We still love each other and we shall continue to do so.*

> *You are not to forget our love. I do not ask that: why should you forget something that is so beautiful? But you must not cling to it. Tear yourself free: let this joy of joys be all for you, but don't let it blind you and prevent you from seeing all the glorious things that still lie before you. Promise me one thing — you owe this to me because of everything for which I have lived — promise me that the thought of me will never stand between you and life; remember that I am in you a reason for being; and if I leave you that means merely that this reason lives on by itself.*

> *It should be a healthy and natural thing, it should not take up too much room, and after a while, when larger and more important things take its place, it should become nothing more than a small element in a soil full of promise of development and happiness.*

> *Miss me but get on with living. Remember me by your happiness, not by sadness. Let me be a happy part of your memories not a lingering grief. Let me never stand between you and life.*

Prayer

Miss me, but let me go.

9 April — Reflecting God's Presence

Some significant events on this day

Year	Event
1867	The US signs a treaty with Russia to purchase Alaska.
1940	Germany invades Norway, a neutral country, during World War II.
2003	As US forces take control of Baghdad, Iraqis celebrate the overthrow of Saddam Hussein's 25 year rule by destroying a huge bronze statue of the dictator.

Key thought for today

A word spoken is past recalling.
— English proverb

Reflection

By Br Bill Firman: I don't know who wrote this piece, as it was given to me with 'anonymous' typed at the bottom, but I think 'Words are Weapons' is a great title which contains an important message.

Take care when you speak in judgement.
Words are powerful weapons
That cause lots of tragedies.
Never make a person look a fool with your tongue.
Never make a person look small with your big mouth.
A hard word, a sharp word can burn a long time,
deep in the heart, leaving a scar.
Accept that others are different,
think differently,
act differently,
feel differently,
speak differently.
Be mild and healing with your words.
Words should be lights.
Words should calm, bring people together, bring peace.
Where words are weapons,
people face each other like enemies.
Life is much too short
and our world is much too tiny
to turn it into a battlefield.
Lord, help me to keep my big mouth shut,
until I know what I want to say.

Prayer

May our thoughts and words be gentle and positive. Amen.

Reflecting God's Presence

Some significant events on this day

Year	Event
1942	After the fall of Luzon to the Japanese, the 'Bataan Death March' begins, in which 75,000 Filipino and American troops were forced to walk 137 km in six days. Hundreds died.
1968	Fifty-three people lose their lives when the NZ inter-island ferry, TEV *Wahine*, founders on Barrett's Reef at the entrance to Wellington Harbour.
1970	Paul McCartney shocks fans by announcing the break-up of The Beatles.
1998	After 30 years of conflict, Protestants, Catholics and the British Government in Northern Ireland sign a peace treaty known as 'The Good Friday Agreement'.

Key thoughts for today

Even the woodpecker owes his success to the fact that he uses his head and keeps pecking away until he finishes the job he starts.
— Coleman Cox

The one who removed the mountain began by carrying away small stones.
— Chinese proverb

Reflection

By Jonathon Hewett

When I was young I believed that every job would be a quick and temporary duty that could be dispatched and forgotten. As I grow older I realise that relationships, bringing up children and careers are all 'works in progress' and should never be left untended. They are all jobs for the long haul. My work on college magazines has taught me that jobs may seem daunting, but are all achievable if they are planned and built piece by piece. If something goes wrong, then you improvise, you never turn back. Instead you put your foot on the accelerator harder until the situation is re-balanced. I have two favourite quotes, from two great men who understood and appreciated the benefits of work and the success it brings:

> *We are continually faced by great opportunities brilliantly disguised as insoluble problems. When nothing seems to help, I go and look at a stonecutter hammering away at his rock, perhaps a hundred times without as much as a crack showing in it. Yet at the hundred and first blow it will split in two, and I know it was not that blow that did it – but all that had gone before (Jacob Riis).*

> *Nothing in the world can take the place of persistence. Talent will not; nothing is more common than unsuccessful men with talent. Genius will not; unrewarded genius is almost a proverb. Education will not; the world is full of educated derelicts. Persistence and determination alone are omnipotent (Calvin Coolidge).*

Prayer

Grant me the gifts of determination and persistance, that I may never give up on what I know to be important but walk towards my goal one step at a time.

11 APRIL

Reflecting God's Presence

Some significant events on this day

Year   Event

1814   Napoleon abdicates the French throne and is exiled to the Isle of Elba.

1951   General Douglas MacArthur is relieved of command of the US forces in Korea by President Harry S. Truman on the grounds of insubordination.

1970   *Apollo 13* is launched, destined for America's third lunar landing. Two days later an oxygen tank explodes and the mission is aborted. The astronauts eventually returned safely to earth.

1979   Ugandan dictator Idi Amin is overthrown.

Key thought for today

My religion has come to mean more to me than ever before. I have come to believe more and more in a personal God – not a process, but a person, a creative power with infinite love who answers prayers.
   — Martin Luther King Jr

Reflection

By Saint John Baptist de La Salle

The gentleness and wisdom of Saint Leo were admirable and won for him the esteem and veneration of those outside the faith, even the most uncivilised. These qualities of the saint had led the pope and the emperor to make use of him in settling a dispute between two generals of the Roman Empire armies, a mission which he concluded successfully. Later, when he became pope, the emperor begged him to meet and plead with Attila, King of the Goths, encamped before Rome and ready to besiege it, in order to get him to give up his plan. The saint acquitted himself of this mission with so much wisdom, eloquence and success that this barbarian prince was led to withdraw and leave Italy in peace.

Is it in this way, by your gentleness and wisdom, that you lead those entrusted to your care to give up bad habits and disorderly conduct and to devote themselves to a sincere disposition? These two means, joined to prayer, are often more effective on souls than any other method you could imagine.

Saint Leo's zeal for the strengthening of the church and the defeat of her enemies and the heresies that arose in his time manifested itself in an extraordinary manner. He was eminently successful in this, for, having assembled several Councils, and especially the Fourth General Council, he confirmed the faith of the entire church in the mystery of the Incarnation.

When we are called to an apostolic work, if we do not know how to join zeal to action, all we do for our neighbour will have little effect (Meditation on Saint Leo – Pope from 440 to 461).

Prayer

Give me the courage to stand up for my faith, secure in the knowledge that God loves me even if others occasionally doubt that I am lovable.

Reflecting God's Presence

Some significant events on this day

Year   Event

1633   Galileo is convicted of heresy for teaching that the earth revolves around the sun.
1861   The American Civil War begins in South Carolina.
1961   The USSR puts the first man, Yuri Gagarin, into orbit around the earth.

Key thought for today

The celestial order and beauty of the universe compel me to admit that there is some excellent and eternal being who deserves our respect and homage.
— Tullius Cicero

Reflection

By Br Bill Firman

The calculations of Ptolemy in Alexandria around 140CE strengthened Aristotle's viewpoint that humankind lived in a geocentric universe, with everything in the sky rotating around the earth. This model of the universe was widely believed for the next 1400 years. Christians were essentially very comfortable with the notion of humanity being on the planet at the centre of the universe. Being at the centre seemed important and sat very easily with the notion of God's special love for humankind.

In 1531, Nicholas Copernicus, a priest, once again argued the case for a heliocentric universe. Protestant theologians objected immediately to the notion of a heliocentric universe on a 'biblical basis'. It was not until 73 years later in 1616, occasioned by the teaching of Galileo, that Copernicus' work *De Revolutionibus Coelestium* ('Revolutions of the Heavenly Spheres') was put on the Index of books that Catholics were forbidden to read.

In Pisa, Italy, in 1604, Galileo Galilei learned of the invention of the telescope in Holland. From the barest of information, Galileo constructed a vastly superior model. His observations led him to support the Copernican theory. He became the Professor of Astronomy at the University of Pisa but, in 1633, the Inquisition convicted him of heresy and forced him to withdraw his support of the notion of a heliocentric universe. Galileo died under house arrest in 1642, the year of the birth of Isaac Newton.

That religion could be so threatened by such an advance in scientific knowledge is a reflection as to how much importance is rightly attached to the personal relationship of God with humanity. After all, people are made in the image and likeness of God and God became a man for our salvation. Any denigration of the centrality and importance of humans in the cosmos was seen as a heretical attack on this central Christian belief.
Yet the shift in belief to a heliocentric universe was a very small one to make compared with our modern knowledge of the vast cosmos in which the earth is a very small and insignificant planet. It is a humbling reality in the presence of the splendour of God.

Prayer

Albert Einstein spoke of his religious feelings taking 'the form of rapturous amazement at the harmony of the natural law'. God, we wonder at the universe you have created and praise you in your glory. Amen.

Some significant events on this day

Year	Event
1829	Roman Catholics are granted freedom to practise their religion in Great Britain.
1945	German SS and Luftwaffe troops kill more than 1000 prisoners of war near the town of Gardlegen in Germany.
1964	Sidney Poitier becomes the first African-American actor to receive an Academy Award for his role in *Lilies of the Field*.
1997	Tiger Woods becomes the youngest golfer to win the US Masters.

Key thoughts for today

I never had an occasion to question colour, therefore I only saw myself as what I was – a human being.
— Sidney Poitier

God does not want us to do extraordinary things; God wants us to do the ordinary things extraordinarily well.
— Charles Gore

Reflection

By Brian Long

Each of us may have had this experience of being led by God. Doors close in our lives and when we turn away from the closed door we see new horizons and possibilities.

Our past mistakes, our past experiments with life, are our teachers and guides towards newness and fulfilment. The unexpected meeting, the chance word, the friend or enemy whose life touched ours – all are possible signposts.

God is gentle and wise and leads us in small steps, turning our sins, our weaknesses, our strengths and talents all to good.

This is the God in the thick of our day-to-day lives trying to get 'messages through our blindness as we move around down here knee-deep in the fragrant muck and misery and marvel of our world' (Frederick Buechner).

Prayer

God of mystery and love, when a door closes in my life, I rejoice and thank you that a new adventure lies before me. Amen.

Reflecting God's Presence

Some significant events on this day

Year   Event

1865   Abraham Lincoln is shot by John Wilkes Booth. He died the next day.
1988   The Soviet Union agrees to withdraw from Afghanistan after a decade of guerrilla fighting.
2003   The Human Genome Project comes to an end after 13 years of research and the identification of the approximately 30,000 genes that make up human DNA.

Key thoughts for today

What does not destroy me makes me strong.
— Friedrich Nietzsche

Reflection

By Br Bill Firman

Children often complain very quickly about the slightest pain; balanced adults learn gradually to put up with increasing amounts with a resignation that recognises the inevitability of pain and suffering. Coping with pain and suffering and using them to strengthen our character and resolve is part of living – and dying! Few of us will suffer as painful a death as did Jesus who died without any bitterness, saying:

> *Father, forgive them, for they know what they do.*

There are many stories of the extraordinary strength people can find when they must confront pain. One man who found such strength was Aron Ralston. Aron, a mountaineer, was trapped for five days with one of his arms stuck under a rock, with no help around and no way to call for help. He eventually decided that if he did not get free he would die. As reported in the *Rocky Mountain News* of 3 May 2003:

> *Using his pocket-knife, he amputated his arm below the elbow, put on a tourniquet and administered first-aid. He then rigged anchors and fixed a rappel to the floor of Blue John Canyon.*

After that, Aron walked out to safety. Such a capacity to inflict pain on oneself in order to survive is almost beyond our normal human expectation. Most of us tend to recoil from suffering, as did Jesus in his full humanity when he prayed in the Garden of Gethsemane: 'If it is possible, let this pass me by.'

Yet, just as Jesus did, ordinary people can cope with suffering and can find incredible, interior strength when it is needed. Like Aron, we will never know what strength we can find when it is needed in a desperate situation.

Prayer

Grant me the strength to cope with adversity and pain, without any bitterness. Amen.

Some significant events on this day

Year	Event
1865	Andrew Johnson becomes the 17th President of the United States after Abraham Lincoln died of a gunshot wound.
1912	The 'unsinkable' luxury liner *The Titanic*, on its maiden voyage, sinks at 2.20 am after hitting an iceberg, drowning all but 706 of the 2223 passengers and crew on board.
1983	Disneyland opens in Tokyo.
1989	During a stampede at a British soccer match in Hillsborough, Sheffield, 96 fans are killed and many more injured.
2008	Archbishop Sir Frank Little dies in Melbourne.

Key thought for today

Hope! Of all the ills that we endure, the only cheap and universal cure.
— Abraham Cowley

Reflection

By Phil Ryan

All of us experience hopes that keep us going from day to day. Two recent events caught my attention as signs and settings for hope, and, importantly, Christian hope.

First, I have been touched by the lives of individuals who have lived by hope and given hope to others, and was reminded of this by the death of the retired Archbishop of Melbourne, Sir Frank Little, on 15 April 2008. He was archbishop of Melbourne for 22 years and retired in 1996. His profound spirituality touched all people who regarded him as a man of great personal holiness. He was a person of humility and compassion who constantly reached out to others to thank them for their work and love of the church. My own memory of Archbishop Little, while I was a university student in the early 1980s and attending a Confirmation at St Damian's Church, Bundoora, is of a kind and approachable man who had a common touch and was easy to talk to.

A second sign of Christian hope I viewed on television recently, when, during Pope Benedict XVI's visit to the United States, I saw him humbly praying in silence at Ground Zero at the site of the September 11, 2001, terrorist attack on the World Trade Centre in New York. One fireman who attended the pope's visit remarked that he had lost a close member of his family in the senseless and brutal attack that day. He had stopped believing in God, thinking that the victims and their families had been forgotten by God. With the pope's visit to the site, to humbly pray and speak to those touched by this terrible tragedy, the fireman's faith in God had been rekindled. By compassionately reaching out to the victims and their families, Pope Benedict was able to show the loving face of God who suffers with us and is present amidst our suffering.

Prayer

Let us show the compassionate face of Christ to all we meet and reveal to them the reason for hope. Amen.

Reflecting God's Presence

Some significant events on this day

Year   Event

1947   At Galveston Bay, Texas, a fire breaks out on a French freighter, igniting chemicals, killing 600 people and almost destroying the city.

1964   The twelve thieves of the Great Train Robbery are sentenced to a total of 307 years gaol.

1901   Apollo 16 carries out the sixth lunar landing mission. The astronauts collect rock samples using a lunar rover before returning safely to earth.

Key thought for today

The measure of a man is not determined by his show of outward strength or the volume of his voice or the thunder of his actions. It is to be seen, rather, in terms of the strength of his commitments, the genuineness of his friendships, the sincerity of his purpose, the quiet courage of his convictions, his capacity to suffer and his willingness to continue 'growing up'.
— Grady E. Poulard

Reflection

By Br Bill Firman

Up until the latter part of the 20th century, morality was more clearly articulated and traditions of right and wrong behaviour were more explicit. Today the prevailing attitude has become more relativistic. There has been a shift from the notion of conforming to a clear set of standards to the idea that society should let us be or do whatever we want. In effect, there has been a shift from the notion that human beings should be focused on what God wants and what society demands to a concept that each of us has a right to be and do whatever we like, provided it doesn't impact too negatively on others. We have moved from an attitude of aspiring to be better citizens in society to an attitude that society should offer us immediate gratification and allow us to express ourselves however we like. The consequences of this shift are enormous.

If life is all about me and my gratification, why bother being faithful to my marriage partner, why bother looking after my ageing parents, why bother helping those less fortunate than myself, why bother showing self-restraint, why bother going to church? This kind of attitude generates values that are materialistic and superficial, placing more emphasis on personal gratification than commitment. We need to counteract such attitudes.

Our Year 12 boys who choose to be 'Coolies' rather than 'Schoolies', or our Year 11s who go to build houses in PNG, accomplish very practical benefits for the people in those countries. Even more important, however, than what is achieved, is the underlying attitude that is finding expression. These young men are developing self-restraint and are becoming 'men for others'. They are raising the level of expectation for their generation and making a statement that unselfishness and concern for others are still values to be espoused.

Prayer

Deaf and blind, Helen Keller said, 'I find life an exciting business, and most exciting when it is lived for others.' Help me, Lord, to live for others. Amen.

Some significant events on this day

Year   Event
1961   The Bay of Pigs invasion of Cuba takes place, intending to oust Fidel Castro. It was a huge failure.
1964   The first Ford Mustang is unveiled at New York's World Fair, the most successful automotive launch in history.
1970   The aborted *Apollo 13* lunar module returns to earth safely, splashing down in the Pacific Ocean.

Key thought for today

We are what we believe.
— Anton Chekhov

Reflection

By Br Bill Firman

William James penned these very apt words:

Be not afraid of life. Believe that life is worth living and your belief will help create the fact.

To my mind that is a wonderful insight. Grasp life and let your beliefs shape your life. James himself elsewhere paraphrases the same idea:

Human beings, by changing the inner attitudes of their minds, can change the outer aspects of their lives.

They can take hold of their lives and shape the future by a positive attitude. It might be timely to recall what I believe is a regulation of the Royal Navy which says:

No officer shall speak discouragingly to another officer in the discharge of his duties.

Perhaps we could replace the word 'officer' with 'teacher' or 'parent'. We all need encouragement. Young people especially need encouragement much more than punishment.

If misconduct must be dealt with, so be it. Correction or censure can be necessary. Reality may demand censure for what has, or hasn't, been done, but let us return again to the insights of William James. He wrote:

The deepest principle in human nature is the craving to be appreciated.

I would dispute that this craving is the 'deepest principle', but I have no doubt that in each of us there is a very strong craving to be appreciated. It is very important for the elderly to feel appreciated. It is also very important for the young. Good teachers, good parents, always have an underlying attitude of appreciation for, and encouragement of, the young people in their care.

Prayer

Lord, let me not fear life, but face it with a positive attitude, confident that I can succeed.

Reflecting God's Presence

Some significant events on this day

Year   Event

1906   The great San Francisco earthquake, measuring 7.8 on the Richter scale, leaves 3000 dead and more than 300,000 homeless.

1955   The outstanding scientist Albert Einstein dies. In the year 2000, *Time* magazine declared him to be Man of the Century.

1980   Rhodesia formally becomes the Republic of Zimbabwe, ending white minority rule.

Key thought for today

First they came for the Jews, and I did not speak out because I was not a Jew. Then they came for the Communists, and I did not speak out because I was not a Communist. Then they came for the trade unionists, and I did not speak out because I was not a trade unionist. Then they came for me, and there was no one left to speak out for me.

— attributed to Pastor Martin Niemöller

Reflection

By Br Denis: I am inspired by the attitude of Martin Niemöller, a German Protestant clergyman (1892–1984), whose life has been described as follows.

> *Niemöller was born in Lippstadt in 1892. He had a very conservative upbringing. In World War I, he was the commander of U-73, a U-boat, and earned the nickname of 'The Scourge of Malta'. Flying a French flag as deception, the U-73 sailed past British warships, and torpedoed two Allied troopships and a British man-of-war. As commander of the U-151, Niemöller set a record by sinking 55,000 tons of Allied ships in 115 days at sea.*
>
> *Although he was a national conservative and initially a supporter of Adolf Hitler, he became one of the founders of the Confessing Church. Despite his own antisemitic attitudes, he vehemently opposed the Nazis' Aryan Paragraph. For his opposition to Nazi state control of the churches, Niemöller was imprisoned in Sachsenhausen and Dachau comcentration camps from 1937 to 1945. He narrowly escaped execution and survived imprisonment. After his imprisonment, he expressed his deep regret about not having done enough to help the victims of the Nazis. He turned away from his earlier antisemitic and nationalistic beliefs and was one of the initiators of the Stuttgart Declaration of Guilt. Since the 1950s, he was a vocal pacifist and anti-war activist, and vice-chair of War Resisters' International from 1966 to 1972. He met with Ho Chi Minh during the Vietnam War and was a committed campaigner for nuclear disarmament.*

Maybe we need to be prepared to be outspoken when justice is not served. Leaving it to others to make a response is being faint-hearted and not Christian.

Prayer

Lord, help me to be considerate to all, to seek to understand and appreciate the needs of minority groups, and to support wholeheartedly those who are unjustly persecuted. Grant that I may not grow accustomed to the oppression of the weakest in our midst. Amen.

Some significant events on this day

Year   Event

1971   Charles Manson, cult leader of 'The Family', is sentenced to death for masterminding the murders of Sharon Tate and others. In 1972, California abolished the death penalty and his sentence automatically became life imprisonment.

1993   About 80 cult members, including leader David Koresh, die when fire breaks out in the Branch Davidian headquarters at Waco, Texas, bringing to an end a 51-day siege.

1995   A car bomb explodes in Oklahoma City, killing 168 people and wounding another 500. Gulf War veteran Timothy McVeigh was later found guilty of the attack and was executed on 11 June 2001.

2005   Cardinal Joseph Ratzinger is elected to be pope and chooses the name Benedict XVI.

Key thought for today

Martyrdom has always been a proof of the intensity, never the correctness, of a belief.
— Arthur Schnitzler

Reflection

By Br Bill Firman

On 9 August 1969, five people, including pregnant actress Sharon Tate, were murdered in gruesome fashion by members of Charles Manson's cult known as the 'The Family'. In November, Susan Atkins, in prison in connection with a car theft, boasted that she was one of those responsible for the murders. This led to the arrest of other cult members. In the seven-month trial that ensued, Manson's followers continued to show remarkable allegiance to him, even to imitating his hairstyle. It left people wondering how otherwise normal people could fall so much under the spell of one man and be induced to commit gruesome murders on his direction.

Similar allegiance was shown by the Branch Davidian followers to David Koresh, leading to stout resistance in the Waco, Texas, siege. In Guyana, almost one thousand people were induced to commit mass suicide by the Reverend Jim Jones. The world was again left to ponder how one man could establish such a hold over others.

Cults are insidious groups. They never describe themselves as cults but masquerade as a church or social service 'front' that appeals to the idealism of people. Cults prey on potential members' moments of vulnerability – their loneliness, hunger, need for shelter. Typical cult danger signs are excessive focus on the personality of the leader and obedience to him or her, bizarre sexual behaviour, collective upbringing and isolation of children from their parents, alienation from one's birth family, heavy demands for money and 'love bombing' in an emotionally charged atmosphere to make a person really feel wanted. There inevitably comes a time when cult behaviour contradicts our common sense and we need to be alert to the fact that we have been 'sucked in'. It can happen. One should hasten to seek counsel outside the group, knowing that it is notoriously difficult to leave a cult but a wonderful retrieval of personal freedom.

Prayer

Let me always have faith in my common sense. If ever my normal understanding be corrupted by group practice let me find the courage to seek advice outside of that group. Lord, help me be free.

Reflecting God's Presence

Some significant events on this day

Year   Event

1862   Louis Pasteur and Claud Bernard complete their first pasteurisation test.

1902   Pierre and Marie Curie isolate radium from pitchblend.

1972   The fifth moon landing occurs when the moon lander *Orion*, from Apollo 16, touches down, the first to do so on the moon's highlands.

1999   In Littleton, Colorado, the Columbine High School massacre occurs as two students open fire on teachers and their fellow students.

Key thought for today

When you have to make a choice and don't make it, that is in itself a choice.
— William James

Reflection

By Br Bill Firman

Frederick Langbridge once wrote:

> *Two men look out through the same bars:*
> *One sees the mud and one the stars.*

How we feel, how we act, can be very much influenced by how we let ourselves see things. Do we look down at the mud or do we look up at the stars? There is another well-used metaphor that implies much the same as Langbridge's reference to the mud and the stars:

> *The optimist looks at a glass which has some water in it and describes it as 'half-full'. The pessimist looks at the same glass and says it is 'half empty'.*

Both describe the same reality but with significantly differing emphases.

I was once travelling on a train from Glasgow to London when I engaged in conversation with an Englishman in the same carriage. The conversation took a political/philosophical turn when he said: 'The trouble with this country is like this. An American stands on the street corner and sees his boss drive past in a Cadillac and says, "One of these days, I'll have a car like that!" An Englishman stands on a street corner and sees his boss drive past in a Rolls Royce and says, "Why isn't he walking like me?"'

The Englishman made the comment against himself. I quote him now not to compare nationalities but to make the point that we can think positively or negatively about our perceived situation. I am a great believer in acting the way you want to feel. Act positively and you will begin to feel positive. If you feel miserable – not uncommon when one gets out of bed on a cold morning – start acting cheerfully and you soon begin to feel much better!

Prayer

Lord, give me the disposition always to light a candle rather than to curse the darkness. Amen.

Some significant events on this day

Year   Event

1944   French women are given the right to vote.

1960   Brasilia replaces Rio de Janeiro as the capital of Brazil.

1985   Brazilian Ayrton Senna wins his first Formula 1 Grand Prix. He went on to win 41 such events until he crashed and died in the San Marino Grand Prix on 1 May 1994.

1994   Polish astronomer Aleksander Wolszczan publishes evidence of the first extra-solar planetary system outside of our own.

Key thoughts for today

Experience is not what happens to a man. It is what a man does with what happens to him.
— Aldous Huxley

Every existing thing is equally upheld in its existence by God's creative love. The friends of God should love him to the point of merging their love into his with regard to all things here below.
— Simone Weil

Reflection

By Brian Long

There is no experience of anything that is not at the same time an encounter with God. We don't always realise this. Potentially, every experience is a 'religious' experience.

God is always calling us 'Beloved' and drawing us into a dialogue of friendship and cooperation and into God's own work of creating a community of people who are sons and daughters of God.

Through reflection on my experiences, I can become fine-tuned to the presence of God – enabling me to discern what is of God and what is not of God in any particular situation.

Even if I cannot be aware of God in an experience, I can try to be aware of the experience itself. This means I am living in the now with full attentiveness. The present moment is always holy ground. It shines with the fullness of God.

To be aware of God, I need to be on the lookout for God. There needs to be a gradual opening of mind, heart and body – a growing sensitisation.

To reach out to each moment with love means to be vulnerable, open, bare-footed, open-hearted to whatever happens – to see each moment as the opportunity to give and receive love, forgiveness and understanding.

Prayer

God, you call me your beloved. May I today create community in my world. Amen.

Reflecting God's Presence

22 APRIL

Some significant events on this day

Year   Event

1509   Henry VIII becomes King of England.

1870   Vladimir Lenin, who would become the first leader of the Soviet Union, is born.

1915   During World War I, German troops fire chlorine gas on French soldiers in the Second Battle of Ypres, the first use of chemical weapons in war.

1994   The death of Richard Nixon, 37th President of the United States.

Key thoughts for today

It is up to us to give ourselves recognition. If we wait for it to come from others, we feel resentful when it doesn't, and when it does we may well reject it.
— Spencer Tracy

Reflection

By Br Bill Firman

Misandry is not a commonly used word. The other-sex equivalent of 'misogyny', it means the hatred of men. 'Misandry' suggests that men are inferior to women. In 'The Misery of Misandry', Dr Christine B. Whelan argues for gender balance but alerts the reader to the underlying misandry of some popular television shows:

> *As our June 16 wedding day approached, my fiancé got a lot of advice from married co-workers and friends about how to navigate his future relationship. It boiled down to two similar messages: 'Do whatever she says' and 'She's always right'. He smiled and nodded at these bits of 'wisdom', but with a few weeks to go before we took our vows, he told me he was getting a little concerned. Was I going to change into some sort of bossy she-monster after our wedding day? Was he signing up for a life-sentence of being wrong and apologising? It's the dead-man-walking trope that is so common in our modern discourse about relationships: Once a man gets married, he's doomed.*
>
> *This is the backbone of situation-comedies. On* Everybody Loves Raymond, *each episode catalogues another bit of husbandly stupidity and the wife saves the day.* King of Queens, The Simpsons – *it's the same thing, cartoon or human: if it's a husband-and-wife combo, the men are portrayed as stupid until they agree to whatever the women want. When we embrace the stereotype that men are mamma's boys, invalids and bumblers, we're falling into a dangerous trap: We're emasculating the men we profess to love ... According to a 2007 study, men in prime time television are viewed far more often than women as sources of marital discontent, as inadequate parents, and as 'corrupt' and 'stupid' ... Gender equality in relationships is the goal, yet somehow we've tipped the balance past the point of equanimity. Now the advice given to a man getting married seems to have a retro ring to it: demur to your wife's wishes and abide by her decisions as mistress of the household.'*

Hopefully, the real experience in most families is that there is deep love and mutual respect between marriage partners and no implied misandry nor misogyny.

Prayer

God, grant that I treat my life-partner as my equal, an adult friend with whom I share responsibility.

Some significant events on this day

Year   Event

1564   Probable birthday of William Shakespeare.
1616   Death of William Shakespeare.
1968   Britain begins using decimal currency.
1975   US President Gerald Ford announces the end of the Vietnam War.

Key thought for today

Fortune brings in some boats that are not steered.
— William Shakespeare, *Cymbeline*

Reflection

By Br Bill Firman

The great English dramatist and poet William Shakespeare was probably born in Stratford-upon-Avon on 23 April 1564. Shakespeare's date of death is conclusively known: 23 April 1616. He lived almost exactly 52 years. Although few plays have been performed or analysed as extensively as the 38 plays ascribed to him, there are not many details known about his life. He was the son of John Shakespeare, a leather trader and the town bailiff. He probably attended the grammar school in Stratford, where he would have studied Latin and read classical literature. He did not go to university but at age 18 married Anne Hathaway, eight years his senior and pregnant at the time of the marriage. They had three children.

In 1593, *Venus and Adonis* was Shakespeare's first published poem. In 1594, having probably composed, among other plays, *Richard III, The Comedy of Errors,* and *The Taming of the Shrew,* he became an actor and playwright for the Lord Chamberlain's Men, which became the King's Men after James I ascended to the throne in 1603. The company grew into England's finest, in no small part because of Shakespeare, who was its principal dramatist. It also had the finest actor of the day, Richard Burbage, and the best theatre, the Globe, located on the south bank of the Thames. Shakespeare stayed with the King's Men until his retirement and often acted in small parts.

By 1596, the company had performed the classic *Romeo and Juliet, Richard II,* and *A Midsummer Night's Dream*. That year, John Shakespeare was granted a coat of arms, a testament to his son's growing wealth and fame. In 1599, after producing his great historical series, *Henry IV* and *Henry V,* he became a partner in the ownership of the Globe Theatre. The beginning of the 17th century saw the performance of the first of his great tragedies, *Hamlet,* and during the next decade, he produced such masterpieces as *Othello, King Lear, Macbeth,* and *The Tempest*. In 1609, his 154 sonnets, probably written during the 1590s, were published.

Shakespeare described the full range of human emotions and conflicts, leaving us a heritage of the use of English in a precise and clever way that has entertained and educated a wide audience down the ages.

Prayer

Lord, help me to appreciate the finer things in life that you offer me. Amen.

Reflecting God's Presence

Some significant events on this day
Year   Event

1184BCE Greeks storm the city of Troy by hiding inside the Trojan Horse.

1967   The Russian Space cosmonaut Vladimir Komarov is killed when the space capsule *Soyuz 1* crashes to earth on re-entry.

2005   German-born Cardinal Josef Ratzinger, taking the name Benedict XVI, is inaugurated as the 265th pope of the Roman Catholic Church.

Key thought for today
The underlying truth is that each person is meant to exist. Each person is God's own idea. Within everything that just for the moment exists factually, a plan and an idea are at work, and this gives meaning to my search for my own ideal self and to my coexistence with the world and with the onward path of history.
— Pope Benedict XVI

Reflection
By Jacinta Ryan: I would like to invite you to reflect on this passage from John Powell's *Will the Real Me Please Stand Up?'*

Persons are the gifts of God to me. They are already wrapped, some beautifully and others less attractively. Some have been mishandled in the mail; others come "Special Delivery"; some are loosely wrapped; others very tightly enclosed.

But the wrapping is not the gift, and this is an important realisation. It is so easy to make a mistake in this regard, to judge the contents by the cover.

Sometimes the gift is opened very easily; sometimes the help of others is needed. Maybe it is because they are afraid. Maybe they have been hurt before and don't want to be hurt again. It could be that they were once opened and then discarded. They may now feel more like 'things' than 'precious humans'.

I am a person: like everyone else, I too am a gift. God filled me with a goodness that is only mine. And yet sometimes I am afraid to look inside my wrapping. Maybe I am afraid I would be disappointed. Maybe I don't trust my own contents. Or it may be that I have never really accepted the gift that I am.

Every meeting and sharing of persons is an exchange of gifts. My gift is me; your gift is you. We are gifts to each other.

Prayer
Lord, help me to see beyond the wrapping and embrace the goodness of each person. By unwrapping myself may I be ready to connect with others. Amen.

25 APRIL

Reflecting God's Presence

Some significant events on this day

Year   Event

        Anzac Day holiday in Australia and New Zealand, commemorating the landing in Gallipoli in 1915 when one third of the Anzac troops were killed.

1859   Work begins on the construction of the 162.5 km Suez Canal, allowing ships access from the Mediterranean Sea to the Indian Ocean via the canal and the Red Sea.

1953   Cambridge University scientists James Watson and Francis Crick announce the discovery of the double helix DNA, the basis of all genetic information and the building block of life.

Key thought for today

They shall grow not old, as we that are left grow old: age shall not weary them, nor the years condemn. At the going down of the sun and in the morning, we will remember them.
   — Laurence Binyon

Reflection

By Br Bill Firman

Anzac Day commemorates the landing, during World War I, at Gallipoli in Turkey in 1915, of the fighting men of the Australian and New Zealand Army Corps. These soldiers were ordered to fight a battle that was impossible to win. The Gallipoli Campaign, which ultimately ended in defeat, brought about the deaths of more than 8700 Australians and 2700 New Zealanders, a massive loss of lives. Far removed from the 'glorious adventure' that many of the men who went off to fight as Anzacs had anticipated, warfare was quickly reduced to a fight for survival in appalling conditions and a brutal equation of kill or be killed.

The discovery, announced on 17 March 2008, of the wreck of HMAS *Sydney*, sunk off the Western Australian coast in November 1941, with the loss of the entire crew of 645, reminded us again how the lives of armed service personnel are at risk. It was an especially poignant discovery because we know a De La Salle old boy, Able Seaman Alwyn Burt, was among the 645. The theme of Anzac Day, 'Lest we forget', has never been more important. We should be grateful for the extraordinary sacrifice of those men, and that made by the other men and women in the various conflicts that have followed since the Great War. We should remember not only the heroism of our service personnel but the horror of war itself. War can bring out the worst in people – on both sides. That is what all violence does.

Anzac Day celebrates the heroic efforts of Australian and New Zealand men and women who fought to protect the great gift of freedom. We have been given freedom and opportunity. We shall be responsible for what we become. Previous generations fought wars, while battles continue to be fought today. What am I going to do with my life to help others, to make our society a better place? That is the proper question for each to ask on Anzac Day.

Prayer

We will remember them and pray for the great gifts of freedom and peace. Amen.

Reflecting God's Presence

Some significant events on this day

Year   Event

1962   The US rocket *Ranger* lands on the far side of the moon but fails to send back pictures as planned.

1986   The world's worst nuclear disaster takes place at Chernobyl in the Ukraine, killing many thousands and causing the relocation of 300,000.

2005   After a 29-year occupation, Syria withdraws the last of its troops from Lebanon.

Key thought for today

Provision for others is a fundamental responsibility of human life.
— Woodrow Wilson

Reflection

By Christine Thompson:

Veronica Brady, a Loreto Sister and an Honorary Senior Research Fellow at the University of Western Australia comments on the notion of disconnection in our society:

> *A society which does not cater for those who are less powerful or less fortunate, or even for those who are different, has forfeited the claim to be properly civilised. Yet in our current culture, the larger world of the human mind and spirit, and the possibilities it opens out, possibilities beyond the mere business of money-making, money-having and money-spending, are largely neglected. Those of us who work for an increase in human dignity and hope for a better future for humankind are deemed as 'do-gooders' or 'bleeding-hearts'. Our concerns are seen as irrelevant and a distraction from the real business of increasing GNP and balancing budgets ... Responsibility, then, is not just an individual matter, but implies a mutual respect and sympathy which comes from understanding who we are and where we belong in the larger scheme of things ... I believe that 'spirited practices' that derive from a sense of respect and responsibility to and for others and for the living world around us will bring us back in tune with reality ... Flowers may then begin to grow in the hard ground of our times.*

The social justice focus in our De La Salle schools is a pertinent example of 'spirited practices'. It is vital that we instil in our students the understanding that it is indeed a responsibility of all to help others less fortunate, those struggling with life or those who just need a friendly look, smile or sympathetic ear. Never underestimate the value of these actions:

> *Much of what we do may seem like planting trees under which we will never sit, but plant we must.*

Prayer

Lord, help us to realise and be sympathetic to the plight of others and then utlise our skills to alleviate their burdens. Amen.

27 APRIL

Reflecting God's Presence

Some significant events on this day

Year	Event
1667	The poet John Milton, blind and destitute, sells the publishing rights to his epic, *Paradise Lost*, for 16 English pounds.
1950	Racial groups are officially segregated in South Africa with the passing of the Group Areas Act.
1994	The first fully democratic multi-racial elections are held in South Africa
2005	The Airbus A380 makes its maiden flight in France, replacing the Boeing 747 jumbo jet as the world's largest passenger plane.

Key thought for today

If you want to make peace with your enemy, you have to work with your enemy. Then he becomes your partner.

— Nelson Mandela

Reflection

By Br Bill Firman

His election as president on this day in 1994 ushered in a remarkable final chapter in the life of Nelson Mandela, 50 years after he began his fight against racism in South Africa. In 1944, Mandela, a lawyer, had joined the African National Congress (ANC). In 1952, he became deputy national president, advocating non-violent resistance to apartheid, South Africa's institutionalised system of white supremacy and racial segregation. After the massacre of peaceful black demonstrators at Sharpeville in 1960, Mandela helped organise a paramilitary branch of the ANC to engage in guerrilla warfare against the white minority government. In June 1964, after a series of doubtful charges, he was convicted and sentenced to life in prison. He spent 27 years in jail, mostly confined to a small cell without a bed or plumbing and forced to do hard labour in a quarry. He could write and receive a letter once every six months, and once a year he was allowed to meet with a visitor for only 30 minutes.

Mandela's resolve remained unbroken and he became the symbolic leader of the anti-apartheid movement. In 1989, F.W. de Klerk, South Africa's president, began dismantling apartheid. In 1990, he ordered the release of Mandela who then led negotiations with the minority government for the establishment of a multiracial government. In 1993, Mandela and de Klerk were jointly awarded the Nobel Peace Prize. One year later, the ANC won an electoral majority in the country's first free elections, and Mandela was elected as South Africa's president, a position he held, with dignity and without evident vindictiveness, until 1999.

Mandela helped bring about change which was only a dream in his childhood. He dared to dream, remained true to his resolve and turned that dream into reality.

Prayer

Nelson Mandela said: 'And as we let our light shine, we unconsciously give other people permission to do the same.' We ask, Lord, for the courage to let our lights also shine, so that, fired by purpose, we might live and work to improve our society.

Reflecting God's Presence

Some significant events on this day

Year   Event

1789   Fletcher Christian and crew members mutiny against Captain Bligh on the sailing ship *Bounty*.

1967   Norwegian marine biologist Thor Heyerdahl sets out from Peru on his raft *Kon-Tiki* to sail to Polynesia. His journey took 101 days.

1996   In a killing spree, Martin Bryant massacres 35 people and wounds 37 more at Port Arthur in Tasmania.

Key thought for today

I feel that God is behind every flower and every tree in the woods. He is behind every mountain rock and every foam-crested wave in the sea.
— Thor Heyerdahl

Reflection

By Br Bill Firman

On this day in 1996, 28-year-old Martin Bryant began a senseless killing spree in the quiet, historic town of Port Arthur, a former penal colony, in Tasmania. Bryant began the day by killing an elderly couple who were the owners of Port Arthur's Seascape guesthouse. He then travelled to the site of the historic Port Arthur prison colony, a tourist destination.

After having lunch on the deck of the Broad Arrow Cafe, Bryant entered the restaurant, removed an automatic rifle from his bag, and began shooting. After killing 22 people, he left the restaurant for the parking lot, where he continued to shoot, killing the drivers of two tour buses, some passengers and a mother and her two small children. As he left the parking area, he shot four people in a BMW and drove the car to a nearby service station, where he shot one woman and took a man hostage, before driving back to the Seascape guesthouse. After an 18-hour stand-off with police, Bryant set the guesthouse on fire, ran outside and was captured. The hostage was dead. By the time the killing ended, Bryant had killed 35 people. Bryant was later given Australia's maximum sentence, life in prison, 'never to be released'. The Broad Arrow Cafe and its environs have been turned into a memorial site. Gun-control laws in Australia were significantly strengthened in the aftermath of the tragedy.

All of this happened before the September 11, 2001, terrorism in New York. People across Australia and the world were horrified by Bryant's actions. Nothing explains such deranged behaviour. It was irrational madness. The tragic effect on the lives of many people cannot be undone but it does make us all reflect on the wonderful gift of life. It was a great surprise this happened in Australia where we live with more security and safety than in most countries. It is worth a prayer that security continues to be part of our future.

Prayer

There is an African proverb that states: 'Smooth seas do not make skilful sailors.' Help us to face challenge and overcome adversity courageously and thereby to be prepared for any storms in our way.

29 APRIL

Reflecting God's Presence

Some significant events on this day

Year   Event

1770   Captain James Cook lands in Australia at Botany Cove.

1945   Dachau, the first concentration camp opened by the Nazis in 1933, is liberated by US forces.

1967   Muhammad Ali refuses induction into the US army. He was stripped of his World Boxing Title and convicted of draft evasion.

1992   In Los Angeles, race riots break out after a mainly white jury acquits police officers of beating African-American Rodney King

Key thought for today

Two kinds of people please God – those who serve him with all their heart because they know him; and those who seek him with all their heart because they know him not.
— Ivan Panin

Reflection

By Saint John Baptist de La Salle

> *Adore this sacred mystery which is entirely above our senses and even above our reason ... Declare that all you can say of it, all you can conceive of it, is that it is the mystery of one God in three Persons, the Father, the Son and the Holy Spirit. This is the object of the church's most profound veneration in heaven as well as on earth ... Today, pay your homage to this divine mystery and acknowledge that this is the mystery above all mysteries, for it is the source of all the others.*

> *With good reason we can call the Holy Trinity the mystery of faith, because nothing but faith can throw light on this mystery. Faith alone can enable us to know it, though only in a superficial manner; nevertheless we do know it as far as it can be grasped in this life. Faith alone keeps our mind fixed on the consideration of this supreme mystery, which is infinitely beyond the range of the human mind.*

> *Ask God, therefore, for a deep faith to believe this sacred mystery, and while firmly professing that God is One in Three Persons, proclaim that blessed are those who have not seen but yet believe ...*

> *Dedicate yourself, entirely, to the Most Holy Trinity to contribute as far as you will be able to extend its glory over all the earth (Meditation on Trinity Sunday).*

Prayer

Louis Evely said that God is not an idea, or a definition that we have committed to memory – God is a presence we experience in our hearts. Be in my heart, O God, and in my mind insofar as I am able to understand this great mystery of the Holy Trinity.

Reflecting God's Presence

Some significant events on this day

Year   Event

1803   France sells Louisiana to the United States for US$15 million.

1945   Adolf Hitler and his new wife Eva Braun commit suicide in Hitler's Berlin bunker by taking cyanide capsules.

1975   The Vietnam War ends as communist forces gain control over Saigon.

1993   The World Wide Web is launched by CERN, the European Organisation for Nuclear Research, which states it would be free for anyone to use.

Key thought for today

The final decision as to what the future of a society shall be depends not on how near its organisation is to perfection, but on the degree of worthiness in its individual members.
— Albert Schweitzer

Reflection

By Br Bill Firman

When historians of future ages look back on the 20th century, it is probable that they will describe it as a period of great social experiment, a time when social organisation was struggling to keep up with the technological revolution. The rise and decline of communism and fascism and the rampant extremes of capitalism - from economic depression to exploitation – have been major occurrences. The imbalance between rich and poor nations and international debt continue to be huge problems.

Not only has a fourth world, as described by Pope John Paul II in 1987, emerged in the USA, Australia and other developed countries but, in Australian society at least, another band has developed at the very wealthy end of the spectrum. Whereas a brick house was once a sign of being 'well to do', never before this era have so many people been able to live in large double storey houses. Never have so many owned holiday homes or units, boats or multiple numbers of cars. It is certainly a 'First World Plus' existence today for many Australians.

There is nothing wrong with prosperity but what becomes a real problem is when wealth in a society becomes so skewed that only the rich can afford the health or justice systems. It is a role of government to ensure that access to legal services, doctors, hospitals and so on exists as a right for all persons in society. Fortunately there are many Australians and New Zealanders, blessed with resources, who, in a spirit of solidarity and wishing to help others, give generously to people in need.

Prayer

Lord, we pray for good government, for civic leaders who will exercise a legitimate social responsibility to ensure the rights and basic needs of all people are respected. We pray that in our own hearts we shall put aside greed and be prepared to respond generously to need. Amen.

1 MAY

Reflecting God's Presence

Some significant events on this day

Year	Event
1707	Scotland and England are united by an Act of Parliament. England, Scotland and Wales together form Great Britain.
1851	The first ever World Fair opens in the Crystal Palace in London.
1964	BASIC, a multi-purpose computer programming language that anyone could use, is introduced at Dartmouth College.
1997	Tony Blair leads Britain's Labour Party to a landslide election victory.

Key thought for today

It is a sublime mystery that Christ should begin to work before he began to teach; a humble workman before being the teacher of all nations.
— Pope Pius XII

Reflection

By Br Bill Firman

May the first is often called May Day, an official public holiday in many countries celebrating workers – a traditional day of special celebration in communist countries particularly. The Catholic Church celebrates 1 May as the feast day of St Joseph the Worker.

Catholic Social Justice teaching was initially developed between 1880 and 1891 as a direct response to the consequences of the Industrial Revolution. At that time, liberalism, capitalism and socialism were competing for intellectual and social allegiance. Pope Leo XIII (1878 –1903) examined the misery and poverty of workers in industrialised countries, noting the destitution of many and the concentration of wealth in the hands of a few. In 1891, Leo published *Rerum Novarum*, 'On the Conditions of Labour'. He rejected what he perceived as socialism's promotion of class warfare and its denial of private property rights. He affirmed private possession, distinguishing just ownership from just use. He taught the obligation to pay a living wage and asserted worker's rights to organise and collaborate rather than class struggle as the fundamental means of social change. Leo wrote of the right of the church to educate citizens to act justly and promote social reconciliation

Since *Rerum Novarum*, there has been a series of social justice encyclicals addressing work and related issues. Three are by Pope John Paul II, including *Centesimus Annus* ('The Hundreth Year' – after *Rerum Novarum*) in 1991. He reiterated the rights and dignity of workers and called for reducing or cancelling third world debt, rejection of consumerism, protection of natural and human ecology, authentic democracy based on human rights, grievance resolution, rejection of war in favour of non-violent resolution of conflicts, free but fair markets, and attention to the needs of those in the fourth world – those marginalised such as the elderly, the young and many women.

Prayer

Pope John Paul II said: 'Work is not a curse; it is a blessing from God.' Bless me with a sound work ethic so that I may be a person of justice and compassion. Amen.

Reflecting God's Presence

Some significant events on this day

Year   Event
1945   As World War II draws to a close in Europe, German forces in Berlin surrender to the Soviet army.
1949   US playwright Arthur Miller wins the Pulitzer Prize for his play *Death of a Salesman*.
1969   The huge liner *Queen Elizabeth II* begins its maiden voyage.
1994   Nelson Mandela is elected President of South Africa in the first democratic election in that country.

Key thought for today

The most terrifying thing is to accept oneself completely.
— Carl Jung

Reflection

By Patrick Jurd.

Accepting the gifts and the limitations we each have is an important part of our personal life journey. I invite you to reflect on the following passage from John Powell's book, *Fully Human, Fully Alive*.

To accept oneself

Fully alive people accept and love themselves as they are. They do not live for the promise of some tomorrow or the potential that may some day be revealed in them.

They usually feel good about themselves, as they have the same warm and glad emotions that you and I feel when we meet someone whom we really like and admire.

Fully alive people are sensitively aware of all that is good in themselves, from the little things, like the way they smile or walk, through the natural talents they have been given, to the virtues they have worked to cultivate.

When these people find imperfections and limitations in themselves, they are compassionate. They try to understand, not to condemn themselves.

'Beyond a wholesome discipline', Desiderata says, 'be gentle with yourself.'

The wellsprings for the fullness of life rise from within a person. Psychologically speaking, a joyful self-acceptance, a good self-image, a sense of self-celebration are the bedrock beginning of the fountain that rises up into the fullness of life.

Prayer

Saint Bernard of Clairvaux wrote: 'First learn to love yourself, and then you can love me.' Grant me, Lord, that I may accept myself the way you made me. Help me to love myself as the first step in being ready to love others. Amen.

Some significant events on this day

Year Event

1937 Margaret Mitchell wins the Pulitzer Prize for her novel *Gone with the Wind*.
1973 The Sears Tower in Chicago is completed. At 520 metres, it was at that time the world's tallest building.
1989 Christine Jorgensen, the first transsexual, dies.

Key thought for today

Every new adjustment is a crisis in self-esteem.
— Eric Hoffer

Reflection

By Br Bill Firman

There were no McDonalds, KFC, Red Rooster, Burger King or other fast food chains in the 50s. Takeaway meant a trip to the hamburger shop, or fish'n'chip shop. Chinese food was just beginning to be popular, but we had never even heard of pizza, kebabs or tortilla. 'Pasta' meant almost exclusively spaghetti, but with many Italian immigrants after the war this was rapidly changing. In Melbourne, the only huge shopping precinct was in the city proper – until Myer led the way with the opening of a new store and associated mall in Chadstone. My dad was mayor and spoke at the opening of Chadstone. As malls with parking were developed, some local councils preserved their traditional shopping streets by buying nearby properties and demolishing them to provide more parking. As more families became two-car families, shopping was adapting on the assumption people would drive to large malls rather than shop at local stores.

In the latter part of the 20th century, many small businesses – butchers, bakers, grocers, greengrocers – closed, while niche market shops developed for antiques, the new technologies and all manner of specialties. Generally, however, shopping became less personal as people shopped in large department stores.

Trouser legs flared and then became stove pipe, just as hemlines went up and down – not quite as frequently as the fad for yo-yos. Fashion fads such as Ivy League, 'Cooks Daks' or striped blazers came and went and suits alternated between double and single breasted with one, two or no vents at the back. If you kept clothing long enough, it would come back into fashion. Of course it wasn't much use by then as most of us had gone up a size or two! The one constant fashion item was formal wear. For both men and women, the change has been minimal.

Fashions, fads, facilities, technologies are always changing and people adapt. At the time, some of these things seem important but my thoughts come back to the great truth: 'All things are passing. God alone remains.' I have always enjoyed change and innovation, but most of the things of my youth I no longer have or need. I have come to understand that all I really need is the love of family, friends and God.

Prayer

Most things come and go, rather like the wind. Let me hold fast to what is really important, the love of God and neighbour. As St Francis demonstrated, the rest is simply not important. Amen.

Reflecting God's Presence

Some significant events on this day

Year	Event
1970	Four students are killed by National Guardsmen at a student rally against the Vietnam War at Kent State University, Ohio, USA.
1979	Margaret Thatcher becomes Britain's first female prime minister.
1994	Israel and the PLO sign a historic accord on Palestinian autonomy, granting self-rule in the Gaza Strip and Jericho.

Key thought for today

Trust is a treasured item and relationship. Once it is tarnished, it is hard to restore it to its original glow.
— William A. Ward

Reflection

By Br Bill Firman

One of my favourite quotations are these words of Peter Ustinov:

> *Parents are the bones on which children sharpen their teeth. And the same can be said too of rectors and teachers. And of what use are these bones if they are too soft?*

There will always be a healthy tension between young people seeking to exercise self-determination and those who feel the young people still need more guidance. All parents will feel 'gnawed at', some time or other, as their children test the limits and feel out the boundaries. At some stage or other most parents are made to feel like an old bone, if not a total fossil!

When the 'tooth sharpening' comes to an end, and teachers are no longer a guiding or goading influence and parental authority is relaxed, how should the young adult react? Teachers now have no say and parents have diminished control. Parents are now trusting their 'emerging adult' to make good decisions. It is important for the future relationship of young people with their parents that this trust not be abused.

With freedom comes responsibility. Some young people will demand freedom but may not be ready to accept the corresponding responsibility. Most will be. Sometimes parents have to balance trusting their child's honesty, integrity and good intentions with the fact they do not yet really trust the judgement of their offspring who still lacks a lot of experience in life. The best thing is to be ready to talk openly about it.

And if parents do observe their young adult making mistakes, it is well to recall the advice of that wonderful pontiff, John XXIII: 'See everything, overlook a great deal, correct a little.'

Prayer

George Eliot said, 'Those who trust us educate us.' May trust be part of my personal integrity and characterise my relationships with others who are close to me.

Some significant events on this day

Year   Event

1893   Panic hits the New York Stock Exchange, causing European investors to withdraw their money. A severe depression ensued with some 500 banks and 15,000 companies going bankrupt.

1961   Alan Shepherd, in the *Freedom 7* capsule as part of the Mercury space exploration program, becomes the first American to travel in space.

1979   *Voyager 1*, 19 months after being launched from earth, passes Jupiter at a speed of 16 km/sec.

Key thoughts for today

In our era, the road to holiness necessarily passes through the world of action.
— Dag Hammarskjöld

When one door of happiness closes, another opens; but often we look so long at the closed door that we do not see the one which has been opened for us.
— Helen Keller

Reflection

By St John Baptist de La Salle

Two things are required of those who have charge of others and should characterise them. First, they should be very virtuous in order to serve as an example. For, unless they walk in the right path, those who follow them would be led astray. Second, they should manifest great tenderness for those persons confided to them, so that anything which might be capable of injuring or wounding these persons will call for their attention' (Meditation for the Second Sunday after Easter).

It is by your gentleness and wisdom that you should induce those who are in your care to give up vice and evil, and become spiritual. These two means, joined with prayer, have often greater effect upon persons than any other measures we can devise (Meditation on Saint Leo).

You must expect to find difficulties all through life, no matter where you are. Hence form an attitude of quiet acceptance of whatever occurs to you in your state in life (Letter to Brother Paulin).

Pray earnestly that God may do with you whatever God pleases. You should be entirely resigned to God's holy will (Letter to Gabriel Drolin).

Prayer

God, lead me on a path through life whereby I may face difficulties with courage and confidence in your abiding support. Amen.

Reflecting God's Presence

Some significant events on this day

Year   Event

1889   The Eiffel Tower is officially opened in Paris.
1914   The British House of Lords rejects giving women the right to vote.
1937   The Hindenburg airship crashes on its arrival in New Jersey, USA.
1954   Roger Bannister becomes the first person to run a mile in under four minutes.
1994   The 50 km long Channel Tunnel is formally opened by Queen Elizabeth II and President François Mitterand.
2001   Pope John Paul II visits and prays in a Muslim mosque in Syria, the first pontiff ever to do so.

Key thought for today

There is a time when we must firmly choose the course we will follow, or the relentless drift of events will make the decision.

— Herbert Prochnow

Reflection

By Br Bill Firman

The French poet, Victor Hugo, who lived from 1802 until 1885, possessed the ability to craft profound wisdom into very few words. One of his memorable statements is:

Have courage for the great sorrows of life and patience for the small ones. And when you have laboriously accomplished your daily task, go to sleep in peace. God is awake.

Mostly, we need patience in dealing with the small difficulties that come our way and, occasionally, in times of great grief or sorrow, we also need courage. These qualities may not always come easily to us, and there will be some laborious hard times. But at the end of the day, knowing we have done all we can, we can sleep in peace, knowing God is awake and watching over us.

Underlying Hugo's wisdom is a vision of persons, each taking hold of life, deciding what kind of person he or she wants to be, what values to live by. Living is not something we soak up like blotting paper: life is not what happens to us. We make a life by what we decide to do, by what we decide to be. Not that we are always aware we are making such decisions. It is easy just to drift until we wake up one day and say, 'How did it all come to this?'

Yes, God is awake and watching over us, but God did not make us as a finished product. God has given us the freedom to make our own decisions. It is up to us to create the kind of person we want to be.

Prayer

Watch over me, God, as I stumble through life. Help me to deal with crises patiently and to rest in peace in the knowledge that you are always awake.

7 May

Reflecting God's Presence

Some significant events on this day

Year   Event

1915   The British Cunard ocean liner *Lusitania*, on a voyage from New York to Liverpool, sinks off the coast of Ireland after being struck by a German U-boat.

1945   Germany formally surrenders to the Allied forces, marking the end of World War II in Europe.

1995   Jacques Chirac, the conservative mayor of Paris, is elected French president.

Key thought for today

A loving person lives in a loving world; a hostile person lives in a hostile world. Everyone you meet is your mirror.

— Ken Keyes Jr

Reflection

By Br Bill Firman

Ronnie spent his early years on Butterworth Air Force base in Malaysia, where his dad was a pilot. Life was good – a fine house, servants, uniforms and planes – the substance of many a boy's dreams. Life was, indeed, very good until Dad spent too much time in the mess and his lonely wife began to drink at home – too much! So Ronnie found himself back in Australia living with an unemployed alcoholic mother who could no longer provide the finer things of life while Dad simply disappeared over the horizon.

I first met Ronnie when he was aged 12 and had been admitted to BoysTown. Even then he had a 'touch of class' about him, a certain arrogance and style and a very clever tongue that earned him the nick-name of 'the Prince'. His penchant for the latest in fashion led him into stealing and he was quick to join the fringe culture where substance abuse was seen to be cool. He was a natural leader and even older boys followed him. His quick wit and sharp words put many an adult on the defensive. My approach was to keep treating him with respect, never to get drawn into a stand-off with him and to help him whenever I could. So it was that I took him to visit his mother. Her circumstances were pretty destitute. I knew I was making progress when tough Ronnie came over and sat on my knee. That was quite a vote of confidence!

Ronnie progressed well at BoysTown and graduated, but was in trouble again as he succumbed to substance abuse. Marijuana led to heroin, resulting in more serious offending and gaol. A few years later we made special provision for Ronnie and took him back onto a property where he could use the horse-riding and farming skills he had learned at BoysTown. With the help of a young farming couple he undertook methadone treatment. I observed his courage as he fought to overthrow the drug demon. The cockiness was now more subdued and the pain was tangible but he won that battle. He has won and lost a few more since. It is incredibly difficult to stay off drugs once you become an addict! Some might condemn him. I see a young man trying to make it against the odds.

Prayer

I have never been tested like Ronnie. Let me be slow to judge others, not knowing their pain and anguish as they try to build their lives in the midst of unforgiving circumstances. Let me be very thankful for my gift of life. Help me use it well. Amen.

Reflecting God's Presence

Some significant events on this day

Year	Event
1943	Mordechai Anielewcz, the leader of the Warsaw Ghetto uprising, dies when the Germans finally discover the uprising command post.
1963	Sean Connery appears in *Dr No*, the first of the James Bond films.
1967	Champion boxer Muhammed Ali is indicted for refusing induction into the US Army.
1984	The Soviet Union announces it will not participate in the Los Angeles summer Olympics.

Key thought for today

It is better to live one day as a lion than a hundred years as a sheep.
— Italian proverb

Reflection

By Christine Thompson

The Warsaw Ghetto uprising, which began on 19 April 1943, demonstrated the determination of the Jewish Fighting Organisation (ZOB) to fight against the evil forces. It was a remarkable act of resistance by the young of the ghetto who refused to give in to the will of the Nazis and the inevitable fate that they knew awaited them. The commander of ZOB, Mordechai Anielewcz, spoke to the band of courageous young people as the Nazis closed in on them: 'We want to preserve one choice – how we die. Whether it be in an airless bunker or elsewhere. But I can assure you of one thing: the spirit of our deaths will shape the soul of a new generation. A new nation of Jews.'

It was these words that spurred on the group to continue their fight. It was this sentiment that gave them courage to find new weapons, practise their fighting skills, continue to teach the children in the bunkers and even volunteer to move between the ghetto and the Aryan side to seek aid from anyone who was sympathetic to the Jewish cause. In spite of the German army, a number of the ghetto fighters managed to escape to the forests surrounding Warsaw. From here, some joined partisan groups to continue the fight, others managed to escape Europe altogether, while others were unfortunately captured and executed by the Gestapo.

However, the memory of their efforts lives on today. What is significant about their efforts is that this band of young, poorly equipped Jews managed to hold out against the might of the German army for longer than did the entire country of Poland. Mordechai Anielewicz reiterates this aspect prior to his death when he says, 'It is now clear to me that what took place exceeded all expectations. In our opposition to the Germans, we did more than our strength allowed ... I feel that great things are happening and that this action which we have dared to take is of enormous value.'

Prayer

Lord, help us to utilise our abilities to make a difference to the lives of those around us.

Some significant events on this day

Year   Event

1914   President Woodrow Wilson proclaims the first national Mothers' Day holiday in the USA.

1960   The US Food and Drug Administration (FDA) approves the first birth control pill, which led to a revolution in the social and economic roles of women in society.

1962   A ruby laser beam is successfully bounced off the moon for the first time by Louis Smullion and Giorgio Foccio from the Massachusetts Institute of Technology.

2006   Tasmanian miners Todd Russell and Brant Webb are freed after being trapped underground for 14 days in a gold mine at Beaconsfield in Tasmania.

Key thought for today

With courage you will dare to take risks, have the strength to be compassionate and the wisdom to be humble. Courage is the foundation of integrity.
— Keshavan Nair

Reflection

By Br Gerald Barrett: I invite you to reflect on these thoughts by Father Anthony Ross OP.

The truly brave man is not the kind who has 'never known fear', or the 'beserker' type who works up to a frenzy, or even the highly trained soldier sure of his skill and perhaps conditioned to fight with little or no thought of danger.

He is rather the man who measures difficulty and danger realistically, understanding what is involved as far as he can, and controlling, in the light of that understanding, feelings naturally aroused in the situation, whether they are feelings of fear or exhilaration, of over-confidence or under-confidence.

Prayer

In the letter to the Hebrews, we read: 'Jesus had to become like his sisters and brothers in every respect, so that he might be a merciful and faithful high priest in the service of God, to make a sacrifice of atonement for the sins of the people. Because he himself was tested by what he suffered, he is able to help those who are being tested' (Hebrews: 2: 17-18). Lord, we ask you to be with us today and to face with us the trials that may come our way. Some of the challenges we may face will need all our strength and courage. With your help we can overcome the hardest of trials. Amen.

Reflecting God's Presence

Some significant events on this day

Year   Event

1901   The flag of Australia is selected from entries in a nation-wide competition.

1908   The first Mothers' Day observance is celebrated in churches in West Virginia and Philadelphia.

1954   The Rock'n'Roll Era begins with the recording of 'Rock Around the Clock' by Bill Haley and His Comets.

Key thought for today

None of us is able of ourselves to grasp the supreme good of eternal life; we need divine help. Hence there is here a two-fold object, the eternal life we hope for, and the divine help we hope by.
— Saint Thomas Aquinas

Reflection

By Phil Ryan

A clear sign of Christian hope was the visit of the World Youth Day Cross and Icon (enduring signs of God's redemption and incarnation in our world) to the Melbourne archdiocese from 25 April until 10 May 2008. This visit offered everyone an opportunity to deepen their love for God and answer God's call to take up their cross and follow Jesus.

What can we learn from such a contemporary sign of Christian hope? First, that prayer, personal witness, and action for justice are schools and practices for learning Christian hope. Second, and fundamentally, that a compassionate God in the person of Jesus Christ redeems all people through his cross and resurrection. Here God suffers with us and compassionately loves us when we are in relationship with others. This is the meaning of Jesus dying on the cross for us. When we experience love, we experience God's absolute and unconditional love in our lives, even if we know it or not.

When someone experiences a great love, they are experiencing a moment of redemption which gives new meaning to their lives. Moments of great love are moments of God's unconditional love and a reminder that Jesus Christ has redeemed us. Finally, this is the ultimate and absolute setting of Christian hope. As Pope Benedict in his encyclical *On Christian Hope* says, when we live in relationship with God's love, the source of all life, 'then we live'.

As one story goes, once upon a time a preacher ran through the streets of the city shouting, 'We must put God into our lives! We must put God into our lives!' Hearing him, an old monastic rose up in the city plaza to say, 'No, sir, you are wrong. You see, God is already in our lives. Our task is simply to recognise that.'

Prayer

Let us pray each of us can be conduits or schools of Christian hope for each other, our friends, their parents, our families and all we meet. Amen.

Some significant events on this day

Year   Event

1949   The name of Siam is changed to Thailand. The word *Thai* represents the country's largest ethnic group and also translates as 'freedom'.

1949   Israel, by a vote of 37 to 12, is admitted to the United Nations as the world body's 59th member.

1998   The first Euro coin is struck in France, the first of the participating 11 European nations to produce the new currency.

Key thought for today

The only cure for suffering is to face it head on, grasp it around the neck and use it.
— Mary Craig

Reflection

By Br Bill Firman

For the first half of Sam Bailey's life, he was an energetic, activity-loving jackaroo, thinking of himself as 'bulletproof'. In 1987, when he was 19, that all changed in a car accident in which he was a passenger. That accident, on an outback Northern Territory road, left him with a severed spinal cord and, consequently, no feeling or movement from the chest down. Sam writes:

> *What kept me going? One big factor was the support of family and friends ... I also had my fellow patients in the spinal unit. While some were better off than me, others would be 24-hour dependent for the rest of their lives. Some couldn't even breathe for themselves. So I figured I was lucky.*
>
> *When I broke it all down to the basics, I had two options – either sink or swim. I couldn't see much life at the bottom of the pool, so I chose to swim. I did wonder, however, if my lifelong dream to be a farmer was shattered. I now know that with persistence and determination anything is possible.*
>
> *Today I'm a farmer, a pilot, an author, a public speaker and a husband. If I could go back to that moment on the Barkley Highway when the accident happened and have it all different, I wouldn't. Thanks to my accident I discovered I had the strength to overcome life-challenging hardship.*
>
> *I had a great life up until the age of 19, but I've got an absolute cracker now and I wouldn't change places with anyone.*

St Therese of Lisieux said of Jesus that 'Suffering is the very best gift he has to give us. He gives it only to his chosen friends.' Most of us, however, would think suffering a gift we could well do without and would rather not be such a 'chosen friend'. But if it comes, as Sam discovered, we may well find we have more strength than we ever realised before – if we can choose positively like Sam.

Prayer

Dietrich Bonhoeffer said: 'A Christian is someone who shares the sufferings of God in the world.' Help me to accept suffering with a positive attitude. Amen.

Reflecting God's Presence

Some significant events on this day

Year   Event

1820   Birth of Florence Nightingale, English nurse (d. 1910).

1949   The Soviet Union lifts its blockade of Berlin during the Cold War.

1967   At Queen Elizabeth Hall, England, Pink Floyd stages the first-ever quadraphonic rock concert.

Key thought for today

You will never be happier than you expect. To change your happiness, change your expectation.
— Bette Davis

Reflection

By Paul Maxted

We convince ourselves that life will be better after we leave school, get a car, get married, have a baby, then another. Then we're frustrated that the kids aren't old enough and we'll be more content when they are. After that, we're frustrated that we have teenagers to deal with. We'll certainly be happy when they're out of that stage. We tell ourselves that our life will be complete when our spouse gets his or her act together, when we get a nicer car, are able to go on a nice vacation, when we retire. The truth is, there's no better time to be happy than right now. If not now, when?

Your life will always be filled with challenges. It's best to admit this to yourself and decide to be happy anyway. It was Alfred D. Souza who said,

> *For a long time it had seemed to me that life was about to begin – real life. But there was always some obstacle in the way, something to be gotten through first, some unfinished business, time still to be served, or a debt to be paid. Then life would begin. At last it dawned on me that these obstacles were my life.*

This perspective has helped me to see that there is no way to happiness. Happiness *is* the way. So, treasure every moment you have and share it with someone special, special enough to spend your time with – and remember that time waits for no one. So, stop waiting – until you finish school, until you go back to school, until you lose a kilo, until you have kids, until your kids leave the house, until you start work, until you retire, until you get married, until you get divorced, until Friday night, until Sunday morning, until you get a new car, or home, until spring, until winter, until you're off social security, until your song comes on, until you've had a drink, until you've sobered up, until you die, until you're born again, to decide that. There is no better time than right now to be happy!

Prayer

Grant to us, O Lord, the royalty of inward happiness, and the serenity which comes from living close to you. Daily renew in us the sense of joy, and let the eternal Spirit of the Father dwell in our souls and bodies, filling every corner of our hearts with light and grace; so that, bearing with us the infection of good courage, we may be diffusers of life, and may meet all ills and cross accidents with gallant and high-hearted happiness, giving you thanks always for all things (Robert Louis Stevenson).

Some significant events on this day

Year   Event

1940   After becoming British Prime Minister three days earlier, Winston Churchill tells the House of Commons: 'I have nothing to offer but blood, toil, tears and sweat.'

1965   The *Luna 5* spacecraft, launched by the USSR, malfunctions and crashes on the moon.

1981   In St Peter's Square, Rome, Pope John Paul II is shot and seriously wounded by Turkish assailant Mehmet Ali Agca.

Key thought for today

Those who would have no trouble in this world must not have been born in it.
    — Italian proverb

Reflection

By Br Bill Firman

My mother used to talk of her great grandmother who left England in the 1820s bound for Australia on a sailing ship with three young children. On the way out the children all died, no doubt causing her great anguish. Yet she resolutely overcame her grief and had several more children. Such women have tremendous strength. They illustrate well the message enunciated by Marcel Proust:

Happiness is beneficial for the body but it is grief that develops the powers of the mind.

Grief in life is inevitable. Loved ones die. I like the sentiment expressed poetically in the Chinese proverb:

You cannot prevent the birds of sorrow from flying over your head, but you can prevent them from building nests in your hair.

We live with a high probability of birds of sorrow, but we can prevent grief from settling on us simply by getting on with life. The power of our minds must carry us forward. There are many challenges in life and always plenty of people advocating caution; but I like these thoughts of John Keats:

> *... I leaped
> headlong into the sea,
> and thereby have become
> better acquainted with the
> surroundings, the quicksand,
> and the rocks, than if I had
> stayed upon the green shore,
> and piped a silly pipe,
> and took tea and
> comfortable advice.*

We can be timid and choose comfort before courage and take 'tea and comfortable advice'. We may well recall that someone once said, 'A leap in the dark often ends in the ditch' – but does that really matter? What matters is that we have the courage to try again. What matters is that we cherish the gift of life and not fear inevitable upsets or even death.

Prayer

Benjamin Disraeli spoke of 'the indulgence of grief, the blunder of a life'. Help me, Lord, to deal with grief and other problems as instants in my life and then to move on without self-indulgence. Amen.

Reflecting God's Presence

Some significant events on this day

Year	Event
1796	Edward Jenner gives the first vaccination against smallpox.
1973	The US Supreme Court approves equal rights for women in the military, leading to more combat-related roles for women.
1978	Sir Robert Menzies, Australia's 12th and longest-serving prime minister, dies.

Key thought for today

If you ever find happiness by hunting for it, you will find it, as the old woman did her best spectacles, safe on her nose all the time.
— Josh Billings

Reflection

By Br Bill Firman

In most sports, you have an opponent – tennis, swimming, athletics races, horse racing, lawn bowls and so on. In team sports you have a team playing with you and an opposing team – cricket, football in its various codes, hockey and so on. Then there are sports wherein you essentially compete against yourself: your real opponent comes from within – golf, shooting, diving, high jump, gymnastics, surfing and so on. In this latter group, you do compare scores, sometimes on a handicap basis, but the sport is based on your individual efforts alone and not on directly vanquishing an opponent.

I am what one might call a 'rusty golfer', one who plays for two or three weeks on a January holiday and then only rarely throughout the year. I dream I could be better than I am if only I could practise more. But when I hit a bad shot I know I can't blame the club, the ball, even the bad lie or the non-existent referee in a social round. It really is my fault, my failing in concentration, my weakness in technique – and my personal frustration! Golf can be quite confronting.

Keep your head and shoulders still, don't swing too fast, don't lift your head, hit through the ball, transfer your weight – and relax – all at the same time. I did it in practice – why it is harder now that I am really addressing the ball? Forget your playing partner – he has a lower handicap anyway and you can't affect his score. All you can do is try to make yourself better by controlling what goes on inside your own head.

A round of golf can be viewed as a metaphor for living. Don't blame others, take control of your life within the set of agreed ethics, accept your handicap and your limited ability, focus on what you are trying to achieve, especially playing it straight and don't get too uptight about it when you are erratic! Calmly refocus. You can't change what has happened; you can shape what you are about to do. You play better when you stay quietly optimistic. Remember your good shots. It brings you back tomorrow with new hope.

Prayer

God, I am conscious of my limitations but struggle sometimes to live within them. Keep me calmly focused on what is important. Help me to be optimistic. Amen.

Some significant events on this day

Year	Event
1940	Nylon stockings, the first successful commercial polymer, made from coal, water and air, go on sale in the USA.
1948	Britain's 28-year mandate over Palestine ends.
1972	Okinawa, a Japanese island under US control since 1945, is returned to the Japanese government.

Key thought for today

What lies behind us and what lies before us are small matters compared with what lies within us.
— Ralph Waldo Emerson

Reflection

By Maria Giacomantonio:

Don't go overboard. Stay cool. Keep an even keel. Virtue lies in the middle.

It would be hard to imagine John Baptist de La Salle making the above statements to his Brothers. Great works are not accomplished by lukewarm people. De La Salle was full on, not half-hearted. He was full of zeal. Nothing of significance can be achieved without zeal – what some people call drive or passionate dedication. It seems impossible to think of great writers, artists, leaders or saints devoid of zeal.

Christian zeal should not be confused with destructive compulsion. Infamous criminals and deranged tyrants are compelled to extreme behaviour by destructive forces from within over which they have little control. The zeal that fired De La Salle, and the zeal that he wanted his Brothers to have, expresses itself as constructive creativity, positive energy and empowerment of other people.

De La Salle radiated zeal and acted dynamically and courageously. Inspired by his faith in a loving God, he zealously acted upon God's call to him.

In the *Power of Myth*, Joseph Campbell remarks:

The influence of a vital person vitalises, there's no doubt about it. The world without spirit is a wasteland ... Any world is a valid world if it's alive ... the thing to do is to bring life to it, and the only way to do that is to find in your own case where the life is and become alive yourself.'

God calls us to be fully alive persons, zealously committed to the Good News and to serving our neighbour.

Prayer

Lord, help me to put into practice, in my life, these words of De La Salle: 'Let it be clear, then, in all your relationships with the children who are entrusted to you that you look upon yourself as minister of God, acting with a sincere and true zeal, accepting with much patience the difficulties you have to suffer' (Meditations for the Time of Retreat).

Reflecting God's Presence

Some significant events on this day

Year   Event

1985   Michael Jordan is named the US National Basketball Association (NBA) Rookie of the Year.

1989   Soviet President Mikhail Gorbachev meets with Chinese leader Deng Xiaoping in China, formally ending a 30 year rift between the two countries. During the visit, 3000 students on a hunger strike filled Tiananmen Square. The protest movement was violently suppressed on 4 June.

1999   The Kuwaiti Cabinet votes to give women the right to vote as from the 2003 elections.

Key thought for today

I can accept failure. Everyone fails at something. But I cannot accept not trying.
— Michael Jordan

Reflection

By Michael Naughton

Michael Jordan was one of my sporting idols. I've never seen an athlete so dominant in a team sport at the elite level. I like his message in today's key thought. Everyone fails at some time – but you have to get out there and have a go! The only failure in life is the failure not to try. If you live your life only attempting what you know you can achieve, then you are probably not going to achieve that much. The fear of failure is paralysing for some people. Louis E Boone said:

'Don't fear failure so much that you refuse to try new things. The saddest summary of a life contains three descriptions: could have, might have, and should have.'

Michael Jordan didn't fear failure. He once said, 'You're going to miss 100 per cent of the shots you don't take.' You've got to admire an attitude like that! In order to succeed, you must be first willing to fail. It is how we learn. By failing, we know what not to do next time. We learn by our mistakes! Malcom S. Forbes said, 'Failure is success if we learn from it.'

So, get out and have a crack today! Michael Jordan will never be remembered for the thousands of shots he missed, but the 25 times he made buzzer-beating shots to win an NBA game will live forever. Michael Jordan overcame obstacles. He summarised his attitude in these words:

> Obstacles don't have to stop you. If you run into a wall, don't turn around and give up. Figure out how to climb it, go through it, or work around it.

Now that is positive!

Prayer

Let me not be paralysed by fear of failure but be energised by the determination to succeed. Let me learn from all my failures to become stronger within and more understanding of those around me who make mistakes. Grant me, O God, the courage to try. Amen.

Reflecting God's Presence

Some significant events on this day

Year   Event

1845   The rubber band is patented.

1846   The saxophone is patented by Adolphe Sax.

1961   Cuban leader Fidel Castro offers to exchange 500 prisoners captured in the abortive Bay of Pigs invasion for 500 bulldozers.

1989   More than one million people converge on the centre of Beijing in support of Chinese students undergoing a hunger strike to advocate democratic reform.

Key thought for today

In peace, sons bury their fathers; in war, fathers bury their sons.
  — Herodotus

Reflection

By Br Bill Firman

The last Anzac, Alec Campbell, died on 16 May 2002, aged 103. He had been born on 26 February 1899. My father, who had been born four years earlier in 1895, also fought in Turkey in the First World War, the so-called 'Great War', but he was not an Anzac. Alec and my dad were two of 324,000 Australians who volunteered to fight overseas, of whom 60,000 died and many more were injured and permanently maimed. My dad was lucky: a bullet which just missed his heart put him out of the war. I was not yet conceived: so I guess that makes me lucky also!

The Second World War (1939–1945) followed the first, only 21 years later. Really it was a shorter period than that if we consider the slaughter in preliminary conflicts such as the Japanese invasion of Nanking in China in which it is believed 370,000 Chinese, men, women and children were killed. Nanking, then the capital of China, fell to the Japanese on 16 December 1937, and, for the next six weeks, there was wholesale slaughter.

Like many of the veterans of World War I, my dad preferred to suppress the memories of the terrible things he experienced and witnessed and would not talk about them to his children. Gallipoli, and the other campaigns of World War I, revealed the stark futility and the absolute horror of war.

The agreed ethics of war used to be that wars were fought by soldiers and that civilians should not be harmed unless they were collaborators. But by the end of World War II both sides had indulged in indiscriminate killing of civilians. The bombing of Hiroshima and Nagasaki undoubtedly hastened the end of the war in the Pacific, but at a horrendous cost. It is almost impossible to adhere to a clear code of morality once war unleashes the wholesale slaughter of other people. Many soldiers are left scarred and traumatised by their role in the carnage and many non-combatants are innocent victims.

Prayer

Make me an advocate of your peace, O God.

Reflecting God's Presence

Some significant events on this day

Year   Event

1920   Birth of Pope John Paul II in Poland.

1982   Unification Church (the Moonies cult) founder, Sun Myung Moon, is convicted of tax evasion.

1990   The French TGV train clocks a record speed of 515.3 km/h.

Key thought for today

The world is far more ready to receive the Gospel than Christians are to hand it out.
— George W. Peters

Reflection

By Br Bill Firman

Even though farming methods today, with large numbers of sheep on vast properties, are now very different from past ages, most of us still understand the image of a shepherd looking after his sheep. The enduring gospel image of the selfless shepherd braving cold and dark to go out in search of the missing sheep from his flock is a powerful one, emphasising Christ's role as the Good Shepherd, as the wise pastor-teacher, as the one who seeks to ensure no sheep is lost. Each sheep is valuable to the shepherd.

But not all the shepherds in the Bible were good shepherds, as Ezekiel was clearly reminded! (Ezekiel 34:3-4)

> *You take care of yourselves, but never tend the sheep ... You have not taken care of the weak ones, healed those that are sick, bandaged those that are hurt, brought back those that have wandered off, or looked for those that were lost.*

God was unable to accept that this was good enough for his people, and he left the poor shepherds in no doubt as to their fate (see Ezekiel 34:10).

The increasing responsibility falling on parents, teachers and leaders – any persons who are responsible for the well-being of other people – is a heavy burden - and at the same time a great privilege. Each of us can be a good shepherd or a poor one. Each of us can either nurture or turn our backs on those who depend on us.

Saint Peter charges us:

> *Be shepherds of the flock that God has given you and take care of it willingly* (1 Peter 5:2).

We are not just responsible each for our own individual lives but especially for all those who depend on us for care and guidance. Our example, our advice, our care, our attitudes are going to help or hinder them. The bad shepherds take care of themselves but are condemned for not taking care of the weak, the sick, the hurt, the strays who have wandered off.

Prayer

May I be aware of my responsibilities to be a good shepherd and look after others I meet. Amen.

Some significant events on this day

Year   Event
1861   Birth of the famous Australian opera singer, Dame Nellie Melba.
1922   In the Soviet Union, the 'Young Pioneer Movement' is established as a communist equivalent to the scouting movement of the Western countries. Scouting had been eliminated because many scout masters had fought with the Bolsheviks during the Russian Civil War.
1965   Death at the age of 192 of Tui Malita, then the world's oldest tortoise, having been born in 1773.

Key thought for today

For the ignorant, old age is a winter; for the learned, it is a harvest.
— Jewish proverb

Reflection

By Brother Bill Firman

Robert Louis Stevenson (1850–1894) told a story from his childhood when he gazed from his window on a dark night as a man came down the street lighting the gas lamps. Robert called out to his mother:

I see something wonderful. There's a man coming down the street poking holes in the dark.

Stevenson's story reminds me of words we read in St John's gospel:

The light shines in the darkness and the darkness did not overcome it (John1:5).

In anyone's life, there can be dark times when burdens, disappointments or depression seem overwhelming. One small light, a candle of hope, is all that is needed to ensure the darkness does not become overwhelming. Life is a gift from God, a journey into God, our light.

We do not choose our parents, our nationality our socio-economic circumstances, our aptitudes. We do not make the circumstances of our unique personalities but we do shape them by our own volition. We decide what we are going to do with the unique gift of this life, how selfish or unselfish, how generous or mean, how inward-looking or outward-loving. It was William Hazlitt who wrote:

Man is the only animal that laughs and weeps: for he is the only animal that is struck by the difference between what things are and what they might have been.

The challenge is to be proud of who we are and the journey we are making. Then we shall come to understand the words of Joseph Joubert:

The evening of a well-spent life brings its lamps with it.

Prayer

Life is a rich harvest for those who decide to make the most of life's journey. Let me never regret who I am or what I have become. Help me, God, if I stray, always to return to the light so that my journey is, indeed, a life well lived. Amen.

Reflecting God's Presence

Some significant events on this day

Year   Event

1773   Captain James Cook releases the first sheep in New Zealand.

1902   Cuba gains independence from the United States.

1996   Iraq and the UN sign the Memorandum for Oil for Food Program, allowing oil revenue to be used for humanitarian aid.

Key thought for today

We are not our own, any more than what we possess is our own. We did not make ourselves; we cannot be supreme over ourselves. We cannot be our own masters. We are God's property by creation, by redemption, by regeneration.

— John Henry Newman

Reflection

By St John Baptist de La Salle

Consider that the account you will have to give to God will not be inconsequential, because it concerns the salvation of the souls of children whom God has entrusted to your care. On the day of judgment, you will answer for them as much as for yourself. You must be convinced of this, that God will begin by making you give an account of their souls before making you give an account of your own. For when you took responsibility for them, you committed yourself at the same time to procure their salvation with as much diligence as your own.

Have you up to the present looked upon the salvation of your students as your personal responsibility during the whole time that they are under your guidance? You have exercises that are arranged for your own sanctification, but if you have an ardent zeal for the salvation of those whom you are called to instruct, you will not fail to perform them and to relate them to this intention. You can be assured that if you act this way for their salvation, God himself will take responsibility for yours. Take on this spirit for the future (Meditations for the Time of Retreat).

There are some children to whose conduct their parents pay very little attention, sometimes none at all. From morning until evening, they do only what they please. They have no respect for their parents. They are disobedient. They grumble at the least thing. Sometimes these faults do not come from an evil disposition of heart or mind; they come from having been left to themselves. If they are of a bold and haughty spirit, they should be given some charge or responsibility in school to inspire them with a liking for school. But along with this they must be corrected and brought into line, never allowed to act as they please (The Conduct of Schools).

Prayer

May I treat all children as special; may I be responsible for helping those who come into my care progress on their path to God. Amen.

Some significant events on this day

Year   Event

1819   The first bicycles, known as 'swift walkers', are introduced in New York City.

1840   The Treaty of Waitangi is signed in New Zealand between Maori chiefs and representatives of Queen Victoria.

1965   The nuclear-powered US submarine *Scorpion* disappear, with 99 men aboard. It was later found on the ocean floor 640 km south-west of the Azores Islands, Portugal.

1991   At a campaign rally near Chenai, a Tamil suicide bomber assassinates Indian Prime Minister Rajiv Gandhi, and 14 other people.

Key thought for today

Short is the road that leads from fear to hate.
— Italian proverb

Reflection

By Brother Bill Firman: From an article published in *Europnews*, 21 May 2008, 'Islamic Extremists Kidnap Christian Girls', I gleaned the following disturbing description that outlines, I am not sure how accurately, the actions of extremist Muslims. I applaud the moderate Muslims who denounce such actions. Such tactics as described here are an incredible abuse of freedom — and also an abuse of the religion they pretend to espouse.

Paramilitary-backed Islamist militants have kidnapped thirteen Christian girls and destroyed six churches in a remote area of south-east Nigeria. Europenews reports police recovered two of the kidnapped Christian girls, aged 14 and 15, on May 12 after Muslims in Ningi kidnapped them three weeks ago in an attempt to expand Islam by marrying them to Muslim men. Police took the two girls, who had been under foster care, to safety in south eastern Nigeria where their biological parents live.

Following the rescue of the girls, Muslims under the auspices of the Hisbah Command, a paramilitary arm of Kano state's Sharia Commission, responsible for enforcing Islamic law, went on a rampage, attacking Christians and setting fire to the churches. The destroyed churches were the Deeper Life Bible Church, St Mary's Catholic Church, All Souls Anglican Church, Church of Christ in Nigeria, Redeemed Christian Church of God, and the Redeemed Peoples Mission.

Joseph Abdu, pastor of Deeper Life Bible Church, told reporters his congregation had shrunk to 40 from the 130 who had attended before the attack. Kidnapping of teenage Christian girls by Muslims, he said, has become a recurring practice in Ningi. Muslims have kidnapped at least 13 Christian girls in the town. 'These girls are usually kidnapped, forcefully converted to Islam, and then married out to other Muslim men against the will of both the girls and their parents', Abdu said.

Prayer

Let me never be so extreme as to try to force my will on others, nor to over-generalise when confronted by the behaviour of fanatics but let me act always with Christian respect for others, conscious of the need to lead others, not force them, in a search for truth. Amen.

Reflecting God's Presence

Some significant events on this day

Year   Event

1843   The first wagon train of pioneering people travelling west departs Missouri heading for Oregon. About 700 out of 1000 people reached their destination safely.

1939   The military alliance between Germany and Italy, known as the Axis, is formed when Adolf Hitler and Benito Mussolini sign the so-called 'Pact of Steel'.

1964   US President Lyndon Johnson proclaims his vision and plans for 'The Great Society'.

Key thoughts for today

The most worthwhile endeavour I have ever undertaken is responsibility for my own life. It's hard and it's worth it.
   — LeVar Burton

We are responsible for the world in which we find ourselves, if only because we are the only sentient force that can change it.
   — James Baldwin

Reflection

By Brother Bill Firman

For a person to lead a good life, it is obvious that he or she must act responsibly. Yet too often the notion of a good life is confused with the notion of being free to do whatever one wants. We are free to choose, but morality is based on making responsible choices, not choices that give us simply pleasure, power or material goods. Bishop Robinson expresses it this way:

> *The aim of morality is that people should grow to become all they are capable of being. Freedom without responsibility is the surest way to prevent growth, while responsibility cannot be exercised without freedom.*
>
> *Placing freedom and responsibility together is a middle ground between the two extremes of freedom without responsibility (I decide to do something and that makes it morally right for me) and responsibility without freedom (don't think, just obey). The terms of the debate in our modern society are all too often either total obedience or unlimited freedom, but both are dead ends that allow no growth and no escape. The only road that opens us to true growth is that of freedom and responsibility taken together.*
>
> *I, and I alone, am finally responsible for the person I become. It would be a pity if, at the end of life, a Christian person had to say to God, 'Lord, I must confess that I largely ignored the death of your son on the cross and I consistently followed the easier way. What I wanted was freedom without responsibility.' What God wants is growth and that must involve a truly responsible use of freedom.*

Prayer

Langston Hughes said, 'My soul has grown deep like the rivers.' Help me to flow and grow through life as a person of deep soul, full of responsibility and integrity.

Some significant events on this day

Year   Event

1958   Mao Zedong starts his ironically titled 'Great Leap Forward' movement in China.
1996   South Korea confirms a North Korean pilot had defected in a MIG-19 jet.
2004   Part of Charles de Gaulle Airport terminal collapses, killing five people.

Key thought for today

Enter into the inner chamber of your mind. Shut out all things save God and whatever may aid you in seeking God; and, having barred the door of your chamber, seek him.
— Saint Anselm of Canterbury

Reflection

By Brian Long

Christian Meditation

Find a quiet place. Sit down with your back upright. Sit still. Gently close your eyes and begin to recite your prayer-word, or mantra, silently, interiorly and lovingly throughout the time of your meditation: 'Ma-ra-na-tha.' Say it as four equally-stressed syllables.

It is an Aramaic word (which is the language that Jesus spoke) and it means 'Come, Lord.' It is found in the scriptures and is one of the earliest prayers in the Christian tradition.

Do not think about the meaning of the word. Just give your attention to the sound of it throughout the time of your meditation, from the beginning to the end. Whenever distractions arise, simply return to your mantra. Meditate for 20 minutes each morning and each evening, every day of your life. Meditation is a way of pure prayer marked by silence, stillness and simplicity (based on the writings of Fr John Main).

Prayer

*I arise today
in the name of silence,
womb of the Word.
In the name of stillness,
home of belonging.
In the name of solitude,
of the soul and the earth.
I arise today
blessed by all things,
wings of breath,
delight of eyes,
wonder of whisper,
intimacy of touch,
eternity of soul,
urgency of thought,
miracle of health,
embrace of God.
May I live this day,
compassionate of heart,
gentle in word,
gracious in awareness,
courageous in thought,
generous in love.*

John O'Donohue
Eternal Echoes

Reflecting God's Presence

Some significant events on this day

Year	Event
1941	Robert Zimmerman, later to be called Bob Dylan, is born in Minnesota USA.
1971	Senator Neville Bonner becomes the first Australian Aboriginal parliamentarian.
2000	Israel withdraws its troops from South Lebanon after two decades of occupation.
2000	A new island is born in the Pacific in the Solomons group following the eruption of the Kavachi volcano.

Key thought for today

Where the spirit does not work with the hand there is no art.
— Leonardo Da Vinci

Reflection

By Br Bill Firman

I came across this poem, 'Unity' (author unknown), which I think captures the delicate work carried out by parents and teachers working together as they fashion the mind of a child. I offer it for prayerful reflection.

> *I dreamed I stood in a studio*
> *And watched two sculptors there.*
> *The clay they used was a child's mind*
> *And they fashioned it with care.*

> *One was a teacher: the tools he used*
> *Were books and music and art.*
> *One was a parent, with a guiding hand*
> *And a gentle, loving heart.*

> *Day after day the teacher toiled*
> *With a touch that was deft and sure,*
> *While the parent laboured at his side*
> *And polished and smoothed it over.*

> *And when at last their work was done*
> *They were proud of what they had wrought*
> *For the things they had moulded into the child*
> *Could neither be sold nor bought.*

> *And they each agreed they would have failed*
> *If they had worked alone,*
> *For behind the parent stood the school,*
> *And behind the teacher the home.*

Prayer

Every person is precious to God. It is our task to help children learn to respect themselves, and others, as precious in our sight and God's sight. May we fashion their minds and hearts well.

Some significant events on this day

Year   Event

1895   Playwright Oscar Wilde is sentenced to two years of hard labour in Reading Gaol for committing acts of gross indecency with other male persons.

1955   UK mountaineers George Band and Joe Brown successfully climb the third highest mountain (after Everest and K2), Kanchenjunga.

1986   An estimated seven million people participate in holding 'Hands across America' for 15 minutes with the aim of helping the homeless. The path stretched 6400 km from New York to California.

Key thought for today

Sex has become one of the most discussed subjects of the modern era. The Victorians pretended it did not exist; the moderns pretend that nothing else exists.

— Bishop Fulton Sheen

Reflection

By Br Bill Firman

In 1895, Oscar Wilde was locked up and sentenced to hard labour for practising homosexuality. There has been a dramatic shift in attitudes since then. In late 1986, the parents of a Year 12 student rang to make an appointment to see me, the Principal. At the interview the conversation went something like this:

> Parents: 'Paul came home last night and declared he was gay.'
> Principal: 'Does he know that you are coming to see me?'
> Parents: 'Yes, we told him we were coming to see you.'
> Principal: 'What was his reaction?'
> Parents: 'Our son said: "If it helps you!"'

At that point I realised how public opinion had shifted. Paul did not believe he had a problem. His parents had the problem. He was happy to see his parents helped with their problem.

The use of language has been incredibly powerful on this issue. Anyone who dares today to question the normalcy of homosexuality is labelled 'homophobic'. All people deserve respect, no matter who they are or whatever their sexual orientation: every person is our brother or sister in Christ, precious to God. So any aggressive or punitive attitude to homosexuals is wrong. But that doesn't mean that I have to accept that homosexuality is simply an alternative and equal lifestyle to heterosexuality. I don't. I see family life – with its implied heterosexuality – as the best basis for our society. So when those parents came to me about Paul, I told them they must keep loving and supporting him. But as parents, they also have to be true to their own integrity.

Prayer

Lord, let us love all people as they are but not to the point of overlooking what is best for humanity. Grant me the strength to argue my convictions. Amen.

Reflecting God's Presence

26 MAY

Some significant events on this day

Year   Event

1521   Martin Luther is banned by the Edict of Worms because of his religious beliefs.

1966   A Buddhist nun sets herself on fire at the US Consulate in Hue, South Vietnam, in protest at the Vietnam War.

1989   The Danish Parliament is one of the first countries to allow legal marriage between homosexuals.

Key thought for today

A love of reconciliation is not weakness or cowardice. It demands courage, nobility, generosity, sometimes heroism, an overcoming of oneself rather than of one's adversary. At times it may even feel like dishonour, but it never offends against true justice, or denies the rights of the poor. In reality, it is the patient, wise art of peace, of loving, of living with one's fellows, after the example of Christ, with a strength of heart and mind modelled on his.

— Pope Paul VI

Reflection

By Br Bill Firman

We, parents and teachers and Lasallian graduates, must aspire to create a better world and reveal values better than the 'anything goes, tolerate everything' mentality advocated by many in today's society who like to pretend any conservative attitude, especially if it is based on a religious tradition, is out of date. It is up to us, parents and teachers, to help the youth of today avoid succumbing to what Brother Damien Harvey used to call, 'the great grey mass of mediocrity' and, as we pray in the Mass, to 'lift up our hearts' with resolute determination.

Alexander Solzhenitsyn bravely chose to speak out against Stalinist oppression. Nelson Mandela was jailed in response to his efforts to develop a more just society in South Africa. Martin Luther King Jr gave his life advocating for equal rights. Mother Teresa dedicated her life to assisting the poor. John Baptist de La Salle gave away his wealth to provide schools for the poor. No doubt some of their peers thought them foolish. They were ordinary people who rose to do extraordinary things: they did not suffer from mediocrity. Christianity challenges us to be better than mediocre, for all of us to give a return on the talents we have been given.

Would that our College produce young men who do not become part of the great grey mass of mediocrity, who will be above average husbands and fathers of their families, or who will follow callings as religious brothers or priests that enable them to touch the hearts of others in an above-average way.

Prayer

Johann von Goethe said: 'If you treat people the way they are, you never improve them. If you treat them the way you want them to be, you will.' Help us to lift up our hearts and the hearts of those whom we meet. Amen.

27 MAY

Reflecting God's Presence

Some significant events on this day

Year   Event

1937   The Golden Gate Bridge, recently completed and connecting San Francisco and Marin County, California, is opened to pedestrians. The bridge rapidly became the principal icon of San Francisco.

1964   Death of India's first prime minister after winning independence from Britain, Jawaharlal Nehru.

1967   With the largest majority of any Australian referendum, voters overwhelmingly support a proposal to count Indigenous people in the national census.

1994   After 20 years of exile in the USA, Alexander Solzhenitsyn, the Nobel prize-winning dissident author, returns to Russia with his citizenship restored and charges of treason dropped.

Key thought for today

We have lost the concept of a Supreme Complete Entity, which used to restrain our passions and our irresponsibility ... We turned our backs upon the Spirit and embraced all that is material with excessive and unwarranted zeal ... Fifty years ago it would have seemed almost impossible that an individual could be granted boundless freedom simply for the satisfaction of instincts and whims ... In the West one almost never sees voluntary self-restraint.
— Alexander Solzhenitsyn, July 1978, at Harvard University

Reflection

By Brother Quentin O'Halloran:

Ivan Turgener, the famous 19th century Russian novelist, whose provocative 'A Sportsman's Sketches' argued for the abolition of serfdom, once saw a ragged, down-and-out beggar in the street.

He stopped beside the man, intending to give him some money, but, to his embarrassment, as he searched his pockets he realised he did not have a single coin.

He grasped the beggar's outstretched hand and said, with real regret in his voice, 'I'm really sorry but I haven't anything to give you.'

'Never mind', said the beggar. 'But thank you for your handshake. It is a gift worth having.'

Prayer

Lord, how rich our life will be if I can give friendship, a smile, a handshake, some encouragement or sympathy to someone each day. Help me to see you in others and to share my gifts with them.

Reflecting God's Presence

Some significant events on this day

Year	Event
1961	Amnesty International is founded by British lawyer Peter Benenson, to protect and promote human rights.
1987	Mathias Rust, aged 19, creates world headlines by landing a small plane on a bridge near Red Square, Moscow, without having been intercepted by Soviet air defences. He was kept in prison for 432 days.
1999	After 22 years of restoration work, Leonardo Da Vinci's masterpiece 'The Last Supper' is put back on display in Milan, Italy.

Key thought for today

Everything can be taken away except the last of the human freedoms – to choose one's attitude in any given set of circumstances, to choose one's own way.
— Viktor Frankl

Reflection

By Br Bill Firman

The sufferings of Jesus Christ, his condemnation to brutal punishment, and death by crucifixion, would appear to be the low point of his life yet it was perhaps the most meaningful act in history. God became a man and died for us because God was asserting that we matter, that God loves us then and now, and invites us to love him in return. In his love for us, even to his death, God gave meaning to suffering. 'There is no greater love', Jesus said, 'than to lay down your life for your friends.'

The Viennese psychotherapist Dr Viktor Frankl, describing his experiences in concentration camps during the Second World War, observed that frequently it was not the physically strong who survived the rigours and privations of the camps but somehow those who found meaning in their suffering.

Frankl explains how he spent many hours thinking of his wife. His love for his wife gave meaning to his desperate struggle for survival. Frankl suggests that what people are really searching for in life is *meaning* and he concludes that this meaning is found in love. He quotes Nietzsche's words:

> *Those who have a why to live for can bear with almost any how.*

The greatest meaning in life is to love and be loved by other people and by God. Happiness in life is found through giving and loving even when, and especially when, we suffer. This is the meaning to be recognised in the death of Christ on the cross. Real meaning in life is found in giving and receiving love, when at least two people make each other feel they matter.

Prayer

Viktor Frankl wrote: 'Ever more people today have the means to live, but no meaning to live for.' Grant me the focus, purpose and meaning that I may enjoy the fullness of living. Amen.

Some significant events on this day

Year   Event

1953   Edmund Hillary of New Zealand and Nepalese Sherpa Tensing Norgay become the first people to reach the summit of Mt Everest.

1963   Timothy Leary and Richard Alpert, both psychology professors at Harvard University in the USA, are fired for experimenting with psychedelic drugs.

1985   Thirty-five people are killed when rioting breaks out between British and Italian spectators at the European Cup soccer final held in Brussels.

Key thought for today

You don't have to be a fantastic hero to do certain things – to compete. You can be just an ordinary chap, sufficiently motivated to reach challenging goals.

— Sir Edmund Hillary

Reflection

By Michael Naughton:

We all have dreams about what we are going to achieve in life. Edmund Hillary was the first man to conquer Everest, the highest mountain on the planet. Wow, what a dream! In 1958 he also became the first explorer to reach the South Pole since Captain Robert Scott in 1912.

Sometimes our dreams seem unattainable and we lose sight of where we are going. To help achieve your dreams, start setting some goals now. Diana Scarf Hunt said: 'Goals are dreams with deadlines.'

Setting smaller and achievable goals is a good way to work towards a final dream. Write them down somewhere. Be specific about what you want to achieve and how you are going to do it. Set some time lines. They need to be realistic, but challenging. Your goals need to stretch you in some way – there's little satisfaction in achieving a goal that is easy. Your goals should be high enough to inspire you but low enough to encourage you.

Be prepared for failure along the way, but use it as a form of motivation. Reward yourself when you achieve a goal, then knuckle down and look towards the next. All great athletes and high achievers set goals in their lives. Aristotle wrote:

Humans are goal seeking animals. Their life only has meaning if they are reaching out and striving for their goals.

What are your goals? Don't be someone who sets sail without a destination in mind. Do it now. You become successful the moment you start moving towards a worthwhile goal.

Prayer

Lord, help me never to be afraid to dream and set lofty goals. Help me to be focused on where I want to go and grant me the courage to take one step at a time in this direction. Amen.

Reflecting God's Presence

Some significant events on this day

Year   Event

1431   Joan of Arc, accused of witchcraft, heresy and wearing male clothing, is burned at the stake, at the age of 19, in Rouen, France. In 1456, after another trial, she was found innocent. She was canonised in 1920.

1896   The first car accident occurs in New York when Henry Wells hits a cyclist.

1911   The first Indianapolis 500 is run.

Key thought for today

There is no more evil thing in this world than race prejudice … It justifies and holds together more baseness, more cruelty and abomination that any other sort of error in the world.
— H.G. Wells

Reflection

By Br Bill Firman (based on an article by Dr Peter Hodge)

'Untouchability' has been outlawed by the Indian Constitution but the reality is far different. The lowest caste (untouchables) are called Dalits. One of them, Moses Vattipalli, is a rare case among Dalits to have escaped the same work as his father. He is assistant to the National Administrator of the All India Christian Council. One of his tasks is to record abuses against Dalits on the organisation's website. 'Every day I have things to report', he says. 'Every day a killing, every day a Dalit is raped, humiliated, beaten up.'

The common perception is that modern India has a booming economy based on an IT revolution, but few Dalits have reaped much benefit because of lack of education and ongoing discrimination. Like most Dalit children, Moses' education about caste status began early. In his own village, he knew not to take water from the well the upper-caste people used. The Dalits in Moses' village are isolated on the eastern side. 'When the wind blows, the wind of the Dalits should not touch the upper-caste people', explained Moses. The general rule in Indian culture that respect should flow to elders is skewed by caste. Children growing up under such conditions develop a sense of inferiority. That is precisely the intention. 'There were many times when I was told I was a Dalit and equal to any other animal', said Moses.

Freedom, to some extent, came when he moved to the city, where his caste identity wasn't so obvious. His study of the Bible also helped, especially the Christian perspective that, contrary to his upbringing, everyone is born equal. The most insidious characteristic of the caste system is the deliberate attempt to brand each human with a designation that determines their dignity and life expectations. 'It's always in the back of my head that I'm a Dalit and not a first class citizen', says Moses. The system he describes as 'evil' continues to haunt him and all Dalits. 'We can run away from it but we can not get rid of it.'

Prayer

God, help me to respect all people as equally precious to you and with the same rights to human dignity as I have, no matter what their race or social status. Amen.

31 MAY

Reflecting God's Presence

Some significant events on this day

Year	Event
1879	The first electric railway opens at the Berlin Trades Exposition.
1902	The Second Boer War, between Great Britain and two Boer republics of South Africa, ends.
1927	The last of more than 15 million T-model Fords is assembled.
1942	A Japanese midget submarine strikes the HMAS *Kuttabul* in Sydney Harbour, killing 19 sailors.
1955	A US Supreme Court decree orders an end to racial segregation in all schools in all states 'with all deliberate speed'.
1987	The member states of the World Health Organisation create World 'No Tobacco Day' to draw attention to deaths and diseases caused by smoking.

Key thoughts for today

Courage consists not in blindly overlooking danger, but in seeing it and conquering it.
— Jean Paul Richter

God is full of compassion. and never fails those who are afflicted and despised if they trust in him alone.
— Saint Teresa of Avila

Reflection

By Brian Long

It is worth reflecting on these words of Eleanor Roosevelt, who said:

> *You gain strength, courage and confidence by every experience in which you really stop to look fear in the face ... You must do the thing you think you cannot do.'*

The key is to take bravely just one step; to make just one move. Then the door will often open before me and my fears will go away because in all things I am being carried by a loving God who can magnify my one small step into one great stride. Everything that happens in life is life-giving somehow, even when I can't see how. I trust that the God who brought me to this point will see me through it. God's love goes before me and walks beside me in a way I can never name.

Saint Julian of Norwich reminds us,

> *All shall be well,*
> *and all shall be well,*
> *and all manner of thing shall be well.*

Prayer

God, I trust that you are with me and that you will never allow me to be faced with more than I can deal with. Walk beside me and give me the courage to take the first step necessary. Help me to accept the reality of the Chinese proverb: 'The gem cannot be polished without friction, nor people perfected without trials.'

Reflecting God's Presence

Some significant events on this day

Year   Event

1942   The first news of the gassing of tens of thousands of Jews at Chelmno death camp in Poland is published in a Warsaw Ghetto underground newspaper.

1968   The deaf and blind humanitarian activist Helen Keller dies in Connecticut at the age of 87.

1979   Ninety years of British Rule in Rhodesia ends as Bishop Muzorewa replaces Ian Smith and the country changes its name to Zimbabwe.

Key thought for today

Science may have found a cure for most evils; but it has found no remedy for the worst of them all – the apathy of human beings.
— Helen Keller

Reflection

By Br Bill Firman

In the 1950s, one could assume most Christians agreed that pre-marital sex, contraception, abortion, pornography, euthanasia, 'swinging', homosexuality and transsexuality were outside the moral code. One of by one the agreement on each of these issues has been eroded, although I cannot recall any coherent debate or dialectic process that has led to this change. Mostly it has simply been the application of remarkably effective pressure by minority groups, some driven by genuine conviction but many by seeking financial gain.

In the late 60s the movie *Blow Up* was given remarkable publicity because, for the first time, a woman's naked breasts were shown on the cinema screen. Agreed levels of permissibility have moved a long way since then. I have no doubt that the 50s, in which I grew up, were tainted with vestiges of Puritanism, especially since my parental generation had grown up under the influence of the values of Victorian England. In some ways we were too prudish and the cause of some problems could well have been an excessive sense of guilt and shame associated with the human body and an unhealthy preoccupation with sexuality as the source of most sins.

Increased openness, in my opinion, has been a healthy change generally, but it has not been healthy when it is accompanied by a loss of respect for others and effective denial of full human dignity. Access to pornography is now so easy for children who, in viewing such material, can confuse bizarrely-sexualised and disrespectful behaviour with sensitive interaction genuinely expressing the mutual love of two people. Today, infidelity and changing partners have become more common and more socially acceptable in some people's eyes, and the number of broken marriages has exploded. Nobody can convince me that this is a change for the better.

Prayer

John MacMurray wrote: 'Love may or may not include sexual attraction. It may express itself in sexual desire. But sexual desire is not love. Desire is quite compatible with personal hatred, or contempt, or indifference.' Help me to be in control of my desires so that I am respectful of all. Amen.

Some significant events on this day

Year   Event

1865   Confederate forces surrender, marking the end of the American Civil War.

1953   The coronation of Queen Elizabeth II, the first to be televised, is held in London.

1994   Death of Ian Phoenix in a helicopter crash on the Mull of Kintyre, off Scotland (see Reflection below).

Key thought for today

A life spent making mistakes is not only more honourable but more useful than a life spent doing nothing.
— George Bernard Shaw

Reflection

By Andrew Wozencroft

While reading the book, *Policing the Shadows: The Secret War against Terrorism in Northern Ireland*, I came across the following passage.

> *On 2 June 1994, a Chinook helicopter, carrying many high ranking police officers from Northern Ireland, crashed on the Mull of Kintyre, a small rocky outcrop between Northern Ireland and Scotland, killing all those on board. One of those killed was Detective Superintendent Ian Phoenix who had spent 25 years working undercover to fight terrorism. Many of the deeds he performed to save lives will never be known and in fact up until his death most of his friends thought he was a hearing-aid salesman, such was the dangerous nature of his work. His family had to be constantly on guard, with every action requiring thought, lest they be targeted. The story of his life in a small part of Ireland torn by fighting for so long is truly amazing. Regardless of who was right or wrong, Ian Phoenix just wanted peace for that small part of the world he called home.*

At Ian's funeral, a quote by Theodore Roosevelt was read that summed up how he had lived his life:

> *It is not the critic who counts nor the man who points out how the strong man stumbles or where the doer of deeds could have done better. The credit belongs to the man who is actually in the arena, whose face is marred by dust and sweat and blood, who knows great enthusiasm, great devotion, and the triumph of achievement, and who, at worst, if he fails at least fails whilst daring greatly. His place will never be with those odd and timid souls who know neither victory nor defeat. You've never lived until you've almost died. For those who have had to fight for it life has truly a flavour the protected shall never know.*

When I read this quote it struck a chord with me. Either we can spend our lives worrying about what others think or, like Ian, we can simply live life, a life that rewards us by considering the needs of others.

Prayer

God, help me never to be fearful of dust and sweat but assist me always to be enthusiastic and committed to what I believe in. Let me not be afraid of the criticism of others but let me always be prepared to try to do my best. Grant me the inward peace of my own integrity so that I may be an agent of just peace among other people. Amen.

Reflecting God's Presence

Some significant events on this day

Year   Event

1923   Italian women are given the right to vote by dictator Benito Mussolini.

1969   HMAS *Melbourne* collides off South Vietnam with the US navy destroyer USS *Frank E. Evans*. Seventy-two US sailors were killed or drowned when the destroyer was cut in two. An inexperienced US officer on the watch was eventually found to be at fault.

1994   The Mabo decision is handed down in the Australian High Court recognising the falsity of *terra nullius* in a landmark decision for Indigenous land rights.

Key thoughts for today

We cultivated our land, but in a way different from the white man. We endeavoured to live with the land; they seemed to live off it.
— Tom Dystra, Australian Aboriginal

Those who lose Dreaming are lost.
— Australian Aboriginal proverb

Reflection

By Br Bill Firman

On 3 June 1992, the High Court of Australia delivered its landmark Mabo decision which rewrote Australian common law and gave a massive boost to the struggle for the recognition of Aboriginal land rights. Put simply, the decision said that, under Australian law, Indigenous people have rights to land – rights that existed before colonisation and which still exist. This right is called 'native title'. By a majority of six to one, the High Court ruled that native title to land is recognised by the common law of Australia, throwing out forever the legal fiction that when Australia was 'discovered' by Captain Cook in 1788 it was *terra nullius*, an empty or uncivilised land.

The case centred on the Murray Islands in the eastern part of the Torres Strait Islands between Australia and Papua New Guinea. The Meriam people, led by Eddie Koiki Mabo, took the action to the High Court to overturn the doctrine of *terra nullius*. The judges in the case declared that 'the Meriam people are entitled as against the whole world to possession, occupation, use and enjoyment of the lands of the Murray Islands'.

It was the first time that the High Court had considered the position of Indigenous people in Australian property law and their judgement was not restricted to the Murray Islands. Justice Brennan said, '… there may be other areas of Australia where Aboriginal people, maintaining their identity and their customs, are entitled to enjoy their native title'.

This was a critical step in restoring the dignity of ownership to our dispossessed first inhabitants.

Prayer

We pray that all Australians may be accorded full human dignity and live together in peace.

Some significant events on this day

Year   Event
1919   The US Congress approves the 19th amendment to the Constitution, giving women the right to vote.
1939   The SS *St Louis*, carrying 963 Jewish refugees, is denied permission to land in Florida. It was forced to return to Europe where most of its passengers later died in concentration camps.
1940   The Battle of Dunkirk ends, with more than 300,000 Allied troops evacuated by ships, many of which were civilian.
1944   Rome surrenders to the Allies – the first Axis capital to fall to the Allies in World War II.
1989   Tanks roll into Tiananmen Square to suppress the peaceful student protest.

Key thought for today

In China, a million people is still only a small number.
— Deng Xiaoping after the Tiananmen massacre

Reflection

By Br Bill Firman

Tiananmen Square is a large public square in Beijing, China, on the southern edge of the inner city. The square, named for its Gate of Heavenly Peace (Tiananmen), contains the monument of the heroes of the revolution, the Great Hall of the People, the museum of history and revolution, and the Mao Zedong Memorial Hall. Mao Zedong proclaimed the founding of the People's Republic in the square on 1 October 1949, an anniversary still observed there.

A massive demonstration by Chinese students began in the Square in April 1989 for democratic reform and to demand the posthumous rehabilitation of former Communist Party Chairman Hu Yaobang. The demonstrators were joined by workers, intellectuals and civil servants, until over a million people filled the square The government was tolerant until after Hu Yaobang's funeral. General Secretary Zhao Ziyang expressed sympathy, but lost out to Deng Xiaoping, who denounced the protests. Martial law was declared on 20 May. The protesters demanded that the leadership resign, but the government answered on the nights of 3 and 4 June with troops and tanks, killing thousands to quell a 'counter-revolutionary rebellion'. Zhao was dismissed and a number of the student leaders were arrested.

The suppression of the protest was immortalised in Western media by famous video footage and photos of a lone man in a white shirt standing in front of a column of tanks, halting their progress. He stood defiantly for some time, then climbed up onto the turret of the lead tank to speak to the soldiers inside. He reportedly said, 'Why are you here? You have caused nothing but misery.' *Time* magazine dubbed him 'The Unknown Rebel' and later named him one of the 100 most influential people of the 20th century. All the world admired his courage.

Prayer

We pray for the courage of the so-called 'Tank Man', the unknown rebel whose image still inspires people who are unjustly oppressed. We pray for peace, justice and freedom. Amen.

Reflecting God's Presence

Some significant events on this day

Year Event

1967 Israel begins the Six-Day War with simultaneous attacks on the air forces of Egypt, Jordan and Syria.

1968 US presidential candidate Robert F. Kennedy is shot in Los Angeles by Sirhan Sirhan. Kennedy died the next day.

1989 After the Tiananmen Square protests in China are forcibly concluded, an unknown rebel stands in front of a column of advancing tanks, halting their progress for more than half an hour. His name and fate have never been disclosed. Nor has the name and fate of the tank driver who refused to run him down.

Key thought for today

A man can accept what Christ has done without knowing how it works; indeed he certainly won't know how it works until he's accepted it.
— C. S. Lewis

Reflection

By Br Gerald Barrett

We all know what it is like when things go wrong.

During my life as a Brother I have always been consoled by the fact that I can rely on someone to help me through those moments when the well runs dry. At times, the last person I seem to turn to is Jesus.

Why? I think that, being human, we tend to think that there is always an earthly or human solution. The difficulty arises, and only when all else fails do we seek out Christ and we knock. He has always been there waiting, but in our stubbornness of heart we aren't ready.

I offer a prayer, called 'Footprints', that I have always found comforting during the difficult moments in my own life's journey.

Prayer

One night I had a dream. I was walking along the beach with the Lord, and across the skies flashed scenes from my life. In each scene I noticed two sets of footprints in the sand. One was mine, and one was the Lord's. When the last scene of my life appeared before me, I looked back at the footprints in the sand, and, to my surprise, I noticed that many times along the path of my life there was only one set of footprints. And I noticed that it was at the lowest and saddest times in my life. I asked the Lord about it: 'Lord, you said that once I decided to follow you, you would walk with me all the way. But I notice that during the most troublesome times in my life there is only one set of footprints. I don't understand why you left my side when I needed you most.' The Lord said, 'My precious child, I never left you during your time of trial. Where you see only one set of footprints, I was carrying you.'

Some significant events on this day

Year Event

1944 Operation Overlord begins, with Allied troops landing in Normandy on D-Day.
1968 Senator Robert Kennedy dies after being shot the previous day.
2002 A small earth-bound asteroid explodes with near nuclear force in the atmosphere over the Mediterranean Sea, leading to many UFO reports.

Key thought for today

There is many a boy here today who looks on war as all glory. But, boys, it is all hell.
— General W. T. Sherman

Reflection

By Br Bill Firman

The terms D-Day and H-Hour are used for the day and hour on which a combat attack or operation is to be initiated where secrecy is essential. By far, the best known D-Day is 6 June 1944 – the day on which the Invasion of Normandy began. Code-named Operation Overlord, it commenced the Western Allied effort to liberate the mainland from Nazi occupation during World War II. The Normandy landings were the first successful opposed landings across the English Channel in nine centuries.

The German high command had been duped into the belief that the invasion would be in the Calais area but the invasion force assembled off the Normandy coast of France as dawn broke on 6 June 1944. There were nine battleships, 23 cruisers, 104 destroyers and 71 large landing craft of various descriptions, as well as troop transports, mine sweepers, and merchant ships – nearly 5000 ships of every type, the largest armada ever assembled. Naval bombardment began at 0550, detonating large minefields along the shoreline and destroying a number of the enemy's defensive positions. In the hours following the bombardment more than 150,000 fighting men swept ashore to begin one of the epic assaults of history, a 'mighty endeavor', as President Franklin D. Roosevelt described it to the American people, 'to preserve our civilisation and to set free a suffering humanity'.

The defeat inflicted on the Germans was one of the largest of the Second World War. Strategically, the campaign led to the loss of the German position in most of France and the secure establishment of a new major front. The Allies Supreme Commander, US General Dwight Eisenhower, said:

> *The tide has turned! The free men of the world are marching together to victory! I have full confidence in your courage, devotion to duty and skill in battle. We will accept nothing less than full victory! Good luck! And let us all beseech the blessings of Almighty God upon this great and noble undertaking.*

We take our freedom very much for granted. Other generations fought for it. It is a blessing to preserve, cherish and appreciate.

Prayer

God, make me truly grateful for the freedom I enjoy in this country. May those who fought to preserve it rest in peace. Amen

Reflecting God's Presence

Some significant events on this day

Year   Event

1862   The ratified treaty between the US and the UK agreeing to suppress the slave trade comes into effect.

1929   The Vatican City becomes a sovereign state by the Lateran Treaty, separating the papal lands from Rome and giving them self-government.

1942   The World War II Battle of Midway ends, resulting in severe losses to the Japanese fleet and the retention of Midway as a vital landing ground for the Pacific allies.

Key thought for today

The greatest need in the world is the transformation of human nature. We need a new heart that will not have lust and greed and hate in it. We need a heart filled with love and peace and joy, and that is why Jesus came into the world.

— Billy Graham, *Just As I Am*

Reflection

By Br Bill Firman

I like this meditation offered by Bishop Geoffrey Robinson. It is a beautiful metaphor describing the handing on of the Gospel message.

> *In everything he did and in everything he said, Jesus Christ sang a song. Sometimes, when he cured a sick person, he sang softly and gently, a song full of love. Sometimes, when he told one of his beautiful stories, he sang a haunting melody, the kind of melody that, once heard, is never forgotten, the sort of melody you hum throughout the day without even knowing that you are doing it. Sometimes, when he defended the rights of the poor, his voice grew strong and powerful, until finally, from the cross, he sang so powerfully that his voice filled the universe.*
>
> *The disciples who heard him thought that this was the most beautiful song they had ever heard, and they began to sing it to others. They didn't sing as well as Jesus had – they forgot some of the words, their voices sometimes went flat – but they sang to the best of their ability, and the people who heard them thought in their turn that this was the most beautiful song they had ever heard. And so the song of Jesus gradually spread out from Jerusalem to other lands. Parents sang it to their children and it began to be passed down through the centuries.*

I believe the song of Jesus makes sense. If the values he taught permeate our lives then we sing a beautiful song, albeit imperfectly. All we need to do to live well is to sing this song to the best of our imperfect ability.

Prayer

Muhammad Ali once said: 'Christianity is a good philosophy if you live it, but it's controlled by white people who preach it but don't practise it.' Help me to sing a true song and to live up to the song I sing.

Some significant events on this day

Year	Event
632	The death of Mohammed, the Prophet of Islam.
1942	Two Japanese submarines fire shells at Sydney and Newcastle.
1949	George Orwell's novel *Nineteen Eighty-Four* is published.
1953	The US Supreme Court rules that Washington DC restaurants may not refuse to serve black customers.
1984	The state of New South Wales decriminalises homosexuality between consenting adults in private.

Key thought for today

Loving relationships are a family's best protection against the challenges of the world.
— Bernie Wiebe

Reflection

By Betty Rudin

A little boy and his younger sister both suffered from a strange disease. They both also had the same rare blood type. The boy had just recovered but his sister was in need of a blood transfusion. With blood from someone who had recently recovered, this made the boy a perfect candidate. The doctor walked into the waiting room and asked the boy if he would give blood for his sister. The boy hesitated at first but then agreed for the sake of his sister. As they walked into the room, they said nothing. At the end of the transfusion the boy turned to the doctor and asked, 'Doctor, when do I die?'

You see, this little boy thought that he was giving up his own life for the sister that he loved so much. Would you give your life for the people you love?

Prayer

> Lord, teach me to be generous.
> Teach me to serve you as you deserve;
> To give and not count the cost;
> To fight and not to heed the wounds;
> To toil and not to seek for rest;
> To labour and not to ask for reward, except to know
> That I am doing your will. Amen.
>
> (Prayer for Generosity by St Ignatius of Loyola)

Reflecting God's Presence

Some significant events on this day

Year   Event

68   The Roman Emperor Nero commits suicide to avoid execution by the Roman Senate.

1870   The death of the author Charles Dickens.

1934   Walt Disney's character Donald Duck debuts in the animated short film *The Wise Little Hen*.

Key thought for today

Have a heart that never hardens, and a temper that never tires, and a touch that never hurts.
— Charles Dickens

Reflection

By Br Bill Firman

A very good friend of mine, Father Chris Gleeson SJ, writing in *Madonna*, reflected on the preoccupation of many people with self-image. He willingly agreed to my including his words in this *Vade mecum*.

> *In mythology, Narcissus was the young man who fell in love with and became captivated by his own image reflected in a lake. That great saint, Teresa of Avila, once remarked that 'It is absurd to think that we can enter heaven without first entering our own souls – without getting to know ourselves.' And if you want to know why we do not reach the intimacy of walking with the Lord in the cool of the evening, it is because we are unwilling to see ourselves as we are.*
>
> *This is not a very popular idea in our post-modernist age of image, where spin predominates over substance, and where style – even lifestyle– is more important than searching for the truth. To quote an excellent newsletter article, by the Dean of Students at Brisbane Girls' Grammar School, ours is a 'culture where narcissism has been repackaged and sold as normal'. We need constantly to return to those words in Samuel: 'We look at the outward appearance but God looks at the heart' (1 Samuel 16:7).*
>
> *While inordinate use of the mirror might reveal a preoccupation with self-image, nonetheless all of us need a strong self-picture, a healthy self-esteem. After all, the Gospel enjoins us to love our neighbours as ourselves. Yet have we gone overboard on self-esteem? Should we be focusing more on self-respect rather than self-esteem? If self-esteem flows from a heartfelt knowledge of how much we are loved by God, it will not be selfish narcissism.*

We need to value ourselves, to have self-respect, though not to be focused on ourselves but rather to be reaching out to others.

Prayer

Lord, help me to reach out to others, secure in who I am, with a heart that never hardens and a touch that never hurts. Amen.

10 JUNE

Reflecting God's Presence

Some significant events on this day

Year	Event
1886	Mount Tarawera volcano erupts in New Zealand, killing 153 people and destroying the famous geological marvels, the 'pink and white terraces'.
1940	Italy declares war on France and Great Britain, joining the German Axis.
1967	Israel accedes to a UN ceasefire and ends the Six-Day War.
2003	The Mars *Spirit Rover* is launched and collects surface data successfully.

Key thought for today

Advice is like snow: the softer it falls, the longer it dwells upon and the deeper it sinks into the mind.
— Samuel Taylor Coleridge

Reflection

By Peter Riordan

There comes a time when teachers and parents have done all they can – all that remains is the act of faith that the young men or women we have helped grow up are developing good judgement, common sense and an understanding of their own personal weaknesses and limitations. As young people leave school, it is a time for them to begin to sort out who their real friends are, which of their acquaintances share the same values, and who will admonish and encourage them down the paths that they know they should travel. Adults know well that having the right friends is very important, but it is young people's right to choose their friends.

As adults, our role continues to be one of offering gentle guidance and encouragement, developed out of our own experiences; but it is less directive than it was when the children were school age. We offer support when, given the impatience and impetuosity of youth, mistakes inevitably happen. Offering such support does not mean we approve of who the friends are or what happened but it is part of our continuing love.

Some adults may still feel compelled to correct every mistake made by those in their care, but often it is better to wait, to give the young people time to recognise themselves that they have made a mistake. I like the words of Johann von Goethe who said:

> *Correction does much, but encouragement does more. Encouragement after censure is as the sun after a shower.*

The sun after a shower brings new growth, which is what we want to see. It is also important never to be so offended that we cannot forgive, forget and get on with living. We keep in mind the wise warning of C.S. Lewis:

> *Everyone says forgiveness is a lovely idea until they have something to forgive.*

Ultimately it is a great gift to have our children as our adult friends who forgive and forget our weaknesses as much as we do theirs.

Prayer

Lord, help me to encourage out of love rather than correct out of anger. Amen.

Reflecting God's Presence

Some significant events on this day

Year   Event

1937   Soviet leader Joseph Stalin begins his purge of the army by executing eight generals, with many more from all ranks to follow.

1955   At the Le Mans 24-hour race, 83 are killed and more than 100 injured when an Austin-Healey explodes after colliding with a Mercedes-Benz. To avoid panic, no announcement was made and the race continued to the end.

1962   Three prisoners, the only ever to 'escape' from the prison on Alcatraz Island, disappear, never to be seen again. It is thought they drowned or were eaten by sharks.

1987   Margaret Thatcher wins her third consecutive term as British Prime Minister.

Key thought for today

If a man hasn't discovered something he will die for, he isn't fit to live.
— Martin Luther King Jr

Reflection

By Br Bill Firman

I invite reflection on these words of former US President Bill Clinton with which he concludes his book *Giving*.

> *Will giving make you happier? You'll have to answer that for yourself. When I was in Africa with Bill and Melinda Gates, watching them talk to villagers whose lives they had improved, they seemed happy ... When Barbra Streisand and Rupert Murdoch, two highly public figures who disagree on nearly everything politically, stood together to give the first contribution to my foundation's fight against climate change, they seemed happy ...*
>
> *So much of modern culture is characterised by stories of self-indulgence and self-destruction. So much of modern politics is focused not on honest differences of policy but on personal attacks. So much of modern media is dominated by people who earn fortunes by demeaning others, defining them by their worst moments, exploiting their agonies. Who's happier? The uniters or the dividers? The builders or the breakers? The givers or the takers?*
>
> *I think you know the answer. There's a whole world out there that needs you, down the street or across the ocean. Give.*

Prayer

> *Lord, help me to be:*
> *a uniter rather than a divider;*
> *a builder rather than breaker;*
> *a giver rather than a taker.*
>
> *Help me to focus on*
> *what can be done rather than what seems too hard;*
> *the needs of others before my own comfort;*
> *the lasting good more than the passing pleasure.*
>
> *Lord, help me to give!*

12 JUNE

Reflecting God's Presence

Some significant events on this day

Year   Event

1963   African-American civil rights leader Medgar Evers is shot dead in Jackson Mississippi by Ku Klux Klan member Byron de la Beckwith. Beckwith was not originally convicted by biased all-white juries but was eventually jailed in 1994, as depicted in the 1996 movie *Ghosts of Mississippi*.

1964   African National Congress leader Nelson Mandela is sentenced to life imprisonment for sabotage. He was released in 1990 and was elected president of South Africa in 1994.

1991   Boris Yeltsin becomes the first democratically elected president of Russia.

Key thought for today

You can kill a man but you cannot kill an idea.
— Medgar Evers

Reflection

By Brother Quentin O'Halloran

When speaking to students about the future, I like to put it in the context of a Peanuts comic strip. Lucy and Linus are having a philosophical discussion about life with Charlie Brown.

'Some people', they say to Charlie, 'like to set up their deck chairs at the front of the ship, so they can see where they are going and scout out new possibilities. Others like to place their deck chairs at the back of the ship to see where they have been and gain wisdom from these observations.'

They ask Charlie, 'Where would you like to put your deck chair?'

'I don't know', Charlie mutters. 'I can never seem to get my deck chair open.'

The world you will face over your lifetime will be vastly different to the one you knew when you first set off to school. Whether you choose to explore possibilities from the front or steer sagely from the back, remember you are your greatest resource. Be aware of your human frailty, like Charlie Brown, but try not to 'fooster around' like him. Strive to be your own person in the knowledge that

> What lies behind you,
> what lies before you,
> are small matters compared
> to what lies within you.

Prayer

Lord, may I become increasingly a person for others, wanting to make a difference and witnessing proudly to more spiritual things.

Reflecting God's Presence

Some significant events on this day

Year   Event

1920   The US Postal Service rules that children may not be sent by parcel post.

1944   Germany first attacks London with V1 flying bombs.

1983   Pioneer 10, launched in 1972, becomes the first artificial object to leave our solar system. Signals continue to be received from it until January 2003.

Key thoughts for today

Try not to become a man of success, but rather try to become a man of value.
— Albert Einstein

It is a sign of strength, not of weakness, to admit that you don't know all the answers.
— John P. Loughrane

Reflection

By Br Bill Firman

Success in life is not to be measured by the wealth or status we achieve in the eyes of others but by our inner integrity. Living with integrity brings happiness in this life – and the ability to face death, when it comes, with confidence.

This was eloquently expressed by Martin Luther King Jr, two months before his assassination in 1968. He said:

> *If any of you are around when I have to meet my day, I don't want a long funeral ... Tell the preacher not to mention that I have a Nobel Peace Prize – that isn't important. Tell him not to mention that I have 300 or 400 other awards – that's not important ...*

> *I'd like somebody to mention that day that Martin Luther King Junior tried to give his life serving others. I'd like somebody to say that Martin Luther King Junior tried to love somebody ... I want you to be able to say that I did try to feed the hungry ... I did try in my life to clothe the naked ... I did try to love and serve humanity ...*

> *I won't have any money to leave behind. I won't have the fine and luxurious things of life to leave behind. But I just want to leave a committed life behind. And that is all I want to say.*

That is what it is to become a Christian: to know what is right, to do something about it, and to keep doing it every passing year.

Prayer

God, I want to be focused on what is really important in my life. Assist me to appreciate my family and friends. Lead me to commit myself to being unselfish and loving. Teach me to live so that everyone who knows me will be grateful to call me their friend. Amen.

Some significant events on this day

Year   Event
1777   The Stars and Stripes is adopted by US Congress as the country's flag.
1789   After a 6400 km journey in an open boat, the 19 survivors of the mutiny on HMAV *Bounty*, including Captain Bligh, reach Timor safely.
1919   John Alcock and Arthur Brown make the first non-stop trans-Atlantic flight.
1982   The Falklands War ends with Argentina's surrender to the UK.

Key thoughts for today

We are a society oppressed not by lack, but by surfeit; not by strife, but by ease.
— George Carey, Archbishop of Canterbury, 1999

Reflection

By Br Denis Loft

I have been to India the last three years with groups of Year 12 students doing a 'Coolies' program. Each time I have been astounded by the impact the children in the orphanage have on the boys from De La Salle.

These children have not had the loving personal care of a parent who dotes on their every move, who is able to satisfy their demands, wishes or even their needs. Yet these children seem to want for nothing. They exude happiness. They long to be with others and share their games, time and talk with somebody else.

I read recently an article quoting Robert Lane's book, *The Loss of Happiness in Market Democracies*. He sums up his argument as follows:

> *When income is plentiful compared with companionship, people who believe that income and wealth are the primary sources of well-being see themselves and others in terms of income and wealth, engage disproportionately in activities they think will bring material success (rather than activities that are intrinsically enjoyable), and derive their life satisfaction from their success or failure in material pursuits, will enjoy relatively lower well-being than others.*

In other words, materialism may make you sick! Don't rely on the approval of others. Accept yourself, have good relations with others, be physically fit, enjoy good health and have a desire to help the community. Sounds a bit like the gospel injunction to love God and one's neighbour as oneself!

Prayer

> Lord, may I seek my own well-being by not being too focused on me.
> May I have friends with whom I enjoy time.
> May I love better, seek less and find more. Amen.

Reflecting God's Presence

Some significant events on this day

Year   Event

- 1215   The Magna Carta is sealed by King John of England.
- 1752   Benjamin Franklin flies a kite with a key attached to it in a thunderstorm to prove that lightning is electricity.
- 1911   The Computing-Tabulating-Recording Company, later known as IBM, is incorporated in the USA.
- 1920   Three African-American youths, falsely accused of rape, are dragged from their cells and lynched in Duluth, Minnesota, by a white mob of about 5000 people.

Key thought for today

Let us work as if success depended upon ourselves alone; but with heartfelt conviction that we are doing nothing and God is doing everything.
— Saint Ignatius Loyola

Reflection

By Brian Long

The Ignation Method of Meditation

Begin with a period of quiet meditation, just paying attention to your breath for a few minutes. Choose a story from the Bible. Notice all the different players in the story. They do not have to be people; a player could be a tree, an animal, a stone ... Now close your eyes and imagine the scene as vividly as possible.

Where is this place? What is the weather like? Are you inside or outside? Are you in the open air or a stuffy room? Once you have a good sense of the environment, imagine that the story is replaying and you are a participant either as one of the players or as an observer of the events. Pay attention to your location in relation to others and how you are feeling.

As you experience the sequence of events, feel free to stop during any part that touches you and dwell in the moment. Being there now, what do you say? How do you feel about what is happening? What do you do? Is there someone there you would like to speak with? Go up to him or her and do so. What do you hear back?

When you feel that you have finished this experience, open your eyes. Then say a prayer of gratitude for any messages you may have received and any connections with Jesus you have felt. You may also want to make a record of what happened by writing a first-person narrative of the story you imagined and drawing pictures of any striking images. This process helps the exercise take root in your heart.

Prayer

Dietrich Bonhoeffer once wrote that 'the figure of the Crucified invalidates all thought which takes success for its standard'. Help me to contemplate my life and judge my progress not by the power, pleasure or wealth I accumulate but my fidelity to the Gospel message to love my God and my neighbour.

Reflecting God's Presence

16 JUNE

Some significant events on this day

Year   Event

1972   Five White House operatives break into the Democratic Party headquarters at the Watergate Hotel, Washington. Investigative reporting eventually revealed a systematic plot to discredit the Democratic Party and led ultimately to the resignation of President Richard Nixon in August 1974.

1976   Thousands of black school children in Soweto, South Africa, protesting against poor education, are fired on by police, causing a riot and many deaths.

1977   Leonid Brezhnev becomes President of the USSR, a role he would hold until his death in 1982.

1999   Thabo Mbecki becomes the second black man to be elected president of South Africa.

Key thought for today

What is actual is actual only for one time, and only for one place.
— T.S. Eliot

Reflection

By Br Bill Firman

Former Israel leader Golda Meir once remarked, almost cynically: 'Moses dragged us for forty years through the desert to bring us to the one place in the Middle East where there was no oil.' Israel is surrounded by oil-rich neighbours who control the major part of world oil supplies. As the price of oil goes up, people are acutely aware of the cost of petrol and transportation. Oil is also the most significant resource from which plastic is made. That makes it an asset almost too precious to burn as fuel.

The first picnic sets I remember were made out of tin, coated with enamel. In the late 1940s I remember Mum bringing home the first plastic picnic set that I had seen. In the early 50s, school desks were made of timber, with ceramic inkwells. By the time I reached Year 12 in 1960, there were some laminate-topped tables in the library. As a teacher in the 70s, I was delighted to welcome the first all-plastic chairs, replacing plastic seats attached to metal frames that often broke or lost their protective stoppers.

I remember holidays with hurricane lamps and kerosene fridges, supplemented by an upright 'ice box'. A large block of ice would be purchased from the local ice works and placed in the space at the top. Some would use a Coolgardie Safe – an upright open box, shaped like a refrigerator, with fly-wire on all sides to let the air through but not the flies! There was no electricity in many farmhouses and holiday spots, even in the 70s.

People coped and enjoyed a lifestyle where family interaction, such as card or board games rather than electronic wizardry, created the principal evening entertainment. The internet began seriously in 1993. Now we lean heavily on it as well as on email and both have become essential tools in industry and education – and, for some, for entertainment. But it is important not to lose the skill of family fun together.

Prayer

Help me, Lord, to initiate simple, family fun that depends on us rather than technology. Amen.

Reflecting God's Presence

Some significant events on this day

Year	Event

1631	Mumtaz Mahal dies in childbirth. The Mughal Emperor, Shah Jahan I, built her a monumental tomb known as the Taj Mahal.

1961	Russian ballet dancer Rudolf Nureyev defects in Paris to the West.

1991	The South African Parliament repeals the Population Registration Act, which had required all South Africans to have their race classified and registered at birth.

Key thought for today

It is not the mountain we conquer but ourselves.
— Sir Edmund Hillary

Reflection

By Br Bill Firman

The American philosopher and twentieth century educational reformer, John Dewey (1859–1952), once wrote words to the effect:

The moral person is the person who, no matter what he or she has done, is moving to become better.

I have always liked this simple definition of morality which is consistent with a Christian viewpoint that God will always forgive us. All we have to do is to put past mistakes behind us, knowing God will forgive us, and then move forward with the determination to do better. It is a position consistent with the cardinal virtue of hope. God loves us and will forgive our mistakes, provided we try to become better.

This definition is also consistent with Dewey's view of education, regarded as progressive at the time he was writing, that

... greater emphasis should be placed on the broadening of the intellect and the development of problem solving and critical thinking skills, rather than on the memorisation of lessons.

Dewey's viewpoint would be accepted much more universally today than it was in Dewey's time. We aim to broaden our intellect not only by acquiring knowledge but by appreciation of the arts. We endeavour to learn to think critically and make sound judgements rather than just memorise answers. We seek to acquire values and standards that are freely embraced rather than imposed. These are our aspirations.

Of course, we shall make mistakes. When things go wrong, it becomes an even bigger mistake to blame others or wallow too long in remorse. It is far more sensible to learn from the mistake and get on with striving to become better.

Prayer

Help me to be always focused on moving forward and becoming better and, if life gets rough, to remember the practical advice of Winston Churchill: 'If you are going through hell, keep going.'

Some significant events on this day

Year   Event

1429   Joan of Arc leads the French to a crushing victory over the English at the Battle of Patay, turning the tide of the Hundred Years' War.

1815   Napoleon is defeated at the Battle of Waterloo by an international army commanded by the Duke of Wellington.

1979   Presidents Jimmy Carter and Leonid Brezhnev sign the SALT II pact which limited the use of nuclear arms.

Key thoughts for today

There are two freedoms – the false, where a man is free to do as he likes; the true, where a man is free to do what he ought.
— Charles Kingsley

Freedom consists not in doing what we like but in having the right to do what we ought.
— Pope John Paul II

Reflection

By Br Bill FIrman

The German theologian Karl Rahner (1904–1984) described people in these words:

> *People are essentially a freedom-event. As established by God, and in their very nature, they are unfinished. They freely determine their own everlasting nature and bear ultimate responsibility for it.*

We are responsible, in large part, for what we become. The philosopher George Hegel (1770–1831), also a German, stated clearly:

> *Freedom is to be in possession of oneself.*

Using drugs, or too much alcohol, is to lose possession of ourselves and to abuse our human dignity, our freedom. We may then make choices we would not normally make. Many good people have compromised themselves when their ability to choose was clouded by the use of alcohol or drugs and their behaviour became crass or even violent. French saint, Francis de Sales (1567–1622), cautioned:

> *We have freedom to do good or evil; yet to make the choice of evil is not to use but to abuse our freedom.*

We have a say in shaping who we are and who we want to be. It is the hope of all parents that their children will become persons of honour and strength who value the freedom to choose, who make right decisions and respect the rights of others. Education involves giving enough freedom so that young people may make their own decisions. Inevitably some will be right and some will be wrong. A good education leaves room for a young person to make mistakes.

Prayer

God, I know you force no one, as love does not compel but invites. Help me to choose to use my freedom well.

Reflecting God's Presence

Some significant events on this day

Year   Event

1870   The rebel Southern states are re-admitted to the United States, marking the end of the Confederated States of America.

1912   After being established in New Zealand and Australia in the 1840s and 1850s, the eight-hour work day is established in the USA where, previously, work days commonly lasted between ten and 16 hours.

1978   English cricketer Ian Botham becomes the first man to score 100 runs and take eight wickets in one innings of a test match.

Key thought for today

God will forgive me. That's his business.
— Heinrich Heine

Reflection

By Fr Chris Gleeson SJ

If we are to love as Jesus loved, we need to be forgiving people. Forgiving people are bridge-builders and reconcilers On this theme of forgiveness and bridge-building, of loving as Jesus loved, Mary McAleese, President of the Irish Republic, has written beautifully about the remarkable reaction of one man, Gordon Wilson, to the brutal killing of his daughter:

> *It is a rare person who arrives at that state of perfect spiritual serenity. I suppose they are saints of sorts, not necessarily beatified and canonised saints but the kind of people in whose presence we intuit the nearness of God because they bring their best friend everywhere with them. God does not accompany them as a bodyguard or go in front of them like a Soviet tank. He accompanies them like a soprano's pure voice accompanies a song, like a dewdrop sits on a rose.*
>
> *One such was Gordon Wilson. He was a man so practised in the discipline of love that when his beautiful daughter Marie died, hard and cruelly, at the slaughter that was the Enniskillen bombing, her hand in his as she slipped away, the words of love and forgiveness sprang as naturally to his lips as a child's eyes are drawn to its mother. His words shamed us, caught us off guard. They sounded so different from what we expected and what we were used to. They brought stillness with them. They carried a sense of the transcendent into a place so ugly we could hardly bear to watch.*

The Christian Brothers have a wonderful saying: 'What we do with our hearts affects the whole universe'. It is so true. Readers might remember the tragic incident in 2006 of Amish school children being slaughtered by a mad gunman in America. The Amish are a very strict religious sect, whose austere way of life was captured in the exciting film Witness. Their response to that horrific tragedy, when their own sons and daughters were murdered, was nothing short of extraordinary. They publicly forgave the murderer and even attended his funeral to give his family support. Their forgiving attitude deeply touched the whole world.

Prayer

God, grant me the serenity that I might always be able to find forgiveness in my heart. Amen.

20 JUNE

Reflecting God's Presence

Some significant events on this day

Year   Event

1837   Victoria is crowned Queen of England. She reigned until her death at the age of 81 in 1902, becoming England's longest serving monarch.

1977   Oil begins to flow through the Trans-Alaska Pipeline System (TAPS)

1991   The German parliament votes to move the re-unified nation's capital back from Bonn to Berlin.

2001   General Pervez Musharraf becomes President of Pakistan following a coup.

Key thought for today

The most important thing a father can do for his children is to love their mother.
— Theodore Hesburgh

Reflection

By Br Bill Firman

Good parent-child relationships require time and effort. We ponder the words of the poet H.W. Longfellow:

> *Between the dark and the daylight,*
> *When the night is beginning to lower,*
> *Comes a pause in the day's occupations*
> *That is known as the children's hour.*

Longfellow was writing with the advantage of living in a pre-television era; but how valuable it is to set aside time each evening to give priority to family life. 'Pause' doesn't necessarily mean inactivity. I would think that a son or daughter sharing time doing chores with Dad or Mum would be establishing this kind of priority. It is good to join in back yard cricket and other activities. It is the doing together, and the being together, which is important.

Not every parent or teacher finds the time for others the way we should because we can succumb to the pressure of having too much to do. Yet it is so important to take time, to 'waste' time for our children if we want them to be happy, secure and to feel they matter and are loved.

Baptist Minister, Tim Costello describes his life this way:

> *Because I am busy and my wife is working, it's very important for us to try and have that family rite of a meal together. And each night, when either my wife or I tuck him [their son] in, we say a prayer together. Whatever has happened during the day, however bruised he might be, whatever he's not told us, we hope at least the rite of saying a prayer every night might communicate, through its ritual, that the world is still a safe place and in its right order. Rituals are fundamentally important in school life and family life.*

Every family needs rituals to celebrate that all members matter. Family prayer can provide that. So can other family gatherings. That's why birthday parties and special gatherings to celebrate achievements or anniversaries are important.

Prayer

May I always find the time to share with those whom I love, especially my family.

Reflecting God's Presence

Some significant events on this day
The winter solstice, the shortest day of the year in the southern hemisphere.

Year   Event

1964   Three civil rights workers, Andrew Goodman, James Chaney and Mickey Schwerner, are murdered in Mississippi by the Ku Klux Klan.

2002   The World Health Organisation declares Europe to be free of polio.

2004   *SpaceShip One* becomes the first privately funded space plane to achieve spaceflight.

Key thoughts for today
One day, in retrospect, the years of struggle will strike you as the most beautiful.
— Sigmund Freud

For our struggle is not against enemies of blood and flesh, but against the rulers, against the authorities, against the cosmic powers of this present darkness, against the spiritual forces of evil in the heavenly places.
— Ephesians 6:12

Reflection
By Paul Maxted

Struggles
One day a small opening appeared on a cocoon, and a man sat and watched the butterfly for several hours as it struggled to force its body through that little hole. Then it seemed to stop making any progress. It appeared as if it had gone as far as it could and it could go no further. The man decided to help the butterfly. He took a pair of scissors and snipped off the remaining bit of the cocoon. The butterfly emerged easily. But it had a swollen body and small, shrivelled wings. The man continued to watch the butterfly because he expected that, at any moment, the wings would enlarge and expand to be able to support the body, which would contract in time.

Neither happened! In fact, the butterfly spent the rest of its life crawling around with a swollen body and shrivelled wings. It never was able to fly. What the man in his kindness and haste did not understand was that the restricting cocoon and the struggle required to get through the tiny opening are God's way of forcing fluid from the body of the butterfly into its wings so that it will be ready to fly once it achieves its freedom from the cocoon.

Sometimes struggles are exactly what we need in our life. If God allowed us to go through our life without any obstacles, it would cripple us. We would not be as strong as we could have been. We could never fly.

Prayer
When prayer is a struggle, do not worry about the prayer that you cannot pray. You yourself are a prayer to God at that moment. All that is within you cries out to him. And he hears all the pleas that your suffering soul and body are making to him with groanings which cannot be uttered (see Romans 8:26).

Some significant events on this day

Year | Event
- 1910 — German bacteriologist Paul Ehrlich announces his cure for syphilis, the first of a new family of drugs leading to modern antibiotics.
- 1970 — The voting age in the USA is lowered to 18.
- 1978 — Astronomer James Christy discovers Charon, Pluto's moon, about half the size of Pluto in diameter.

Key thought for today

Posterity will some day laugh at the foolishness of modern materialistic philosophy. The more I study nature, the more I am amazed at the creator.
— Louis Pasteur

Reflection

By Br Bill Firman

The almost infinite expanse of the universe, the almost infinite numbers of stars and other celestial bodies, stretches the human intellect. The incomprehensibility of 'infinite' in number or in distance, and of 'eternity', are unavoidable mysteries. They are mysteries of mathematics and science defying neat, transparent explanation.

We have come to a point in time where no one can legitimately claim that science, given enough time, can solve the mysteries of everything that exists. The only feasible explanation is the existence of an eternal, infinite being we call 'God.' I find it hard to accept that any informed, intelligent person can be an atheist. There is no other feasible explanation for the existence of a cosmos full of such vastness, mystery and wonder. Frederick Burnham, a science-historian, referring to the modern understanding of the cosmos, has said,

> *These findings, now available, make the idea that God created the universe a more respectable hypothesis today than at any time in the last 100 years.*

On the other hand, it is logical enough to be an agnostic. In fact it is quite reasonable to ask the challenging question that if the universe is so vast, how can God love each of us personally? We still need the gospels to answer that question. Nonetheless, as Vincent McNabb has written,

> *Agnosticism solves not, but merely shelves the mysteries of life. When agnosticism has done its withering work in the mind of man, the mysteries remain as before; all that has been added to them is a settled despair.*

Agnosticism is not an answer to the mysteries of the universe. At best it is a question; at worst a cry of despair. Faith provides answers and creates hope. Faith comes from the person of Jesus —and, for me, from the fact that so much of what Jesus taught is filled with true insight. Further, the odd miracle, contravening the laws of science, also helps one to believe in a personal God who cares for us, as opposed to the God of the agnostic, who may have made us but is not really interested in us! It is ironic that as science reveals more and more of the vast cosmos in which we live, some people retreat into denial of a God who turns out to be as infinite, ubiquitous and eternal as Christians have always believed.

Prayer

Great God of this immense universe, hold me gently in the 'palm of your hand'. Amen.

Reflecting God's Presence

Some significant events on this day

Year   Event

1960   Japan signs the Treaty of Mutual Cooperation and Security with the USA.

1983   Polish-born Pope John Paul II meets with Solidarity Leader Lech Walesa in Poland, with a mutual interest in ending communism in Poland.

1991   The character and video game 'Sonic the Hedgehog' is launched; it subsequently became one of the most popular games ever.

Key thought for today

Smother the feelings of annoyance at humiliations, for humiliations will do you much good if you accept them in good part.
— Saint John Baptist de La Salle

Reflection

By St John Baptist de La Salle

The Pharisees and Herodians, as today's gospel relates, approached Our Lord, praising him because he taught the way of God in truth, without considering who a person was and without paying attention to a person's status ... If you perform your actions to please others you will not receive any reward for them except what people will give you, which is very low, very fragile and very fleeting ... So when the thought of human respect crosses your mind, remember the words of St Paul: 'If I were pleasing people, I would not be a servant of Jesus Christ.'

It is not enough to avoid acting to please other people; but it is required that you act with the single view of pleasing God and, as Saint Paul says, that you perform your actions and do everything in a manner worthy of God ... for, he adds, the will of God is that you be holy and pure, meaning your actions should be pure, having no other motive than to please God.

This will be the true and surest means to walk in the way of God and make more and more progress. For since God in the next life is the purpose and goal of all your actions, he should be this also in this life ... For God did not call you, says Saint Paul, to be impure, that is, to do things unworthy of your state, actions degraded and corrupted by the bad ends you will give them; rather he has called you to be holy. Therefore, whoever does not apply himself to do his actions with a view to God is despising not a man, but God himself (Meditation for the 22nd Sunday after Pentecost).

Prayer

John Baptist de La Salle wrote in his meditation on St Catherine of Siena: 'Even in this life God rewards us a hundredfold for what is done for him. How this thought should encourage you to endure willingly, for his love, any suffering you may have.' Help me to live my life confident in the love of God and determined to assist my neighbour. Amen.

24 JUNE

Reflecting God's Presence

Some significant events on this day

Year   Event
1441   Eton College is founded by King Henry VI of England.
1901   Pablo Picasso's first exhibition opens in Paris.
1948   The Berlin Blockade is put in place by the USSR. The USA responded with a massive airlift until the blockade was lifted on 12 May 1949.
1978   The first Gay and Lesbian Mardi Gras is held in Sydney, with 53 marchers arrested when a peaceful protest degenerated into a near-riot.

Key thoughts for today

No one learns to make right decisions without being free to make wrong ones.
— Kenneth Sollitt

Speak when you are angry and you will make the best speech you will ever regret.
— Ambrose Bierce

Reflection

By Br Bill Firman

Some tension, and give and take, is an inevitable part of every relationship. Children experience this as they grow up with their parents. Paul Sweeney commented, with an apt sense of humour:

Children are very adept at comprehending modern statistics. When they say, 'Everyone else is allowed to', it is usually based on a survey of one.

Most parents understand this type of generalisation and do not hesitate to impose some limits or say 'No' but parents must be prepared to explain why that is their response. To explain is to educate; but to impose and refuse to explain is to bully! In adult conversations, we will meet people who, from our viewpoint, express prejudice, make sweeping generalisations, offer differing opinions on what should happen or not, and state varying convictions on what is reasonable or acceptable and what is not. The expression of such differences should not be a concern. As Mahatma Gandhi once said:

Honest differences are often a healthy sign of progress.

Mature people expect differences of opinion. There does need, however, to be the trust of integrity on both sides. Especially in the work situation, where one person may be more empowered by promotional position than the other. A good boss should value the employee who speaks his or her mind plainly but civilly. Yes, some bosses are bullies and may react angrily to the expression of an alternative viewpoint, but in the healthy work environment all opinions are respected.

Prayer

May I express my opinions plainly, sensitive to the viewpoints of others, but never angrily. Goethe said: 'Insinuations are the rhetoric of the devil'. Let me be open and honest in expressing my opinions, but never resort to dark insinuations.

Reflecting God's Presence

Some significant events on this day

Year   Event

1876   General George Custer and 260 men are killed by Sioux and Cheyenne Indians at the Battle of Little Big Horn in Montana, USA.

1903   Marie Curie announces that she and her husband Pierre had discovered radium.

1950   In a surprise attack, North Korea invades South Korea, leading to the subsequent deaths of 2.5 million people in the three years of the Korean War.

Key thought for today

The habit of thinking ill of everything and everyone is tiresome to ourselves and to all around us.
— Pope John XXIII

Reflection

By Br Bill Firman

Many years ago, a traveller in the north of Ireland came across a rock on which was painted in big letters: *To hell with all popes.* Underneath someone had added: *Except Pope John.* The reference was to Pope John XXIII, whose simple goodness somehow cut through the strong Protestant/Catholic sectarian bitterness of his era. John XXIII was one of the true 'giants' of the last century who understood clearly that every other person – no matter what colour they are or creed they follow – is our brother or sister, loved by God, equally precious and deserving of our love. John XXIII expressed a profound respect for others, yet instead of respect our society often promotes criticism of others – and the right of the media to pass harsh, and often speculative, judgement.

The poet, Robert Graves once wrote:

> *Bullfight critics ranked in rows*
> *Crowd the enormous plaza full,*
> *But only one is there who knows*
> *And he's the one who fights the bull.*

Most of us are not bullfighters but each of us has a unique experience of life. Nobody has walked or can walk in your or my shoes. Each of us has a unique personality, family situation, friendship pattern and personal history. All of us, to varying degrees, live with our inadequacies and our feelings of self-doubt and uncertainty.

Some may have similar jobs and responsibilities but each lives a life that no one else has ever lived and makes a unique life journey. It is easy to be critical of others while failing to understand the unique difficulties they are facing. As each of us leads his or her life, we shall do some things well and some things that we would rather not have done. Such is human judgement and human failing. Why think ill of others?

Prayer

God, grant me an attitude of being positive and welcoming to all whom I meet. Amen.

Some significant events on this day

Year   Event

1934   The first helicopter, the Focke-Wulf Fw 61, flies for the first time.

1945   The United Nations Charter is signed by 50 founding nations in San Francisco, California.

1959   The St Lawrence Seaway linking North America's Great Lakes with the Atlantic is opened by Queen Elizabeth II and US President Eisenhower.

1974   A ten-pack of chewing gum in Ohio, USA, is the first product to be sold using a barcode scanner.

Key thoughts for today

It is better for a man to go wrong in freedom than to go right in chains.
  — Thomas Henry Huxley

You must recognise as brothers and sisters all who live; and free to will, free to act, free to enjoy, you shall know the worth of existence.
  — Richard Wagner

Reflection

By Patrick Jurd: Here is some more wisdom from John Powell's book *Fully Human, Fully Alive*.

To Be Oneself

Fully alive people are liberated by their self-acceptance to be authentic and real. Only people who have joyfully accepted themselves can take all the risks and responsibilities of being themselves.

'I gotta be me!' the song lyrics insist, but most of us get seduced into wearing masks and playing games. The old ego defence mechanisms are built up to protect us from further vulnerability. But they buffer us from reality and reduce our visibility. They diminish our capacity for living.

Being ourselves has many implications. It means that we are free to have and to report our emotions, ideas, and preferences. Authentic individuals can think their own thoughts and make their own choices. They have risen above the nagging need for the approval of others. They do not sell out to anyone.

Their feelings, thoughts and choices are simply not for hire. 'To thine own self be true' is their life principle and life style.

Prayer

Albert Schweitzer said 'the tragedy of life is what dies in someone while they live'. I pray, Lord, to be fully alive, fully myself and free to make my own choices. Amen.

Reflecting God's Presence

Some significant events on this day

Year   Event

1929   The first public demonstration of colour television is given at the Bell Laboratories in New York.

1954   The world's first nuclear power station opens in Obninsk, near Moscow.

1959   The world's first ATM is installed at a branch of Barclay's Bank in North London.

Key thought for today

There is no cure for birth and death, save to enjoy the interval.
— George Santayana

Reflection

By Br Bill Firman

In former times, when family homes did not have freezers or refrigerators and mass transportation had not been developed, people were more conscious of the seasons, especially as regards the food that was available and the way in which living had to be adapted to the time of the year. We now take it for granted that almost every type of food is available all year round, shipped in from some part of the globe, preserved in freezers or cool storage and brought out as 'fresh' even when it is not in season. It is similar with the temperature inside our homes or cars. Modern technology allows us to heat or cool almost at will – if we can afford it. While there are clear benefits in the introduction of much of the global technology, there is an increasing sense of sameness.

Imperceptibly, we can lose sight of the natural rhythm of life and one season blends into another. If we lose a sense of the seasons, if there is nothing awesome or wondrous in our lives, we can begin to lose the sense of the rhythm of life – and of death. High points and low spots are part of the rhythm of life that we need to expect and accept. Henry Thoreau (1817–1862) expressed this very beautifully. He said quite simply:

> *Do not think that winter, with its ice and snow, is a problem to be solved.*

Winter is one of the seasons of life. Pain and suffering and doubt and eventual death are part of every person's rhythm of life. We cannot avoid pain and suffering. We cannot avoid dying. Life brings winter and summer moments, and other seasons in between. Pain, grief, suffering and death are not problems to be solved.

Too many people seek to avoid the wintry moments of life and avoid personal sacrifice in an unreal dream of personal satisfaction. How many marriages have broken down because the relationship did not measure up to its promised hope of immediate fulfilment? Yet how many marriages have survived because the partners are prepared to put up with personal deprivation, to work to overcome difficulties, to accept the pain of failure, to support each other in weaknesses as well as enjoy each other's strengths? Real joy only comes when we are prepared to give until it hurts.

Prayer

Help me to welcome and enjoy the springtime moments when they come, to accept the warmth of summer moments and the beautiful calm of autumn, but also to embrace the purification and strength that winter brings.

Some significant events on this day

Year   Event

1880   Australian bushranger Ned Kelly is captured after a day-long siege at Glenrowan, with the rest of his gang killed. Ned was later tried and hanged.

1914   Archduke Ferdinand of Austria and his wife are killed in Sarajevo.

1919   The Treaty of Versailles is signed, ending World War I with Germany.

Key thought for today

What is the good of your speeches? I come to Sarajevo on a visit and I get bombs thrown at me. It is outrageous.
— Archduke Franz Ferdinand

Reflection

By Br Bill Firman

World War I, from 1914 to 1918, began as a local war between Austria-Hungary and Serbia. The immediate cause was the assassination on 28 June in Sarajevo of Archduke Francis Ferdinand, heir-presumptive to the Austrian and Hungarian thrones, and his wife Sophie. The assassination set off a rapid chain of events, as Austria-Hungary immediately blamed the Serbian government for the attack. As large and powerful Russia supported Serbia, Austria asked for assurances that Germany would step in on its side against Russia and its allies, including France and Great Britain. The conflict escalated into a general European struggle by Germany's declaration of war against Russia on 1 August and eventually became a global war involving 32 nations. Twenty-eight of these nations, known as the Allies and the Associated Powers (including Great Britain, France and Russia, with Italy joining in April 1915, and the United States in April 1917) opposed the coalition known as the Central Powers, consisting initially of Germany, Austria-Hungary and Turkey, and, a year later, Bulgaria.

The fighting mostly took place along several fronts that broadly encircled Europe. The Western Front was marked by a system of trenches, breastworks and fortifications separated by an area known as 'no man's land'. These stretched 600 kilometres and precipitated a style of fighting known as trench warfare. On the Eastern Front, the vastness of the eastern plains and the limited railroad network prevented the stalemate of the Western Front, though the scale of the conflict was just as large. There was heavy fighting on the Balkan, the Middle Eastern and the Italian fronts. There were also hostilities at sea and in the air.

Over 40 million casualties resulted, including 20 million civilian deaths. Over 60 million European soldiers were mobilised from 1914 to 1918. The war was ended by several treaties, most notably the Treaty of Versailles, signed on 28 June 1919, though the Allied powers had an armistice with Germany in place since 11 November 1918. The harsh terms imposed on Germany, the war's biggest loser, led to widespread resentment, that would culminate in the outbreak of the Second World War. One of the most striking results of the war was a redrawing of the map of Europe. All of the Central Powers lost territory, and many new nations were created.

Prayer

God, preserve us from the futility of war, with so many lives lost. Grant us your peace. Amen.

Reflecting God's Presence

Some significant events on this day

Year	Event
1967	Following victory in the Six-Day War, Israel removes the barricades between Israel-controlled West Jerusalem and the formerly Jordanian-controlled East Jerusalem, reunifying the city.
1974	Isabella Peron, widow of Juan Peron, is sworn in as Argentina's first female president. She was later deposed in 1976 and exiled to Spain in 1981.
1995	The NASA space shuttle *Atlantis* docks with the Russian *Mir* space station for the first time.

Key thought for today

When a finger points to the moon, it is foolish to look at the finger.
— Buddhist proverb

Reflection

By Br Bill Firman

A story is told of a farmer who approached Professor Grundvig, founder of the famous Folk School in Denmark, concerning the possible enrolment of his son. The farmer said, 'I've looked over your course of studies, and I see only courses such as history, literature, civics, geography, and science. Nothing about farming. Tell me, will my son be a better farmer after he takes a program with you?'

The professor replied, 'No, your son won't learn how to make better butter at Folk School. But all his life he will be ashamed to make bad butter.'

Often in life we look for the practical outcomes and lose sight of the real values implicit in what we are doing. A good education is more concerned with the development of values and attitudes than the simple delivery of the facts that we call 'knowledge'. It is, of course, far easier to examine whether or not a person knows how to make butter than to assess whether or not that person would be ashamed to make bad butter.

So this is a problem. Society tends to want to measure outcomes, growth, profit rather than how decently it treats its members. Australian society is healthy if the underpinning values are healthy and the best indicator is the level of care for those less gifted or underprivileged. This is the 'moon' reflecting the light of the society in which we live. Do we care and share resources with those who are needy?

Prayer

God, help us to keep perspective, to recognise that many qualities worth cherishing are not so easily measured as some less valuable commodities. Integrity of the process and honesty of the participants are more important than simple statistical gain.

30 JUNE

Some significant events on this day

Year   Event

1934   In the 'Night of the Long Knives', Adolf Hitler orders the murder of hundreds of senior Nazis to remove any leadership rivals.

1936   *Gone with the Wind* by Margaret Mitchell is published and becomes the second best selling book after the Bible in the USA. She never wrote another book and died in 1949 after being hit by a cab.

1950   In accord with a UN Security Council resolution, President Truman orders US forces to Korea.

Key thought for today

The usual masculine disillusionment is discovering that a woman has a brain.
— Margaret Mitchell

Reflection

By Br Bill Firman

There is no other person in the gospels that is so strongly told off by Jesus as St Peter. Jesus even says to him, 'Get behind me, Satan.' Put simply, Peter often gets its wrong. He makes mistakes, even to the point of denying that he knows Jesus. So why did Jesus make him the leader of the apostles? It certainly wasn't because he had the best knowledge, or the most wisdom, or never made mistakes. Perhaps it was because he was strong enough to lead and because he had incredible good will and love. He was passionate and honest. What you saw was what you got, mistakes and all. If he made a mistake, he sought forgiveness and got on with living as well as he could.

Jesus made Peter the first pope, head of his church, yet Jesus told off the first pope in no uncertain terms. If the first pope could get it so wrong, why are we afraid to admit we may be wrong? Why do some church leaders today like to pretend they don't make mistakes? It is in the gospels for all to see that the first pope made major mistakes. The one, and possibly only, good thing to come out of the child abuse scandal that has rocked the church is the reminder that even the wisest and best trained church leaders have not consistently handled this devastating crisis well and have indeed made mistakes. It is an old but true cliché: 'To err is human.'

We usually think of the Gospel as a call to imitate Christ. This is at the level of aspiration, because Christ is God and only God is always right. Maybe we should recognise that at the level of reality we are more likely to imitate Peter. We are called, like Peter, to be honest, forgiving, loving, seekers after truth, very much aware of our own weaknesses and fragility. We can aspire to be perfect like Jesus but we shall live more like Peter. We can study, pray and become better informed and hopefully increase our chances of being right more often, but sometimes we shall be wrong. Jesus possibly thought that Matthew might have been a better businessman or John a more profound theologian but he recognised in Peter a good, though imperfect, man who would lead his church honestly and courageously but humanly.

Prayer

God, I know I shall sometimes be wrong. Help me to live humbly with this knowledge. Amen.

Reflecting God's Presence

Some significant events on this day

Year   Event

1916   The World War I Battle of the Somme begins in France when British troops leave their trenches to advance towards the Germans. By the end of the battle, in mid-November, 1,265,000 lives had been lost for a gain of only 11 kilometres.

1969   At the age of nine, Prince Charles is invested as Prince of Wales.

1979   The first Sony Walkman goes on sale in Japan.

1997   Britain hands the colony of Hong Kong back to China, ending 156 years of British sovereignty.

Key thought for today

Conscience, illuminated by the presence of Jesus Christ in the heart, must be the guide of everyone.
— Robert Hugh Benson

Reflection

By Br Bill Firman

The great statement of the Second Vatican Council *Gaudium et Spes* (1965) asserted:

> *Human dignity requires us to act out of conscience and free choice, as moved and drawn in a personal way from within, and not by blind impulses in ourselves or by mere external constraints.*

The *Catechism of the Catholic Church* states that

> *The right to the exercise of freedom, especially in moral and religious matters, is an inalienable requirement of the dignity of the human person.*

While Christianity teaches this freedom, Islam takes a radically different viewpoint, seeking to impose Islamic beliefs and punishing anyone who seeks to make other choices. It is far harder to convert from Islam to Christianity than the opposite. Bishop Robinson says:

> *We grow in moral and spiritual stature when we do two things together: seek to act according to God's truth and goodness despite the cost to ourselves, and take responsibility for our actions. It is possible to move beyond a subjective understanding of goodness to a more objective understanding of what God's goodness asks of us, but it involves a serious and never-ending search, both for individuals and for the whole human race. We should spend our whole life in this search, while also constantly making decisions and acting on the basis of our present and often inadequate understanding of that goodness. The relationship between our conscience and God's goodness should be a constant, humble and loving dialogue.*

We not only enjoy the freedom to follow our conscience but have a life-long responsibility to shape our conscience in loving acknowledgment of God's love for us. It is a matter of acting responsibly in our full dignity as human beings.

Prayer

God, you have made us as restless beings whose hearts will never rest until we rest in you. Amen.

Some significant events on this day

Year   Event

1818   The Factory Act is passed in Britain, banning children under nine years from working in cotton mills and limiting older children, between the ages of nine and 16, to 12 hours work each day.

1922   The first water skis, invented by 18-year-old Ralph Samuelson, are used on Lake Pepin, Minnesota.

1964   The US Civil Rights Bill, making discrimination on the basis of race, country of origin or religion, illegal, is signed by President Lyndon Johnson.

1990   In a stampede in a pedestrian tunnel, 1426 Muslim pilgrims are killed attending the Hajj in Mecca.

Key thought for today

You can't love God with your arms folded.
— South African proverb

Reflection

By Br Bill Firman

In chapter 3 of St Luke's Gospel, Jesus is in the synagogue, preaching a message of justice for all people, respecting others as being worthy to walk with God and giving people the freedom to live with this dignity. The gospels tend to be economical in the use of words, so I find it fascinating that in verse 22 we read:

They were all very impressed with him and marvelled at the eloquent words he spoke.

Yet by the time we reach verse 29, after Jesus has said a few more things, we read:

... they were filled with anger. They rose up, dragged Jesus out of the town, and took him to the top of the hill on which the town was built. They meant to throw him over the cliff, but he walked through the crowd and went his way.

After the initial good impression, Jesus offended some of the self-righteous citizens in the synagogue. There are self-righteous people today who take offence at being asked to help others. Some even get angry with those who are generous in helping others. Such people point out the inconsistency and lack of prioritisation of those who confuse needs and wants and who may have made irrational decisions such as to buy electronic gadgetry before food. In seeking to help others, we cannot always act with a consistent ideology but must modify our practice to confront the practical reality. We must be wary of the rationalism that concludes, 'I'll never give a hand-out'. Those who deliver welfare often do not share the same viewpoint as those who receive it. If we think we are going to find a perfect recipient, we may be keeping our arms folded for a long time.

The grumblers in the synagogue remind me of a further problem. There are also self-righteous people in charge of helping others but doing it badly. Conflict can arise when those delivering a welfare service, such as prison visitation, believe they need to advocate for change. Ideally we should speak out, but the practical reality is that our voices may need to be muted – at least for a time – if we are to gain access to the prisoners. Modern society puts complicated barriers in the way that may demand our patience in trying to demolish them.

Prayer

God, show me how to unfold my arms so that I may bring your love to those most in need.

Reflecting God's Presence

Some significant events on this day

Year   Event

1844   Three Icelandic fisherman kill the last pair of great auks, large flightless birds hunted to extinction for their meat and feathers

1886   In Germany, Karl Benz first demonstrates his automobile in public. It travelled at 16 km/hr.

1927   Inventor John Logie Baird makes the first colour television transmission across the Atlantic.

1988   During the Iran-Iraq war, an American jet fighter mistakes an Iran Air jet airliner for an Iranian F-14 fighter and shoots it down, killing 290 people.

Key thought for today

If we wish to have true peace, we must give it a soul. The soul of peace is love, which for us believers comes from the love of God and expresses itself in the love of others.
     — Pope Paul VI

Reflection

By Brian Long

Here are two passages that emphasise, from different angles, the value of relationships and home.

According to Celtic spiritual tradition, the soul shines all around the body like a luminous cloud. When you are very open – appreciative and trusting – with another person, your two souls flow together. This deeply felt bond with another person means you have found your anam cara, *or 'soul friend'. Your* anam cara *always beholds your light and beauty, and accepts you for who you truly are. In Celtic spirituality, the* anam cara *friendship awakens the fullness and mystery of your life. You are joined in an ancient and eternal union with humanity that cuts across all barriers of time, convention, philosophy and definition. When you are blessed with an* anam cara, *the Irish believe, you have arrived at that most sacred place – home (John O'Donaghue).*

We are always near to home. Every moment is full of the deliciousness of God, every relationship is sacred: in Safeway, in touching the squirming child in a mother's tummy, in pirouetting with the ball in the soccer field, in making your last mortgage payment, in having a Friday night meal with friends. God is there with you in every moment, offering a quiet, intimate and thrilling companionship. Be glad. Rejoice. Be transformed. Become the whispering friend (Terry Monagle).

Prayer

Nurturing Mother God, lead each of us to find our anam cara, the beloved of our soul. God, open our eyes to see you today. Amen

4 JULY

Some significant events on this day

Year   Event

1776   The Declaration of Independence, prepared by US statesman Thomas Jefferson, is signed.

1826   Thomas Jefferson, the third US president, dies, exactly 50 years after the signing of the Declaration of Independence. The second President, John Adams, also died on the same day.

1946   The Philippines becomes independent for the first time in 400 years.

1954   Rationing ends in Britain, 15 years after it had begun and nine years after the end of the war.

Key thought for today

Grief is the agony of an instant; the indulgence of grief, the blunder of a lifetime.
— Benjamin Disraeli

Reflection

By Br Bill Firman

Death is not a problem for us to solve. Death is part of the natural cycle of life which we have to accept when it comes, grieve, and then move on. If we indulge in grief too long, it can destroy us. I was taken by the dialogue in the film *Chocolat*:

> *'He's still grieving for his wife who died during the war.'*
> *'But it's thirteen years since the war ended.'*
> *'Not that war. The first world war!'*

What a mistake. Dying is part of the natural cycle of life. It is inevitable for each of us. Many of us hope, for ourselves and for our loved ones, for a longer period on this earth than we may be granted. That is only natural. When death comes, however, it is wrong to grieve too long. It is the quality of the life we are living that is the most important: we have some control over that. There is great wisdom in the words of Edmund Burke:

> *The true way to mourn the dead is to take care of the living who belong to them.*

There are various aphorisms that relate to this:

> *Live each day well, for you know not what tomorrow brings.*
>
> *Be on your watch, for you know not the day nor the hour.*

I like the phrase I heard once – the 'sacrament of the present moment'. Each moment in life is a time to be cherished and enjoyed, not in a shallow hedonistic way but with a faith-filled attitude by which we value those with whom we share life's journey – our families, our friends and our God who gave us this great gift. Gratitude for the gift we had can be as profound as the agony of the grief we now feel. Focus on the gratitude for moments shared – and move on.

Prayer

Lord, let me grieve deeply at the death of those whom I love but help me to move on quickly to honour their memory by the way I care for those who are living. Amen.

Reflecting God's Presence

Some significant events on this day

Year   Event

1865   William Booth holds the first meeting of the East London Christian Mission in a tent in London. In 1878 he changed the name to The Salvation Army.

1945   The Australian Prime Minister John Curtain dies in office. He was replaced on 13 July by Ben Chifley.

1946   The first bikini is presented at a fashion show in Paris.

Key thought for today

Thus let me praise you in the way you love best,
by shining on those around me.
Let me preach without preaching,
not by words but by example,
by the loving influence of what I do,
by the evident love my heart bears to you. Amen.
— John Henry Newman

Reflection

By St John Baptist de La Salle

Let it be clear, then, in all your relationships with the children who are entrusted to you that you look upon yourself as a minister of God, acting with a sincere and true zeal, accepting with much patience the difficulties you have to suffer (Meditations for Time of Retreat, No. 9).

Strive to manifest as much kindness and love for the children whom you instruct as St Barnabas showed for those whom he sought to convert. The greater the tenderness you show for the members of Jesus Christ and of the church, the more wonderful will be the effects of grace that God will produce in them (Meditation No. 124).

Since you are required by your duty of state to instruct children, try to profit by the wise words and gentle manners of St Anselm towards the young ... You should esteem it an obligation on your part to win their hearts because this is one of the best ways of inducing them to live a Christian life (Meditation No. 115).

Prayer

God, grant me a profound understanding of Lasallian ideals. Help me to make these values an instinctive part of my life. Grant me, O God, a hopeful vision and clear understanding of the kind of person I wish to be. Assist me to act consistently with a strong but gentle disposition that reflects a deep respect for the value of every person. Amen.

Reflecting God's Presence

Some significant events on this day

Year Event

1535 After refusing to accept Henry VIII as the head of the Church in England, Sir Thomas More is charged with treason and beheaded in the Tower of London. He was declared a saint in 1886.

1926 In retaliation for the death of a white boundary rider, speared by an Aboriginal man he was beating with a stockwhip, Western Australian police kill about 100 Aboriginal people in a week in the East Kimberley area.

1967 Nigerian forces invade the breakaway state of Biafra. Almost one million people died in the Biafran War which lasted two and a half years.

Key thought for today

Those who judge others condemn themselves.
— English proverb

Reflection

By Br Bill Firman

When Giuseppi Zangara emptied his pistol in the direction of US President Theodore Roosevelt in 1931, he was apprehended, tried and executed within a month. When John Hinckley Jr shot President Ronald Reagan in 1981, the legal proceedings dragged on for over a year. No one doubted Hinckley had shot the president, but he was eventually acquitted of murder on the grounds of insanity at the time.

The notions of temporary insanity and diminished responsibility have become commonplace in 20th century courtrooms, making it far more difficult to obtain convictions. The state of mind and subjective motivation of offenders have become just as critical as what the defendant actually did. Those who have lived through the second half of the 20th century have observed this and, if they are like me, have some misgivings about it.

I don't doubt sanity and motivation are important, but when it comes to the point that people can avoid responsibility for actions in which they made no effort at self-control, I wonder. The problem is we cannot see inside the mind and the best psychologists are open to manipulation.

Someone guilty of road rage, which puts other people under threat, might claim diminished responsibility on the grounds of tiredness, tension at home, stress at work, psychological impairment caused by a previous accident, and so on – though such a defence may not work because the prosecution can argue you should not be driving if you do not have self-control. A similar raft of reasons may help gain an acquittal if, say, a mother kills a baby. Suppose a difficult child is the cause of sleep deprivation and stress for which the mother has sought help – does this then excuse her?

There are no simple or clear-cut answers. That is a major reason of the cause of such unease when a jury or judge is called upon to judge the guilt of another human being.

Prayer

Thomas à Kempis cautioned, 'How rarely we weigh our neighbour in the same balance in which we weigh ourselves.' Help me not to judge others, and certainly not more harshly than I judge myself. Amen.

Reflecting God's Presence

Some significant events on this day

Year   Event

1456   In a retrial, Joan of Arc is acquitted of heresy 25 years after her death.

2005   Influenced by the Live 8 concerts held on 2 July, the G8 leaders pledge to double 2004 levels of aid to Africa from US$25 to US$50 billion by the year 2010.

2005   During London's peak hour, three terrorist bombs are exploded in the London Underground and one on a bus, killing 52 innocent people. Al-Qaeda claimed responsibility on 1 September.

Key thought for today

Violence is always an offence, an insult to human beings, both to those who perpetrate it and to those who suffer it.

— Pope John Paul II

Reflection

By Br Bill Firman:

Billy Graham once wrote:

> *God gives us two hands – one for receiving and the other for giving.*

It is important that the hand we hold out to help others is available to every person we meet because each of those persons is precious to God. All people are loved by God, not just those of a particular race or creed.

One of the great signs of hope of this era is the decline of sectarianism within Christianity and a willingness to acknowledge that there is a path to God for adherents of other major religions. Meetings between Muslim and Christian leaders, once a rare event, are becoming more frequent.

Following the terrorist bombings in London on 7 July 2005, the Archbishop of Canterbury, Rowan Williams, was at pains to stress that he had been meeting that day with Muslim leaders who deplored, like him, the senseless violence. There is no doubt, I believe, that the most dangerous people are religious fanatics who lose balance, if they ever had it. Some people are convinced suicide bombing is a heroic act, a form of martyrdom. It is most disturbing that human thought can become so confused that violence towards others can be seen as a religious act.

The basic value for people in every healthy society is for them to love their neighbour whom they can see and thereby their God whom they cannot see. Real martyrdom is an act of love, not terror. The basis of every valid religious act is love of God and neighbour.

Prayer

God, we pray for peace and an end to violence. May we learn to live in your love.

Reflecting God's Presence

Some significant events on this day

Year   Event

1889   The first issue of *The Wall Street Journal* is published in New York.

1965   Ronald Biggs, one of the members of the gang who carried out the Great Train Robbery of 1963, escapes from Wandsworth Prison. His subsequent life on the run took him to Spain, Australia and Brazil. He returned voluntarily to prison in England and for medical treatment in 2001.

1994   Death of the so-called 'Great Leader' of North Korea, Kim Il Sung.

Key thought for today

There were many injured people, and I thought, 'How am I alive when everyone is dying around me?'
— George Psaradakis, driver of the bus blown up by terrorists in London in 2005

Reflection

By Peppe Di Ciccio

Success

*That man is a success
who has lived well
laughed often and loved much;
who has gained the respect
of intelligent people
and the love of children;
who has filled his niche
and accomplished his task;
who leaves the world better
than he found it,
whether by an improved poppy,
 a perfect poem
or a rescued soul;
who never lacked appreciation
of earth's beauty
or failed to express it;
who looked for the best in others
and gave the best he had.*

The origins of this poem are hard to trace. It has been attributed to Robert Louis Stevenson, Ralph Waldo Emerson, Bessie Stanley (who won a contest with it in 1904), Harry Emerson Fosdick (1878–1969) and William Henry Channing (1810–1884). At this point the writer of the poem is not confirmed but evidence is mounting for Bessie Stanley to be the original writer (of a slightly different version). After all, she won the competition with it …

Prayer

*Dear God,
Help me to always act with integrity and do the things I love to do,
Like love, laugh, travel and, of course, learn.
Help me to do them as well as I possibly can.
In my own little, or big, way, help me to make a difference.
But, when I am doing the things I don't really want to do,
Give me the strength to do them well too,
for I know there is a positive in everything. Amen.*

Reflecting God's Presence

Some significant events on this day

Year   Event

1900   Queen Victoria consents to the Commonwealth of Australia Constitution Act, uniting Australian colonies under a federal government.

1960   Seven-year-old Roger Woodward, wearing a life jacket after a boat capsized, becomes the first person to survive an accidental drop over Niagara Falls.

1977   Death of Loren Eiseley, American author and scientist, who wrote the original famous story 'The Star Thrower'.

Key thought for today

Strength does not come from physical capacity. It comes from an indomitable will. You must be the change that you want to see in the world.
— Mahatma Gandhi

Reflection

By Georgina Dwyer

In 2002, a girl from country Australia worked with volunteers and local people to establish St Jude's school in Tanzania. Her aim was to provide free education for the poorest children, whose destiny would have been to remain trapped in a cycle of inadequate education, illiteracy and poverty. Her story is about the joy and hope that education could bring to these children. At times, this goal seemed insurmountable and she wondered if all their efforts would make a difference. She writes about confiding this fear to a friend:

'You know, Rosemary', I said, 'this project is such a small drop. It's not even a drop. It's not even a grain of sand. It's the smallest thing in the biggest area you can imagine. When I travel away from Arusha, if I'm looking around myself at an airport in Kenya or Australia, I realise that our little school is so tiny, and what it can achieve is so limited, that it's almost a joke.'

Rosemary listened to me thoughtfully. 'Gemma, have you ever heard the story of the starfish?'

'No, I haven't', I said. 'Is it any good?'

'Two men were once walking along a beach together. It was just after a storm and the beach was strewn with flotsam and jetsam. Stranded all the way along the beach were thousands and thousands of starfish, still alive but slowly drying out in the sun's heat. One of the men walked over them but the other stopped every few paces, picked up a starfish and threw it back into the sea.

'"What are you doing that for?" asked the first man. "You know it's not going to make a difference. There are too many starfish and only one of you."

'"I know", agreed his friend, bending down and picking up a starfish. As he placed it in the shallows, he picked up another and said, "But it makes a difference to this one. And this one. And this one."'

Prayer

Lord, help us to remain courageous in the face of our doubts. Amen.

Some significant events on this day

Year   Event

1924   Finnish runner Paavo Nurmi wins the 1500 metres race at the Paris Olympics. Fifty-five minutes later he returned to win the 5000 metres.

1929   Charles Kingsford Smith and his *Southern Cross* aircrew arrive in England after flying from Australia in the record time of 12 days, 21 hours and 18 minutes.

1985   Greenpeace flagship *Rainbow Warrior* is blown up in Auckland Harbour, NZ, by French secret agents shortly before it is to lead a protest against French nuclear testing at Mururoa Atoll. One man was killed.

Key thought for today

In the main it is not by introspection but by reflecting on our living in common with others that we come to know ourselves. What is revealed? It is an original creation. Freely the subject makes himself what he is. Never in this life is the making finished, always it is in process, always it is a precarious achievement that can slip and fall and shatter.
— Bernard Lonergan

Reflection

By Br Bill Firman

There is an excitement in life, a mystery, a mission of discovery, especially as children near adulthood. No parent has ever succeeded in passing on all the wisdom gleaned from personal experience to his or her children. Children have to search out life for themselves, to dream their own dreams and fight their own fights.

As Mary Molloy says of life, when one of her children became pregnant unintentionally:

> *Life continues to be basically mysterious. Copulating, birthing, dying, continue to fill us with awe when we encounter them in the raw, and it is important that they should. It is in these moments of mystery that God touches us most powerfully. When our children fail in their understanding of the power they have unleashed, we can offer them, along with our support and comfort, that equally baffling mystery: the endless, unremitting and forgiving love of God.'*

Parents need to give children scope to make their own decisions – with the consequence that the children will make mistakes, even very serious ones. Mary Molloy's words offer insight into how to react to such mistakes. Parents further need to recognise that almost all young people wish to appear mature and adult. It does no harm but much good if parental support is discreet and sensitive to the young person's feelings. It is not worth an argument if a son or daughter wants to be picked up a block away rather than at the front door of a disco. Emerging adult sons and daughters often want to appear to their friends to be more independent than they really are

Excitement, and exasperation, for parents can come from the fact that they witness an emerging independence in their offspring. Better to give thanks that one has not parented a spineless 'jellyfish' rather than an assertive human being. To change the metaphor, it is timely to laugh and 'enjoy the ride' than to get upset at the 'thrills and spills'. It is time to be the agent for the forgiving love of God when things go wrong.

Prayer

Lord, help me to continue to manifest love even when I feel challenged. Amen.

Reflecting God's Presence

Some significant events on this day

Year	Event
1960	One of the best selling novels ever, *To Kill a Mockingbird* by Harper Lee, is published, revealing a gripping image of racism in southern USA.
1975	The discovery of the tomb of about 600 life-sized 'terracotta warriors' in China is announced to the world.
1979	*Skylab* falls back to earth after six years in orbit, scattering debris across the southern Indian Ocean and desert regions of Western Australia.

Key thought for today

Love stretches your heart and makes you big inside.
— Margaret Walker

Reflection

By Br Bill Firman

Love is a word often used, and misused, in the English language. Bishop Geoffrey Robinson points out that the ancient Greeks had three different words to express three different aspects of love: *eros* (desire), *philia* (affection) and *agape* (self-giving love).

Eros is the desire within, the energy or pull towards others, beauty, creativity. *Eros* is a broader desire than the sexual connotation the word 'erotic' denotes. We can desire something with all our being (*eros*) which may not be at all sexual (for example, a Ferrari), yet if we gain it we come to the realisation that we are seeking more.

Philia is the affection we feel for those close to us. We want them to be an important part of our life and we want all that is good for them. We have spontaneous, strong feelings for those close to us. *Philia* can include 'all the feelings of romantic love and all the tenderness of true friendship'.

Agape is the love that goes out to others without people looking for anything for themselves. It is the genuine love we feel, for example, for people on the far side of the world who are dying of hunger. It is altruistic. 'It does not exclude affection (for example, the self-giving love of parents) but it extends even to people for whom we have no feelings of love' writes Bishop Robinson. He goes on to say:

> *All true love starts as desire, leads to affection and culminates in self-giving love. For example, a couple desire a child (eros), are overwhelmed by feelings of affection and tenderness when they first hold their baby in their arms (philia) ... but quickly discover that this love involves tremendous self-giving (agape).*

All people seek meaning in life. All religions, as well as nearly every modern theory of psychology, recognise that love, in its various aspects, is the only source of that meaning. Love is the deepest longing of the human heart. All people want to feel they matter to someone.

Prayer

Lord, fill our lives with the shared love of family and good friends. Amen.

Reflecting God's Presence

12 JULY

Some significant events on this day

Year   Event

1776   Captain James Cook sails from Plymouth, England, in the *Resolution* on his third and final voyage of discovery.

1957   US Surgeon General Leroy Burney announces that there is a direct link between lung cancer and smoking.

1986   Rioting occurs in Northern Ireland at several of the annual Orange Parades which commemorate the victory of Protestant William of Orange over Catholic James II at the Battle of the Boyne in Ireland in July 1690.

Key thought for today

I feel the capacity to care is the thing that gives life its deepest significance.
— Pablo Casals

Reflection

By Euan Walmsley

For more than 30 years, Ken Evans, a university lecturer, ran camps during school holidays for children and adults from Yooralla at Yarra Junction. He would ask two university students to each camp. I began attending when I was at university at the goading of a fellow student. Those from Yooralla had a wide range of illnesses and problems: spina bifida, cerebral palsy, muscular dystrophy, arthrogryphosis, cystic fibrosis, among many other conditions. Some children only occasionally visited home because their parents could not cope effectively with managing their child's condition. Hence the camps were important for both children and parents.

I cannot recall Ken Evans ever raising his voice towards the children, even when many of us would have been tempted. My good friend Peter Ross was playing chess with a boy suffering from spina bifida. Matthew, the boy involved, became increasingly frustrated that he had not beaten Peter after several games. Had I been playing, I think I would have let him win a couple of games. Matthew picked up a Duralex glass and donged Peter on the head with it. Duralex are those glasses that seem impossible to break. Ken did offer Peter consolation and muttered some words of reproach to Matthew who remained somewhat irritable for the rest of the day.

Another young man, Tim, suffered from arthrogryphosis, which led his arms to twitch on occasions and his gait was rather unsteady. Tim enjoyed photography and rejoiced in showing his photos. Many were somewhat blurred, because of his condition. His enthusiasm and delight in his work led everyone to enjoy them whether they were clear or not. Even when his lawn bowls hit the side of the wall he would call out, 'What a beauty!'

After archery, swimming, inside lawn bowls, chess, cards, bushwalking with wheelchairs and trips through the forest, there were often tears in the eyes of children at the end of the camp. It was important that they could mix with others who did not share their physical problems and to enjoy food, games and jokes together.

Prayer

Open my heart, Lord, help me to see your face. Open my heart, Lord, help me to hear your word. Amen.

Reflecting God's Presence

Some significant events on this day

Year   Event

1947   At a Paris conference, European leaders agree to the Marshall Plan proposed by the US for the rebuilding of Europe after the Second World War.

1984   In Arkansas, USA, 19-year-old Terry Wallis is injured in a car accident and becomes comatose. Nineteen years later, in June 2003, he came out of the coma and gradually began to speak.

1986   The Live Aid concerts, organised by Bob Geldof, raise more than $60 million for Ethiopian famine victims.

Key thoughts for today

Those who give to me teach me to give.
— Danish proverb

Complete possession is proved only by giving. Everything that you are unable to give possesses you.
— Andre Gide

Reflection

By Br Bill Firman

The image of pop stars enjoying the adulation of millions and making huge sums of money was improved greatly by the efforts of one man, and those who rallied around him, in 1984. Bob Geldof, lead singer of the British band the Boomtown Rats, saw a television news report about famine-stricken Ethiopia. There simply wasn't enough food for everyone. Aid workers would dab with a pen those who looked like they had the most chance of survival and they would be fed. What a tragic decision confronted those workers!

Geldof and Mitch Ure from the band Ultravox wrote the song 'Do they know it is Christmas?' Many famous artists joined in recording it and it raised $16 million for famine relief. When Geldof visited Ethiopia in 1985 he realised the aid was not reaching many who needed it. He decided to organise a world-wide telethon to raise money for a fleet of trucks and food. On 13 July 1985, two 16-hour concerts were held simultaneously in Wembley Stadium, London, with the Prince and Princess of Wales attending, and JFK stadium in Philadelphia, with bands from other places joining in by satellite. Seventy-five acts participated, including Elton John, U2, Paul Simon, Paul McCartney, Madonna, David Bowie, The Who, Tina Turner, The Beach Boys and Phil Collins. The two main concerts attracted 170,000 people while 1.5 billion watched on television. Bob Geldof urged viewers, 'Don't go to the pub tonight – please stay in and give us your money.'

It worked. The event raised more than $60 million and people became much more conscious of African poverty and starvation. One man's conscience and generous response made a remarkable difference to suffering people who were previously out of sight and out of mind. Good people are prepared to help others if someone shows them how.

Prayer

May I always remember that many things are more important than a trip to the pub. Amen.

Reflecting God's Presence

Some significant events on this day

Year   Event

1789   The French Revolution is triggered by the storming of the Bastille.

1867   Alfred Nobel demonstrates dynamite in a quarry in Surrey, England. He was an explosives manufacturer whose legacy endows the Nobel Prize.

2002   An assassination attempt is made on French President Jacques Chirac during Bastille Day celebrations.

Key thought for today

The strongest principle of growth lies in human choice.
— George Eliot

Reflection

By Br Bill Firman

A Lasallian school aspires to produce 'men for others', people who freely chose to place high value on reverencing and helping others. Be it by participation in Mission Action Day, helping at Sacred Heart Mission or St Vincent De Paul, going to India as a 'Coolie' or any other activity in which we help others, we are on a journey of discovering our own capacities – and our likeness to God, who has given so generously to us in the first place. Learning to use our freedom to choose the positive is very important.

A Spanish proverb says:

God made us and we wonder at it.'

People are more than biological machines. Our capacity to think, our capability of loving and being loved, our freedom to choose and shape who we are, generates a sense of wonder and some comprehension of the sacredness of God's work in creating us.

Most parents understand intuitively, or have learned from the example of their own parents, that it is important to make choices that are unselfish, considerate and conducive to love. Most parents patiently teach their children to use their freedom well and encourage them to become persons of principle.

The 'Coolies' chose very well. They gave and, in turn, they received. They took a risk and found a new level of possession of themselves in their sharing with and for others. They not only provided houses for Indian families, they made themselves better men. St Gregory of Nyssa (who died about 385) speaks of life as a 'journey into God'. It sometimes takes a brave decision to take a step on that journey.

Prayer

Augustus Hare wrote that 'in darkness there is no choice. It is light that enables us to see the differences between things; and it is Christ who gives us light.' Let me live in the light of Christ, learning from the wisdom of the gospels to choose well.

Reflecting God's Presence

Some significant events on this day

Year   Event

1799   A soldier in Napoleon's army, Captain Bouchard, finds the Rosetta Stone in the Egyptian village of Rosetta near Alexandria. The stone proved to be the key to deciphering Egyptian hieroglyphics.

1995   Jeff Bezos opens amazon.com for business, one of the first and largest online retailers. He began by selling books.

1997   Fashion guru Gianni Versace is murdered outside his Miami home by a man he had never met, Andrew Cunanan. Cunanan was found dead eight days later.

Key thought for today

Human brotherhood is not just a goal. It is a condition on which our way of life depends.
— John F. Kennedy

Reflection

By Br Bill Firman

Story telling is a strong part of the Jewish tradition. Jesus was a Jew and the gospels are full of the stories he told to get his message across. Such stories we call parables. They are repeated so often we frequently have no idea who first told the story. I would be guessing to say that some of the gospel parables may not have been made up by Jesus. He may have re-told stories he had heard or adapted stories he had heard. What mattered to Jesus then, and to us now, is not the specific details of the story but the message we should take from it. Here is a Jewish story. I don't know who wrote it, but I think the message is very clear.

> *An ancient rabbi asked his students how they could tell when night had ended and day was on its way back.*
>
> *'Could it be when you see an animal in the distance and can tell whether or not it is a sheep or a dog?'*
>
> *'No', answered the rabbi.*
>
> *'Could it be when you look at a tree in the distance and can tell whether or not it is a fig tree or a peach tree?'*
>
> *'No.'*
>
> *'Well then', his students demanded, 'when is it?'*
>
> *'It is when you look on the face of any man or woman and see that he or she is your brother or sister. Because if you cannot do that, then, no matter what time it is, it is still night.'*

Prayer

In every face may I see my sister or brother humans who deserve my respect and love. Amen.

Some significant events on this day

Year	Event
1945	The US detonates the first atomic bomb, nicknamed 'the gadget', in a test near Alamogondo, New Mexico.
1965	The Mont Blanc Tunnel connecting Italy and France is opened. This tunnel, the world's deepest at 2480 metres, took six years to build and is 11.6 kilometres long.
1979	General Saddam Hussein comes to power in Iraq following the resignation of President Hassan al-Bakr. A week later, Hussein sends his opponents in his own party to a firing squad.

Key thought for today

We can only find meaning for our existence in something outside ourselves.
— Viktor Frankl

Reflection

By Patrick Jurd

John Powell, in *Fully Human, Fully Alive*, writes of how it is essential that we find meaning in our lives. He refers to Viktor Frankl's book, *Man's Search for Meaning*, which describes how Frankl found meaning in the midst of terrible experiences in a concentration camp during World War II.

To Believe

Having learning to transcend purely self-directed concern, fully alive people discover 'meaning' in their lives. This meaning is found in what Viktor Frankl calls 'a specific vocation or mission in life'. It is a matter of commitment to a person or cause in which one can believe and to which one can be dedicated.

This faith commitment shapes the lives of fully alive individuals, making all of their efforts seem significant and worthwhile. Devotion to this life task raises them above the pettiness and paltriness that necessarily devour meaningless lives.

When there is no such meaning in a human life, one is left almost entirely to the pursuit of sensations. One can only experiment, looking for new 'kicks', new ways to break the monotony and boredom of a stagnant life. A person without meaning usually gets lost in the forest of chemically induced delusions, the alcoholic fog, the prolonged orgy, the restless eagerness to scratch without even having an itch.

Human nature abhors a vacuum. We must find a cause to believe in or spend the rest of our lives compensating ourselves for failure.

Prayer

Lord, help me to avoid being absorbed in myself and lost in self-pity and selfishness. May I find the ultimate meaning in learning to love you and my neighbour. Amen.

Reflecting God's Presence

Some significant events on this day

Year   Event

1955   The world's first theme park, Disneyland, is opened at Anaheim, California.

1996   Trans-World Airlines flight 800 explodes after takeoff from New York, killing all 230 on board. The cause was later announced as mechanical failure.

1997   Three tsunamis, the last 14 metres high, strike Papua New Guinea, sweeping away ten low-lying villages and killing at least 3000 people.

Key thought for today

I want to live my life so that my nights are not full of regret.
— D.H. Lawrence

Reflection

By Joan Ferguson: 'No Regrets' presents us with food for thought.

> *Some people, if they had the chance, would relive a certain part of their lives*
>   *This is a regret.*
> *Some people wished they had worked harder at school.*
>   *This is a regret.*
> *Some people wished they had not committed that crime.*
>   *This is a regret.*
> *Some people wished they had taken up an offer that had been too hard at the time.*
>   *This is a regret.*
> *Some people wished they had chosen a different profession.*
>   *This is a regret.*
> *Some people wished they hadn't bet.*
>   *This is a regret.*
> *Everyone has regrets of some sort.*
>   *That is why my motto for the year is*
>   *No regrets.*
>   *Daniel Lagastes, Year 8, July 2006 (RIP)*

Daniel Lagastes wrote this poem shortly before he died. He appeared a healthy student, but returning from a cross-country training run he collapsed. He had no warning that his young life would be cut short. What he did know and write in this poem is that we need to live each moment as if it was our last and not come to a point when all we have is regrets for what we failed to do or how we behaved.

Prayer (read by Luke Frazzetto at Daniel's funeral)

Dear Lord, All people are able to discover their talents, whether academic, sporting or social, and use them to the best of their ability. Daniel always strived to do his best and made the most of every opportunity he had. Help us to follow in his footsteps and not to waste the gifts we possess, but make the most of them. Amen.

Some significant events on this day

Year	Event
1814	On the day before he died, Matthew Flinders publishes his book *A Voyage to Terra Australis*, in which he advocates naming the southern continent 'Australia'.
1925	The first volume of *Mein Kampf* by Adolf Hitler is published.
1936	The Spanish Civil War begins with General Franco leading an uprising in Spanish North Africa.

Key thought for today

My aim is to put down on paper what I see and what I feel in the best and simplest way.
— Ernest Hemingway

Reflection

By Margaret McPhee

This reflection comes from a book given to me by my yoga teacher. The reflections in the book are spiritual and uplifting and offer common-sense ideas that relate to the world we live in and the world we create for ourselves.

> **One Catchword**
>
> Keep at least one catchword for your life.
> It can be anything that will remind you always of the highest truth.
> It need not be the same for everyone.
> If there is some inspiring phrase or word
> that particularly strikes you,
> that's your catchword.
> In any situation where you feel a little shaky,
> think of that catchword.
> It will immediately elevate you
> and lift you above the problem.
>
> From *The Golden Present: Daily Inspirational Readings*
> by Sri Swami Satchidananda

Prayer

James Hunter wrote: 'Everyone has a religion. We all have some sort of beliefs about the cause, nature and purpose of the universe. Our religion is simply our map, our paradigm, our beliefs, that answers the difficult existential questions.'

Help me, Kord, to be an honest seeker after truth. Help me to have some catchwords to which I can cling as I chart my way through life. Help me to rise above the inevitable small problems of life to be happy with who I am and who I am becoming. May I grow closer to God and act more consistently with my beliefs, day by day. Amen.

Reflecting God's Presence

Some significant events on this day

Year   Event

64CE   The Great Fire of Rome begins, burning for six days. Some believe the Emperor Nero was responsible.

1903   Frenchman Maurice Garin wins the first Tour de France.

1935   The world's first parking meters are introduced in Oklahoma city, USA.

1946   Marilyn Monroe takes her first screen test.

Key thought for today

Hollywood is a place where they will pay you a thousand dollars for a kiss and fifty cents for your soul.
— Marilyn Monroe

Reflection

By Br Bill Firman

Gough Whitlam, when ejected from the office of Prime Minister of Australia in 1995, uttered the words: 'Maintain your rage.'

There are people who go through life accumulating the baggage of feeling they have been unjustly treated: 'This person did that to me. This organisation did that. It was most unjust that ...'

Some people want to maintain the rage of being poorly treated. They build up bitterness towards certain people and over incidents that seemed negative to them. They accumulate unnecessary baggage on the journey of life. Unfortunately their bitterness, over time, can build until it consumes them. These are angry people internally and, sometimes, externally. They never forget and they never forgive and they create their own chalice of poison. Life becomes a withering, shrivelling existence of carrying a consuming bitterness. It is always someone else's fault.

Other people accept that there will be setbacks and injustices along the pathway of life, but feel there is no use brooding over them. They forgive and forget and get on with life. They look to the future. Life is an expanding bloom. They acknowledge their own weakness but have confidence in their own strength. They maintain not rage but hope. Even physical aches and pains, inevitable with age, do not prevent them being positive, because they have developed indomitable spirit. They use strength of mind and soul to remain always hopeful. They believe in a fortunate life.

Prayer

Victor Hugo said that 'the word God has written on the brow of every individual is hope'. Make me hopeful, positive and forward-looking. Never let me brood over past hurts.

Some significant events on this day

Year   Event

356BCE   Alexander the Great is born on this day (or 11 August, depending on which calendar is followed) in Macedonia. By age 21 he had conquered and ruled a large portion of the known world. He died in 323 BCE, aged only 33.

1969   Neil Armstrong becomes the first man to walk on the moon. Buzz Aldrin followed 19 minutes later. *The Eagle* lander blasted off to re-join *Columbia* after 22 hours on the moon's surface.

2003   Working elephants in Delhi begin wearing reflectors on their flanks and ankles to avoid being hit by cars when working during the night.

2008   Almost half a million people attend a Mass celebrated by Pope Benedict XVI at Randwick Racecourse as the culminating event of World Youth Day in Sydney.

Key thought for today

Be not afraid of life. Believe that life is worth living, and your belief will help create the fact.
— Henry James

Reflection

By Brother Quentin O'Halloran

The renowned Macedonian general of the ancient world, Alexander the Great, while not an admirable character in some respects, was a wizard with horses. A friend of Alexander was having great difficulty in controlling a valuable, beautifully bred but frightened colt. Alexander told him to turn the young horse's head towards the sun because he was frightened by his dancing shadow. Once his friend did so, the colt calmed down.

As you young people step from the training track of school onto the course proper of life, I encourage you not to let the shadows of your fears dominate your life. You are your greatest resource! While always being mindful of your human frailty, strive to use the unique gifts God has given you.

Each day, like you, your parents and teachers have to face the fears and challenges of life. A source of inspiration for me in this battle is the following reflective prayer which might also help you.

> *I am only one,*
> *but I am one.*
> *I cannot do everything,*
> *but I can do something.*
> *The something I can do*
> *I ought to do.*
> *What I ought to do,*
> *with the grace of God*
> *I will do.*

If you can live this out in your life, you might not end up a wizard with horses but you'll be a 'top person'.

Prayer

Lord, I can do something if I really want to. Help me to be what I want to be. Amen.

Reflecting God's Presence

Some significant events on this day

Year   Event

1873   English explorer William Gosse announces the discovery of Ayers Rock, which he named after the South Australian Premier Sir Henry Ayers. In 1985 it was officially renamed Uluru, the traditional name used by the Mutitjulu Indigenous people.

1944   US troops land on Guam. By 10 August they had reclaimed it from the Japanese forces.

1970   The Aswan High Dam is completed in Egypt, controlling the floodwaters of the Nile.

Key thought for today

Faith keeps many doubts in her pay. If I could not doubt, I should not believe.
— Henry Thoreau

Reflection

By Br Bill Firman

In the Gospel of Luke, writing about the women visiting the tomb of Jesus, Luke is very explicit about the resurrection of Jesus. The angel at the tomb says:

'Why look among the dead for someone who is alive? He is not here; he has risen' (Luke 24:5).

Shortly after, two disciples were walking to the little village of Emmaus when, as Luke describes it:

Jesus himself came up and walked by their side, but something prevented them from recognising him (Luke 24:15).

Mark's description of the same event is that

He showed himself under another form to two of them as they were on their way into the country'(Mark 16:12).

There are other examples where it is clear that the apostles did not at first recognise the risen Jesus when he came among them (see Luke 24:26). In fact, when Jesus later appeared to the eleven apostles, Mark records:

He reproached them for their incredulity and obstinacy (Mark 16:14).

Somehow the risen Jesus was different and not immediately recognisable. The reaction of the apostles was sceptical – which is not really surprising since they had witnessed the crucifixion and death of Jesus. Yet Jesus reproached them, perhaps because he knew they had seen enough of him in their lives to know who he was yet they still did not believe.

Faith is like that. Faith is not certainty. There may be plenty of evidence and even experience of God in our lives, yet there is also doubt. It is the human condition to have doubts and difficulties. We are not all-knowing as God is.

Prayer

Sometimes, Lord, it is hard to see your presence in the world. Lord, increase my faith.

Some significant events on this day

Year   Event

        The feast day of St Mary Magdalene. For mathematicians it is Pi Approximation Day, which some Maths departments celebrate by eating pies, pizza, pineapples and the like.

1983   Australian adventurer Dick Smith becomes the first person to fly a helicopter around the world.

1991   American serial killer Jeffrey Dahmer is arrested after one of his would-be victims escapes and leads police back to his house.

Key thought for today

It is never too late to repent.
   — English proverb

Reflection

By Br Bill Firman

Mary Magdalene was a close follower of Jesus, the first person to greet him after his resurrection. In his meditation for this day, St John Baptist de La Salle has this to say:

> *One cannot admire too greatly the tender love that St Mary Magdalene had for Jesus Christ. Attracted by the sight of his miracles and by his very moving discourses, she left the world in which she had been involved and gave herself entirely to Jesus Christ. Nothing held her back, neither human respect, which might have made her think of what people would say about the sudden change in her conduct, nor her attachment to the pleasures and comforts of life, nor her concern for status (since Jesus Christ's followers were for the most part drawn from the outcasts of people).*

De La Salle is alluding to the commonly held belief at that time that Mary had indeed been a sinner and not a person known for high standards and acceptable values. Yet it is obvious that Mary, once she found Jesus, followed him wholeheartedly. With no evidence, some writers try to distort her relationship with Jesus into a sexual one. Yes, she was given to public display of affection for him, but Jesus handled that always with appreciation but restraint. I find it most encouraging that Jesus welcomed Mary. He was comfortable in his own integrity and did not worry what others might say.

Like Peter, that very imperfect and headstrong man whom Jesus made the leader of the church, Mary is the very imperfect woman, an excellent role model for all of us who are far from perfect. The gospels are not just about Jesus, the perfect person, and Mary his immaculate mother: they are also about imperfect people such as Peter and Mary Magdalene. Their saintliness comes not from being perfect but from being wholehearted, faults and weakness notwithstanding, in their willingness to embrace the message of Jesus.

We are not expected to be perfect. We are simply expected to be open and honest in responding to God's love.

Prayer

In all my weakness, Lord, welcome me and help me to journey down right paths. Amen.

Reflecting God's Presence

Some significant events on this day

Year   Event

1903   The Ford Motor Company of Detroit sells its first car, a Model A Ford, designed by Henry Ford.

1952   In a bloodless coup, King Farouk of Egypt is overthrown by military leaders.

1983   In Sri Lanka, the majority Sinhalese Buddhists begin rioting and massacre about 3000 Tamils. Some 400,000 Tamils fled to the part of the island nation called Tamil Nadu.

Key thought for today

Never cease loving a person, and never give up hope for that person, for even the Prodigal Son, who had fallen most low, could still be saved. The bitterest enemy, even one who was your friend, could again be your friend; love that has grown cold can be kindled again.
— Søren Kierkegaard

Reflection

By Br Bill Firman

When Pope John Paul II died in 2005, many people of different creeds and nationalities were united to pay homage at his funeral. Not all had agreed with the strong beliefs of John Paul II as he had expressed them, but all respected him as a good and decent man who had touched the lives of many in his respect for all people on earth. Present also at the Pope's funeral was the Archbishop of Canterbury. It wouldn't have happened in the days of King Henry VIII!

A few years ago in New Zealand, the recently appointed Anglican Bishop, Philip, came to live in our Brothers' community. He stayed with us for sixth months until his family could join him from southern New Zealand. He was a great support to and friend of our resident Catholic chaplain, Father Dave, who was in the last stages of his life. The bishop and his family became good friends of the Brothers and each Christmas we shared the main Christmas meal. I had many late night discussions with him and discovered how close are our Christian faiths and the values we cherished. When Philip was ordained into the Anglican Church, the homily was preached by his good friend and Catholic priest Peter. I am sure that also wouldn't have happened if Henry were king!

On one occasion Anglican Bishop Philip presided and preached at a school Mass while his Catholic friend Peter was the celebrant. They did not concelebrate but it possibly looked that way to some of the students. I was ready for complaints. There was not a single one. All I heard were positive comments to the effect that it is great to see the unity of the Christian faiths rather than the division. When Father Dave died, the attending Catholic Bishop Owen welcomed Philip's significant participation in the funeral services. In their commonsense approach to unity, the local people of both denominations in that part of the world were way ahead of the official churches. What unites is far more important than what divides.

Prayer

With profound respect for all people, may I seek union always before division. Amen.

Some significant events on this day

Year   Event

1704   British forces, led by Sir George Rooke, capture Gibraltar. The Rock of Gibraltar has remained in British hands ever since.

1911   The ancient ruined Inca settlement of Machu Pichu is rediscovered by Hiram Bingham III, a Yale University professor.

2005   Lance Armstrong wins his seventh successive Tour de France bike race.

Key thought for today

Success consists of getting up just one more time than you fall.
— Oliver Goldsmith

Reflection

By Br Bill Firman

One of the athletes who has fascinated me by his commitment and ability is Lance Armstrong. He won his seventh Tour de France on this day in 2005. He had been diagnosed in October 1996 with advanced testicular cancer. The disease had spread to his brain and lungs and doctors gave him a less than 40 per cent chance of survival. After he underwent surgery, hoping to keep cycling, he chose a form of chemotherapy that was less likely to damage his lungs. He could well have felt very sorry for himself and settled for no more bike racing, but first he 'defeated' the cancer and then went on to a record number of wins in the toughest cycling event in the world.

Each gruelling tour lasts three weeks and covers approximately 3640 km, including stages over high mountain passes. Often, as in life, Armstrong simply stayed with the group, the *peleton*, but unlike lesser riders, he never dropped off the back. His desire, and his extraordinary personal discipline, carried him on.

Every tour, he would watch others break away but still he would mostly keep riding calmly with the *peleton*. He knew not to confuse brief flashes of satisfaction with the long term goal. Armstrong himself described the tour as 'actually a high-speed chess match on bikes'. He prepared thoroughly for each race and knew when he would have to make that special effort – usually on the toughest stages. That is when his will power and the long hours of training made him better than the rest. He knew the pain of discipline. He would not suffer the pain of regret. Successful people must be schooled in discipline. If they do not learn discipline and desire, then one day they will awaken to deep regret.

Real strength is in the heart, not in the legs. Such strength is cultivated in a family when parents insist the children learn to be unselfish, to give up things for others and to share with others. Good parents place demands on their children and insist they live up to them. We grow in strength every time we are unselfish and each time we make a commitment and live up to that commitment. Good schools also foster discipline and commitment and become a school of no regrets.

Prayer

Grant me, God, the determination to live life as well as I can, and always to keep trying.

Reflecting God's Presence

Some significant events on this day

Year   Event

1959   The hovercraft, invented by Christopher Cockerill, makes its first journey from England to France in two hours and three minutes.

1978   The first person conceived by in vitro fertilisation (IVF), Louise Joy Brown, is born in England.

2000   The supersonic passenger plane Concorde, Flight 4590, crashes just after take-off from Paris, killing all 109 people on board, along with four people in the hotel the plane hit.

Key thought for today

A guilty conscience needs no accuser.
   — English proverb

Reflection

By Gemma Austin

Don't ever try to understand everything – some things will just never make sense.

Don't ever be reluctant to show your feelings – when you're happy, give into it; when you're not, live with it.

Don't ever be afraid to try to make things better – you might be surprised at the results.

Don't ever take the weight of the world on your shoulders.

Don't ever feel threatened by the future – take life one day at a time.

Don't ever feel guilty about the past – what's done is done. Learn from any mistakes you might have made.

Don't ever feel that you are alone – there is always somebody there for you to reach out to.

Don't ever forget that you can achieve so many of the things you can imagine – imagine that! It's not as hard as it seems.

Don't ever stop loving, don't ever stop believing, don't ever stop dreaming your dreams.

Prayer

May we be blessed with gratitude for the gift of another new day of life.

May we be blessed with love, love for God and for all people.

May we be blessed with hope; the possibility of growth in each moment.

May we be blessed with compassion for all of creation and for our deep connection.

May we be blessed with generosity in all that shall be asked of us this day.

May we be blessed with laughter; the joy that will refresh our hearts.

May we be blessed with patience in the difficult challenges that may arise.

And may all who hear the Word of God be blessed forever.

Reflecting God's Presence

Some significant events on this day

Year   Event

1959   Egypt's President Nasser nationalises the Suez Canal.

1963   The first geosynchronous satellite *Syncom 2* is launched from Cape Canaveral, Florida.

2005   In 24 hours, Mumbai, India, receives 995 millimetres (39 inches) of rain, the heaviest monsoon rain on record. More than 1000 people died as the heavy rain, causing severe flooding, continued into August.

Key thought for today

One thing I know: the only ones among you who will be really happy are those who have sought and learned how to serve.

— Albert Schweitzer

Reflection

By Br Bill Firman

In our Malvern Brothers' community, and well known to staff and boys at De La Salle, is a man of short stature and solid build, Brother Gabriel O'Shea. Most boys know him as the cheerful person who greets latecomers to the Tiverton campus and the keeper of locks, keys, stationery and other goods required for the running of the College. Not all realise Br Gabriel has also worked in remote places where there was real need. Brother Gabriel spent nine years at Tapini, a very isolated village in the Goilala District of Papua New Guinea.

The shower in the house was simply a hessian bag with a nozzle. The Brothers would leave a black plastic bag full of water in the sun on the septic tank. When the water had been heated by the sun, one tipped it into the hessian bag and washed fast before the water ran out. There was no hot or cold running water. I still recall lying on my mattress in the small dining room, the only space for a guest to sleep, listening to the rats running around inside the walls of this small house which had a roof but no ceiling.

I stayed at Tapini for brief periods on a few occasions, but Brother Gabriel lived there and taught in the local high school for nine years. I witnessed the respectful relationships that the Brothers and a Brigidine Sister established with the local people. I was able to arrange for a teacher friend, Paul Swannie, who is also a qualified plumber, to go to Tapini for a few weeks. Paul generously gave up his time to extend the Brothers' house, with assistance from another couple of volunteer teachers from Australia, and installed hot and cold running water. One local boy called Celsus, whom I had come to know, wrote to me later: 'Never in my life have I seen such a wonder. There are two taps and hot water comes out of one and cold out of the other.'

This was when the power was on and power was available for only a few hours each day. Life was very basic, but Brother Gabriel and the two other Brothers in that school made an enormous difference to the quality of education and life of those remote people. Life at Tapini was a genuinely happy time.

Prayer

Grant that I may learn how to serve well and put the needs of others before my own.

Reflecting God's Presence

Some significant events on this day

Year	Event
1586	Sir Walter Raleigh's colonists return to England from Virginia with tobacco and potatoes. These were then planted in the UK for the first time.
1866	The laying of a 3200 km long transatlantic telegraph cable between Newfoundland and Ireland is completed.
1953	The Korean War ends after three years, with both sides claiming victory and neither having made any territorial gains.
1996	A bomb made of explosives and nails is detonated during an outdoor concert at the Atlanta Olympics, killing one woman and injuring 100 people.

Key thought for today

Every man has a train of thought on which he rides when he is alone. The dignity and nobility of his life, as well as his happiness, depend upon the direction that train is going, the baggage it carries and the scenery through which it travels.

— Joseph Fort Newton

Reflection

By Brian Long: Each day is a new opportunity, a gift, a time for expanding our hearts to embrace the love of God.

Once again you are gifted with a whole new day, twenty four priceless hours for you to fill as you will. Free of charge, and offered once only, they can be lived in a cul-de-sac of fear or against an infinite horizon.

Let today be a day for reaching out in thanksgiving, a day of expansion for your heart, a day for breathing out of your system the suffocating baggage of yesterday's and yesteryear's left-over baggage.

So reflect for a little while this morning on the power of blessing and praising that we all carry. Just as your heart and breath bless your body with life and energy, so too you can bless the world and its people with your love and compassion.

Today, as you meditate, in the still centre of your being encircle in a halo of light, one by one, all those you wish to bless, including your friends, the members of your family, the people you will encounter wherever they may be. Look at their faces with a heart full of compassion. Let the powerful love of God vibrate outwards from your still self today, bringing relief and joy to their lives.

I know people who, as they walk along the street, drive their cars or ride on a tram, send out blessings on everybody and everything, with every breath and touch.

Daniel O'Leary in *Travelling Light*

Prayer

God, as you have blessed and loved me, may I breathe out a blessing to each person I meet today. Amen.

Some significant events on this day

Year   Event

1914   World War I begins when the Austro-Hungarian Empire declares war on Serbia for failing to meet an ultimatum to find the killer of the Archduke Francis Ferdinand.

1945   In foggy conditions, the pilot of a US bomber accidentally crashes into the Empire State building in New York, killing the three men in the plane and ten people in the building.

1976   As many as 750,000 people die in the worst earthquake of the 20th century that struck the city of Tangshan in China, about 150 km from Beijing.

Key thought for today

Only love lasts forever. It alone constructs the shape of eternity in the earthly and short-lived dimensions of the history of man on the earth.
— Pope John Paul II

Reflection

By Br Bill Firman

I have often been asked, 'What is a Brother?' A popular misconception is that brothers are on the way to becoming priests but aren't there yet, while another wrong idea is that brothers and priests are the same but simply focus on different ministries. Some religious congregations contain both priests and brothers and some of these brothers go on to become priests, but for the De la Salle Brothers, and for other congregations of teaching brothers such as the Christian Brothers and the Marist Brothers, all our members are brothers and not priests.

A priest leads other Christians in the celebration of the sacraments. The priest brings the sacrament of Baptism to the new-born, the sacrament of Marriage to those who are marrying and the sacrament of Anointing to a person in danger of death. The priest also provides regularly the sacraments of the Eucharist and Reconciliation. A brother is not ordained and does not lead the celebration of sacraments. Teaching brothers do not focus on sacramental ministry but on an educational ministry. (Of course it is possible to be both priest and educator, as are, for example, some Jesuits, Salesians and Carmelites.)

John Baptist De La Salle was a priest, but he founded our brothers more than 300 years ago (c. 1682) in France for the explicit purpose of teaching. We venture wherever the need is greatest to provide education, guidance and inspiration to youth in need. Our commitment is to help young people, especially the marginalised, regardless of their religion or race. Often our mission may take us to inhospitable areas, where even the local government cannot persuade teachers and administrators to go. We endeavour to live our Catholic faith through the values of love, compassion, justice and belief in the human dignity of each person. We like to say that we are ordinary men leading extraordinary lives, not because we have extraordinary talents but because becoming a Brother gives us an extraordinary opportunity to obtain a solid spiritual grounding for our work and great support in our ministry, especially through community life.

Prayer

I am an ordinary person. May I find a way to make a difference with my life and to use my talents as well as I can. Amen.

Reflecting God's Presence

Some significant events on this day

Year   Event

1907   The Boy Scout Movement is launched by Boer War veteran Robert Baden-Powell.

1954   *The Fellowship of the Ring*, the first part of J.R.R. Tolkein's *Lord of the Rings,* is published in Britain.

1981   A national holiday is declared in Britain when Charles Prince of Wales and Lady Diana Spencer marry in St Paul's Cathedral, London.

Key thought for today

Men are what their mothers made them.
— Ralph Waldo Emerson

Reflection

By Br Bill Firman

Douglas Wilson, the pastor of Christ Church, Moscow, in Idaho, USA, has written several books, one of which is called *Future Men*. He advertises the book this way:

> As much as it may distress us, our boys are future men. When Theodore Roosevelt taught Sunday school, a boy showed up one Sunday with a black eye. He admitted he had been fighting, and on a Sunday too. He told the future president that a bigger boy had been pinching his sister, and so he fought him. TR told him that he had done perfectly right and gave him a dollar. The stodgy vestrymen thought this was a bit much, and so they let their exuberant Sunday school teacher go. What a loss!
>
> Unbelief cannot look past surfaces. Unbelief squashes; faith teaches. Faith takes a boy aside and tells him that this part of what he did was good, while that other part of what he did got in the way. 'And this is how to do it better next time.'

Inside the book, these thoughts are expanded. It is a great advice for creating 'future men'.

> The faith exhibited by the wise parents of boys is the faith of the farmer, or a sculptor, or anyone else engaged in the work of unfolding possibilities. Say a boy breaks a chair because he was jumping onto it from the bunk bed. Unbelief sees the cost of replacing the chair. Faith sees aggressiveness and courage, both of which obviously need to be challenged and disciplined. Suppose a boy gets into a fight protecting his sister. Unbelief sees the lack of wisdom that created a situation that could easily have been avoided; faith sees an immature masculinity that is starting to assume the burden of manhood.
>
> Unbelief squashes; faith teaches. Faith takes a boy aside and says, this part of what you did was good, while that other part of what you did got in the way. This is how to do it better next time.

Prayer

How to be a man is shown perfectly in the life of Jesus. He is the one who demonstrates friendship, courage, loyalty and integrity, for being a man. Help me, Lord, to be like you. Amen.

Some significant events on this day

Year	Event
1629	An earthquake in Naples, Italy, kills 10,000 people.
1954	Elvis Presley makes his debut as a public performer.
1997	A landslide at Thredbo in Australia leads to the loss of 13 lives. The extraordinary survival of one man, Stuart Diver, rescued 66 hours later, captured the attention of the nation.
2003	Some 490,000 rock fans attend the Sarsfest concert at Downsview Park in Toronto, Canada, headlined by The Rolling Stones, AC/DC and 14 other rock acts.

Key thought for today

I felt it better to speak to God than about him.
— Saint Therese of Lisieux

Reflection

By Paul Marshall

Prayer can range from a simple silent openness to a very personal dialogue with God. Here is an almost formless approach to prayer as described by St John of the Cross. It's an invitation to place oneself simply and humbly before God, in faith:

> *When you go apart to be alone for prayer, put from your mind everything you have been doing or plan to do. Do not pray with words unless you are really drawn to this: or if you do pray with words, pay no attention to whether they are many or few. Do not weigh them or their meaning. Do not be concerned about what kind of prayers you use, or whether you formulate them interiorly, by thoughts, or express them aloud in words. See that nothing remains in your conscious mind save a naked intent stretching out toward God. Leave it stripped of every particular idea about God (what he is like in himself or in his works) and keep only the simple awareness that he is as he is. Let him be thus, and force him not to be otherwise. Search into him no further, but rest in this faith as on solid ground.*

> *Leave your thought quite naked, your affection uninvolved, and your self simply as you are, so that grace may touch and nourish you with the experienced knowledge of God as he really is. Look up joyfully, and say to your Lord, in words or desire: That which I am, I offer to you, O Lord.*

> *Go no further, but rest in this naked, stark, elemental awareness that you are as you are* (St John of the Cross in The Ascent of Mount Carmel)

Prayer

Many times at school I prayed, 'Live Jesus in our hearts, forever.' Let me live with the simple awareness that he is as he is, and that we are naked in his presence. We offer to you, Lord, what we are with all our strengths and weaknesses. Amen.

Reflecting God's Presence

Some significant events on this day

Year   Event

1902   An explosion at the Mt Kembla coal mine in NSW causes a landslide, trapping some 250 men and boys and killing 96 of them.

1945   The former leader of Vichy France, Pierre Laval, gives himself up to Allied soldiers in Austria. After a trial, he was executed on 15 October.

1991   Presidents Gorbachev and George W. Bush sign the first Strategic Arms Reduction Treaty (START 1) which agreed to cut the number of long-range nuclear warheads by almost half.

Key thought for today

Henceforth the adequacy of any military establishment will be tested by its ability to preserve the peace.
— Henry Kissinger

Reflection

By Br Bill Firman

Baptist minister Tim Costello calculates that by the time children turn 16 they will have watched half a million TV ads.

> *And all these ads have told them one thing: that they shouldn't feel satisfied with themselves. The aim of advertising is to make you feel dissatisfied with yourself - your looks, your image and what you are wearing. That's the aim. Because then the product can be associated with good feelings of belonging, of intimacy, of sexuality, of beauty, or whatever it is will make you feel better. Once you need to have it to improve your feelings about yourself, you're more likely to buy it.*

I will feel that I am a better sportsman if I dress like Michael Jordan or wear Nike shoes – so the ads would persuade us. Worse still, if I don't wear the latest and most popular style of clothing I will feel inferior – or, if I don't have sex with my girl friend, there is something wrong with me, or her, or our relationship. If I don't fit the stereotype of the beautiful, then I am not quite a full-value person.

Further, some advertising pressures children to grow up too fast. Fortunately, the incipient, promotional practice of sexualisation of young girls, some pre-teens, in some advertising, is rightly provoking a reaction by thinking adults who believe it is wrong to create a social environment in which young children are pressured to look 'sexy'.

Advertising creates its own myths and fantasies. Older persons need to react strongly to distorted life views so that young people have safe childhoods that are not destroyed by those seeking profit.

Prayer

I pray that children are able to enjoy being kids without being pressured to act older than they are. Amen.

1 AUGUST

Reflecting God's Presence

Some significant events on this day

Year   Event

1834   Slavery is abolished throughout the British Empire.

1914   Germany declares war on Russia, marking the start of World War I.

1966   Charles Whitman shoots 15 passers-by from a tower at the university of Texas before he himself is killed by police.

1976   Niki Lauda crashes his F1 racing car in the German Grand Prix. He was rushed to hospital in a critical condition. He was back racing six weeks later.

Key thought for today

The healing acts of Jesus were themselves the message that he had come to set us free.
— Francis MacNutt

Reflection

By Br Bill Firman

Differences of opinion, if badly handled, can easily grow into hurtful ridicule or sarcasm. Ridicule, scorn, sarcasm, cynicism are very powerful, destructive verbal weapons which some people employ unthinkingly. The Scottish author Thomas Carlyle (1795–1881) once wrote:

If Jesus Christ were to come today, people wouldn't even crucify him. They would ask him to dinner, hear what he had to say, and make fun of it.

Much of what Carlyle wrote I do not accept, but I agree wholeheartedly with him when he describes sarcasm as 'the language of the devil'. I have met the occasional person who can use sarcasm constructively for humour but mostly it causes hurt and even longer-lasting harm. Nobody likes to be laughed at. Carlyle implies that being made fun of is almost a form of crucifixion. That is strong and insightful language.

One of my favourite scriptural sayings is from the Book of Proverbs:

The tongue of the wise person brings healing.

Every person dealing with people in need, especially children, should ask themselves: 'Do I have a healing tongue or a wounding tongue?'

I have often asked myself does my language heal or wound? Am I sensitive to the feelings of others, especially the young people in my care? When the young people in my life make mistakes, am I careful to laugh with them rather than at them? Do I focus on healing and soothing, on helping them overcome their mistake, or does my anger, or impatience, get in the way? It easy to make excuses and assert, 'I had a right to be angry.' Maybe, maybe not; but we have an obligation to heal. A just anger does not create a right to wound and pierce the soul. Understanding, correction and forgiveness are not generated by a wounding tongue, but by a forgiving one.

Prayer

Jesus, you were the great healer. Grant me the gift of healing words that I may be able to soothe anger and unrest and find the right words to convey your message of hope. Amen.

Reflecting God's Presence

Some significant events on this day

Year   Event

1492   The last ships carrying Jews expelled by King Ferdinand leave Spain. Almost 200,000 people, the entire community, were forced to leave. Many died.

1870   The world's first underground tube railway opens in London.

1934   Adolf Hitler becomes Führer of Germany.

Key thought for today

Getting ahead in a difficult profession requires avid faith in yourself. That is why some people with mediocre talent but with great inner drive go much further than people with vastly superior talent.
— Sophia Loren, actress

Reflection

By Br Quentin O'Halloran

Being your own man or woman

Some of the well-known 'demons' people will have to confront when young are associated with:

— a lack of self-esteem;
— image: how you measure up in the good looks stakes;
— pressure from your peers;
— success in tertiary studies;
— gaining satisfying employment.

A real danger is to be trapped into thinking about personal deficiencies and concentrating on negatives about yourself. When all is said and done, Jesus was the boy next door, the carpenter's son; Mother Teresa was a frail, tiny, wrinkled old lady; Ben Chifley started life as a train driver and lived in a tiny home in Bathurst. These were very real human beings who accepted themselves and made a significant difference to people's lives.

So, strive 'to be your own man or woman', remembering that what lies before you is a small matter compared to what lies within you.

Prayer

Lord, each of us has different talents and enthusiasms.
We ask you to inspire us
to develop what is best within us.
Lead us to be humble and generous
in praising others, especially friends,
for the brave use of their talents.
May we all make use of our talents in the service of others. Amen.

Some significant events on this day

Year   Event

1492   Christopher Columbus sets sail from Spain on his first voyage, returning with previously unknown goods such as tobacco, pineapples and turkeys.

2003   Although many bishops around the world opposed the appointment, the Anglican Church elected its first openly gay bishop, causing a major crisis with the potential to divide the church.

2005   Adidas purchases Reebok for US$3.8 billion.

Key thought for today

There is no virtue without effort, and we must not aim at a mere veneer. Yours must be a solid virtue, but it is not by seeking and taking one's ease that it will be acquired.
— Saint John Baptist de La Salle in a letter to Br Denis

Reflection

By Br Bill Firman

Balgo Hills is approximately one thousand km north-west of Alice Springs or 220 km south of Halls Creek, at the junction of the Simpson and Tanamai deserts in the Tjurabalan region of Western Australia. There are no grassy hills – just a stony, red gibber plain overlooking another large sunken pound at the foot of red stone cliffs. Just on 460 Indigenous Australians call Balgo home. I spent a month there there just on 25 years ago, working with five other Brothers to get the school ready.

The old people I met then were the generation who literally had made first contact with white people. Balgo began as a mission established by the Pallotine Fathers. Some of the priests and nuns stayed for many years, but I recall that before the De La Salle Brothers and Mercy Sisters took over the school, no teacher, including the principal, had been on the staff for more than two years. Few white people wanted to stay in this very isolated place.

The Brothers and Sisters brought commitment to Balgo and stability to education. Modern technology has now brought television, telephone and all types of information apparatus. With technology have come other problems such as easy access to pornography in which a very distorted view of the world is portrayed. No wonder there are significant problems that led to government intervention in some communities in 2007.

In the early years, the Pallotine mission employed the people who worked to get money to buy food from the store to supplement their 'bush tucker', but when the Australian government made a broad policy decision to give unemployment benefits directly to the people, the motivation to work disappeared for many of them. I recall one industrious local man making the remark: 'See those men over there, they get sit-down money'. The Brothers, and as from 2008 BoysTown, are there to help the people find their place as full and respected citizens in our society so that they have a future built on their own productivity and resourcefulness. We want to create a 'stand up' society, not a 'sit down' mentality.

Prayer

Lord, may we be ready to assist the first custodians of our land to stand with us as equal citizens.

Reflecting God's Presence

Some significant events on this day

Year   Event

1693   Dom Pierre Pérignon, a Benedictine monk, reputedly invents champagne, stating, 'Come quickly, I am drinking the stars.'

1914   Germany invades Belgium. In response, Great Britain declares war on Germany.

1944   The Nazi Gestapo capture Anne Frank and her family in an Amsterdam warehouse.

Key thought for today

By the accident of fortune, someone may rule the world for a time, but by virtue of love and kindness, another may rule the world forever.
— Lao-Tse

Reflection

By Murray Enniss: This reflection describes a great approach to living.

Life goes on!
I have learned that, no matter what happens, how bad it seems today, life goes on and it will be better tomorrow.
I've learned, that you can tell a lot about people by the way they handle three things – a rainy day, lost luggage and tangled Christmas lights.
I've learned that, regardless of your relationship with your parents, you will miss them when they are gone from your life.
I've learned that making a living is not the same as making a life. I've learned that life sometimes gives you a second chance.
I've learned that you shouldn't go through life with a catcher's mitt on both hands. You need to be able to throw something back.
I've learned that if you pursue happiness, it will elude you. But if you focus on your family, your friends and the needs of others, your work and doing the very best you can, happiness will find you.
I've learned that whenever I decide something with an open heart, I usually make the right decision.
I've learned that every day you should reach out and touch someone. People love those human touches – holding hands, a warm hug or just a friendly pat on the back.
I've learned that I still have a lot to learn.
I've learned that you should pass this on to everyone that you care about – I just did.
Sometimes they just need a little something to make them smile.
People will forget what you said, people will forget what you did, but people will never forget how you made them feel.
(Source unknown)

Prayer

May I live out today with the conviction expressed in the words of Anne Frank: 'It's really a wonder that I haven't dropped all my ideals, because they seem so impossible and absurd to carry out. Yet I keep them, because in spite of everything, I still believe people are really good at heart.'

Some significant events on this day

Year   Event

1884   The cornerstone of the Statue of Liberty is laid on Bedloe's Island, New York City.

1944   Some 545 Japanese prisoners attempt to escape from the POW camp near Cowra, NSW, with 234 prisoners killed and 108 wounded. Four Australian soldiers are also killed.

2003   Terrorists bomb the Australian Embassy in Jakarta, Indonesia.

Key thought for today

We should ever conduct ourselves towards our enemies as if they were one day to be our friends.
— John Henry Newman

Reflection

By Br Bill Firman

My five years as Director of BoysTown in Beaudesert, Queensland, brought me into frequent contact with young offenders and the impact of the justice system upon their lives. Whereas I would have hoped to find a system that assisted the growth and rehabilitation of the young offenders, I found a punitive and clumsy adaptation of an adult structure - The Westminster system of justice - that was neither in touch with modern understanding of the psychology of children nor applied with any consistent attempt at behaviour rectification.

The justice system is adversarial in nature – arguments by the prosecution and counter arguments by the defence sometimes become more important than truth. The process of the law can appear more important than the rehabilitation of the young person. As a school principal I have always been concerned to educate young people to be truthful, to face the consequences of their actions, to develop respect for others and the laws of the society in which they live. Yet if I were a lawyer guarding their legal rights, in this adversarial legal system, I would be more or less obliged to give them advice that makes conviction least likely – never agree to be interviewed, never admit to anything, never answer any questions – in other words, deny and lie your way out if you can. Dreadful education but reasonable legal advice (if you are not under oath). This is an irreconcilable tension, a fatal flaw in the system.

I recall an occasion when two boys were appearing in court represented by Legal Aid. The report came back from the social worker: 'The solicitor thinks he may be able to get them off on a technicality that the police interviews were not carried out quite correctly.' Why was the Legal Aid solicitor trying to get them off? They were guilty and had admitted their guilt. In our adversarial system, the solicitor correctly saw it as his task to get them off or to obtain the minimum sentence for them. I believe in treating the mistakes of the young with compassion; but I also believe young people must learn to face the consequences of their actions.

I have seen boys represented in court by solicitors who had never spoken to them. Recommendations were made based purely on legal considerations – not on the wishes of the child, nor of his guardian. Legal argument and process took priority over the truth – and the wishes of the accused or the guardian of the accused.

Prayer

Help me to be just and compassionate, no matter what outcome the legal system permits. Grant me always to behave with integrity. Amen.

Reflecting God's Presence

Some significant events on this day

Year   Event

1890   In New York, William Kemmler becomes the first person to be executed in the electric chair.

1926   American Gertrude Ederle becomes the first woman to swim the English Channel, taking 14.5 hours to complete the crossing.

1945   At 8.15 am, an American B-29, the *Enola Gay,* flies over the Japanese city of Hiroshima and drops the 'Little Boy' atomic bomb. In a flash, approximately 70,000 people are killed.

Key thought for today

Those who have the faith of children have also the troubles of children.
— Robert Hugh Benson

Reflection

By Br Bill Firman

If God is recognised as the being who is pure uncreated spirit, and men and women are known to be created beings who are both spiritual and material, I don't believe it is difficult to accept that there are also created beings who are pure spirits – the angels. Yet in throwing out fairies and the other false images of childhood, we also often throw out angels and hell-fire and the like but never replace them with a mature religious understanding of the realities these images are supposed to reflect.

Research indicates that many Christians do believe in Satan – the devil – who is a fallen angel, but at the same time say they do not believe in angels. Perhaps the greater willingness to believe in Satan derives from the awareness of our own inclinations to weakness and our personal experience of sin.

In more extreme form, this has given rise to the heretical notion of there being two gods, one good and one evil. Originally called 'Oriental dualism', this was part of the false teaching of the Manichees, opposed by St Augustine in the 4th century, and of the Albigenses, opposed by St Dominic in the 13th century.

Notions of good and evil, incarnation, salvation and resurrection and the characteristics of the Triune God require deep reflection and insight. They have challenged some of the greatest minds down the ages. It is not surprising that we may find such notions hard to understand.

Yet we cannot stay as children in our thinking. As St Paul reminded us:

> *When I was a child, I used to talk like a child, and think like a child, and argue like a child, but now I am a man all childish ways are put behind me. Now we are seeing a dim reflection as in a mirror; but then we shall be seeing face to face (1 Corinthians 13:11-12).*

Prayer

Saint Paul points to the core of the Christian message when he says,'There are three things that last: faith, hope and love; and the greatest of these is love.' May these three things fill my life and take me closer to seeing God face to face.

Some significant events on this day

Year   Event

1944   IBM donates the first automatic digital calculator to Harvard University; it weighed 5000 kg.

1987   America's Lynn Cox swims 2.7 km from Alaska to Siberia.

2003   The 'smiling assassin' Amrozi bin Nurhasyim is sentenced to death for the 2002 Bali bombings, which killed 202 people.

Key thought for today

A teacher affects eternity; he can never tell where his influence stops.
— Henry Adams

Reflection

By St John Baptist de La Salle

What scripture tells us about the ancient patriarchs can also be said of St Cajetan, namely, that his days were full and that he died full of days. As soon as he was ordained he devoted himself to the saving of souls such that the day and the night did not seem long enough. He spent all day administering the sacraments, visiting and encouraging the sick, and in other acts of piety, while the greater part of the night was devoted to penance, study and prayer.

Since you are obliged to work for the salvation of your neighbour, bring to the exercise of your work the same preparation that St Cajetan brought to fulfil his ministry well. Therefore, study your religion, read good books, apply yourself to prayer with fervour. You must learn the truths of religion thoroughly by study, for your ignorance would be criminal, since it would cause ignorance in those whom you instruct (Meditations for Sundays and Feasts).

The zeal shown by St Cassian cannot be praised too much. The Emperor Julian the Apostate had forbidden any Catholic to teach youth. St Cassian nonetheless thought that he could not take on a work more useful for the church than that of a schoolteacher. He devoted himself with all possible care to instruct children, and while teaching them reading and writing, he trained them in piety.

The emperor, for his part, was working to destroy religion by destroying schools, and this saint was trying to establish religion through the education of the young. How often it happens that work which people consider lowly produces much more good than the most brilliant work. Look upon your work as one of the most important and most excellent in the church, for it is one most able to strengthen it by giving it a solid foundation (Meditations for Sundays and Feasts).

Prayer

Lord, we all teach one another by what we say and what we do. May I be an honest seeker after truth, so that my thoughts, words and deeds may reveal your love to all I meet. Amen.

Reflecting God's Presence

Some significant events on this day

Year   Event

        Feast day of Blessed Mary MacKillop (See 15 January), the first Australian to be beatified.

1972   Richard Nixon accepts nomination as candidate for the US presidency.

1974   Facing possible impeachment for his role in the Watergate scandal, US President Richard Nixon announces his resignation, effective the next day.

Key thought for today

No individual, for any considerable period, can wear one face to himself and another to the multitude, without getting bewildered as to which may be true.
  — Nathaniel Hawthorne

Reflection

By Br Bill Firman

Leading up to 1960, Richard Nixon was Vice-President to President Eisenhower. As Eisenhower's term came to an end, Nixon was nominated as the Republican candidate and was opposed to a young Democrat nominee, John Fitzgerald Kennedy, who went on to win the election narrowly and become president. In the normal course of events, defeated candidates move on to other things, as Nixon did for a while. In 1968, however, Richard Nixon again won the Republican nomination and was elected president. In 1972, Nixon was re-elected but in the lead-up to the election five men were caught breaking into the Democrats' National Committee's offices in the Watergate Hotel in Washington. Some persistent investigative reporting eventually threaded its way through attempted cover-ups to expose that the break-in had been authorised by the White House.

Since 1971, the White House had been commissioning political spying and sabotage by a unit known as 'The Plumbers', so called because of its role of plugging leaks in the Nixon administration. It was also revealed that in September 1971 the Plumbers had sought to discredit former defence analyst Daniel Ellsberg, who had leaked the Pentagon papers – a top secret report detailing US involvement in the Vietnam War – to the newspapers.

With his integrity totally compromised and impeachment likely, Richard Nixon resigned, handing the presidency to his Vice-President, Gerald Ford. Since Watergate, all political leaders have been subject to much sharper scrutiny. While sad for Nixon, the increased awareness of accountability of leaders and expectations of personal integrity have been positive outcomes of Watergate. Good leaders are expected to be honest, trustworthy people. As Nixon himself said: 'People have got to know whether or not their President is a crook.' The public concluded he was and, no matter what good things he achieved, that is how he is now remembered.

Prayer

Lord, may I be an upright person whose words are always truthful, whose mistakes are always honest, whose attitude is always helpful and whose integrity is never compromised. Amen.

Some significant events on this day

Year	Event
1483	Pope Sixtus IV celebrates the first Mass in the Sistine Chapel, opened in the Vatican in Rome.
1936	African-American sprinter Jesse Owens becomes the first American to win four Gold medals at one Olympic Games in Berlin.
1945	An atomic bomb is dropped on Nagasaki in Japan, killing more than 70,000 people.
1969	Members of Charles Manson's 'Family' murder five people, including pregnant actress Sharon Tate.
1974	US President Richard Nixon resigns from office, to be replaced by Gerald Ford.

Key thought for today

The more unintelligent people are, the less mysterious existence seems to them.
— Arthur Schopenhauer

Reflection

By Br Bill Firman

In 1997, the comet Hale-Bopp reached its closest point to our sun. Comet Hale-Bopp's speed varies according to what part of its orbit it is in, from 4000 km per hour to 156,800 km per hour. Its fastest, 156,800 km per hour, sounds very fast. It is, in fact, about five times faster than a speeding bullet, and about six times faster than the greatest speed at which any human has ever travelled (in the space shuttle) but this is still not quite one hundredth of the speed of light.

If by some unimaginable cataclysm Hale-Bopp was 'kicked out' of the Milky Way Galaxy and headed off to the Andromeda Galaxy, our nearest neighbouring galaxy, then it would take Hale-Bopp, travelling at its maximum speed, 2200 million years to swap galaxies. Of course, how it would find an energy source to do this would be a major problem as its present maximum speed is generated by drawing on the gravity of the planets it passes.

It is not seriously conceivable that it will ever be possible to visit the Andromeda Galaxy nor any of the fifty million or so galaxies outside our own Milky Way, each containing billions of stars and planets. Such numbers of stars and planets are so immense the numbers are incomprehensible. In mathematical terms it is correct to say the number of stars is approaching, but not equal to, infinity.

The distance to the more distant stars might as well be infinite. In fact, at least one scientist has postulated that since the rate of expansion of the universe is increasing, some of the more distant galaxies are 'disappearing over the horizon'. In other words, the galaxies are so far away and moving away increasingly faster, that the light from those galaxies will never reach earth. So we will never be able to see them and never know they exist.

Prayer

Thomas Carlyle wrote: 'Wonder is the basis of worship.' I wonder at the universe you have created, O God, and, indeed, pray to you in humble worship. Amen

Reflecting God's Presence

Some significant events on this day

Year   Event

1519   Portuguese explorer Ferdinand Magellan begins his epic journey, the first person to circumnavigate the earth. Of the 270 men who left with him, only 18 returned.

1969   Members of Charles Manson's cult kill Leno and Rosemary La Bianca.

1990   The *Magellan* space probe, launched by NASA, reaches Venus.

Key thought for today

The thought manifests as the word;
The word manifests as the deed;
The deed develops into habit;
And habit hardens into character.
So watch the thought and its ways with care,
And let it spring from love
Born out of concern for all beings ...
As the shadow follows the body,
as we think, so we become.

     — From the Dhammapada (*Sayings of the Buddha*)

Reflection

By Troy Potter

Upon completion of your secondary schooling, some might say that your formative years have ended. You have left adolescence behind and have become an adult. Throughout the past six years, you have learnt from family, friends and teachers, and have developed your sense of identity. Some people might ask, 'Who are you?' You may even offer these people an answer.

It is said that, over a span of seven years, every cell in your body is replaced. Whether cells are replaced in seven seconds or seven years, we know that the cells which make up our bodies are constantly regenerating. This means that we are never the exact same person we were a year ago, a day ago, even a second ago. A liberating notion: we are always in the process of becoming.

Like our bodies, our thoughts and beliefs are constantly being renewed. Examine your thoughts and seek to colour them with love, tolerance and selflessness. Look to become someone who is liberated by independence of mind, someone who embodies the best qualities and values of humanity. With a simple thought, you can become whoever it is you want to be.

The question, therefore, should not be 'Who am I?', but 'Who will I become?'

Prayer

Lord, help me to become the best that I can be. Amen.

Some significant events on this day

Year   Event

1934   Alcatraz Prison opens in San Francisco Bay. In its 29 years of operation there was not one known successful escape.

1984   In the 3000 metres final at the Los Angeles Olympics, British athlete Zola Budd accidentally trips American Mary Decker.

2003   The North Atlantic Treaty Organisation (NATO) takes command of peace-keeping in Afghanistan, the first time it has operated outside Europe.

Key thought for today

Be careful that nobody spoils your faith through intellectualism or high sounding nonsense.
— Saint Paul in his letter to the people of Colossae in Asia Minor

Reflection

By Br Bill Firman

The faithful man or woman is the honest seeker after truth, the person who finds a path through the grey, searching for God in the midst of uncertainty and even confusion. Not even the apostles always saw Jesus clearly. The faithful man or woman suffers the same anguish as the man in the gospels who prayed:

'Lord, I do believe; please help my unbelief.'

We should not expect our faith to give us absolute certitude but it should make us better people – more caring, compassionate, forgiving, loving. Our faith should not make us rigid, dogmatic, judgemental people but people aware of personal weakness who seek God in prayer and try to help others. Our Church, the people of God, should be a supportive community in which our love of God is shared and nourished.

Our faith should not make us intolerant or unsympathetic to human weakness nor should it make us apathetic. Our faith is a commitment to love people, to care for them in their needs, even to be exceptionally concerned for those who have been unfaithful, bearing in mind that

'There is more joy in heaven over one sinner who repents than over ninety-nine who do not need to repent.'

Our faith is nourished by time spent in prayer as we place our lives, our relationships, our needs before God. In prayer we reflect on the insights we have into what God expects of us – the scripture, homilies, whatever we read – and balance that against what we find ourselves doing.

Prayer

My God, I know that faith is not conformity to a set of rules but the genuine seeking for truth. I seek to be true to who I am and to whatever you ask of me. Help me to love others as part of your community on earth. Amen.

Reflecting God's Presence

Some significant events on this day

Year   Event

1908   The first Model T Ford is built. By the end of production in 1927 more than 15 million had been sold and more than half the number of cars on the road were T-model Fords.

1952   In a night later dubbed 'The Night of the Murdered Poets', on the orders of Soviet leader Joseph Stalin, 13 prominent Jewish intellectuals in Moscow are murdered.

2000   After a massive explosion on board, the Russian Navy submarine *K-141 Kursk* sinks in the Barents Sea, with the death of all 118 sailors.

Key thought for today

As for the best leaders, the people do not notice their existence. The next best the people honour and praise. The next the people fear, and the next the people hate. When the best leader's work is done, the people say, 'We did it ourselves.'
— Lao Tzu

Reflection

By Br Bill Firman

There are many kinds of leadership. I illustrate some of them by a parable about the five principal leaders of the former Soviet Union which goes like this.

The Soviet Union may be compared to a train rolling across Siberia. In the days of Lenin, the train started to grind to a halt. The people asked Lenin what to do. He gave an inspirational address asking them to work harder for the country. And so they did. And the train started rolling again. In the days of Stalin, the train was again grinding to a halt, so they asked Stalin what to do. He replied: 'Shoot half the passengers, and lighten the load, and tell the other half they'll be shot if they don't push like hell.' And once again the train started rolling.

In the days of Krushchev, with the country running out of resources, they asked Krushchev what to do. He hit on the ingenious short-term solution: 'Tear up the tracks behind and re-lay them in front.' And again the train was able to roll on. In the days of Brezhnev, the train again ground to a halt and they asked Brezhnev what to do. 'Pull down the shutters', he said, 'and shake like hell. And make believe the train is rolling'.

When Gorbachev came to power, he said: 'Open the shutters. See, we have stopped. This train is not going'. And he opened the windows and set off across the paddocks to find a new way forward. The people resented that they had to walk for quite some days but once again they began to make progress.

There are many ways to control people but not all ways and not all kinds of leadership are good. The best leadership is a leadership of service to the people – powerfully illustrated by the image of Jesus washing the feet of his disciples. In the Soviet Union, he would be the steward on the train!

Prayer

Lord, if I lead, may it not be by fear, cunning or deceit, but by honest service. Amen.

12 AUGUST

Some significant events on this day

Year   Event

        Feast of Saint Benilde, one of the De La Salle Brothers officially declared holy by the church, .

1940   The Battle of Britain begins, with almost 1500 German aircraft bombing southern England in an attempt to destroy the RAF and British radar stations. The Germans called it 'The Day of the Eagle'. The Battle of Britain lasted until 31 October.

1961   Shortly after midnight, East German soldiers begin constructing a 153 kilometre wall between Soviet-controlled East Berlin and the democratic Western section of the city to prevent the exodus of Eastern citizens to the West. The wall, a stark reminder of the Cold War, stood until 9 November 1989.

Key thought for today

I expect to pass through this world but once; any good thing therefore that I can do, or any kindness that I can show to any fellow creature, let me do it now; let me not defer or neglect it, for I shall not pass this way again.

— Stephen Grellet, Quaker missionary

Reflection

By Patrick Jurd (from the De La Salle Brothers' website)

Pierre Romançon was born in Thuret, France, on 14 June 1805. When he joined the De La Salle Brothers, he was given the name Brother Benilde and assigned to teach children in the primary grades. This would be his life's work. He was noted for his spirit of prayer and care for others and was director of a primary school at Sauges, France, for 20 years. Brother Benilde's extraordinary religious sense was evident to everyone: at Mass with the students in the parish church, teaching catechism, preparing boys for first communion, visiting and praying with the sick. There were even rumours of near-miraculous cures.

Br Benilde died at Sauges on 13 August 1862, aged 57. At his beatification in 1948, Pope Pius XII stressed that his sanctification was attained by enduring 'the terrible daily grind' and by 'doing common things in an uncommon way'. Pope Paul VI canonised this humble De La Salle Brother on 29 October, 1967. *Chalk Dust Halo*, the title of a book written about him after his death, is an admirable epithet describing the life of this apostle of the catechism.

Prayer

Dear Lord, may we be inspired to help others in the many ordinary moments of our lives. Doing the ordinary things well, day after day, can test our perseverance but can often lead to extraordinary achievement. May we learn patient goodness from Saint Benilde. Amen.

Reflecting God's Presence

Some significant events on this day

Year	Event
1880	The Cologne Cathedral in Germany is finally completed after more than 600 years. Construction began in 1248.
1947	Pakistan gains independence from the United Kingdom.
1979	Fifteen crewmen die when freak storms hit the Fastnet Yacht Race in the Irish Sea.
2003	A huge power failure blacks out large parts of the USA and Canada.

Key thought for today

True Christianity is love in action.
— David O. McKay

Reflection

By Peter Riordan

My life has been a good news story. I think of myself as having been extremely blessed. I grew up with the loving care and guidance of great parents and grandparents. My twin brother has always been my best friend – so there was always someone with whom to share the adventures of youth. The rest of my family are also precious to me and to one another. My parents sent me to great schools where I learned values and attitudes I cherish. I am married to a wonderful wife and have two terrific children – a son and a daughter who are also great friends to one another. I live in a prime location where my neighbours are also my friends. I count my blessings and thank God for them.

My work is my chance to pay God back, to share the gift of God's love. At work I enjoy the loyal friendship of staff and the company of the students whom I try to treat with respect and with sensitivity for their feelings – what John Baptist de La Salle calls a 'tender regard'. I try to call each by name so that I know each as a person. My parents were both teachers. I guess that was part of the reason I also felt called to teach. But does this mean there has never been, or never will be, upsets, problems or disappointments? Of course not. No matter how blessed our lives may be there will always be challenges along the way. What do we do about them?

It seems to me we have a very clear choice. Either brood about them and be angry, bitter and resentful, or get on with life. Sadly, I meet people who do not cope well with 'knock-backs' and who seem to accumulate the baggage of bitterness and lingering hurt. So my attitude is never to fret about what went wrong, what I missed out on, what could have been. I can do without carrying the burden of past disappointments. It is far better to face each problem and either to turn it into an opportunity, or to look for the next opportunity.

Look forward, not back. It is much easier to progress if we face where we want to go.

Prayer

May I accept disappointments without being hurt and look forward positively to the next opportunity.

Some significant events on this day

Year   Event

         Feast day of the Assumption of Mary.
1877   The first sound recording is made by Thomas Edison with his phonograph.
1914   The 64 kilometre-long Panama Canal is opened.
1945   Emperor Hirohito broadcasts the news of Japan's defeat to the Japanese people, the first time they had heard his voice over the air-waves. He retained his title but was forced to disclaim his divine status.

Key thought for today

When you were born, you cried and the world rejoiced. Live your life so that when you die, the world cries and you rejoice.
— Cherokee expression

Reflection

By Patrick Jurd

On this great feast of the church, also marked by Orthodox churches, Mary's faith is celebrated. As mother of Jesus, she is set apart from the rest of humanity. Her body did not remain on earth but was assumed into heaven in anticipation of the general resurrection of the dead.

> *Mary, how much did you understand at the Annunciation?*
> *Did you know, could you know, all that was to happen*
> *To the baby you breast-fed and whose nappies you changed?*
> *To the boy who fell over and came to you crying?*
> *To the young man who startled you in the Temple?*
> *To the man who loved as no other, but whose words of love, truth and justice*
> *Were as bitter gall in the mouths of those*
> *Motivated by fear, fame, power and control?*
> *Well you may have pondered these things in your heart.*
> *What mother would not be cut in pieces*
> *Watching all that happened to her son?*
> *But this was not your only response.*
> *You were a rock to the community that gathered around your son*
> *Before and after his death and resurrection.*
> *Your faith, your courage, your goodness*
> *Are a stunning example to all.*

Today is a celebration of the goodness of God, a goodness, a divinity which we see in each person around us when, as the Lasallian maxim says, 'we remember we are in the holy presence of God'.

Prayer

Let us remember we are in the holy presence of God. Let us see God in those around us. Amen.

Reflecting God's Presence

Some significant events on this day

Year	Event
1868	Seventy thousand South Americans die in a tsunami, caused by an earthquake of 8.5 on the Richter scale off the coast of Peru.
1977	Elvis Presley, aged 42, is found dead in his Graceland mansion in Memphis, Tennessee. His death was attributed to heart failure.
2003	The former Ugandan dictator Idi Amin, who was responsible for the deaths of more than 400,000 people, dies in exile in Saudi Arabia.

Key thought for today

The image is one thing and the human being is another. It's very hard to live up to an image.
— Elvis Presley

Reflection

By Br Bill Firman

Elvis Aaron Presley was born to Vernon and Gladys Presley in humble circumstances in a two-roomed house in Tupelo, Mississippi, on 8 January 1935. His twin brother Jessie Garon was stillborn, leaving Elvis to grow up as an only child. One biographer said: 'Presley was bullied at school; classmates threw things at him – rotten fruit and stuff – because he was different, quiet and he stuttered, and he was a mama's boy.'

In November 1948, the family moved to Memphis, Tennessee, allegedly because Vernon, in addition to needing work, had to escape the law for transporting bootleg liquor. Elvis graduated from Humes High School there in 1953. Fellow students apparently viewed his performing unfavorably. One recalled that he was 'a sad, shy, not especially attractive boy' whose guitar playing was not likely to win any prizes. Many of the other children made fun of him as 'a trashy kind of boy playing trashy hillbilly music'.

Nonetheless, by 1956 he was an international sensation. He starred in 33 successful films, made history with his television appearances and specials, and knew great acclaim through his many, often record-breaking, live concert performances. He has sold over one billion records, more than any other artist. As his fame grew, his mother continued to drink excessively In early August 1958, doctors diagnosed hepatitis and her condition worsened. Two days later, she died of heart failure, aged 46. Elvis was distraught, 'grieving almost constantly' for days.

Elvis overcame his unpopularity and awkwardness at school. He did not let bullying or criticism get him down. His very successful music career lifted his family out of poverty. To many, he was a created hero. Today he is still imitated abundantly. Yet there was a lack of reality and perspective in his life. The outward success was not balanced by an inner serenity. Society still embraces his music, but the personal cost was high. He died aged only 42.

Prayer

At times we may feel 'all shook up', but may we find peace and security in the love of family and good friends.

Some significant events on this day

Year	Event
1962	Peter Fechter, aged 18, is shot by East German border guards. He was the first person killed trying to cross the Berlin Wall into West Germany.
1980	Baby Azaria Chamberlain disappears from her tent at Uluru, NT, presumably taken by a dingo.
1991	At Strathfield shopping centre in Sydney, Wade Frankum, aged 33, shoots and kills seven people before shooting himself.
2005	Brother Roger Schultz, founder of the Taizé ecumenical community in central France, is stabbed to death in the chapel at Taizé.

Key thought for today

Do not protect yourself by a fence, but rather by your friends.
— Czech proverb

Reflection

By Patrick Jurd. Here is another valuable reflection from John Powell's *Fully Human, Fully Alive*.

To belong

The fifth and final component of the full life would no doubt be a 'place called home', a sense of community. A community is a union of persons who 'have in common', who share in mutuality their most precious possessions – themselves. They know and are open to one another. They are 'for' one another. They share in love their persons and their lives.

Fully alive people have such a sense of belonging – to their families, to their church, to the human family. There are others with whom such people feel completely comfortable and at home, with whom they experience a sense of mutual belonging. There is a place where their absence would be felt and their deaths mourned. When they are with these others, fully alive people find equal satisfaction in giving and receiving.

A contrary sense of isolation is always diminishing and destructive. It drives us into the pits of loneliness and alienation, where we can only perish. The inescapable law built into human nature is this: We are never less than individuals but we are never merely individuals. No man is an island. Butterflies are free, but we need the heart of another as a home for our hearts. Fully alive people have the deep peace and contentment that can be experienced only in such a home.

Prayer

Thank you, Lord, for family and friends, for those who welcome me into their community circle, who recognise me as important to them and share their lives with me. I pray that I may return their friendship and love and help build our community of warmth and support. Amen.

Reflecting God's Presence

Some significant events on this day

Year   Event

1964   The International Olympic Committee bans South Africa from the Tokyo Games because of its apartheid policies.

1971   Australia and New Zealand announce they are withdrawing their troops from Vietnam.

1991   Soviet hard-liners launch a coup against President Gorbachev, which fails thanks to assistance from Boris Yeltsin and his backers from the Russian parliament.

Key thought for today

Bear in mind that the wonderful things you learn in schools are the work of many generations. All this is put in your hands as your inheritance in order that you may receive it, honour it, add to it, and one day faithfully hand it on to your children.
    — Albert Einstein

Reflection

By Br Bill Firman

Adults had the answers and schools existed to help children learn them. Perhaps that is too brief a summary but I suspect I began life as a student at De La Salle with that kind of simplistic notion in mind. In religion classes, we learned a catechism of questions and answers – the important questions and the right answers. I knew I would change, but I had no idea the world around me would change so much and so many cherished beliefs would be challenged. I expected some changes, as had occurred in previous eras, but not the incredible rate of change that would characterise the second half of the twentieth century.

Some Catholics look back to the 1950s and earlier, before the Second Vatican Council, and yearn for the monumental solidarity, the uniform certainty, the triumphalistic rectitude that was a part of the Catholic mentality of that era. Some even look back wistfully with the thought, 'If only there had not been a Vatican Council.'

It would be just as valid to say if only TV sets, the internet, the Hubble telescope, mobile phones, or any number of technological developments had not been invented. There have been many drivers of change that have created the world in which we now live and many difficult issues ensue from developments outside the church, not from within. Today, it is not only each person making a personal journey, it is society itself, and the churches within it, that are moving, changing, journeying. I once thought all the 'unbelief' came from my end, but now I recognise that some of the unbelief can be caused by the changing society, or even the changing attitudes in the church, not just my own personal convictions. Each of us is on a personal journey but we are also on a collective journey where the currents sometimes ebb and flow and throw us off balance.

Prayer

Anwar Sadat once said: 'There can be hope only for a society which acts as one big family, not as many separate ones.' May there be unity in the diversity of our modern society and a strong commitment to the universal brotherhood and sisterhood of all people. May we live by the unchanging values of love of God and of our neighbours. Amen.

Some significant events on this day

Year	Event
1768	Saint Isaac's Cathedral is founded in St Petersburg, Russia.
1909	The first car race is held at the Indianapolis Speedway. The winner averaged a speed of just under 100 km per hour.
1930	Frank McCourt, Irish-American author of the best-selling *Angela's Ashes*, is born.
1967	The Beatles' single 'All You Need is Love' hits #1 on the charts.
2003	A massive bomb destroys the UN Headquarters in Baghdad, killing 17 people.

Key thought for today

The important thing is not to stop questioning. Curiosity has its own reason for existing.
— Albert Einstein

Reflection

By Sandra Troise: Here are eight thoughts I find useful and would like to share with you.

> **Peace**: Blessed are the peacemakers, for they shall be called the children of God (Matthew 5:9).
>
> **Integrity**: Integrity is one of several paths. It distinguishes itself from the others because it is the right path and the only one upon which you will never get lost (M.H. McKee).
>
> **Joy**: If the sight of the blue skies fills you with joy, if the simple things of nature have a message that you understand, rejoice, for your soul is alive (Eleonora Duse).
>
> **Kindness**: Kindness is the language which the deaf can hear and the blind can see' (Mark Twain).
>
> **Faith**: Faith is the strength by which a shattered world shall emerge into the light (Helen Keller).
>
> **Courage**: 'This is courage ... to bear unflinchingly what heaven sends' (Euripedes).
>
> **Hope**: Hope is faith holding out its hand in the dark (George Iles).
>
> **Charity**: We must not only give what we have; we must also give what we are (Désiré-Joseph Mercier).

Prayer

Lord Jesus, may everything I do begin with you, continue with your help, and be done under your guidance. May my sharing in the Mass free me from my sins, and make me worthy of your healing. May I grow in your love and your service, and become a pleasing offering to you and with you to the Father. May the mystery I celebrate help me to reach eternal life with you. Amen.

Reflecting God's Presence

Some significant events on this day

Year   Event

1912   The death of William Booth, founder of the Salvation Army.

1997   Guerrillas massacre more than 60 people and kidnap 15 women in Algeria. People fled the town of Souhane, reducing its population from 4000 to 103.

2003   Controversial Queensland politician Pauline Hanson is sentenced to three years gaol for electoral fraud. In November an appeal court quashed her conviction.

Key thought for today

Anger is often more hurtful than the injury that caused it.
— American proverb

Reflection

By Br Bill Firman

Will Rogers once pointed out the futility of getting angry by this metaphor:

People who fly into a rage always make a bad landing.'

I think of anger as generally a destructive emotion simply because we get back what we give out. If we act angrily, violently or aggressively towards others, that is what we will receive back. Two angry people shouting at each other is a rough situation. It is hard to resolve an angry confrontation. Give out negativity and that is what comes back in bigger doses. Thus, anger begets anger, violence begets violence, aggressiveness begets aggressiveness.

But if we are calm, controlled, reasonable and caring, that is the kind of response we are more likely to receive. As Edmund Burke once said:

Our patience will achieve more than our force.

Patience is usually far more effective than any attempt to be seen as tough or threatening.

I am not one who says a parent should never hit a child. There are situations, such as in tantrum throwing or where kids act very angrily towards others, where a child may have effectively thrown reason and calm out the window. A short sharp smack may be the sensible remedy, especially for a young child, but the sooner one can revert to the use of reason and restraint the better. There is, however, never a place for aggression or violence by adults towards kids. A smack should never be delivered simply because we are angry or upset. Nor should we be 'physical' with other adults. It takes far more strength to control anger than to give in to it. Good humour and patience are the most valuable weapons in defusing situations where anger has developed. Deliberately seeing the funny side is a great way of dispelling tension. So if ever your boss annoys you, don't get angry. Respond with good humour and the landing should be softer.

Prayer

Help me to be good humoured, calm and patient, a maker of peace not war.

21 AUGUST

Reflecting God's Presence

Some significant events on this day

Year Event

1911 Leonardo da Vinci's painting *Mona Lisa* is stolen from the Louvre in Paris. It was not recovered until 1913.

1983 Moments after the exiled Philippines opposition leader Benigno Aquino returns home, he is assassinated by a gunman.

2005 Approximately one million people attend the Mass celebrated by Pope Benedict XVI in Cologne, Germany, to mark the end of World Youth Day.

Key thought for today

Life is a flame that is always burning itself out, but it catches fire again every time a child is born.
— George Bernard Shaw

Reflection

By Br Bill Firman

In August 2008, a pro-abortion bill was introduced into the Victorian state parliament. The controversial bill was introduced by Women's Affairs Minister Maxine Morand who said, 'I have a very solid view that men should not be telling women what to do with their bodies.' The bill permits pharmacists and nurses to supply or administer drugs to women up to 24 weeks of pregnancy, without the supervision of a medical practitioner. Melbourne Archbishop Denis Hart spoke out strongly against the bill.

> *Treating abortion as an ordinary medical procedure deprives the unborn, our most vulnerable human beings, of the legal protection which the law should afford them, An abortion is not like any other medical procedure and any attempt to treat it as such should be opposed both for the sake of the unborn and for the sake of women who may be pressured to have an abortion. Abortion, understood as the intentional destruction of the unborn child in the womb, is always wrong and unjust. The unborn child is a human being entitled to the protection of the law no less than any of us. Every attempt to harm an innocent human person violates principles of justice and is always wrong.'*

MP Matthew Guy pointed out the confused values of our society: 'Tail docking a dog would be illegal, putting a lobster in boiling water would be illegal, but it will be legal to abort a six-month-old child if this bill passes.

The Archbishop also said,

> *The Bill is a clear breach of the human rights of doctors and nurses, forcing them to act against conscientiously held moral, cultural or religious beliefs.*

The unborn cannot speak for themselves. I ask myself why is it that people seeking to destroy the key value of respect for all human life are presented as progressive when those seeking to conserve and protect need not only the courage of their personal convictions but the courage to resist public opinion.

Prayer

Lord, we pray for respect for all human life, for the protection of the unborn and of all who cannot protect themselves. Amen.

Reflecting God's Presence

Some significant events on this day

Year	Event

1770	Captain James Cook lands in Botany Bay.

1864	Twelve nations sign the first Geneva Convention, designed to protect vulnerable people in times of war.

1910	Japan annexes Korea and changes its name to Chosen, meaning 'ancient'.

Key thought for today

I lose my respect for the man who can make the mystery of sex the subject of a coarse jest, yet, when you speak earnestly and seriously on the subject, is silent.
— Henry Thoreau

Reflection

By Br Bill Firman

Many psychologists have attempted to put forward suitable models to describe how and why people act. Freud depicted life in terms of the innate pleasure-seeking and aggression drives of each individual person. Erik Erikson, initially a follower of Freud, thought that we must also look outside ourselves to our interaction with those around us if we are to understand our growth and development. Erikson developed the notion that we pass through eight psychosocial crises as we pass from infancy to mature age. One of these he described as 'Intimacy' versus 'Isolation': wanting to be close to people but yet wanting one's own space.

Sometimes the balance point for the sexes is not the same. Girls in their late teens are often seeking a steady, close relationship of 'intimacy' – in another word, love – whereas boys at that age are more often still at a stage of wanting to be more with their mates, 'isolated' in Erikson's terms, rather than 'tied down' into an intimate relationship. Of course, both boys and girls have sexual feelings as well as psychosocial needs but the approach of the sexes is somewhat different. A woman doctor, Mary Calderone described it this way:

> *Both the boy and the girl are seeking love and sex, but their needs are somewhat different. For the sake of clarifying the point, we can say the girl plays at sex, for which she is not ready, because she fundamentally wants love; and the boy plays at love, for which he is not ready, because what he wants is sex. We must understand that in reality the boy and girl seek love and sex, tenderness and passion, but in the early years their drives are rarely synchronised. A girl usually has a greater need for a feeling of legitimacy about the relationship before she can give herself to a boy, a legitimacy rooted in her belief that the boy loves her and that she loves him, for it is this belief that frees her to express the sexual side of her nature.*

So some boys pretend to have feelings they don't really have and walk away after sex leaving a disillusioned girl who thought she had a meaningful relationship. It is only after the event that the girl realises she has been used and regrets her compliance. Such boys taking advantage of the feelings of a girl can hurt that girl badly.

Prayer

Grant me the integrity to treat other people with profound respect, rather than take advantage of their needs. Amen.

Reflecting God's Presence

Some significant events on this day

Year   Event

1305   The death of William Wallace, Scottish national hero.

1939   The Molotov-Ribbentrop Pact, also known as the Hitler-Stalin Pact, is signed. Described as a non-aggression treaty between the USSR and Germany, it incorporated an additional secret protocol for the sharing between the two the nations of Finland and Poland.

1990   East and West Germany announce plans to re-unite on 3 October.

2005   Israeli troops remove the last Jewish settlers in the Gaza strip.

Key thoughts for today

Every person dies. Not every person really lives.
— William Wallace

Those who save one life, it is as if they saved the entire world.
— The Talmud

Reflection

By Haylene Peipert

The Talmud, the great book of Jewish law and mythology, poses the following question:

Why did God choose to begin the human race by creating one man, Adam?

Surely the world would have been populated more easily had God chosen to create many humans at once. The Talmud answers that God created one man to teach that all human beings are individuals.

Throughout the passage of human history the individual has suffered under stifling collectivism. Our ancestors were forced to be part of a nation, a religion or a group.

We of the modern era are given the choice to seize our individual paths. This is an awesome privilege and responsibility. Although the lure of individuality can be exciting, it is not without its darker side. For the one who is obsessed with individuality may suffer disconnectedness, fragmentation and loneliness.

In the 21st century it is our challenge to be true to our unique selves but also to remember that, although God began creation with a single human being, we all share the same ancestry and are therefore part of a single family, which is humankind.

Prayer

May I find my place within your world, not for my sake but for all.

Reflecting God's Presence

Some significant events on this day

Year   Event

1981   In New York, Mark David Chapman is sentenced to more than 20 years gaol for shooting former Beatles member John Lennon.

1991   Soviet President Mikhail Gorbachev suspends the Communist Party and resigns as General Secretary.

2004   An independent panel substantiates the occurrence of authorised abuse of prisoners by American soldiers at Abu Ghraib prison in Iraq.

Key thought for today

The greatest fault is to be conscious of none.
— Thomas Carlyle

Reflection

By Br Bill Firman

Dan Mintie describes society as one in which 'sin has lost its bite'. In our increasingly secular, and media-influenced world, all kinds of attitudes are depicted as permissible or normal. Profit-making interests seem to be shaping public opinion more than agreed moral principles. Many of the attitudes promoted by the media emanate from people who have no clear conscientious position but are driven by material gain. The secular press publishes what sells papers or is in its own self-interest, not what promotes understanding of right and wrong.

Many people have experienced a loss of conviction of what is right and wrong and a tolerance and indifference that blurs any sense of sin. Yet we all face the fundamental option of choosing to live a moral life of integrity or succumbing to selfish temptation. There is a distinct choice to be made: to love God and neighbour or to seek our own advantage, no matter what the cost.

To steal from someone else, to take for one's own use what belongs to another, is very plainly sinful. It is indefensible. It is one of the clearest signs that one is choosing the selfishness of sin above the love of God and other people. Cheating on a marriage partner is another clear sign. Violence to others is yet another. Some people know this in varying degrees; others are in denial and their personal level of moral understanding has been reduced to the lowest level of 'Can I get away with it or not?'

Using another person to satisfy one's own sexual urges rather than to express love is also a disorder once clearly classified as sin but now intentionally overlooked by those with fuzzy consciences. We need strong convictions on what is right and what is wrong and a clear mind-set on how we should treat others with full respect for their rights and dignity as human beings. A sense of right behaviour and of the opposite, sinful behaviour, is fundamental to functioning as full human beings.

Prayer

May we be keen to develop a strong sense of right and wrong. Amen.

Some significant events on this day

Year   Event

1875   Captain Matthew Webb becomes the first person to swim the English Channel.

1944   The Allies liberate Paris from the Germans during World War II.

2005   Hurricane Katrina hits Florida, killing three people and leaving one million residents without electricity.

Key thought for today

Fear can be headier than whisky, once a man has acquired a taste for it.
— Donald Downes

Reflection

By Br Bill Firman

The following news report, abbreviated here, appeared on the internet on this day in 2008.

> Friends and family of Australian BASE jumper Ben Cannon have left grief-filled messages of love following the death of their 'angel' in Switzerland. The 31-year-old NSW man died on Thursday after a base jump in Switzerland went wrong and he plummeted to his death. Eyewitnesses told World Radio Switzerland that Mr Cannon was late opening his parachute after leaping off a cliff face in the Lauterbrunnen Valley in the Bernese Oberland. He fell into a tree before hitting the ground and was taken to hospital where he died a short time later.
>
> Countless messages from friends and family wished their 'angel' all the best on his next journey. They referred to his 'infectious smile' and told him to enjoy the 'eternal skies' and 'fly free' ... 'Why did you have to go already? Too many nice jumps left undone, too many good times that we never had time to have. Play hard wherever you are and keep some beers in the fridge! I'll see you when I get there', reads another. World Radio Switzerland said at least 14 base jumpers had been killed in Lauterbrunnen Valley in recent years.

It seems to me that the rise of modern ultra sports – 'kamikaze sports' may be one apt epithet – where one challenges death is almost a modern version of Russian roulette. Little value is placed on human life, even though one death can cause extraordinary grief for the loved ones left behind. Life's purpose is reduced to a search for the exhilarating pleasure of a moment, rather than a seeking for meaning and the establishment of enduring, meaningful, loving relationships.

Of course, risk is relative and these risk-takers try to minimise risk; but even a small risk often repeated becomes a large risk. There is something immature, selfish and pointless in repeated and increasingly dangerous risk taking just for the thrill of it. Death is only one possible consequence. A life time of quadriplegia can also result – leaving the risk-taker to depend on future lifelong care bestowed by others less selfish.

Prayer

I pray for enduring meaning in my life, in loving and being loved, and not just in seeking passing thrills. Amen.

Reflecting God's Presence

Some significant events on this day

Year   Event

1498   Pope Alexander VI commissions Michelangelo, aged 23, to carve the Pietà for St Peter's Basilica in Rome.

1883   Mt Krakatoa, an Indonesian volcanic island, erupts, causing the loudest noise reported in history, heard 3000 miles away in Turkey and Japan. The residual dust in the atmosphere caused red sunsets into the following year.

1920   In the 19th amendment to the US Constitution, women are given the right to vote.

1995   The International Rugby Board brings the game's amateur status to an end to stem the flow of players transferring to Rugby League.

Key thought for today

If people knew how hard I worked to get my mastery, it wouldn't seem so wonderful at all.
— Michelangelo

Reflection

By Ewan Walmsley

Open minds and open hearts

Of course we teachers are such strange creatures: we seem to wish that we might have stayed at university, in the library, at the exhibition, within the laboratory, at the summit or within the canoe. Strangely enough we watch the ABC or SBS, or switch the television off.

Foreign films appeal to us. Characters in novels and plays jump into our dreams. We are aware of how severe our foreign debt is and wonder about reducing it. The growing inequalities in our country disturb us so we look for how to reduce them.

Like Albert Einstein, I hope that young men retain a sense of curiosity, a capacity to wonder, speculate, imagine and resolve. He says:

> *The important thing is not to stop questioning. Curiosity has its own reason for existing. One cannot help but be in awe when one contemplates the mysteries of eternity, of life, of the marvellous structure of reality. It is enough if one tries merely to comprehend a little of this mystery every day. Never lose a holy curiosity.*

Prayer

May we never lose our sense of wonder, our innate curiosity, our capacity to imagine and dream, our hope that life can be better because God is walking with us on the journey of life. May every step reveal a little more of God's splendour to us and sustain us in the difficult times when problems seem larger than the answers. Amen.

Reflecting God's Presence

Some significant events on this day

Year   Event

1813   Napoleon Bonaparte, with a force of 100,000 men at the Battle of Dresden, defeats the combined forces of Austria, Prussia and Russia, numbering 150,000.

1910   Birth of Mother Teresa, humanitarian, Nobel Prize recipient and saint.

1939   The first turbine-powered jet aircraft flight takes place.

2003   Mars and Earth are at their closest for 60,000 years, passing within 56 million kilometres of each other.

Key thought for today

Everybody can be great ... because anybody can serve. You don't have to have a college degree to serve. You don't have to make your subject and verb agree to serve ... You only need a heart full of grace, a soul generated by love.
 — Martin Luther King Jr

Reflection

By Shane Mackintosh

Mother Teresa (1910–1997), the Albanian-born Roman Catholic missionary, has inspired many people around the world through the work she did for the poor, sick and underprivileged. She was a remarkable woman who lived by her vow to give wholeheartedly to the poorest of the poor. Her love and devotion towards those in greatest need has inspired many to carry her flame in reaching out to people who are in greater need than they are.

Stephan Waugh, former Australian cricket captain, had the privilege of meeting her on one of his extended tours of India. He writes in his autobiography, *Out Of My Comfort Zone*, about his encounter with her:

> Her face was wrinkled and weathered, yet soft and welcoming, and she radiated a tremendous inner strength and sense of compassion. She walked towards me, stopping about a metre away from me. She passed to me a piece of paper. It was one of her business cards. In that fleeting moment I turned the card over to read the text. It read:
>
> 'The fruit of silence is prayer, the fruit of prayer is faith, the fruit of faith is love, the fruit of love is service.'

Prayer

God, all of us have the capacities to live out the Mother Teresa mantra of serving others who are in greater need than ourselves. Guide me in my silent prayers and my actions as I walk in her shadow, continuing to assist those who are in greater need than I am. Amen.

Reflecting God's Presence

Some significant events on this day

Year   Event

1963   Martin Luther King Jr leads a march of 250,000 to the Lincoln Memorial in Washington where he delivers his famous speech: 'I have a dream ...'

1981   The US national centre for disease control begins investigations to find out why rare diseases are afflicting gay men, which leads to the recognition that the diseases are symptoms of AIDS.

1990   Saddam Hussein proclaims Kuwait is Iraq's nineteenth province, which subsequently leads to the Gulf War.

Key thought for today

The quality, not the longevity, of one's life is what is important. If you are in a moment that is designed to save the soul of a nation, then no other death could be more redemptive.
— Martin Luther King Jr

Reflection

By Br Bill Firman

I like the attitude expressed in the following poem I was given by a friend in 1994 and which is generally listed as 'author unknown' - although I did find one source who indicated it was written by Deirdre Love Graham in 2003. Whoever wrote it, I think it speaks very well to the grieving family and friends of one who has died.

> *When I come to the end of the road*
> *And the sun has set for me,*
> *I want no rites in a gloom-filled room.*
> *Why cry for a soul set free?*
>
> *Miss me a little, but not too long,*
> *And not with your head bowed low,*
> *Remember the love that we once shared.*
> *Miss me, but let me go.*
>
> *For this is a journey we all must take*
> *And each must go alone,*
> *It's all a part of the Master's plan,*
> *A step on the road to home.*
>
> *When you are lonely or sick of heart,*
> *Go to the friends we know*
> *And bury your sorrows in doing good deeds.*
> *Miss me – but let me go.*

Life goes on. If the person who died loved you, he or she would want you to go on living happily. We do not show genuine love by mourning too long. To do so can be to indulge in bathos. Miss the dead person but get on with life very positively. It is a good attitude, since dying is part of living.

Prayer

I pray for enduring meaning in my life, in loving and being loved, in contributing to our society. Amen.

Some significant events on this day

Year Event

1885 The world's first motorcycle, invented by German Gottlieb Daimler, is patented.
1966 The Beatles give their last public performance in Candlestick Park, San Francisco.
2005 More than 1600 people are killed and 80 per cent of New Orleans flooded when hurricane Katrina hits the south-east coast of America with winds of up to 250 km per hour. The estimated damage was US$75 billion.

Key thought for today

Our highest endeavour must be to develop individuals who are able out of their own initiative to impart purpose and direction to their lives.
— Rudolph Steiner

Reflection

By Br Bill Firman

Maggie Dent wrote:

> *The first essay I ever failed was during my first year at university and within an hour of experiencing this failure I attempted to take my own life. I was just 18, a successful student, a former school leader, a very capable netball and basketball player, and I had friends, family and a stable relationship.*
>
> *The moment of epiphany that followed while I was covered in vomit, snot and tears has shaped my life every day since. I began a journey of inquiry, searching for answers to what had triggered that almost tragic decision on that chilly May day. I became concerned and committed to help other young people struggling with low self-esteem, disconnectedness and deep feelings of inadequacy.'*

The trouble with suicide is that one poorly reasoned decision, when one is feeling low, can be so final. Maggie speaks of 'learning to read the masks of the kids who lived without love, who felt useless, ugly and unlovable'.

There are many kids like that but each of them feels isolated and desperately alone. Maggie describes what we need to do in simple but beautiful words:

> *I came to see and understand that every child, teenager and adult secretly wants someone to shine a light on the invisible sign that sits on their chest, that reads 'make me feel I matter'. Once individuals experience this they can change their way of interpreting the world to a more positive one.*

Prayer

Today, let me show the people in my life that they matter. And let me do the same again tomorrow. Amen.

Reflecting God's Presence

Some significant events on this day

Year   Event

1945   British troops liberate Hong Kong from Japan, whose troops had been in occupation for almost four years.

1984   The space shuttle *Discovery* is launched. It made 97 orbits of the earth and travelled 3.6 million kilometres in six days and 56 minutes.

1999   After 23 years of Indonesian occupation, the people of East Timor vote for independence in a UN-supported referendum.

Key thought for today

The true test of civilisation is not the census, nor the size of cities, nor the crops, but the kind of person that the country turns out.
— Ralph Waldo Emerson

Reflection

By Brian Long

What shall I do with my life? This is the big question for any of us. It is a question that is there whether we are young or old. The answer at one stage may not be the same at another. We follow many different paths in any one life.

Sometimes the word 'vocation' is used to describe what I do with my life. The heart of this word is the sense of being called to do something and be someone.

One of my favourite writers, Frederick Buechner, defines vocation as 'the place where our deep gladness meets the needs of the world'. We can't start with what the world needs, says Buechner, because the world needs everything, and it will lead us out and away. Instead, we start with the soul we were born with, the gifts we were given, what makes us deeply glad.

If I can find the path that enables my heart to sing, that gives me the sense that in my work and daily living I am being my best and most beautiful self, I am truly blessed.

The real question is, 'What is the life that is trying to live in me?' Sometimes I try to wear the faces of others. I try to be what others expect me to be. Instead I am called to discover my true self and spend my life becoming that. I have my particular bundle of gifts and weakness. My uniqueness is what the world needs most of all.

Prayer

God, you call me to be my best and most beautiful self. Help me to find my path so that always I may be your loving face in the world. Amen.

Reflecting God's Presence

Some significant events on this day

Year   Event

1994   After 25 years of fighting to force the British out of Northern Ireland, the IRA announces a ceasefire and their willingness to begin peace talks.

1997   Diana, Princess of Wales, dies in a car crash in Paris.

2004   Mel Gibson's film *The Passion of Christ* sells about 4.1 million copies in the USA on the first day it is released on DVD.

2005   Rumours that there were suicide bombers among them start a panic among Shiite Muslims on their way to a holy shrine in Baghdad, Iraq, leading to the death of more than 1000 in the stampede.

Key thought for today

It was a storm in a tea cup, but in politics we sail in paper boats.
— Harold Macmillan

Reflection

By Br Bill Firman

The Panama Canal, opened in 1914, crosses the Central American isthmus joining North and South America; but before it was built there was a long debate about where it should be built – in Panama or in Nicaragua. In 1898 the estimated cost of building a Nicaraguan canal was US$65 million dollars (a huge sum at that time) as opposed to $130 million for a Panama canal. The proposed Nicaraguan one would have used Lake Nicaragua and the San Juan River as part of the canal system, reducing construction costs. So why was the canal built in Panama?

In 1902, a lobbyist for Panama, William Nelson, chanced upon a Nicaraguan stamp depicting a fuming Mount Momotombo volcano. Thirty thousand people had died earlier that year in the Caribbean when the St Martinque volcano erupted. So death by volcanic explosion was clearly a possibility in the minds of many people. Mt Momotombo was nearly dormant and a long way from the proposed canal, but Nelson obtained and circulated copies of the postage stamp to all who were to vote. The decision to build in Panama passed by only four votes, with many politicians clearly influenced by the image of the fuming volcano. The irony is that many modern ships are too big for the Panama Canal and there is debate again about building a Nicaraguan Canal.

It should be clear that little things do sometimes make a difference – a kind word, a small gift, a smile, a postage stamp. Even a few misspelt words in a job application might suggest to a potential employer looking for reasons to make a decision to choose another applicant. Turning up a few minutes late for an appointment may be minor but it can influence a person trying to select from among several applicants.

Take the trouble to get the little things right. Little things, like the postage stamp, or a rumour, may take on more significance than we expect.

Prayer

Rumours and postage stamps can cause decisions and actions of great consequence. Help me to keep a true and just perspective on the events of life.

Reflecting God's Presence

Some significant events on this day

Year   Event

1923   The Great Kanto Earthquake of Japan, measuring 8.4 on the Richter scale, devastates Tokyo and Yohohama, killing 140,000 people.

1939   Nazi Germany attacks Poland, beginning World War II.

1983   A Korean Airlines Boeing 747, flying from the USA to Seoul, is shot down by the Soviet Union, killing all 269 people on board.

2004   More than 1100 people, mostly children, are taken hostage by Chechen militants at a school in Beslan, in southern Russia, the beginning of a three-day siege in which 344 people were killed.

Key thought for today

It needs but one foe to breed a war, and those who have not swords can still die upon them.
—J.R.R. Tolkien

Reflection

By Br Bill Firman

Common sense tells us that slaughtering innocent people, no matter what your cause, is wrong. The dreadful tragedy of Beslan took terrorism to a new low when innocent children were subject to incredible treatment – even to girls having to drink the urine of the boys! Nothing justifies doing to kids what happened at Beslan.

Most people are good and kind. Almost all people care about children and are protective of them. The simple trust of children in the adults they love is a sacred bond. All kids are entitled to know that they are precious because human life is precious. No child should ever be exposed to such stark horror and terror as happened at Beslan.

One wonders how many of the surviving children of Beslan, in the years ahead, will cope psychologically with the nightmare of what they experienced. I guess some will but some won't and that is most unfortunate.

Beslan was counter to human dignity and counter to our human instinct to protect the young. Beslan was totally unjust to innocent people and contrary to common sense. Motivation cannot make such a heinous act right. It is a distortion of religious values to depict terrorism as a kind of 'martyrdom' for the perpetrators.

Trying to justify terrorism of any kind, let alone against children, is a great lie. Convincing suicide volunteers that they are martyrs is a great lie. It is heroic to give one's life to save others, not to kill others.

Prayer

Help me, God, to use my life to help others, not to harm them. Make me a person of peace. Let my credo be to do good to all. Amen.

2 SEPTEMBER

Reflecting God's Presence

Some significant events on this day

Year   Event

1666   The Great Fire of London breaks out, burning for three days and destroying 10,000 buildings, including St Paul's Cathedral.

1792   Death of Blessed Brother Solomon.

1945   Japanese officials sign the act of unconditional surrender aboard the battleship USS *Missouri* in Tokyo Bay, bringing to an end the six years of World War II.

1973   Death of J.R.R. Tolkien, author of the renowned *The Hobbit* and *The Lord of the Rings*.

Key thoughts for today

Vision sees the invisible, believes the incredible and achieves the impossible.
— Bill Newman

Reflection

By Brother Quentin O'Halloran

In Thomas Bolt's preface to his compelling and highly acclaimed play *A Man For All Seasons*, he gives several reasons why he regards St Thomas More a hero of selflessness and a Christian saint. His reasons can be summed up as follows: More had an adamantine sense of his own self; he seized life in great variety; he possessed a sound adjustment to life; he refused to state that he believed what he didn't believe, as required on oath.

If Bolt had been aware of the life of Blessed Brother Solomon, I'm confident he would ascribe the same personal qualities to him and liken his martyrdom to More's death at the hands of Henry VIII. The fifth of nine children, Brother Solomon (Nicholas Le Clercq) was born in 1745 in Boulogne sur Mer where his father ran a business in the busy harbour district. Hoping Nicholas would succeed him, his father organised business studies courses for him in Boulogne and then Paris. However, Nicholas was attracted to the life of the Brothers whom he joined in 1767. Gradually, his character and giftedness led to his being appointed to leadership roles, culminating in his becoming the right-hand man of the Brother Superior General in 1787.

Fortunately, 138 of Brother Solomon's letters to various members of his family have survived. In them, his love of people, his wisdom and prayerfulness shine through. Like Thomas More, Brother Solomon became personally affected by the political upheaval around him. This was associated with the French Revolution and the passing of the law requiring religious and clergy to swear the Oath of the Civil Constitution of the Clergy.

Having refused to sign the oath, Brother Solomon was arrested on 15 August 1792 and placed in an improvised prison in a Carmelite convent with 150 other 'suspects'. On 2 September 1792, armed assassins broke into the convent. Prisoners were massacred while others were given the chance to take the oath before being bludgeoned to death. Carts were piled high with naked bodies. Remaining bodies were thrown down a well in the grounds and covered with lime. Brother Solomon was one of the victims of the massacre. He was beatified along with his other companion martyrs in 1926.

Prayer

Lord, like St Thomas More, the way Blessed Brother Solomon lived his life prepared him for the martyrdom which crowned it. We pray that we also may be ready for whatever comes to us.

Reflecting God's Presence

Some significant events on this day

Year   Event

1783   The American War of Independence ends after eight years of fighting.

1895   After a 25-year transformation from English rugby, the first professional American football game is played in Pennsylvania.

1984   More than 4300 people are killed and one million left homeless when a powerful typhoon sweeps through the southern Philippines.

2004   Shooting breaks out on the third and final day of the Beslan school massacre, resulting in the deaths of more than 300 people, many of them children.

Key thought for today

No one can develop freely in this world and find a full life without feeling understood by at least one person.
    — Paul Tournier

Reflection

By Patrick Jurd: Father's Day in Australia is celebrated on the first Sunday in September. This passage about Father's Day is quoted by Afshawn Towfighi of Fort Lauderdale, Florida, USA.

> *Father's Day is this weekend, and to honour how important dads are in our lives, here is a reflection about feeling close to Dad from 'She Said ... He Said: Teens Speak Out on Life and Faith':*
>
> > *I am happy when I have something to talk about with my dad. When I was younger, my dad and I used to talk to each other all the time. However, now that I am older, I don't have as much free time with my dad as I used to. We just say 'good morning' when we wake up and 'good night' when we go to bed. The rest of the time, there is little communication between us.*
> >
> > *However, when we talk about different things, whether it's cars, computers, or anything at all, I feel happy inside. It is a special feeling that makes me feel like I'm on top of the world. It makes me feel a lot closer to my dad, and I would like to have that feeling more often. I also know he feels better too, and that's what makes me feel happy.*

As we get older, our dad is still our dad but he is also one of our most special friends.

Prayer

> *Thank you, friend Jesus, for my father who loves me,*
> *for my grandfather who cares for me,*
> *and for God, your father and mine,*
> *who made me and is always with me.*
> *How lucky I am!*

Some significant events on this day

Year   Event

476   The Western Roman Empire falls when Romulus Augustus, the last emperor, is forced to abdicate by Eastern rival, Odoacer, who proclaimed himself King of Italy.

1886   The wars in North America between the white settlers and the Native Americans effectively come to an end with the surrender in Arizona of the Apache leader Geronimo.

1965   Death of Albert Schweitzer, physician, anthropologist, musician and Nobel laureate.

1972   US swimmer Mark Spitz wins his seventh gold medal at the Munich Olympics.

Key thought for today

God does not die on the day when we cease to believe in a personal deity, but we die on the day when our lives cease to be illuminated by the steady radiance, renewed daily, of a wonder, the source of which is beyond all reason.
— Dag Hammarskjöld

Reflection

By Fr Chris Gleeson SJ

I was listening to the Reverend Graham Long, Pastor at the Wayside Chapel in Sydney, being interviewed on the radio. In talking about his life and his ministry, he described himself at one point as a lapsed atheist, adding that in his brief time as a 'postie' he had learnt the valuable skill of riding a motorcycle down stairs.

Graham also talked about his life as a prison chaplain, and I was really moved by his attitude to the hundreds of people who come to the Wayside Chapel each day. He said his challenge was to see the beauty in every face, even when the owner of that face had long given up on it. Surely, that is to love others as Jesus did – Jesus the one who never gives up on us ...

Timothy Radcliffe, the former general superior of the Dominicans, has a beautiful phrase for this unconditional love of God for us. He refers to God as the one for whom

> ... *no one is on the edge because God's centre is everywhere and his circumference is nowhere. It is in the spaciousness of God that we will be completely at home because everyone will be.*

Cardinal Basil Hume put it another way:

> *God can't count – everybody is number one.*

One of the great stories of our time, surely, is that of Blessed Mary MacKillop, soon, we trust, to be Saint Mary ... Like Mary MacKillop, who was so at home with God, who loved as Jesus did, may we experience God like a best friend we take everywhere with us.'

Prayer

God, be a part of my life by helping me be a good person in the sense of William Wordsworth's verse: 'That best portion of a good man's life / His little, nameless, unremembered acts / Of kindness and of love.'

Reflecting God's Presence

Some significant events on this day

Year   Event

1960   In the Rome Olympics, the first televised to the USA, boxer Cassius Clay, aged 18, wins the gold medal. He later changes his name to Muhammed Ali and becomes World Heavyweight Champion.

1972   A Palestinian terrorist group attacks Israeli athletes at the Munich Olympic Games.

1997   Death of Mother Teresa, born in Albania in 1910, and well known as a living saint for her work with the poor in Calcutta. She was beatified only six years after her death.

Key thought for today

I want to be thoroughly used up when I die, for the harder I work the more I live. I rejoice in life for its sake. Life is no brief candle to me. It is a sort of splendid torch which I've got hold of for the moment and I want to make it burn as brightly as possible before handing it on to the next generation.
— George Bernard Shaw

Reflection

By Br Bill Firman

I am inspired by the words of Mother Teresa. In 1979, the year in which she was awarded the Nobel Peace Prize, she said to a group of De La Salle Brothers in Rome:

> *My prayer to you Brothers ... I beg of you, be faithful to the gift of God that has been entrusted to you to teach. You are the only light today amongst the young people.*
>
> *The future of the whole world depends on what you make them. You can make them and you can break them. You are the only ones that can, as teachers, stand before them as a presence of Christ. May the young people entrusted to you be able always to see Christ in you and be filled with his purity and goodness, with his justice, because today, especially, the young are misled and you are the people who have to lead them.*
>
> *Be that light to them. Be the light that will lead them to God. People are hungry – especially the young people – hungry for God, and you are there to satisfy that hunger.*
>
> *Be faithful to the great gift of God to you ... to be teachers, to be the light: his light in the world amongst young people.'*

We are called to be the light of the world, a splendid torch. It is worth a try.

Prayer

Mother Teresa, you once said: 'Do not wait for leaders; do it alone, person to person.' I ask God, through your intercession, to make me a person for others who will be a light for good in the world, who will encourage and bring hope to others. Be with me on this journey, Lord. Amen.

6 SEPTEMBER

Reflecting God's Presence

Some significant events on this day

Year   Event

1620   The Pilgrims, a group of Puritans seeking religious freedom, set sail from Plymouth, England, on the *Mayflower* to settle in North America.

1936   Benjamin, the last known surviving member of the *Thylacine* species, the Tasmanian Tiger, dies alone in his cage at Hobart Zoo.

1997   A million people line the route for the funeral of Princess Diana from Westminster Abbey, while an estimated 2.5 billion watch on television.

Key thought for today

Twenty years from now, you will be more disappointed by the things that you didn't do than by the ones you did do. So throw off the bowlines. Sail away from the safe harbour. Catch the trade winds in your sails. Explore. Dream. Discover.
— Mark Twain

Reflection

By Stephen Young

Do something

How often do we feel overwhelmed by the enormity of what is in front of us? We feel inadequate knowing the complexity and volume of the things to be done. How often does this feeling of being overwhelmed then lead to paralysis and inaction?

In 1969, Hawthorn legendary coach and former De La Salle student John Kennedy Snr famously told his team in a rousing half-time speech to 'Do something!' At that time, Kennedy knew his charges were thinking of the enormity of the task of hauling back a significant deficit. He wanted his players to ignore the bigger picture for the moment and to do the individual things for which they were well trained and highly practised. In this way the bigger picture would take care of itself. It is now history that his booming voice imploring the players to do the little things – handball, chase, tackle – produced a great turnaround and a great victory.

Archbishop Oscar Romero may have been to AFL football what John Kennedy was to theology, but he said something very similar.

> *It helps now and then to step back and take the long view. The Kingdom is not only beyond our efforts, it is even beyond our vision. We accomplish in our lifetime only a tiny fraction of the magnificent enterprise that is God's work. Nothing we do is complete, which is another way of saying that the kingdom always lies beyond us ... We cannot do everything, and there is a sense of liberation in realising that. This enables us to do something, and to do it very well.*

Prayer

Lord, as I start my day knowing how much there is to be done, I give thanks for my own small gifts. I pray for the courage to use my gifts and in so doing to make my contribution to the magnificent enterprise that is God's work.

Reflecting God's Presence

Some significant events on this day

Year   Event

1979   The Entertainment and Sports Programming Network (ESPN) opens as a 24 hour per day cable television sports station.

1986   Desmond Tutu is appointed Archbishop of Cape Town so becoming the first black South African to lead the Anglican Church in his country.

1998   University students Larry Page and Sergey Brin, as a research project, found the Google Search engine, which develops to become the largest on the web.

Key thought for today

Always try to speak to the goodness that is in people. Nothing is lost in the attempt.
— Pope John XXIII

Reflection

By Br Bill Firman

There is a succinct Chines proverb that points to the value of human life:

Saving one human life is better than building a seven storey pagoda to the Buddha.

Balanced people, be they Buddhist or Christian or professing any other religious or humanist adherence, place a very high value on human life. The novelist James Baldwin expresses the need for holding on to one another, for joining the pieces together, in this beautiful, poetic way:

The sea rises, the light fails, lovers cling to each other, and children cling to us. The moment we cease to hold each other, the sea engulfs us and the light goes out.

The need for people to work together and especially to help a child to fit all the pieces of life's puzzle together is succinctly expressed in an African proverb:

It takes a village to raise a child.

For children to grow, supportive family and friends – indeed a 'village' – are a necessity. Too many children lack supportive adults in their lives and are in danger of being engulfed by the sea or having the light go out. Too many have experienced inadequate parenting where abuse is more common than tender love. Someone has to provide the encouragement that luckier children are blessed with in their families. Hubert Humphrey, former US vice president, stated in one of his speeches:

Each child is an adventure into a better life – an opportunity to change the old pattern and make it new.

When we deal with children it is well to remember the profound words of Mother Teresa who said:

It is not how much we give but how much love we put into giving.

Prayer

Lord, let me be gentle with children and convey the message to each child that he or she is, indeed, very lovable.

Some significant events on this day

Year   Event

1504   Michelangelo's 5.2 metre high statue of David, which took three years to complete, is unveiled in Florence.

1565   A Spanish expedition establishes the first permanent European settlement in North America, at St Augustine in Florida.

1930   The US company 3M begins marketing transparent Scotch Tape.

1966   The first episode of *Star Trek*, the science fiction series starring Captain Kirk and Mr Spock, is screened on US television.

1986   General Augusto Pinochet, the President of Chile, survives an assassination attempt that kills five of his bodyguards.

Key thought for today

Blessed are those who hunger for friends – for, though they may not realise it, their souls are crying out for God.

— Habib Sahabib

Reflection

By Donna-Maree Yorgey

Co-author of the book *Affluenza*, Clive Hamilton, wrote in a newspaper article:

> *It is widely accepted that people believe they need more money than they have, no matter how wealthy they are. Most people act as if more money means more happiness. But when people reach the financial goals they aspire to, they do not feel any happier ... According to a Newspoll survey, 62 per cent of Australians – nearly two-thirds – believe they can't afford to buy everything they really need.*

Most of us are full of contradictions in one way or another because we confuse what we want with what we need. Ultimately, happiness comes when we learn to cherish and be grateful for what we have. Family and friends we do not buy.

The love of family and friends is what we really need. We can be poor financially but very rich indeed. It is then that happiness will tap us on the shoulder. Someone said it in these simple but beautiful words:

> *Happiness is like a butterfly:*
> *the more you chase it the more it will elude you.*
> *But if you turn your attention to other things.*
> *it will come and sit softly on your shoulder.*

Prayer

Lord, help me to accept life as it comes, cherishing family and friends. Grant us good health and peace so that we may share the gift of happiness landing gently upon us and sitting softly on our shoulders.

Reflecting God's Presence

Some significant events on this day

Year   Event

1850   After being ceded by Mexico in 1848, California becomes the 31st state of the USA.

1971   The Attica Prison riot in New York State breaks out, leading to 42 deaths.

2004   A car bomb explodes outside the Australian Embassy in Jakarta, Indonesia, leaving 10 dead, 160 injured and a crater three metres deep.

Key thought for today

Create your own dreams and follow them until they are a reality.
  — Susan Polis Schutz

Reflection

By Kathie Holmes

Susan Polis Schutz's inspirational works are everywhere – in books, on greeting cards, in magazines. Many times I have referred to them to help me express my feelings or to give me that extra drive to follow my dreams and have faith in myself. Her words encourage others to believe in themselves, to discover what is important to them and to not be afraid of making mistakes.

Susan began her writing career at age seven, when she put together a handwritten newspaper in Peekskill, New York. As she grew older, she wrote some of her earliest poems about her feelings and experiences. Following high school, she enrolled at Rider University in New Jersey and majored in English and Biology. She went on to do social work and teach in Harlem for several years while studying physiology in graduate school. She continued her writing and worked as a freelance reporter for newspapers and magazines.

Throughout Susan's life, she has shared her feelings on love, nature, friendship, family and motherhood. She has a love of life and a fervent wish to make the world a better place. She has always been a staunch supporter of equality and an advocate of the elderly. Susan and her husband Stephen have been involved in peace-oriented groups, worked for civil rights and opposed nuclear war. Susan has championed women's health issues and the sanctity of the family in our society. Over 12 million books have been sold containing Susan's poems and Stephen's artwork, and her poetry has been published worldwide. Poems by Susan have appeared on more greeting cards than those of any other writer in history.

As we move forward in our lives, we need to remember to be honest with ourselves and determine goals that reflect our abilities and dreams. Of course we need to work hard to achieve our goals, remembering that mistakes along the way are an inevitable part of the journey towards success and happiness. Know that God always walks beside us.

Prayer

Susan Polis Schutz wrote: 'Love is being honest with yourself at all times, being honest with the other person at all times, telling, listening, respecting the truth and never pretending.' We pray that we might learn to love like that.

10 SEPTEMBER

Reflecting God's Presence

Some significant events on this day

Year   Event

1963   The era of credit cards begins when American Express, one of the world's biggest banks, introduces its credit card to the United Kingdom.

1977   The last execution by guillotine takes place in France in Marseille.

1990   The largest church in Africa and the tallest Christian place of worship on earth, the Basilica of Our Lady of Peace, is consecrated by Pope John Paul II on a visit to the Ivory Coast.

2002   Switzerland finally joins the United Nations, after being assured its historic neutrality will be maintained.

Key thought for today

It is impossible to be just if one is not generous.
— Joseph Roux

Reflection

By Br Bill Firman

In dealing with the needy in our society – sometimes described as 'the last, the lost and the least' – we should view them not as victims, nor as welfare consumers, but as fellow citizens who have rights and responsibilities. The needy person before us is our brother or sister in the eyes of God, just as important as we are, equally precious. He or she may just happen to be younger, poorer, have been abused or marginalised in some other way. Deep, mutual, human respect, not pity, should be the underlying motive and emotion in any help we offer.

Rarely do the problems ensue solely from the actions of the needy themselves. Usually society has disadvantaged them in some way . Our efforts should be directed to helping them overcome the barriers that prevent their full and meaningful participation in society. All too often we hear political debate about harsher penalties for juvenile offenders. A harsher penalty may be akin to treating only the symptoms of an illness but ultimately it is necessary to eradicate the root cause of the illness itself. Often the cause is unemployment and the solution is found in enterprise training or providing employment. Political band-aids are never enough unless they address the causes. Not often enough do we hear politicians speaking of the need to eradicate drug abuse, youth unemployment and homelessness, the biggest factors leading to juvenile offending. What is called for is a rehabilitative mindset rather than more emphasis on punitive measures or retributive justice.

I have lost count of the number of young people on the fringe of society whom I met through BoysTown, who longed for the dignity of earning their way but who succumbed to stealing as the only way available to them. For some it was a chosen lifestyle but for many no more than a habit born out of desperation rather than desire. God loves everybody but certainly not the injustice they perpetrate. We are called to do the same.

Prayer

Give me the courage, O my God, to reach out with respect to the last, the lost and the least in our society, to help them overcome the obstacles that prevent them from assuming their rightful place as full and positive citizens in our society. Amen.

Reflecting God's Presence

Some significant events on this day

Year   Event

1989   Communist Hungary opens its borders with Austria, signalling the opening of the Iron Curtain and the end of the Cold War.

1997   Scotland votes for home rule and the re-establishment of its own parliament after 290 years of union with England.

2001   Two planes, hijacked by Al-Qaeda terrorists, fly into the World Trade Centre towers in New York; two other planes are also hijacked, one hitting the Pentagon. Almost 3000 people died.

2005   The state of Israel declares an end to 38 years of occupation and military rule of the Gaza Strip.

Key thought for today

My religion is based on truth and non-violence. Truth is my God and non-violence is the way to reach him.
— Mahatma Gandhi

Reflection

By Br Bill Firman

September 11, 2001 is a date burned firmly into the memory of this generation. The stark horror of terrorism is the outstanding social issue of this 21st century. Human liberty and the solidarity of humankind came under attack when terrorists deliberately inflicted the carnage of September 11, Bali or Beslan. We are left to wonder how human beings could randomly slaughter so many innocent people. Portraying such acts as 'religious martyrdom' is a sham.

As a child I wondered at the stories I heard of the atrocities committed under Hitler's leadership. How could people be so cruel to others? The First World War was followed quickly by the Second World War, with smaller conflicts ensuing in other places such as Korea and Vietnam. As years passed, however, and with the ending of the so-called Cold War, most of us were optimistic for a more peaceful planet.

The Second Vatican Council, speaking through *Gaudium et Spes* in 1965, made the point that war should never be directed at population centres. What needs to be said today concerning the innocent victims of terrorism? Perhaps the unique challenge of this century is for Christians to hold fast to Gospel values in their own hearts. If we overreact against innocent Muslims – not the terrorist extremists – or begin to urge reckless vengeance on a principle of 'an eye for an eye', then we ourselves are losing perspective and balance.

The Gospel urges us to feed the hungry, visit the sick, care for the lonely and all such acts of social concern that reflect the central truth of loving God and our neighbour. There is absolutely no justification for the opposite.

Prayer

Saint Thomas Aquinas wrote that 'reason in human beings is rather like God in the world.' Let us pray that reason, not terrorism, and God, not hatred, may grow in our world. Amen.

12 SEPTEMBER

Reflecting God's Presence

Some significant events on this day

Year   Event

1953   John F. Kennedy, destined to become US president, marries Jacqueline Bouvier.
1977   Anti-apartheid activist Steve Biko is beaten to death in police custody in South Africa.
2005   The fifth Disneyland theme park opens on Lantau Island, Hong Kong.

Key thought for today

Ethics and equity and the principles of justice do not change with the calendar.
—D. H. Lawrence

Reflection

By Larry Evans

At times it can be too easy to see the difficulties of the world as overwhelming and to adopt a disconsolate attitude. At these times it can be hard to see how the efforts of the average person can have any impact at all. But this is the only way an individual can have an impact and fight against social wrongs. You can only affect that part of the world that you are involved in, by the way you conduct yourself, relate to others, are for others. If you truly want world peace start by bringing peace to the people you relate to. If you truly want justice, be just in the way you deal with people. Today is the day to start towards this better world.

Just for today

Today ... I will not be a party to pessimism nor join the indifferent.

Today ... I will love my enemies. I will pray for them. I will try to see our differences from their point of view.

Today ... I will disarm myself of rage by extending my hand in help and forgiveness.

Today ... I will know that peace is the child of justice – that peace is more than the absence of war.

Today ... I will plant a seed of justice in this global village, in my city, in my neighbourhood, in my family and in my heart.

Today ... I will pray for peace for all those with whom I come into contact.

Today ... I will test my love of peace by doing one act for peace.

Today ... I will live in peace with God, my neighbour and myself. I will bring peace to my patch of this earth.

Today ... I will believe that world peace is possible. I will remember that hope is the most important gift I can give my world.

Prayer

God, give me the grace and courage to live a life of non-violence. Help me to be an instrument of your peace; to respond with love and not retaliate with violence; to resist death and to choose life for all your children. Guide me along the way of non-violence. Disarm my heart and I shall be your instrument to disarm other hearts. Lead me, God of non-violence, into your reign of love and peace, where there is no fear and no violence.

Reflecting God's Presence

Some significant events on this day

Year   Event

1993   Yitzak Rabin and Yasser Arafat shake hands on the White House lawn, influenced by President Bill Clinton, to sign the declaration of principles, mapped out in the Oslo Accord, to bring about peace between Arabs and Israelis.

1994   Launched in 1990, the unmanned *Ulysses* probe passes the Sun's south pole.

1999   A second bomb within the week explodes in a Moscow apartment building. The two blasts killed more than 200 people. The government blamed Chechen rebels and sent troops back into Chechnya, which they had left in 1997.

Key thought for today

It is much easier to be critical than correct.
— Benjamin Disraeli

Reflection

By Br Bill Firman

I recall a parent who impressed me greatly with her passion for her son. She said: 'I know he is not working as well as he could. I even initiated a meeting with his teachers to address the issue. Some were positive and some were quite negative. I don't mind the criticisms – so long as it comes across that they care about him. It is a Christian school. He needs to feel teachers like him, not condemn him.'

Self-righteousness is a particular problem for those of us who are teachers. We are in the privileged position of standing in front of a class as an authority. One would hope that, given the prerequisite training, it is largely true that teachers are experts in their field of teaching. Nonetheless, this can also be a problem. Teachers are so used to being 'right' and can be so insistent on consistent standards that we fail to show the loving care of Jesus and too readily condemn the failings of individual pupils. The same can be said of some parents with their children.

Some adults have a great way of challenging children. Even when rebuking children, they make them feel cared about, not 'put down'. Dismissive adults, adults who never seem to have time enough to help kids, are not good teachers or mentors. Caring adults use words to heal and know when to back off if the child reacts emotionally to well-intentioned banter. A healing tongue and a sizeable dose of good humour are great tools for loving. Sarcasm, scorn, cynicism are tools of torture. All healthy human relationships are built on respect and kindness to the other. Although there will always be some competitive behaviour among emerging men, which we try to address whenever it occurs inappropriately, the ethos of De La Salle College is generally one of healing rather than bruising, of kindness rather than hurt, of forgiveness more than retribution. We try to make it so and hope the young men will carry that spirit with them for a life time.

Prayer

Help me to remember that my rights are not as important as my relationships, that how I say something is often more important than what I actually say. Amen.

Some significant events on this day

Year Event

1901 US President William McKinley dies after having been being shot twice on 6 September. Vice-President Theodore Roosevelt then became president.

1975 The first US saint, Elizabeth Seaton, is canonised by Pope Paul VI.

1982 Following a car crash, Princess Grace of Monaco, formerly American actress Grace Kelly, dies in Monte Carlo.

Key thought for today

Your sole concern ... should be the establishment of God's reign in your heart.
— Saint John Baptist de La Salle

Reflection

By Br Bill Firman

Dan Mintie describes the dilemma of the 1970s in these terms:

In the decade following the Second Vatican Council, many notions about sin did go out the window – the general consensus being 'happily so'. A 'laundry list' notion of evil, an introspective examination of conscience, a whole geography of heaven and hell and the stopovers in between went out with a whoosh.

By the early 1970s, however, thoughtful people throughout the church began to realise that many more issues had been raised than had been resolved. Suddenly Catholics found themselves facing some tough questions about human nature, evil and the quality of their Christian lives. People are again yearning for some kind of yardstick against which to measure their experience.

One consequence of this yearning in the 80s and 90s has been the rise of fundamentalism - the literal interpretation of the Bible and the false presupposition that the Bible teaches a scientific understanding of the world in the cosmos. There is something attractive about tenets that are easy to grasp and understand. The increase in the number of Christians of all denominations who are fundamentalist has been quite startling.

Genuine faith, however, must rise above such simplistic notions to the central truth of a God who loves us, who became human in the person of Jesus and died in the greatest act of love, an act that gives us hope. It is a mistake to try to oversimplify our notions of the God who is beyond all understanding. It is a gross error to try to use religious belief to justify terrorism. How we act towards others is the central issue. If we become self-righteous to the point that our actions are judgemental, harsh, unkind or even violent, something is wrong. Good people have a fundamental disposition to love others and treat them kindly. If we are not that way, our values are distorted.

Prayer

Grant to us, O Lord, a heart renewed. Re-create in us your own Spirit.

Reflecting God's Presence

Some significant events on this day

Year   Event

1835   Charles Darwin reaches the Galapagos Islands off the South American coast aboard the HMS *Beagle*. There he developed his theory of natural selection and evolution.

1984   Prince Harry, the second son of Charles and Diana, is born in London.

2000   The 27th Summer Olympics opens in Sydney, Australia.

Key thought for today

We do not act rightly because we have virtue or excellence, but we rather have those because we have acted rightly.
— Aristotle

Reflection

By Martin Tuelan, National Director, Catholic Mission

In 1995, for the first time ever, three Catholics held the three most senior positions in Australian public life simultaneously. Sir William Deane was Governor-General, Paul Keating was Prime Minister and Sir Gerard Brennan was Chief Justice of the High Court. It seemed that Australian Catholics had finally made it into the mainstream of Australian society. It will seem ironic that now Australian Catholics are fully integrated into Australian society I am advocating that we now must be different from other Australians. In *Evangelisation in the Modern World*, Pope Paul VI wrote:

> *The first means of evangelisation is the witness of an authentically Christian life, given over to God in a communion that nothing should destroy and at the same time given to one's neighbour with limitless zeal ... People today listen more willingly to witnesses than to teachers, and if they do listen to teachers, it is because they are witnesses.*

How can you or I be witnesses if we blend into the life of other Australians, without any particular distinctiveness? We need to be seen to love God and our neighbour in ways that go far beyond the norm. We must take the risk of being different. First, we must try to be exceedingly generous people. We must try to give our time and our money to others in a way that is far beyond the norm. We must give, not because our help or our money is needed, but because we need to give to grow more Christ-like, and to be authentic witnesses.

Our three senior statesmen of 1995 are very different men, but they are all distinctive in one particular way. They have been three of the most effective advocates for justice for Aboriginal people in Australia. Brennan and Deane were both in the majority in the High Court in the Mabo decision, and before and after their terms in the courts were passionate advocates of Aboriginal rights. Keating led Australians to make Mabo a reality and deliver land rights. Those actions were brave, often unpopular, and generous. Whether we agree with their politics or not, these Catholics stand out as genuine witnesses to an authentic Christian life. In our family, neighbourhood, parish and workplace, our actions must make you and me stand out as witnesses too.

Prayer

Give me the courage to act justly and be motivated by values rather than profit.

Some significant events on this day

Year   Event

1812   Rather than surrender to Napoleon and be ruled by the French, the Russians set fire to Moscow. Within two days 90 per cent of houses and more than 1000 churches were destroyed.

1975   Papua New Guinea declares itself free from Australia's rule, and on this date each year PNG celebrates Independence Day.

1976   The US Episcopal Church approves the ordination of women.

1978   More than 26,000 people die when an earthquake measuring 7.7 on the Richter scale hits the town of Tabas, in south-eastern Iran.

1987   The Montreal Protocol is signed by 24 nations to protect the Ozone layer. By 2006 another 180 countries had added their support.

Key thought for today

If you can solve your problem, then what is the need of worrying? If you cannot solve it, then what is the use of worrying?

— Shantideva, 8th century Indian Buddhist scholar

Reflection

By Troy Potter

Far too often we go through life thinking about what we have done or what we will do. We are either lost in the past, reliving or regretting moments in our lives that have already occurred, or we are thinking about the future, considering the myriad possibilities ahead of us. Very rarely do we think about the present moment.

All the experiences that we have had are in the past. We cannot alter them.

Every experience that we may have is yet to come. It is one among an infinite set of possibilities which may not eventuate.

The only moment we actually exist in is the present. Thus, it is only the present moment which we have the ability to influence. Bring your awareness to this present moment and achieve your best, for it is only within the now that you truly exist.

Prayer

Grant to us, O God, to use the present moment as a sacrament, an opportunity to be true to who we are as creatures of God, to do good to others as our brothers and sisters in Christ and to love God by the quality of the life we lead. Amen.

Reflecting God's Presence

Some significant events on this day

Year   Event

1787   The US Constitution, creating a federal union of sovereign states and a federal government, is adopted at a convention held in Philadelphia.

1976   After more than two years of construction, the first NASA space shuttle *Enterprise* is unveiled.

1983   Vanessa Williams is crowned Miss America, the first African-American winner of the title. Ten months later she resigned when *Penthouse* magazine announced it would print nude photos of her taken long before she had entered the competition. She went on to become a successful R&B singer.

Key thought for today

Racism is a contempt for life, an arrogant assertion that one race is the centre of value and object of devotion, before which other races must kneel in submission.
— Martin Luther King Jr

Reflection

By Br Bill Firman

I love that pithy phrase 'Men for Others'. It sums up an attitude of unselfishness and willing generosity. Learn to be so and you are a long way down the road to genuine happiness. Br Bede Mackrell was living comfortably in retirement in the Malvern Brothers' house in 2005 but answered the plea of the people of Bereina for the Brothers to return to a place they had left a decade ago and to get Mainohana High School running properly again. Well into his seventies, Bede responded.

Br Joe Gabel was a schoolboy at De La Salle Malvern. He trained to be a Brother in the same group as myself. We have never been stationed together except that we both volunteered almost 25 years ago to be part of a small group who spent their Christmas holidays at Balgo Hills, a remote Western Australian Aboriginal community. We spent long hours every day improving the school. Joe was the skills man who could weld and operate almost all machinery and tools; I was one of the labourers! Brother Joe was Principal at St James' College, Bentleigh. He offered to give up that post and has now spent 20 years, 13 at Balgo and eight in Port Moresby where he now works, as an ordinary man making an extraordinary difference.

Brother Gerry was principal of Holy Rosary School in Derby, a remote township in north-west Australia, where most students are Aboriginal. I witnessed the deep appreciation of the Derby people for the tender yet direct and firm approach of this large man. Many De La Salle students also experienced his care and generosity.

These are ordinary men doing extraordinary things – men for others – who value all people as their brothers and sisters in Christ. The Brothers, along with others who have been inspired and imbued with this Lasallian ethos, endeavour to bring care and hope to people in developing regions and countries. There is nothing more fulfilling than using the gifts God gave us to help others, to be men for others, to be ordinary people doing extraordinary things.

Prayer

God, grant me the generosity to be a 'man for others', one who is willing to make a difference for the better. Amen.

Some significant events on this day

Year   Event

1919   The Netherlands gives women the right to vote.

1970   American guitarist Jimi Hendrix dies of a sleeping pill overdose in London at the age of only 27.

1979   Bolshoi Ballet's star dancers Leonid and Valentina Kozlov defect from Russia while on tour in the USA.

1987   US President Ronald Reagan and Soviet leader Mikhail Gorbachev agree to the first reduction of nuclear weapons since their invention 50 years earlier.

Key thought for today

Perhaps with charity one shouldn't think. Charity, like love, should be blind.
— Graham Greene

Reflection

By St John Baptist de La Salle

Charity is kind. Indeed, it is not by scolding, murmuring, complaining about or quarrelling that we show our love and union. It is by speaking in a kind and affable way. A kind word, says the wise man, turns away wrath, while a harsh reply stirs up fury. For this reason Our Lord said to his apostles, 'Blessed are those who show kindness toward others, for they shall possess the land.' This means the whole earth, because those who possess the hearts of others do possess the whole earth, which is what persons whose temperament is kind and moderate easily achieve. They gain entry so well into the hearts of those with whom they speak and relate that they win them over little by little. Ah! What a great advantage it is to learn well and to practise well the lesson given us by Our Lord: 'Learn of me, for I am kind and humble of heart.' Never speak to anyone except with kindness, and if you fear to speak otherwise, keep silent (Meditations for Sundays and Feasts, 12th Sunday after Pentecost).

Frequently spend time in prayer, and during periods of dryness try to find your consolation in it, for it is there you will find God most surely. In periods of dryness and darkness, when you feel no attraction, remain constantly faithful to prayer. Be all the more faithful to prayer when you feel, on the one hand, God deep in your heart drawing you to it, and, on the other, the devil making every effort to dissuade you from it. Your prayer is good just as you are making it. God is in your prayer, making it for you. All you have to do is, from time to time, disown with peace and tranquillity of heart all the distractions you experience. Put yourself completely in the hands of Our Lord, so that he may come and live in you (Letter)

Prayer

The poet John Donne, says, 'This is charity, to do all, all that we can.' I pray that I do all that I can to help others.

Reflecting God's Presence

Some significant events on this day

Year Event

1893 All women in New Zealand receive the right to vote. New Zealand was the first country in the world to grant that right to women.

1985 An earthquake hits Mexico City, killing more than 4500 people. Tenor Placido Domingo was among those who dug through rubble to find his dead relatives.

1991 Otzi the Iceman, a very well-preserved mummy of a Stone Age man from 3300 BCE, is discovered inside a glacier in the Italian mountains. Scientists have since learned a great deal about human life 5000 years ago by their research on this unique mummy.

Key thought for today

In order to fulfil your responsibility with as much perfection and care as God requires of you, frequently give yourself to the Spirit of our Lord to act only under his influence and not through any self-seeking.
— Saint John Baptist de La Salle

Reflection

By Br Bill Firman

The story is told of a man who never married. His friend said to him, 'How is it that you have never married?'

The man replied, 'I have spent all of my life looking for the perfect woman.'

'Oh', said the friend, 'didn't you find her?'

'Oh, I found her all right', said the man.

'Well', responded the friend, 'why didn't you marry her?'

'She was looking for the perfect man.'

I like this story. It speaks of more than just marriage. None of us is perfect. Yet we can be so judgemental and unforgiving when meeting others. We should not expect in others what we do not possess ourselves. We should appreciate the good in others rather than be self-seeking.

Still on the subject of marriage, Benjamin Franklin once wrote:

Keep your eyes wide open before marriage and half shut afterwards.

'Wide open', no doubt, in Franklin's use of words is a warning not to let infatuation get in the way of really looking carefully at the person one is marrying. In more general terms, however, I like to think that we keep our eyes wide open to see the good points in others and half shut when looking at their imperfections.

Prayer

Long ago Confucius warned: 'Seek not every quality in one individual.' Teach me to cope with my weaknesses and those of others. Help me to accept my humanity.

Some significant events on this day

Year Event

1519 Portuguese explorer Ferdinand Magellan sets sail in his ship the *Victoria* on a three year journey which became the first circumnavigation of the world. Magellan himself did not complete the journey, dying in a skirmish with natives in the Philippines.

1893 In Massachusetts, Charles and Frank Duryea build and drive the first gasoline-powered vehicle in America.

1999 A UN peace-keeping force is sent to East Timor to end the violence that had seen thousands killed since the country voted for independence two weeks earlier.

Key thoughts for today

I could not point to any need in childhood as strong as that for a father's protection.
— Sigmund Freud

Christians should offer their brothers and sisters simple and unpretentious hospitality.
— Saint Basil

Reflection

By Phil Ryan

One chilly spring morning in late October, holding my beautiful ten-week-old daughter Rebecca in my arms for a 5 am feed, I was reminded of the presence of God in this little newborn. I was reminded that God loves me abundantly and unconditionally. For me Rebecca's presence is pure gift and one I give thanks to God for every day. In fact, God's love is like a child held lovingly in its parent's arms.

Such God-filled moments have given me ample time to reflect on the nature of hospitality. We generally think of hospitality as something we give to guests, but we can show hospitality to everyone we meet. We can receive people in hospitality every day, every hour, and not just for a meal. St Benedict, in his order's Rule, invites us to live a life of love and service, reaching out to others because we see Christ in everyone. So when you and I receive a guest at home, or a colleague in the staff room or a student in the classroom we are receiving Christ.

This is a hard thing to do at times. We can be very protective of our space and can sometimes become annoyed at events and at others. Sometimes we fail to see the need around us. When we acknowledge Christ in others we acknowledge the part of them connected to God in Christ. This means attending to people with our hearts. Not only are we to receive Christ in others as our guest; we are to *be* Christ to others.

Prayer

Martin Buber wrote: 'People became what they are – children of God – by becoming what they are, brothers of their brothers, sisters of their sisters.' Help us to become sons or daughters of God by being a welcoming and supportive brother or sister who greets others with an open heart. Amen.

Reflecting God's Presence

Some significant events on this day

Year   Event

1998   Olympic gold medal track star Florence Griffith Joyner, known as Flo-Jo, dies in her sleep after suffering an epileptic seizure at the age of 38.

1999   A brief but powerful earthquake kills more than 2000 people in Taiwan, injuring more than 4000 and leaving 100,000 homeless.

2001   The United Nations declares that henceforth this date will be recognised as the International Day of Peace, a worldwide day for ceasefire and non-violence.

Key thought for today

It is cynicism and fear that freezes life; it is faith that thaws it out, releases it, sets it free.
— Harry E. Fosdick

Reflection

By Br Bill Firman

In his 1985 annual report, Brother Damien Harvey, one of the most enthusiastic and hopeful men I have known, wrote:

> *Every human being is only young once and if in that period we do not provide them with a sense of satisfaction which comes from achievement in some form of human endeavour, there is much thinking to be done. We grow old not by having birthdays but by deserting ideals. Passing years may wrinkle the skin but lost enthusiasms wrinkle the spirit. We are old indeed when the central places of our heart are covered by the snows of pessimism and the ice of cynicism. One of the world's saddest sights is a person grown old at 15. We Christians live with the virtue of hope, which is the ability to dream, and when we lose this we begin to die by centimetres.*

Maintain the hope. It is important to continue to dream, to live and to hope for a better world. Sometimes we may wake up feeling we are on a grey road and recognise it is time to take a new direction or to make a renewed effort. It may take a conscious effort to cast off the cloak of depression and gloom or to throw away our security blanket to take a new direction, but we need to be idealistic and visionary, along with having a good dose of enthusiasm.

Of course, there are some things in life that should never change. We need to adhere courageously to Gospel values and live by a consistent set of ideals, principles and standards. The new directions, the renewed effort, to which I am referring are not meant to imply an alteration of our principles and personal values, but rather to signal using resolute energy to shape our lives in accord with the principles we hold dear. We do not abandon our ideals. The idea is to make a conscious drive to live and act consistently with our ideals. Hope comes from a clear vision – and renewed efforts to move energetically in that direction.

Prayer

Carl Schurz wrote that 'Ideals are like the stars – we never reach them, but like the mariners of the sea we chart our course by them.' Grant me the strength to hold to lofty ideals.

22 SEPTEMBER

Reflecting God's Presence

Some significant events on this day

Year   Event

1980   Iraq invades Iran and war breaks out between these neighbouring countries. By the time the UN organised a ceasefire in 1988, there were 400,000 casualties.

1991   The Dead Sea Scrolls, the only surviving biblical documents from before 100 CE, are made available for the first time by Huntington Library in California.

2004   CBC-owned television stations in America are fined US$550,000 for showing pop star Janet Jackson's exposed breast for one second during the Super Bowl half-time show. She blamed a wardrobe malfunction.

Key thought for today

Time is too slow for those who wait, too swift for those who fear, too long for those who grieve, too short for those who rejoice. But for those who love, time is eternity.
— Henry van Dyke

Reflection

By Brother Quentin O'Halloran

One of the world's finest conductors in the 20th century was Sir Malcolm Sargent, who guided several British orchestras to distinction. At a workshop prior to a performance, he was asked which instrument he considered was the most difficult to play. Somewhat surprisingly, he responded: 'The second violin, because it takes a rare type of person to play such a role with enthusiasm and not seek the limelight.'

In all avenues of life, 'second fiddles' are very important and we all admire people who do not hit the headlines but give of their best day after day. Using the skills we have to the best of our ability and praising others for their giftedness are daily challenges we face.

A plaque hanging above my desk sums up the challenge facing this 'second stringer' each day:

> *Use*
> *what talents you possess.*
> *The world would be*
> *very silent*
> *if no birds sang*
> *except those who sang best.*
>   *Henry Van Dyke*

Prayer

Henry Van Dyke also said: 'Happiness is inward and not outward; and so it does not depend on what we have but on what we are.' Help me to be the best I can with what I have. Amen.

Reflecting God's Presence

Some significant events on this day

Year   Event

1846   Neptune is discovered and named after the Roman god of the sea because of its blue methane clouds.

1968   Modern-day saint, Padre Pio of Pietrelcina, dies at the age of 81. The funeral of this humble priest was attended by more than 100,000 people.

2004   Hurricane Jeanne rages for two weeks, killing more than 3000 people in Haiti and leaving 300,000 without basic shelter or supplies.

Key thoughts for today

The way of the world is to praise dead saints and persecute living ones.
— Nathaniel Howe

The serene beauty of a holy life is the most powerful influence in the world next to the power of God.
— Blaise Pascal

Reflection

By Br Bill Firman

Padre Pio was an Italian Franciscan priest who became famous not only for his holiness but because of supernatural events associated with him. With illiterate parents, who memorised the scriptures, related Bible stories to their children and made a living as shepherds, he became known as a modern wonder worker.

After a period of invisible stigmata when he felt the pain but did not have the wounds of Christ in his hands, feet and side, the visible stigmata appeared on 20 September 1918 and stayed with him for 50 years, disappearing at his death in 1968. These wounds never healed and could not be explained by doctors who made thorough investigations. Through his life Padre Pio coped with extraordinary suffering.

There is abundant evidence of his special spiritual gifts which included bi-location, levitation, prophecy, miracles, periods of extraordinary abstinence from sleep and food, and the ability to read what is in the hearts and minds of others. For many years he had to cope with scepticism and criticism from within the Catholic Church and was even banned from the public celebration of the Eucharist and from hearing confessions. When the bans were lifted, thousands flocked to him for confession and guidance and to be in his presence when he celebrated the Eucharist.

In 1947, a young polish priest Karol Wojtyla, later to become Pope John Paul II, visited Padre Pio who heard his confession and apparently told him that he would one day ascend to 'the highest post in the church'. Many miracles that defy normal explanation have been worked in the name of Padre Pio and he was canonised a saint on 16 June 2002 by Pope John Paul II.

Prayer

Thank you, God, for the gift of Padre Pio whose life was evidence of your power and the spiritual level to which we can only aspire in faith. Help us in our doubts.

24 SEPTEMBER

Reflecting God's Presence

Some significant events on this day

Year   Event

1899   Birth of the renowned Australian artist Sir William Dobell.

1948   The Honda Motor Company is founded in Tokyo, Japan.

1975   Dougal Haston and Doug Scott, the first Britons to do so, climb Mt Everest in the record-breaking time of 33 days.

1976   The Rhodesian government reluctantly agrees to introduce black majority rule within two years, leading to the change of leadership in 1980 to Robert Mugabe. The country was renamed Zimbabwe.

Key thought for today

God only asks you to do your best.
— Robert Hugh Benson

Reflection

By Betty Rudin: Here are some thoughts well worth pondering, called 'Things God won't ask'.

God won't ask what kind of car you drove.
    He'll ask how many people you drove who did not have transportation.
God won't ask the square footage of your house.
    He will ask how many people you welcomed into your home.
God won't ask about the clothes you had in your wardrobe.
    He will ask how many people you helped clothe.
God won't ask what your highest salary was.
    He will ask if you compromised your character to obtain it.
God won't ask what your job title was.
    He will ask if you performed your job to the best of your ability.
God won't ask how many friends you had.
    He will ask how many people you were a friend to.
God won't ask in what neighbourhood you lived.
    He will ask how you treated your neighbours.
God won't ask the colour of your skin.
    He will ask about the content of your character.
God won't ask why it took you so long to seek salvation.
    He will lovingly welcome you to your home in heaven.

Prayer

There is a French proverb which says, 'God often visits us, but most of the time we are not at home.' We pray that we be ready to welcome you, God, with the right answers. Amen.

Reflecting God's Presence

Some significant events on this day

Year	Event
1957	With the Arkansas state governor defying desegregation laws, US President Eisenhower orders more than 1000 paratroopers to escort nine black children to school in Little Rock.
1977	More than 15,000 people attend the funeral of South African anti-apartheid activist Steve Biko, killed in police custody on 12 September. Thousands more were barred from attending.
2003	A report is released by France revealing that 14,800 people had died during a recent summer heatwave.

Key thought for today

To see what is right, and not to do it, is want of courage.
— Confucius

Reflection

By Br Bill Firman

The murder of black activist, Steve Biko, in police custody caused outrage in South Africa and brought international condemnation. White officials tried to claim he killed himself, but a post-mortem examination revealed he died from severe brain damage caused by harsh beatings. The funeral service was conducted by Reverend Desmond Tutu and attended by representatives of governments from around the world. Many credit Biko's death as being the catalyst for serious change in South Africa.

White South African newspaper editor Donald Wood, who had met Biko and had been greatly moved by him, fled to the UK where he campaigned for justice. This is starkly portrayed in the moving book and film *Cry Freedom*, which brought Biko's message and life story to the world. The plight of the many black and coloured political prisoners under the brutal apartheid regime of the country, who were subject to gruesome torture and endless detention without trial, was exposed to the international community.

The courage of Steve Biko, Donald Wood and other activists such as Nelson Mandela and Archbishop Desmond Tutu, brought about great change in South Africa so that there is no longer repressive white majority rule. The determination of good people, who never lost hope and refused to be diverted from the pursuit of justice proved to be an irresistible force. It was a seismic change in South Africa and a major step forward for all cultures in the recognition of the equal rights of black and white people.

Prayer

Abraham Heschel described racism as 'the maximum of hatred for a minimum of reason'. I pray for love, not hatred, in my heart for all people. Grant me the courage, whenever confronted by racial prejudice, to act by my conviction that people should be loved, not hated, just as Christ loved us. Amen.

Some significant events on this day

Year   Event

1973   Concorde makes its first non-stop crossing of the Atlantic in just three hours 32 minutes, flying at an average speed of 1535 km/h.

1983   *Australia II* becomes the first non-American winner in the 132-year history of the America's Cup yacht race.

1984   Britain agrees to hand Hong Kong back to China in 1997.

Key thought for today

Reflect on your present blessings, of which every man has many; not on your past misfortunes of which all men have some.
— Charles Dickens

Reflection

By Br Bill Firman: I was taken with these thoughts expressed in an article entitled 'The Struggle to Bless' by Ron Rolheiser OMI in which he discussed the tension that may exist between the young and older people.

It would seem that many of the young do not want our blessing. But is this so? Not really. We must distinguish between the various levels at which we want something.

On the surface, clearly, young persons often do not want the blessing of their parents, elders, teachers, and clergy. But that is the surface; they have deeper wants and needs. Someone once said that a true missionary is someone who goes where he or she is not wanted but is needed; and leaves when he or she is wanted but not needed. That is true too for parenting, teaching, coaching and ministry. We should not identify what someone wants at the surface of his or her life with that which they need and want at a deeper level. Young people may not overtly want the blessing of their elders, but they desperately need it. Later on, after they have matured, they will want that blessing but, paradoxically, then they will no longer need it to the same extent. We should not be put off by the surface of things, where youth, naturally, push elders away and give the impression we have nothing to offer them. They desperately need our blessing ...

To bless someone literally means to speak well of that person. More deeply, that means to see someone's energy and honour it as a source of joy and delight rather than as an intrusion or a threat. To bless a young person is to look at him or her and, without exploitation of any kind, give back to him or her an appreciative gaze that says his or her life and actions are a source of delight and joy for us rather than a threat and irritation ... When the young people in our lives give us the impression that they neither want nor need our blessing, it is precisely the time when, ironically, they probably need it the most. Their very aloofness is partly a symptom of the lack of blessing in their lives and a plea for that blessing. We need to give that blessing. God blesses. When we act like God we will get to feel like God – and God is never depressed.

Prayer

May God bless us, and those whom we love. Amen.

Reflecting God's Presence

Some significant events on this day

Year   Event

1660   The death of Vincent de Paul, a French priest from a peasant family who spent his life helping the poor. He is venerated as a saint.

1822   French linguist Jean-François Champollion deciphers the Rosetta Stone, a slab of granite found in Egypt with three inscribed scripts. His work unlocked the secrets of the hieroglyphs and revealed much about ancient Egypt.

1988   The National League for Democracy, led by Aung San Suu Kyi, is founded in Burma to fight for freedom from the military regime.

Key thought for today

The only real prison is fear, and the only real freedom is freedom from fear.
— Aung San Suu Kyi

Reflection

By Br Bill Firman

The Latin phrase *Quae nocent, saepe docent* translates literally as 'What hurts, often instructs'. This is not quite as severe as the aphorism, often used by coaches of sporting teams: 'No pain, no gain'.

In former days, 'What hurts, often instructs' might have been taken as an excuse for corporal punishment! I certainly do not advocate a return to that practice, but other things such as dressing correctly, being properly groomed and well presented, have long been expectations in the armed forces where such an imposed discipline is seen to instruct. Families, schools and businesses are not the army, but there the ability to accept personal discipline in small things flows over into other areas of more consequence in life. Feeling good about oneself gives one the strength to exercise self-discipline when it is required. As children grow up, imposed compliance becomes less important than possessing self-discipline.

In the school or work context, if people present themselves with personal pride they will more likely do well in important areas such as scholastic achievement or business productivity. The converse is more obvious: if people present as lazy and undisciplined, it is very unlikely that they will do well.

In a more dramatic way, the lengthy detentions experienced by Aung San Suu Kyi, and Nelson Mandela, would have been most unpleasant, yet these leaders emerged stronger, not weaker, as a consequence. For people of lesser character, such experiences might have destroyed them. It is not automatic that what hurts often instructs. Often – not always. Sometimes a weaker person simply gives up and gains nothing. There is an element of personal choice in how we cope with what hurts us.

Prayer

God, help me to learn to cope with the small hurts in life that I may be ready to face the bigger ones when they inevitably come.

28 SEPTEMBER

Reflecting God's Presence

Some significant events on this day

Year   Event

551BCE Birth of Chinese philosopher Confucius.
1887   Brazil passes the Law of the Free Womb, which emancipates the children of slaves.
1978   Pope John Paul I is found dead only 33 days after his election.
1994   The car ferry MS *Estonia* sinks in the Baltic Sea while sailing from Estonia to Sweden, with 852 people killed.

Key thought for today

The more we learn about the wonders of our universe, the more clearly we are going to perceive the hand of God.

— Astronaut Frank Bormann

Reflection

By Br Bill Firman

Neptune is about 4.5 billion km from the sun. Pluto orbits at roughly 5.87 billion km from the sun. In fact, as a consequence of Pluto's orbit occasionally crossing over Neptune's, and not being in the same plane as all the other planets in our solar system, Pluto was closer than Neptune to the sun from 1979 through to 1999. This happens from time to time. Pluto is so far from the sun that it takes 250 earth years for Pluto to make one revolution around the sun.

On Pluto, the sun would appear not much more than a bright star. Beyond Pluto, although there are myriads of 'stars' to be seen in all directions, there is little 'sunlight' and it is very dark indeed. If one tends to think of Pluto as the distant edge of the solar system, it is wise to remember it is only one 68th of the way to our nearest neighbouring star, Proxima Centauri.

A probe from Earth travelling to Pluto will take 12 years to get there. Let us suppose that somehow we were on that unmanned probe and we decided to travel on to visit our nearest star neighbour. After arriving at Pluto we would have a further 39.2 trillion kilometres to go. Travelling at the same average speed that applied for our trip from Earth to Pluto, it would take us another 802 years to reach Proxima Centauri!

The logistics of staying alive this long or of taking enough food for the journey are further problems which we shall ignore! The time required is sufficient to indicate that we are a long way from the reality of stellar travel.

Prayer

The earth we know is only a small part of your creation, O God. Jonathon Swift said: 'That the universe was formed by a fortuitous concourse of atoms – I will no more believe that than the accidental jumbling of the alphabet would fall into a most ingenious treatise of philosophy.' I see your hand in the wonders of this earth in this universe and I praise and thank you for your awesome gift of life. Amen.

Reflecting God's Presence

Some significant events on this day

Year   Event

1952   John Cobb, who held the land speed record, dies on Loch Ness attempting to beat the world water speed record.

1960   Soviet leader Nikita Khrushchev disrupts a UN meeting by pounding his desk and shouting during a speech by British Prime Minister Harold Macmillan.

1979   Pope John Paul II makes the first visit by a pope to Ireland, addressing 1.25 million people in Dublin, nearly a third of the country's population.

1998   Stacey Allison become the first American woman to climb the 8848 metres high Mt Everest, one year after having to turn back after being trapped in a snow cave at 7163 metres during a blizzard lasting five days.

Key thought for today

I wanted to hug someone. This [climbing Everest] is an experience you want to turn around and share with someone. Unfortunately, when I turned around, there was no one there.
— Stacey Allison

Reflection

By Brian Long: We all have special moments of insight, shining experiences that help us realise what is important to us. Daniel O'Leary describes this.

Into every life, the wise ones say, comes one shining moment. It is a moment of glory. The curtains part, the vision is granted, and something is changed forever. That single experience, in one way or another, stays with us always and colours the whole of our lives. It is the timeless moment when the veil is drawn from the mystery of our existence, when our essence is disclosed to us, when we discover – even if only fleetingly – who we really are. It is a highly personal moment of truth.

Your one bright shining moment may have to do with naming what or who you really love; with discerning the job or relationship that is slowly destroying you; with becoming aware that all your decisions and reactions spring from a deeply hidden anxiety, anger or fear; that you need no longer be afraid because you are unconditionally loved by a God who delights in you; that, without a doubt, the universe and life itself are safe places for yourself, your children and all you love; that everything that has happened to you was not random happen-chance but part of a carefully crafted love story; that God comes to you usually disguised as your life, in all its bits and pieces; that, apart from one or two cherished beliefs, nothing matters very much; that it is in our weakness and sinfulness that we are strongest of all; that we are indestructible and untouchable as long as we remain close to God (Daniel O'Leary, Prism of Light*)*

Prayer

Lord God, help me to see the truth of each moment of my life and especially to recognise that one shining moment when it comes. Amen.

Reflecting God's Presence

Some significant events on this day

Year Event

1846 The first use of ether as an anaesthetic is recorded by a Boston dentist, William Morton, removing a patient's tooth.

1938 British Prime Minister Neville Chamberlain is applauded for bringing peace to Europe when he signs the Munich Pact, a non-aggression deal with Hitler. Eleven months later, Hitler invaded Poland, saying the agreement was 'just a scrap of paper'.

1955 Rising Hollywood star James Dean dies in a car crash, aged 24. Dean was driving his rare Porsch 550 Spyder but, contrary to legend, was not speeding and was not at fault. A student driver came around a corner on the wrong side of the road and smashed into him. A month later, his acclaimed film *Rebel Without a Cause* was released.

Key thought for today

Shared laughter creates a bond of friendship. When people laugh together, they cease to be young and old, master and pupil, worker and driver. They have become a single group of human beings enjoying their existence.

— W. Grant Lee

Reflection

By Br Bill Firman

Life as a teacher can have its poignant moments which reveal aspects of human nature. Here are three that I recall clearly.

A particularly difficult student was summoned, with his mother, to the principal's office. The boy gave his version of recent incidents, after which the principal recounted a somewhat different description. The mother then declared: 'Well one of youse is lying!' To which the principal retorted: 'I assure you, madam, it's not me.'

Another teacher was rather concerned at the lack of personal hygiene of one of his pupils. After several attempts to get the boy to address the problem himself, the concerned teacher sent a note home to his parents that the boy needed to wash more often and more thoroughly. The teacher received a note back from the boy's mother: 'My boy ain't no bunch of violets. Don't smell him. Teach him!'

The Brother in charge of boarders met Year 11 student Gerard on the stairs. Gerard looked upset. The kindly Brother said to him: 'Are you okay?' Gerard began to cry and the Brother took him aside. When the boy partially regained his composure, he volunteered, 'I got 2 out of 30 for my Geography assignment'. The Brother began to console Gerard over his poor mark. 'It's not the mark', Gerard said. 'I can accept that. But he [the teacher] didn't have to carry on and on about it and make me feel a fool in front of the whole class!'

Prayer

Lord God, help me to listen sympathetically and understandingly, and to respond with good humour rather than anger. Amen.

Reflecting God's Presence

Some significant events on this day

Year	Event
1964	The first Shinkansen, the Japanese bullet train travelling at speeds up to 321 km/hr, goes into service between Tokyo and Osaka, just prior to the Tokyo Olympics.
1971	The second Disney theme park, Disney World, opens in Florida, following the opening of Disneyland, Los Angeles, in 1955.
1975	Muhammed Ali defeats Joe Frazier in their third fight, the 'Thriller in Manila', to retain the world heavyweight boxing title.

Key thought for today

Christianity is a good philosophy if you live it, but it is controlled by white people who preach it but don't practise it. They just organise it and use it any which way they want to.
— Muhammed Ali

Reflection

By Br Bill Firman

C.S. Lewis, the powerful thinker, author and committed Christian, who desired early in his life to be an atheist, had this to say about Christianity:

> *Christianity, if false, is of no importance, and, if true, of infinite importance. The one thing it cannot be is moderately important.*

It is one of the great paradoxes of Christianity that it embodies the power of God's revelation, yet that message is so often twisted and distorted by people. 'True Christianity', wrote David McKay, 'is love in action.' Samuel Johnson called Christianity 'the highest perfection of humanity'. The problem is that all too often Christians are pharisaic and do not rise to the level demanded of them. The experience of black people in America, who suffered slavery and racism at the hands of white Christians, illustrates one way the message of Jesus can be rationalised and moderated. That eloquent black man, Adam Clayton Powell Jr, described the importance of Christ this way:

> *Once a man walked this earth and spoke with such uncommon power that he separated history into BC and AD ... the teachings he proclaimed become newer and more challenging as the centuries roll.'*

Powell, however, also said:

> *America is not a Christian country. It is a country of pretensions, of 'churchianity' where the institution of Christianity has been perverted to propagate the doctrines of segregation and discrimination.*

Black preacher, Jesse Jackson, described the problem this way:

> *The white Christian church never raised to the heights of Christ. It stayed within the limits of culture.*

Prayer

God, help me accept the full wisdom expressed through the teaching of your son, Jesus, not a version distorted by culture and history. God forbid that I be a modern Pharisee. Amen.

2 OCTOBER

Reflecting God's Presence

Some significant events on this day

Year   Event

1836   Charles Darwin completes his journey of four years, nine months and five days on HMS *Beagle* to South America. There he collected specimens and data in support of his theory of evolution.

1869   Birthday of Mahatma Gandhi, the Indian leader who helped secure Indian independence from Britain.

1950   Charles Schultz' comic strip *Peanuts* first appears. It continued to be published until the year 2000.

Key thought for today

Action expresses priorities.
— Mahatma Gandhi

Reflection

By Br Bill Firman

Occasionally, some people have to make very radical choices. Andrew Harris, an old boy of Francis Douglas Memorial College, in New Plymouth, NZ, successfully climbed Mt Everest and was on his way down when bad weather closed in. A newspaper editorial, under the heading, 'Humble heroes in an age dominated by selfishness', had this to say:

> *Consider New Plymouth climber Andrew Harris as he escaped the almost unimaginable fury of a freezing storm near the summit of Mt Everest. In conditions where he knew there was no margin for error, no mercy, he heard the radioed cry for help from above him. Below was life. Above was death. Andrew Harris climbed.*

Andrew Harris was not heard of again. He made the heroic choice to offer his life in the faint hope of helping others. I imagine Andrew Harris never thought of himself as a hero but he found the strength to do what he had to do when the time of challenge came.

He is an example of a grander vision of the human spirit and its capacity to respond. It was the same with St John Baptist de la Salle. He was a priest, enjoying a relatively comfortable priesthood, a nobleman who found himself drawn into the education of the poor children of Rheims. No doubt he could think of reasons why he could turn away from this lower class. But he also found the heart to respond to need when he saw it.

Every day we make choices. There are always going to be things more glorious and more immediately attractive. It is always tempting to attend to our own needs rather than make sacrifices to help others. If we help others to overcome disadvantage and transform futility into direction and purpose, we are sharing with them a great gift indeed. Extending a helping hand to others is the practical expression of loving God in a very effective way. I am sure, in the eyes of God, it makes up for any number of personal weaknesses.

Prayer

Help me to make good choices in the little things of life so that I may be ready to respond correctly when bigger choices must be made.

Reflecting God's Presence

Some significant events on this day

Year   Event

1226   The death of Saint Francis of Assisi.

1942   Germany launches the first artificial object to reach space – an A4 rocket.

1990   East and West Germany formally reunite. The border between East and West Germany was closed in 1952 and the Berlin Wall erected in 1961. The wall was demolished on 9 November 1989.

Key thought for today

Love is a condition in which the happiness of another person is essential to your own.
  — Robert Heinlein

Reflection

By Joy Bew: At a fund-raising dinner for a school in Brooklyn that serves children with learning disabilities, a father engaged the group with story, of his son, told here in an edited version. .

My son, Shay and I walked past a park where some boys Shay knew were playing baseball. Shay asked, 'Do you think they'll let me play?' I knew that most of the boys would not want someone like Shay on their team, but as a father I also understood that if my son were allowed to play, it would give him a much-needed sense of belonging and some confidence to be accepted by others in spite of his handicaps. I approached one of the boys on the field and asked (not expecting much) if Shay could play. The boy said, 'I guess he can be on our team'. Shay struggled over to the team's bench and, with a broad smile, put on a team shirt.

With two outs and the bases loaded, the potential winning run was on base and Shay was scheduled to be next at bat. Surprisingly, Shay was given the bat. Everyone knew that a hit was all but impossible because Shay didn't even know how to hold the bat properly, much less connect with the ball. However, as Shay stepped up to the plate, the pitcher, recognising that the other team was putting winning aside for this moment in Shay's life, moved in a few steps to lob the ball in softly so Shay could at least make contact. As the pitch came in, Shay swung at the ball and hit a slow ground ball right back to the pitcher. The pitcher picked up the soft grounder and could have easily thrown the ball to the first baseman. Shay would have been out and that would have been the end of the game. Instead, the pitcher threw the ball right over the first baseman's head, out of reach. Everyone started yelling, 'Shay, run to first! Run to first!'

The second baseman understood the pitcher's intentions so he too threw the ball high and far over the third-baseman's head. All were screaming, 'Shay, Shay, Shay, all the way Shay!' Shay reached third base because the opposing shortstop ran to help him by turning him in the direction of third base, and shouted, 'Run to third! Shay, run to third!' Shay finally ran to home, stepped on the plate, and was cheered as the hero who won the game for his team. 'That day', said the father softly with tears rolling down his face, 'the boys from both teams helped bring a piece of true love and humanity into this world.'

Shay didn't make it to another summer. He died that winter, having never forgotten being the hero.

A wise man once said: 'Every society is judged by how it treats its least fortunate amongst them.'

Prayer

Lord, may my day be a Shay Day.

Some significant events on this day

Year   Event

1582   The Gregorian Calendar is decreed by Pope Gregory XIII. (Technically, the length of a year is 365.2422 days per year, not 365.25. So, even with leap years every four years, this small difference of .0078 of one day means the average length of every year is 11 minutes 15 seconds too long – which amounts to one whole day in 128 years. To get the vernal equinoxes back in line, Gregory decreed 4 October in 1582 would be followed by 15 October.)

1957   The first artificial object to leave the earth's atmosphere, the Russian satellite *Sputnik* is launched.

1983   In his vehicle *Thrust 2*, Richard Noble sets the land speed record in the Nevada desert of 1019.44 km per hr (633.468 mph).

Key thought for today

Know that courtesy is one of the properties of God, who gives his sun and rain to the just and the unjust by courtesy; and courtesy is the sister of charity, by which hatred is vanquished and love is cherished.
— Saint Francis of Assisi

Reflection

By Marg McPhee

> *Use what talents you possess;*
> *Be kind to those around you;*
> *Strive to be the best you can.*
>
> *Ask for help when you need it;*
> *Always be there for others;*
> *Enjoy the challenges that life will bring.*
>
> *Embrace the future;*
> *Have confidence in yourself;*
> *Be proud of who you are.*
>
> *Enjoy the laughter of friends and family;*
> *Take time to notice nature's beauty;*
> *May inner peace, a positive attitude and happiness be forever yours.*

Prayer

On this feast day of St Francis of Assisi, we recall his words: 'It is no use walking anywhere to preach unless we preach as we walk.' We remember that we must live with integrity so that our public image reflects who we truly are. We ask you, God, to help us to be persons of integrity who are always willing to be there for others, especially our family and friends. Assist us to be proud of who we are, confident, kind, aware of the world around us and filled with the gift of your peace. In the words of the hymn attributed to St Francis: 'Make us a channel of your peace ...' Amen.

Reflecting God's Presence

Some significant events on this day

Year   Event

1947   US President Harry S. Truman gives the very first White House televised address.

1962   The Beatles release their first hit 'Love Me Do'.

1994   Forty-eight members of the religious cult Order of the Solar Temple die in an apparent mass suicide in Switzerland.

2001   A Florida man dies of anthrax poisoning when he received contaminated mail. This was one of a number of bio-terrorism attacks at this time that have not been solved.

Key thought for today

Children have never been very good at listening to their elders, but they have never failed to imitate them.

— James Baldwin

Reflection

By Br Bill Firman

Dorothy Holte reminds us that our attitudes generate the responses that come back to us from children (and others). Generally, if we are positive, a child will respond positively; but, if we are negative, so will be the response.

> *If a child lives with criticism, he learns to condemn.*
> *If a child lives with hostility, he learns to fight.*
> *If a child lives with ridicule, he learns to be shy.*
> *If a child lives with shame, he learns to feel guilty.*
> *If a child lives with tolerance, he learns to be patient.*
> *If a child lives with encouragement, he learns confidence.*
> *If a child lives with praise, he learns to appreciate.*
> *If a child lives with fairness, he learns justice.*
> *If a child lives with security, he learns to have faith.*
> *If a child lives with approval, he learns to like himself.*
> *If a child lives with acceptance and friendship, he learns to find love in the world.*
>
> Dorothy Law Holte

Prayer

Harold Hulbert said that 'Children need love, especially when they do not deserve it.' Help me, God, to be ready to love even when I feel affronted. Amen.

Reflecting God's Presence

Some significant events on this day

Year   Event

1889   Inventor Thomas Edison shows the first motion picture on a machine which was the predecessor of the movie projector.

1927   The first feature-length talking movie, *The Jazz Singer* (starring Al Jolson), opens on Broadway, New York.

1995   The first planet found outside our own solar system, Bellerophon, is detected orbiting the star, 51 Pegasi, 50.1 light years from the Earth.

Key thought for today

The universe is but one vast symbol of God.
— Thomas Carlyle

Reflection

By Br Bill Firman

Scientists now estimate the number of galaxies to be near to fifty million. Yet everything we see in the night sky by naked eye, with the exception of the Andromeda Galaxy which appears as one small fuzzy dot, is part of our own galaxy, the Milky Way Galaxy. The Milky Way Galaxy is a relatively small, spiral-shaped galaxy. It is approximately 100,000 light years in diameter and 2000 light years from top to bottom. Our solar system is located in one of the four spiralling arms of this galaxy, called the Orion arm. Our sun, a relatively young star, lies about 30,000 light years from the centre of the Milky Way Galaxy. The sun, together with the planets, asteroids and comets orbiting around it make up our solar system.

In 1995, the first planets in our galaxy but outside our own solar system were discovered. By December 2000, the number of such planets identified had increased to 46. By mid-2005, the number of planets, identified by 'gravitational wobble' of stars, had increased to 130. These early discoveries were all of gas giants at least as big as Jupiter and Saturn. Up until the discovery of such planets, most scientists had thought very few stars had planets. In 2000, the common estimate was significantly increased to about a third of the stars having planets.

On 4 May 2005, scientists in Chile photographed a planet five times the size of Jupiter, orbiting a star 200 light years from earth, the first planet that has ever been imaged outside our solar system. To date it has only been possible to look at relatively few stars within a hundred or so light years of earth. That leaves stars within another 99,900 light years in this galaxy to examine! I am exaggerating as knowledge is not yet that accurate but it gives an idea of the order of magnitude.

Statistically, the likelihood of other planets, with conditions like earth, existing in the universe has gone from very low to very high.

Prayer

God, you are infinite and I am very small in one tiny part of the cosmos. I thank you for not only supporting life everywhere but for being all-loving. Amen.

Reflecting God's Presence

7 OCTOBER

Some significant events on this day

Year   Event

1769   Captain James Cook discovers and maps New Zealand. Abel Tasman had charted the west coast in 1642, unaware of the extent of the land.

1982   The Andrew Lloyd Webber musical *Cats* opens on Broadway and runs for 18 years.

2001   The US and British forces launch air strikes against the Taliban in Afghanistan.

2003   Arnold Schwarzenegger is elected Governor of California.

Key thought for today

The human mind, stretched to a new idea, never goes back to its original dimensions.
— Oliver Wendell Holmes

Reflection

By Br Quentin O'Halloran

In October 1994, I spoke to Year 12 students at an assembly about the inscription above the main door of the centuries-old and battle-scarred Cathedral of St Quentin in Picardy, north of Paris. It reads: 'People are worth what they seek.'

Afterwards, one of the young men, Peter Pacalt, came up and spoke to me at some length about the inscription and its relevance in his life. When I received a phone call from his family in 1996 to inform me that he had been tragically killed in a car accident while visiting his brother in South America, I recalled our conversation. Privileged to be asked to give the eulogy at his requiem, I thought it appropriate to speak in general terms about our conversation concerning 'people are worth what they seek'.

What Peter sought was integrity, and that was his measure as a young man. With a frankness and maturity beyond his 18 years, he talked to me about integrity in terms of

— the person he was trying to be;
— fidelity to his studies;
— his relationships with his family, friends and young women.

Peter, like each of us, was a bit battle-scarred because of human frailty, but his basic integrity shone through. So too, as you young men strive to find meaning in your lives, may what you seek make you a person of integrity and bring you closer to God.

Prayer

Ralph Waldo Emerson said that 'Nothing is at last sacred but the integrity of your own mind.' Help me to seek and find that sacred wholeness.

Some significant events on this day

Year   Event

1871   The Great Chicago Fire kills 300 people and leaves another 100,000 homeless.

1978   The world water speed record is set by Ken Warby at 511.11 km/h on Blowering Dam, NSW.

2005   In northern Pakistan and India, 87,350 people are killed by an earthquake of magnitude 7.6 with its epicentre in Kashmir.

Key thought for today

Only love can bring individual beings to their perfect completion as individuals because only love takes possession of them and unites them by what lies deepest within them.
— Teilhard de Chardin

Reflection

By Patrick Jurd: Here is some further wisdom from John Powell's *Fully Human, Fully Alive*.

To forget oneself in loving

Having learned to accept and to be themselves, fully alive people proceed to master the art of forgetting themselves – the art of loving. They learn to go out of themselves in genuine caring and concern for others. The size of a person's world is the size of his or her heart. We can be at home in the world of reality only to the extent that we have learned to love it. Fully alive men and women escape from the dark and diminished world of egocentricity, which always has a population of one. They are filled with an empathy that enables them to feel deeply and spontaneously with others.

Because they can enter into the feeling world of others – almost as if they were inside others or others were inside them – their world is greatly enlarged and their potential for human experience greatly enhanced. They have become 'persons for others', and there are others so dear to them that they have personally experienced a 'no greater love than this' sense of commitment. They would protect their loved ones with their own lives.

Being a loving person is far different from being a so-called 'do-gooder'. Do-gooders merely use other people as opportunities for practising their acts of virtue, of which they keep a careful count. Loving people learn to move the focus of their attention and concern from themselves out to others. They care deeply about others. The difference between do-gooders and people who love is the difference between a life which is an on-stage performance and a life which is an act of love. Real love cannot be successfully imitated. Our care and concern for others must be genuine, or our love means nothing. This much is certain: there is no learning to live without learning to love.

Prayer

Mystical spiritual writer, St John of the Cross, wrote that 'in the evening of our lives we shall be examined in love'. Lord, help me to be ready.

Reflecting God's Presence

Some significant events on this day

Year   Event

1958   The 260th pope, Pius XII, born Eugenio Pacelli, dies after 19 years as pontiff.

1974   German businessman Oskar Schindler, credited with saving 1200 Jews from the Holocaust, dies at the age of 66.

1992   A 1.4 kg meteorite lands in a New York driveway, destroying Michelle Knapp's Chevy Malibu car.

Key thought for today

Take the first step in faith. You don't have to see the whole staircase, just the first step.
— Martin Luther King Jr

Reflection

By Patrick Jurd (from the De La Salle Brothers' website)

Feast of the Martyrs of Turón and St Jaime Hilario

In 1934 Turón, a coal-mining town in the Asturias province of north-western Spain, was the centre of anti-government and anticlerical hostility in the years prior to the outbreak of the Spanish Civil War. The Brothers' school there was an irritant to the radicals in charge of the town because of the religious influence it exerted on the young. The Brothers defied the ban on teaching religion and openly escorted their students to Sunday Mass. On the first Friday of October, the authorities broke into the Brothers' house on the pretext that arms had been hidden there. They and their chaplain, Father Inocencio, a Passionist, were arrested, detained over the weekend without trial, and in the middle of the night were marched out to the cemetery where they were shot. They were victims of the hatred and violence against the church, and witnessed by their death to the faith they so courageously professed and so effectively communicated to their students.

Manuel Barbal Cosan was born on 2 January 1898 in Enviny, a small town at the foot of the Pyrenees in northern Spain. He joined the Brothers at the age of 19 and was given the name of Jaime Hilario. After 16 years in various teaching assignments, his hearing problems forced him to abandon the classroom to work in the garden at the house of formation at San José, in Tarragona.

In July of 1936 he was at Mollerosa on his way to visit his family at Enviny when the civil war broke out. Recognised as a Brother, he was arrested and gaoled. In December he was transferred to Tarragona and confined in a prison ship with several other Brothers. On 15 January 1937 he was given a summary trial. Though he could have been freed by claiming to be only a gardener, he insisted on his identity as a religious and thereby sealed his doom. He was brought to the cemetery known as the Mount of Olives on 18 January to face execution. His last words to his assailants were, 'To die for Christ, my young friends, is to live.'

Prayer

May we be inspired by the life and death of these martyrs to give our lives in faithful service.

10 OCTOBER

Reflecting God's Presence

Some significant events on this day

Year   Event

1933   The first proven case of commercial airline sabotage occurs when a United Airlines Boeing 247 explodes en route from Cleveland to Chicago.

1971   The rebuilding of London Bridge, in Lake Havasu City, Arizona, is completed. A new London Bridge across the Thames was completed in March 1973 at the same place where the old bridge had stood.

1979   *Pac-man*, destined to become a world-wide craze, is released to the Japanese market by Namco.

Key thought for today

When you're troubled and worried and sick at heart
And your plans are upset and your world falls apart.
Remember God's ready and waiting to share
The burden you find much too heavy to bear.
So, with faith, 'Let Go' and 'Let God' lead the way
Into a brighter and less troubled day.
— Helen Steiner Rice

Reflection

By Matt Breen: These words, 'Brighten the corner where you are', are my gift to you.

> *We cannot all be famous or be listed in Who's Who,*
> *But every person, great or small, has important work to do,*
> *For seldom do we realise the importance of small deeds*
> *Or to what degree of greatness unnoticed kindness leads.*
> *For it's not the big celebrity in a world of fame and praise,*
> *But it's doing unpretentiously in undistinguished ways*
> *The work that God assigns to us, unimportant as it seems,*
> *That makes our task outstanding and brings reality to dreams.*
> *So do not sit and idly wish for wider, new dimensions*
> *Where you can put into practice your many 'Good Intentions',*
> *But at the spot God placed you begin at once to do*
> *Little things to brighten up the lives surrounding you.*
> *For if everybody brightened up the spot on which they're standing*
> *By being more considerate and a little less demanding,*
> *If everybody brightened up the corner where they are,*
> *This dark old world would very soon eclipse the Evening Star.*

Prayer

God, may we learn to let go and let you lead the way. May we not be idle but work conscientiously at the tasks you give us to do. Help us to be aware always of the needs of others and to brighten their days by our kindness, courtesy and consideration. Let me demand more of myself than I expect of others. Amen.

Reflecting God's Presence

Some significant events on this day

Year   Event

1910   Theodore Roosevelt becomes the first US President to fly in a plane.

1968   *Apollo 7*, the first successful Apollo flight with a three-man crew on an 11-day earth orbital mission, is launched.

1999   Filming begins on the very successful *Lord of The Rings* trilogy.

Key thought for today

The day will come when, after harnessing space, the winds, the tides and gravitation, we shall harness for God the energies of love. And on that day, for the second time in the history of the world, we shall have discovered fire.
— Pierre Teilhard de Chardin

Reflection

By Br Bill Firman

The Anglican Church, with its low church to high church variations, has always allowed for more diversity than the Catholic Church, but recent divisions over the issues of women priests and bishops and of gay clergy have left some longing for more solidarity and raised debate on matters once considered certain and clear cut.

The Uniting Church in Australia was born of the amalgamation of various Protestant fellowships including the former Presbyterians. This caused division within the Presbyterian Church that was highlighted in Melbourne by the Continuing Presbyterian Church maintaining ownership and control of the prestige schools Scotch College and Presbyterian Ladies College.

The various Christian denominations were more clearly defined and divided in the Melbourne of my childhood. It was a very sectarian era, with the churches emphasising more what distinguished them from other churches rather than what they had in common. Catholics were urged to marry Catholics and there were only two churches in Melbourne at which 'mixed marriages' were permitted – before a side altar of St Patrick's Cathedral or in the Catholic parish church in South Yarra. Today there are far more options for interfaith marriages, and what unites is emphasised more than sectarian differences. The relationship and interaction between the churches has improved greatly at all levels. The Vatican Council emphasised that the church is the People of God. The church exists not in its buildings, not in rules and practices, but in the faith of the people. We respect the faith of people of other denominations as honest seekers of God.

Schools should be places where young people are offered the gift of the Catholic faith and a disposition of reaching out to all as our brothers and sisters in Christ, with an attitude that is inclusive and uniting, places where honest seekers after truth are nourished on their journeys.

Prayer

Lord, as I try to lead my life well and make this a better world, may I remember what is important as expressed in the words of Henry Van Dyke: 'Be glad of life because it gives you the chance to love and to work and to play and to look up at the stars.'

12 OCTOBER

Reflecting God's Presence

Some significant events on this day

Year	Event
1931	Champion Olympic swimmer Johnny Weissmuller is offered the role of Tarzan; he went on to make 12 movies in that role.
1994	NASA's *Magellan* probe's mission to Venus ends when the spacecraft burns up in the atmosphere of the planet.
2002	Terrorists detonate bombs at the Sari Club and Paddy's Bar in Bali, Indonesia, killing 202 people, many of them Australians, and wounding hundreds more.

Key thought for today

In darkness there is no choice. It is light that enables us to see the differences between things. And it is Christ who gives us light.
— C.T. Whitmell

Reflection

By Sally Buick: Peppe Di Ciccio has already commented on these words of R.L. Stevenson (8 July). Let us reflect on them again, along with a passage from St Matthew's Gospel.

Robert Louis Stevenson wrote

> *That man is a success who has lived well, laughed often, and loved much; who has gained the respect of intelligent people and the love of children; who has filled his niche and accomplished his task; who leaves the world better than he found it, whether by an improved poppy, a perfect poem or a rescued soul, who never lacked appreciation of earth's beauty, or failed to express it; who looked for the best in others and gave the best he had; his memory is a benediction.*

Saint Matthew quotes Jesus:

> *You are the light of the world.*
> *A city built on a hill cannot be hidden.*
> *No one lights a lamp and puts it under a basket;*
> *Instead the lamp is put on a lamp stand,*
> *where it gives light to everyone in the house.*
> *In the same way, your light must shine before all people (5:14-16).*

Both Stevenson and Matthew remind us that we are all here to shine our light. For some of us, this may mean producing a beautiful piece of art, capturing a perfect moment in a photo, playing a musical instrument to bring joy into someone else's life, writing a poem, singing a song, rescuing a soul … Whatever your light may be, my prayer for you is that you give the best you have to give, and that your time at De La Salle has given you the courage, determination and spirit to do so.

Prayer

God, help me to let my light shine. Amen.

Reflecting God's Presence

Some significant events on this day

Year   Event

1792   The cornerstone of the White House is laid in Washington, DC.

1972   An Aeroflot Ilyushin-62 plane crashes near Moscow, killing 176 people.

1972   Thirty-three people out of 45 survive the crash in the Andes of a plane carrying a rugby union team from Uruguay to Chile. By the time two men trekked out, 62 days later, only 16 had survived, after resorting to cannibalism to stay alive.

Key thought for today

Whatever you can do or dream, begin it. Boldness has genius, magic and power in it. Begin it now.
— Goethe

Reflection

By Br Bill Firman

Even saints get discouraged at times and run into problems they never expected. John Baptist de La Salle looked back over his life and realised that some of the difficulties he faced came from prelates, clergy in the church. In fact, De La Salle stated the difficulties were so great his courage would have failed if he had known they lay ahead of him. He wrote:

> *For my part, I own to you that if God had shown me the labours and crosses that were to accompany any good I was to do in founding the Institute, my courage would have failed; and far from undertaking it, I would not have dared to put my hand to the work. A prey to opposition, I have been persecuted even by prelates – by those from whom I had the most right to expect help.*

John Baptist de La Salle established and trained the first Brothers. As a priest, he did not marry and had no children of his own. But, as their father figure, he calls them his 'children'. De La Salle continues on from the above passage:

> *My own children, those whom I begot in Jesus Christ, and cherished with the utmost tenderness, whom I trained with the utmost care, and to whom I looked for great services, rose up against me, and added to exterior trials those interior ones which are so much more acute.*

De La Salle concludes with a statement of faith in the sustaining love of God:

> *In a word, if God had not held out his hand and visibly sustained the edifice, it would long ago have been buried under its own ruins.*

If we really are doing God's work, God may not make it easy but God will help us carry the burden.

Prayer

Grant me a share of the courage and faith of St John Baptist de La Salle, that I might respond with similar generosity when faced with the challenge to help others. Amen.

Some significant events on this day

Year	Event
1066	Duke William of Normandy defeats Harold II of England in the Battle of Hastings and is known henceforth as 'William the Conqueror'.
1947	Chuck Yeager, flying the *Bell X-1*, becomes the first man to fly faster than sound in level flight.
1968	At the Mexico City Olympics, US athlete Jim Hines becomes the first man to break ten seconds in a 100 metres race. His record stood until 1983.

Key thought for today

He truly knows God perfectly that finds him incomprehensible and unable to be known.
— Richard Rolle

Reflection

By Br Bill Firman

Albert Einstein introduced the notion of a space-time continuum. It takes time for light to travel through the vast distances of space. Every time we look at the night sky, we are not only looking into a three-dimensional universe, we are looking back in time. The light from our nearest neighbouring star, Proxima Centauri, left that star 4.2 years ago. Scientists describe Proxima Centauri as 4.2 light years away. A light year is a measure of distance. Proxima Centauri is actually 39.9 trillion kilometres away! The speed of light is 2.99792×10^8 metres per second, commonly stated as 3×10^8 metres per second (or 186,282 miles per second). The circumference of the earth is just on 40,000 km. If we could travel at the speed of light, we would be able to travel around the earth 7.5 times in one second. If we could maintain that incredible speed for 4.2 years, we would reach our nearest star neighbour.

The most distant object in the sky, without a telescope, is the Andromeda Galaxy: the light left there 2.2 million years ago. Again, we are looking back in time. If someone from that galaxy is doing the same as us and sending out signals trying to contact other life in the universe, they would have had to have sent the signal 2.2 million years ago for us to receive it now. Their civilisation would have to be more advanced than ours by at least 2.2 million years. Suppose we received a signal and wanted to reply. Our reply would take 2.2 million years since radio waves travel at the speed of light. It would be a painfully slow conversation!

Hugh Ross, an astrophysicist, has written very persuasively of the philosophical implications of all this:

> *Time is that dimension in which cause and effect phenomena take place ... If time's beginning is concurrent with the beginning of the universe, then the cause of the universe must be some entity operating in a time dimension completely independent of and pre-existent to the time dimension of the cosmos. This conclusion is powerfully important to our understanding of who God is ... It tells us that the creator is transcendent, operating beyond the dimensional limits of the universe. It tells us that God is not the universe itself, nor is God contained within the universe.*

Prayer

God of the universe, I offer you my faithful service in gratitude for all you have made. Amen.

Reflecting God's Presence

Some significant events on this day

Year | Event

1815 | Napoleon I, Emperor of France, begins his exile on the island of St Helena, in the South Atlantic, where he died six years later

1990 | USSR President Mikhael Gorbachev is awarded the Nobel Peace Prize.

2001 | The Cassini-Huygens space probe begins its seven year journey to Titan, one of Saturn's moons.

Key thought for today

Take away love and our earth is a tomb.
— Robert Browning

Reflection

By Joan Ferguson: I believe our perceptions guide our response to others and I pray that you find guidance in this ancient story.

The Greek philosopher Socrates was sitting by the roadside one day, when he was approached by a traveller who was making his way towards Athens. The traveller asked, 'What sort of people live in Athens?'

In response, Socrates asked him, 'What sort of people live in your own town?' 'Awful', the traveller said. 'They are horrible, lying layabouts.'

Socrates replied, 'I am sorry to tell you that you will find the people of Athens to be just the same as you have found your own people.'

Soon, another traveller came by, who also asked, 'What sort of people live in Athens?'

Socrates asked him, 'What sort of people live in your own town?' 'Marvellous people', the second traveller said. 'Kind, generous, friendly, honest people.'

Socrates smiled and said, 'I am pleased to tell you that you will find the people of Athens to be just the same as you have found your own people!'

Prayer

Lord, we come before you as we are.
We ask you to take away from us all
that makes us less than human.
Strengthen us
with the power of your Spirit
that our attitude and outlook may develop,
and our way of looking may become more like yours.
Help us to remain positive –
encouraging and appreciating one another,
looking upon people in the same way that you do. Amen.

16 OCTOBER

Reflecting God's Presence

Some significant events on this day

Year   Event

1978   Polish cardinal, Karol Wojtyla, is elected Pope, choosing the name John Paul II, the first non-Italian pope since Pope Adrian VI in 1523.

1984   Archbishop Desmond Tutu is awarded the Nobel Peace Prize, for his promotion of civil rights and racial equality

1996   More than 80 people are crushed to death when 47,000 soccer fans were squeezed into the 36,000 seat Mateo Flores Stadium in Guatemala City.

Key thought for today

Success in marriage is more than just finding the right person; it is a matter of being the right person.
— Rabbi B.R. Birckner

Reflection

By Br Bill Firman

Helen Rowland once wrote:

'Marriage is like twirling a baton, turning handsprings or eating with chopsticks. It looks so easy till you try it'

As one who has never married, who am I to write about marriage? I have never tried it but I did grow up in a good family with excellent parents. Marriage doesn't look easy to me, as it takes two to make it work. All too often I have witnessed, especially when I was in charge of BoysTown, the effects on children of marriages that have failed and of families where something is badly amiss. Family is the central arena of life for most people. I shall never know if I could make a good marriage and family but I do know what I would be seeking to avoid! The anthropologist Margaret Mead said:

There is no lonelier person than the one who lives with a spouse with whom he or she cannot communicate.

Marriage and family life demands a willingness to share and communicate - easily said but only achievable if there is genuine trust and openness. The best families, if one can make that judgement, are ones in which members are good at communication, rich in basic human respect and noteworthy for a binding loyalty that engenders security and the knowledge that each family member is wanted and loved. Further, for love to grow, there needs to be a climate of understanding of human fragility and a willingness to forgive. A quaint French proverb says:

A good husband should be deaf and a good wife blind.

The central intent of this proverb, I believe, is not to make sexist distinctions – although there may be some implications that I'll leave to the imagination of the reader. Rather, this proverb is succinctly suggesting both partners must have a willingness to overlook faults and not be upset when something is said that is less than kind. We all have our poorly considered and grumpy moments which we regret later.

Prayer

Joseph Barth said, 'Marriage is our last, best chance to grow up.' Help me to find the maturity to commit myself, in sickness and in health, to a person I shall love and cherish for my life time. Amen.

Reflecting God's Presence

Some significant events on this day

Year   Event

1968   At the Mexico Olympics, athletes Tommy Smith and John Carlos protest against discrimination by giving the black power salute from the medal podium. The third man on the podium was Australian 200 metre silver medallist Peter Norman.

1979   Mother Teresa is awarded the Nobel Peace Prize for her services to humanity as leader of the order of the Missionaries of Charity.

2003   At 509 metres when the pinnacle was placed on top and 101 floors above ground, Taipei 101 becomes the world's tallest building, taking over from Kuala Lumpur's Petronas Twin Towers.

Key thought for today

It is not hard to make decisions when you know what your values are.
— Roy Disney

Reflection

By Br Bill Firman

A 17-year-old once described his education in these terms:

I walk into the school and lie down on a conveyor belt. I am carried along, stamped, have pieces cut off me, bits stuck on, am encased in exam certificates and emerge at the other end capable of being top of any profession I go into.

I would like to think the educational process at all schools, not only De La Salle, is actually quite different from a one pace, non-stop conveyor belt carrying along passive participants. Education is more about learning to think and form opinions and judgements based on knowledge, leading students to develop a sound system of values and beliefs. All young persons need a clear system of values and principles if they are to be ready to step out from the security of the protected school environment. The psychologist Lawrence Kohlberg says that it is necessary, as we grow up, 'to transform concepts of rules from external things to internal principles'.

In other words, education must help a child develop a system of values. It is not a case of imposing discipline but of the child coming to know what is right and freely choosing what is right. External pressure may produce conformity for a time but, longer term, a mature moral sense, based on internal principles, must be developed.

The French psychologist, Jean Piaget, lists the following as among the most important transitions a person must make in developing a mature moral sense:

— *a shift from morals based on specific rules to more general conceptions of right and wrong;*
— *a shift from a 'morality of constraint' to a 'morality of co-operation';*
— *an increased ability to perceive rules of the game as based on mutual respect and consent rather than arbitrary edicts;*
— *an increased willingness to take account of the circumstances in which acts occur.*

I think these are very good signposts towards developing a mature moral sense.

Prayer

Lord, give me the moral sense to know what is right and the strength to do what is right. Amen.

18 OCTOBER

Reflecting God's Presence

Some significant events on this day

Year	Event
1851	Herman Melville's *Moby Dick* is published in London. It is recognised as one of the greatest English literary works.
1859	Henri Bergson, later to win the 1927 Nobel Prize for literature and become an influential philosopher, is born in Paris. He died in 1941.
1954	The manufacture of the first transistor radio is announced.
1968	Bob Beamon sets a world record of 8.9 metres (29.2 feet) in the long jump at the Mexico City Olympics, breaking the existing record by 53 centimetres (21 inches). The record stood for 23 years until beaten by Mike Powell who jumped 8.95 metres at the 1991 world championships in Tokyo.

Key thought for today

The eye sees only what the mind is prepared to comprehend.
— Henri Bergson

Reflection

By Br Quentin O'Halloran

Integrity

After the Nazi occupation of France in 1940, Jewish people were forced to wear a visible yellow Star of David, setting them apart from their fellow citizens. Sadly, some French people treated them as outcasts, but not Henri Bergson, a philosopher of international repute and highly respected as a scholar of integrity.

In Paris, the venerable old man, although not a Jew, wore the Star of David with quiet dignity. Asking for no privileges, he lined up in the queues for food and was an embarrassment to the Nazi leaders because of his high standing in Europe.

When influential friends urged him to be careful because of possible arrest, his response was along the following lines: 'I'm unable to do more than wear the Star of David so I'll show my integrity by giving witness and so protesting the injustice to the Jewish people.'

As a philosopher, who taught integrity of thought and action, he also lived his integrity. To let you in on a secret – no trumpets will sound when you take courageous decisions in your life. There will be no clapping or pats on the back. Only in the silence of your soul will you know you are doing the right thing and possess integrity as Henri Bergson did.

Prayer

Lord, may my attitude, and all that I think and say, always be based on a spirit of love and care. As a person of integrity, may I make a difference in my own part of the world by respecting and treating people as individuals. Amen.

Reflecting God's Presence

Some significant events on this day

Year   Event

1954   A significant finding of 'metal fatigue', following the crash of two Comet airliners, leads to improved understanding of air travel safety

1987   The Black Monday crash occurs on Wall Street, wiping 22.6 per cent off the Dow Jones Industrial Average, in dollar terms a loss of $500 billion in one day.

2005   The trial of former Iraq leader Saddam Hussein commences in Baghdad.

Key thoughts for today

Be not afraid of growing slowly. Be afraid only of standing still.
— Chinese proverb

The secret of success is getting started. The secret of getting started is breaking your complex overwhelming tasks into small manageable tasks, and then starting on the first one.
— Mark Twain

Reflection

By Br Bill Firman

Most students, when they come to the end of Year 12, have completed at least 12 years of schooling. In each school year there are some 190 days of school. So each graduating student has been to school about 2280 times. I am reminded of the boy who went to school for the first time and when he came home his mother asked him, 'How did you go?' 'Not too well', he replied, 'I've got to go back again tomorrow.'

School soon, however, becomes a familiar routine, a meeting place with friends, a place where we adapt so that we get along better with others, where we give and take, learn and enquire. I would hope you have come to the end of your secondary schooling knowing that your education is still at the beginning. We never have all the answers: all our lives we continue to learn. In fact, the hunger even increases. At De La Salle you have made a good beginning. I know that because every day I witness an atmosphere of mutual respect between students and teachers, of growing together as brothers and sisters, equally precious before God in the Lasallian way.

Do not expect life to be easy but have faith in your own ability to go forward one step at a time. It is the courage in your heart which will lift you up. When stormy times come, be calm and practical as expressed in the Danish proverb:

Pray to God in the storm, but keep on rowing.

God is with us all the way and will give us the strength we need; but, nonetheless, God expects us to do the rowing.

Prayer

Winston Churchill wrote: 'Kites rise highest against the wind – not with it.' Help me, Lord, to fly high no matter what winds blow in my face in the years ahead.

Some significant events on this day

Year   Event

1803   The US Senate approves a treaty with France who had gained control of Louisiana from Spain in 1801. By this treaty the US purchased Louisiana for $15 million (less than three cents per acre) and doubled the size of the United States.

1827   The Battle of Navarino ends the Greek Liberation War against their Turkish Rulers, marking the beginning of modern Greece.

1955   *The Lord of the Rings,* written by J.R.R. Tolkien, is published.

1973   The Sydney Opera House is opened by Queen Elizabeth II.

Key thought for today

Go confidently in the direction of your dreams. Live the life you have imagined.
— Henry Thoreau

Reflection

By Sandra Troise: Here are some thoughts that I think are good advice.

Love. *I have found the paradox that if I love until it hurts, then there is no hurt, but only more love* (Mother Teresa).

Patience. *Never think that God's delays are God's denials. Hold on, Hold fast, Hold out. Patience is genius* (Comte Georges Louis de Buffon).

Determination. *The great thing in this world is not so much where we are, but in what direction we are moving* (Oliver Wendell Holmes).

Gratitude. *A single grateful thought raised to heaven is the most perfect prayer* (Gotthold Ephraim Lessing).

Humility. *Pride is concerned with who is right. Humility is concerned with what is right* (Ezra Taft Benson).

Forgiveness. *Forgiveness is the answer to the child's dream of a miracle by which what is broken is made whole again, what is soiled is again made clean* (Dag Hammarskjöld).

Peace. *We must come to see that peace is not merely a distant goal we seek, but is a means by which we arrive at that goal. We must pursue peaceful ends through peaceful means* (Martin Luther King Jr).

Prayer

Lord, may I always keep perspective so that I am never too big to apologise or too small to forgive. Amen.

Reflecting God's Presence

Some significant events on this day

Year   Event

1805   Admiral Lord Nelson leads the British fleet to defeat the French and Spanish at the Battle of Trafalgar.

1973   The ear of John Paul Getty III, grandson of the oil billionaire, is cut off by kidnappers and sent to a newspaper.

1978   Australian pilot Frederick Valentich reports seeing a UFO over Bass Straight and then disappears never to be seen again.

Key thought for today

Coming together is a beginning, staying together is progress, and working together is success.
— Henry Ford

Reflection

By Bryan Smith and Felicity MacDonald

The satisfaction of good teamwork

Many people do not realise that the arts, especially the performing arts, as much as sport, rely on good teamwork.

When watching a compelling team game such as footy, rugby, soccer or basketball, it is easy to see the cooperation between players to thwart the opposition, kick or shoot goals, and surge to victory. Seeing coaches, runners and medicos on the sidelines reminds us of the greater team that supports those on the field.

In the same way, the work that goes on in the process of creating a production requires the intricate cooperation of a whole team of players who work towards a common goal. Not only the key players out the front, but all who contribute hours of labour behind the scenes, share in the 'victory' of a successful production.

When we pull together as a team we learn to contribute to a vision, to input ideas, to listen to the ideas of others, to hang on to some things and let go of others. We commit part of ourselves, at the same time learning more about the art of selflessness.

The satisfactions of having made a worthwhile contribution to a team are many.

Prayer

Mahatma Gandhi once said, 'I suppose leadership at one time meant muscles; but today it means getting along with people.' Help me to be a genuine team player who appreciates others and is mutually supportive of all team members. Amen

Some significant events on this day

Year   Event

1797   André-Jacques Garnerin makes the first recorded jump with a silk parachute from 1000 metres above Paris.

1960   Ed Yost flies the first modern manned hot air balloon at an air base in Nebraska.

1975   Sergeant Leonard Matlovich of the US Air Force is discharged after appearing on the cover of *Time* magazine stating he was homosexual.

Key thought for today

It is always spring time in the heart that loves God.
— Saint John Vianney

Reflection

By Br Bill Firman

Pope John XXIII wrote the following when, as Archbishop Roncalli before he became pope, he was appointed Cardinal Patriarch of Venice:

I have been blessed with good physical health and enough common sense to grasp things quickly and clearly; I also have an inclination to love people, which keeps me faithful to the law of the Gospel and respectful of my own rights and those of others. It stops me doing harm to anyone; it encourages me to do good to all.

These words express the simple, holy faith of a wonderful man. Faith does not demand miracles nor command certitude. Faith is the cultivation of our goodness, inspired by the love of God and modelled on the life of Christ. Faith should warm our hearts, not chill our souls.

Saint Teresa of Avila once wrote:

The Lord asks two things of us: love of God and love of our neighbour ... We cannot be sure if we are loving God – though we may have good reasons to think so – whereas we can know if we love our neighbour.

There is always room to become better at loving our neighbour, and thereby our God as well. Many people do not see themselves as very religious, but if they exercise genuine, neighbourly love, they are more religious than they realise. Not all see God clearly but we all see the needs of our neighbours.

Prayer

Lord, keep me respectful of my own rights and those of others. Encourage me to do good to all.

Reflecting God's Presence

Some significant events on this day

Year	Event
1973	US President Richard Nixon agrees to hand over audiotapes of his Oval Office conversations about the Watergate scandal.
2001	The first iPod, a portable hard drive capable of carrying 1000 songs, is released in the USA.
2002	Chechen rebels take 900 people hostage in the House of Culture Theatre in Moscow. When Russian soldiers raided the building two days later, 42 rebels and 130 hostages were killed.

Key thought for today

When I meditate, I clearly see that God is already seated inside my heart.
— Sri Chinmoy

Reflection

By Cathy Loft: I really like this poem by Russell Kelfer. I invite you, too, to think and reflect on these words.

> *You are who you are for a reason.*
> *You're part of an intricate plan.*
> *You're a precious and perfect unique design,*
> *Called God's special woman or man.*
>
> *You look like you look for a reason.*
> *Our God made no mistake.*
> *He knit you together within the womb,*
> *You're just what he wanted to make.*
>
> *The parents you had were the ones he chose,*
> *And no matter how you may feel,*
> *They were custom-designed with God's plan in mind*
> *And they bear the Master's seal.*
>
> *No, that trauma you faced was not easy,*
> *And God wept that it hurt you so,*
> *But it was allowed to shape your heart*
> *So that into his likeness you'd grow.*
>
> *You are who you are for a reason,*
> *You've been formed by the Master's rod*
> *you are who you are, beloved,*
> *Because there is a God!*

Prayer

Henry Thoreau said: 'Live your beliefs and you can turn the world around.' God, help me to live with belief in myself knowing I am made and loved by you. Amen.

24 OCTOBER

Reflecting God's Presence

Some significant events on this day

Year   Event

1929   On this day, 'Black Thursday' on the New York Stock Exchange, stocks fall leading to the Great Depression.

1945   The five founding United Nations members ratify the UN Charter in Washington, DC.

1973   The Yom Kippur War between Israel and a number of Arab nations ends.

2003   Supersonic passenger air travel comes to an end, with the Concorde making its last commercial flight from New York to London.

Key thought for today

We must not only give what we have; we must also give what we are.
— Désiré Joseph Mercier

Reflection

By Brian Long

It's great to be able to give. It's great to be in a relationship where another is able to receive one's gift. I know that when I'm giving, I am most fully alive. To be myself, I need to give.

What is it that makes giving such a joy? It is because we are made in the image of the God whose love is continually pouring out on all of us.

De La Salle says in his *Meditations* that

The greatest joy in your life is to proclaim the Gospel free of charge ... solely for the love of God (207.2).

This is the basis of the Lasallian value of *gratuity*. To proclaim the Gospel is not just to speak words, it is to be the face of the loving God to the people we meet each day in our lives and work. The challenge is to offer this open-hearted, open-handed love to all without discrimination or reserve and without expectation of reward.

To act out of gratuity means to empty oneself of ego, of acting in such a way as to meet one's own needs for fulfilment or control or whatever. De La Salle's life is one of just such emptying – of his position as Canon of Rheims, of his status, of the wealth that set him apart from his Brothers because it gave him a security which they did not have. He described this abandonment to Providence as being like the situation of 'a man who puts himself out on the high sea without sails or oars' (*Meditations* 134.1).

Prayer

God of gratuitous love, fill me with your own open heart so that I can be generous and open-handed to all those I meet. Let me set sail on open seas with faith. Amen.

Reflecting God's Presence

Some significant events on this day

Year   Event

1415   King Henry V of England defeats the French at the Battle of Agincourt in France.

1936   The Rome-Berlin Axis agreement is signed by the respective German and Italian leaders, Adolf Hitler and Benito Mussolini.

2003   A lost deer hunter, Sergio Martinez, sets a fire to signal for help. Driven by desert winds, the fire became the largest wildfire in California's history. The Cedar Fire, as it has since been called, destroyed 2232 homes, burned out 109,000 hectares and resulted in the deaths of 15 people.

Key thought for today

Work and love – these are the basics. Without them there is neurosis.
— Theodor Reik

Reflection

By Br Bill Firman

When one applies for jobs time and again and is found wanting, it is most discouraging. Long-term unemployment destroys the human spirit. I was intrigued to read this in a prayer of Pope John Paul II:

> *We entrust to you all people, beginning with the weakest: the babies yet unborn, and those born into poverty and suffering, the young in search of meaning, the unemployed, and those suffering hunger and disease. We entrust to you all troubled families, the elderly with no one to help them, and all who are alone and without hope.*

The Pope said he was beginning with the weakest. Whom did he then list third and fourth? – 'the young in search of meaning, the unemployed'. Although Australia is currently in one of its most prosperous periods with a strong economy and generally low unemployment, youth unemployment is a very significant problem and in some areas is as high as 22 per cent. It is a mistake to think young people do not want to work. I have often witnessed the real joy of young persons when they find jobs, when they gain the dignity of supporting themselves, when they no longer have to depend on social security. Henry Ford once said wisely:

> *There is joy in work. There is no happiness except in the realisation that we have accomplished something.*

There is no greater gift to a child than security and love. There is no greater gift to a hungry person than to appease that hunger. There is no greater gift to a cold and homeless person than the gift of shelter. There is no greater gift to the unemployed than the dignity that comes with a job and the capacity to earn a living. Work helps us to feel we matter. Work brings the joy of a meaningful existence. Every unemployed person who crosses the divide from receiver of a social security benefit to contributor through taxation builds a stronger Australian society, not just economically but in terms of the self-worth of the individual citizens.

It is well known that youth crime rates drop when youth unemployment drops. Yes, there are some lazy people who don't want to work but there are many more who want to work if only they had the opportunity.

Prayer

God of opportunity, help me to find a suitable pathway to make my contribution to the society in which I live. Amen.

Some significant events on this day

Year   Event

1958   Pan American Airways flies the first direct commercial flight from New York to Paris, using a Boeing 707.

1977   The last case of smallpox is diagnosed in Somalia. After this, the World Health Organisation declared the disease to be officially eradicated.

1994   The leaders of Jordan and Israel, with President Clinton in attendance, sign a peace treaty ending 46 years of war.

Key thought for today

The Eucharist is the means whereby those who once received the Spirit in baptism are constantly renewed in the Spirit until their life's end.
— Alan Richardson

Reflection

By St John Baptist de La Salle

Jesus Christ told his apostles that it was better for them that he was leaving. Those who have given themselves to God often believe that God's sensible presence is the only thing that can confirm them in piety. They think that when they experience interior difficulty and dryness they have completely lost the degree of holiness to which God has raised them. Having lost a certain relish for prayer and a facility for praying, they imagine that they have lost everything and that God has completely rejected them. Their inner life is desolate and they suppose that all the paths leading to God are blocked before them.

Such persons should be told what Jesus Christ said to his apostles, that it is better for them that God withdraws from them on a feeling level, and that what they consider a loss is for them a real gain if they willingly endure this trial (Meditations for Feasts, 4th Sunday after Easter).

Some fear to receive Communion because they are convinced, falsely, that they obtain no benefit from it, and that it is an abuse to go so often without any profit for the good of their soul. Do they count for nothing the fact that Communion preserves them from mortal sin? This is without doubt a priceless favour which should make you desire to receive Communion every day.

But, you may say, as others do, this sacrament contains the essence of holiness, and demands great holiness in those who receive it so often. To reason in this way is to mistake the effect and purpose of this sacrament for what is merely the preparation. We go to Communion to become holy, not because we are holy.

If you were to say that you need to be a saint in order to live in community, you would be told that people come to religious life to become saints, not because they are saints. Is not the union with Jesus Christ capable of making you share in his holiness? This is precisely the reason why you should receive Communion often (Meditations for Sundays and Feasts).

Prayer

Lord Jesus, we thank you for the gifts you have given us to help us follow you. Amen.

Reflecting God's Presence

Some significant events on this day

Year   Event

1728   James Cook, later to become a significant sea captain, is born on this day.

1904   The New York subway, the biggest in the USA, is opened.

1973   The 1.4 kg Canon City meteorite, made of chondrite, comes to earth in Colorado, USA.

Key thought for today

The greatest discovery of my generation is that human beings can alter their lives by altering their attitude of mind.

— William James

Reflection

By Br Bill Firman

One of the very influential writers of the late 19th century was the American pragmatist philosopher and psychologist William James (1842–1910). Many of his conclusions I disagree with but some of his aphorisms are very clever in their pithy content and aptness of description of human behaviour.

A clever statement of James', which may be true, is:

> *A great many people think they are thinking when they are really rearranging their prejudices.*

One of his genuinely insightful statements, which I believe and have often quoted to parents, is:

> *The art of being wise is the art of knowing what to overlook.*

Very sound advice when dealing with the uncertain and sometimes mischievous behaviour of children.

Montaigne counselled much the same when he said:

> *Wise people see as much as they ought, not as much as they can.*

Of course, how we act towards others often relates to how we feel at the time. It helps if we can develop consistent good humour and an underlying cheerful attitude. I have often given this advice to students:

> *Too many people get up in the morning and start acting the way they feel – which is pretty miserable. But if they consciously act the way they want to feel, they soon start feeling that way. So act happy and you will begin to feel more cheerful.*

Prayer

Lord, help me to think positive so that I might be positive. Help me to act the way I want to feel.

Some significant events on this day

Year   Event

1886   The Statue of Liberty, a gift from France to the USA, is dedicated by President Grover Cleveland.

1948   Swiss chemist Paul Muller is awarded the Nobel Prize in Chemistry for his discovery of the insecticidal properties of DDT.

1962   The Cuban Missile Crisis ends with the USSR promising to dismantle its bases in Cuba.

Key thought for today

A laugh is like a love affair in that it carries a man completely off his feet; a laugh is like a creed or a church in that it asks that a man should trust himself to it.
— G.K. Chesterton

Reflection

By Br Bill Firman

Martin Luther once said:

> *If you're not allowed to laugh in heaven, I don't want to go there."*

Laughter provides moments of happiness to be enjoyed, as if we were in heaven. Everybody likes people who laugh a lot. Not long after I became a principal, a teacher came to inspect the homework of the students in his class. When he came to his own son, who was in the class, he found that the boy had not done his homework. The teacher sent his son to me with a note saying he had not done his homework. I had serious reservations about the willingness of this teacher to fulfil normal responsibilities, so I sent the boy back to him with a note to his parents saying they needed to make sure their son did his homework!

Jewish accumulated wisdom is well summed up in the Yiddish proverb:

> *What soap is to the body, laughter is to the soul.*

When things go wrong, it often helps to see the funny side. My memories of growing up include making plenty of mistakes but the normal reaction of my parents was to see the funny side. They never got too uptight about what I might call 'teenage human error'. There were never threats of big punishment or heavy sanctions. They laughed with their children mostly, not at us.

Herbert Hoover described children, drily but correctly, in economic terms: 'Children are our most valuable natural resource.' The message that I consistently received was that nothing was more precious to my parents than their children. Being at home was good humour and good fun. Milton Berle called laughter 'an instant vacation'. Henry Ward Beecher gave very good advice when he said:

> *Laughter is God's medicine. Everybody ought to bathe in it.*

Prayer

Thank you, God, for the blessed gift of laughter. I'm sure we give you great entertainment!

Reflecting God's Presence

Some significant events on this day

Year	Event
1863	Agreement is reached at an international conference in Geneva, Switzerland, to form the Red Cross.
1929	The New York Stock Exchange crashes, causing mass panic, the loss of millions of dollars and acting as the trigger that started The Great Depression.
1991	The *Galileo* spacecraft becomes the first probe to reach an asteroid, photographing Gaspra.
1998	John Glenn was the first American to orbit the earth on 20 February 1962. Thirty-six years later, aged 77, Glenn and seven other crew on the shuttle *Discovery* return to space for nine days, orbiting the earth 134 times. This made Glenn the oldest person to go into space.
2004	On Arabic Al Jazeera TV, a video of Osama bin Laden is shown in which he admits direct responsibility for the September 11, 2001, attacks on New York.

Key thought for today

Change has a considerable psychological impact on the human mind. To the fearful it is threatening because it means that things may get worse. To the hopeful it is encouraging because things may get better. To the confident it is inspiring because the challenge exists to make things better.

— King Whitney Jr

Reflection

By Marty Mahy

If I were to offer something for Year 12 students to depart with, it would be the idea of change — how much does one have to change oneself in order to get to where one should be.

Brain research tells us that a teenager has an undeveloped frontal cortex, so rational thinking is inhibited and emotions dominate. As we grow into our twenties we are able to think more rationally. This needs to be consciously worked on. We need to get to the point where we make our big decisions in life by standing back and weighing up the whole picture. No rushing in. No knee-jerk reactions. No spitting the dummy!

I have to admit that I was about 30 when I finally cottoned on to the idea of changing myself into somebody better. Don't waste as much time as we did before we got on to the job! The most important thing in life for most of us is our relationship with those close to us. To get this to work (we remember that the divorce rate is currently some 45 per cent), we cannot afford to stay the same person we were when leaving school after Year 12.

Prayer

Andy Warhol (1928–1987) once wrote that 'they say time changes things, but you actually have to change them yourself'. Lord, help me to make the changes I need to in order to become the best that I can be. Amen.

30 OCTOBER

Reflecting God's Presence

Some significant events on this day

Year	Event
1918	World War I ends in the Middle East when the Ottoman Empire signs an armistice with the Allies.
1974	Muhammad Ali knocks out George Foreman in the 'Rumble in the Jungle' in Zaire, regaining the world heavyweight boxing title.
1975	After the death of long-serving ruler General Francisco Franco, Prince Juan Carlos officially becomes Spain's acting head of state.

Key thought for today

Someone asked Maurice Chevalier on his eightieth birthday: 'How do you feel?'
'Pretty good', he replied, 'when you consider the alternatives.'

Reflection

By Br Bill Firman

The adult Christian is called to be solid in his or her faith. St Paul in his letter to the people of Ephesus says:

> *Then we shall not be children any longer, or tossed one way and another and carried along by every wind of doctrine, at the mercy of all the tricks people play and their cleverness in practising deceit. If we live by the truth and in love, we shall grow in all ways into Christ (Ephesians 4:11).*

We all know elderly people who are wonderfully integral, fulfilled persons who have grown in truth and in love. As they approach the end of their lives, they seem complete. They have grown into Christ and are ready, as much as it is possible, to meet their Maker. St Thomas More was such a man, even though death came early for him. On the other hand, there are people who fear to let go of life. Queen Elizabeth I, for example, after a long reign from 1558 to 1603, experienced great remorse and despair at the end of her life. With all her power, she could not halt the approach of death. None of us can.

As the poet James Shirley has said:

> *Sceptre and crown*
> *Must tumble down*
> *And in the dust be equal made*
> *With the poor crooked scythe and spade.*

We are all 'equalised' at the point of death – but not afterwards! It is well to keep in mind the oft-quoted question posed by Jesus in one of his parables:

> *What does it profit us if we gain the whole world but suffer the loss of our own soul?*

Yet, since the love of God is limitless, we should never lose hope. We are not just depending on our own will power and efforts: we have a loving God wanting to reach out and help us.

Prayer

A Greek proverb says: 'To die well is the chief part of virtue.' Help me to live well so that I may be ready to die well when the time inevitably comes.

Reflecting God's Presence

31 OCTOBER

Some significant events on this day

Year	Event
1876	More than 100,000 people are killed when a tidal wave engulfs the Magna River Delta in India. A further 100,000 died from the ensuing disease.
1941	After 14 years of work, drilling is finally completed to create the giant faces on Mt Rushmore, South Dakota.
1999	Egypt Air flight 990 from New York to Cairo crashes into the Atlantic Ocean just south of Nantucket Island, Massachusetts, killing all 217 on board.

Key thought for today

Convictions are the mainsprings of action, the driving powers of life. What a man lives are his convictions.
— Bishop Francis Kelly

Reflection

By Br Bill Firman

World War II began on 1 September 1939. Just over two years into that war, on 29 October 1941, the British Prime Minister Sir Winston Churchill returned to Harrow, the school he had attended as a boy, to speak to the students. The popular myth is that Churchill stood before the students and said, 'Never, ever, ever, ever, ever, ever, give up. Never give up. Never give up. Never give up.' And then he sat down.

In reality, he made a complete speech that included words similar to ones often quoted above. Before speaking, Churchill discovered that the students had added a verse to one of the school songs, in his honour:

Not less we praise in darker days / The leader of our nation.

Churchill commented:

You sang here a verse of a school song written in my honor, which I was very greatly complimented by. But there is one word in it I want to alter. 'Not less we praise in darker days.' Do not let us speak of darker days: let us speak rather of sterner days. These are not dark days; these are great days – the greatest days our country has ever lived – and we must all thank God that we have been allowed, each of us according to our station, to play a part in making these days memorable in the history of our race.

'Never give up' is good advice in most circumstances. It is amazing what can be achieved with persistence. The distinction between darker and sterner is also well made. What may appear as a dark danger can often be no more than a stern test - greatness and glory may be achieved by overcoming such challenges.

Prayer

God, give me the courage never to give up when faced with stern tests, but simply to do my best with conviction and persistence. Amen.

Some significant events on this day

Year   Event

1512   The 5120 square metre ceiling of the Sistine Chapel, painted by Michelangelo and begun in July 1508, is exhibited to the public for the first time.

1755   A massive earthquake strikes Lisbon, Portugal, leading to fires and tsunamis that kill an estimated 100,000 people.

1986   The Rhine River turns red, killing millions of fish, as a fire in a factory near Basel, Switzerland, causes tons of toxic chemicals to spill into the river.

1993   The Maastricht Treaty comes into effect, creating the European Union.

Key thought for today

The glory of God is men and women fully alive.
— Saint Irenaeus

Reflection

By Paul Marshall

Today is the feast of All Saints, a feast day instituted in the early church to honour and commemorate 'the holy apostles and all the saints, martyrs and confessors, and all the just made perfect who are at rest throughout the world'.

When I was a boy in a Catholic boarding school, each evening meal began with a reading from the *Lives of the Saints* or from *The Roman Martyrology*. These readings were always stirring and edifying accounts of lives lived in an exemplary manner, often heroically – sometimes to the point of giving up one's life for one's faith. These were the stories of good people who had been formally canonised by the church, officially declared to be saints.

But there came a time when it occurred to me to wonder why we also did not hear about the lives of 'ordinary' people, folks like my grandfather Bartholomew, who lived through two world wars in Belgium and made many sacrifices to keep his family together, and who sheltered downed Allied pilots in the barns of his farm behind enemy lines, at great personal peril. I thought about all the other students in that dining room and the lives of their deceased relatives, people who had lived good lives. How many stories of goodness and saintliness were we missing out on? Let us remember today all those whose lives have enriched and blessed others, the known and the unrecognised – all saints in their own right.

Prayer

Let us now sing the praises of famous men and women, our ancestors in their generations. The Lord apportioned to them great glory, his majesty from the beginning ... All these were honored in their generations, and were the pride of their times. But of others there is little memory, and some have perished as though they had never been born. But these also were godly men and women, whose righteous deeds have not been forgotten; their offspring will continue forever, and their glory will never be blotted out. Their bodies are buried in peace, but their name lives on, generation after generation. (Ecclesiaticus 44:1-10, 13, 14).

Reflecting God's Presence

Some significant events on this day

Year   Event

          All Souls' Day – the traditional church day to remember and pray for the dead.

1950   The death of George Bernard Shaw, the only writer to be awarded the Nobel Prize and an Oscar.

1963   South Vietnamese President Ngo Dinh Diem is assassinated after a military coup.

2000   The first crew – two Russians and two Americans – arrive at the International Space Station where they will live for four months.

Key thought for today

What really flatters a man is that you think him worth flattering.
— George Bernard Shaw

Reflection

By Br Bill Firman

The long-lived, irascible playwright and good-humoured commentator on life, George Bernard Shaw, wrote:

> *I was taught when I was young that if people would only love one another, all would be well in the world. This seemed simple and very nice; but I found when I tried to put it into practice not only that other people were seldom lovable but that I was not very lovable myself.*

It is, of course, the Gospel imperative that we should love one another: Jesus told us to love one another as he, Jesus, has loved us. The trouble is that none of us is perfect. People can be greedy, selfish, insensitive and blinded by the pursuit of power or money. Our human weakness does get in the way. If it gets in the way too much, then our greed, our anger, our desire to acquire, can become sinful, a serious disorder. Shaw also said:

> *The worst sin towards our fellow creatures is not to hate them but to be indifferent to them; that's the essence of inhumanity.*

There is no irony here – just a very insightful observation that it is sinful human behaviour to ignore other people and their needs. People are made to care for other people. He uses strong words concerning deliberate indifference to others, calling it 'the essence of inhumanity'. Elsewhere he expressed a kindred sentiment:

> *Silence is the most perfect expression of scorn.*

It does sound simple to love other people and for them to love us. That is something to look forward to in heaven. In this life we may be disappointed but should not be surprised at the selfishness or indifference of others. Other desires get in the way, especially desire for money, sex or power.

Shaw says other people are seldom loveable. In my experience, 'loving one another' is more common that that. I would say rather that other people are 'often lovable' but then, compared with Shaw, I think I have led a more sheltered life. Deliberately!

Prayer

Help me never to give up on trying to love other people, even when I disappoint myself. Amen.

Some significant events on this day

Year   Event

1954   The first *Godzilla* movie is released in Japan.

1957   *Sputnik II* is launched by the USSR, carrying a dog called Laika, the first animal to enter space.

1966   After weeks of wet weather in Northern Italy and water being released from over-filling dams, the Arno River breaks its banks, flooding Florence for three days up to depths of 6.7 metres, the highest water levels since 1333. Close to 150 people drowned and many art treasures were damaged.

Key thought for today

When it is dark enough, you can see the stars.
— Charles A. Beard

Reflection

By Br Bill Firman

There is an old English proverb that strikes a chord with our experience in drought-stricken Australia. It says:

'We never know the worth of water until the well is dry.'

This proverb refers to far more than water, of course. It's a comment on our tendency to take other people and things for granted. When we live with a full larder, we forget what it is like to be hungry; if we have loving family and friends, we forget what it is like to be lonely; and, literally, if we are short of water, it affects us significantly – as we have come to understand. If we had always lived with drought, we would not miss abundant water so much but we do tend to make our judgements in the light of past experiences and present conditions. If we are strong enough, past experience, even the most unpleasant variety, may teach us and be a step on the road to greater wisdom. Abraham Lincoln once wryly remarked that 'The best thing about the future is that it comes only one day at a time.' Yet the future also depends on a longer-term view. The most important steps are the achievement of secure accommodation, a regular income and loyal family or friends. These are the things most people take for granted. These are the metaphorical 'water' that we do not appreciate until the 'well is dry' – until we face life without them.

Too many people, in this era of high property prices, cannot find rental properties at the lower end of the market. Too many cannot hold down a permanent job because they lack confidence or qualifications. Too many are lonely. That is where many social problems begin. The water crisis is something we must face and adapt to. It is similar with the developing shortage of oil. There will be a solution if we look forward and create one. We won't find an answer simply by longing for the way things were. George Bernard Shaw expressed this notion when he said: 'Life isn't about finding yourself. Life is about creating yourself'.

A problem is simply an opportunity to be creative and a challenge to adapt.

Prayer

Lord, help me to recognise that there will always be problems. Give me the courage to change, adapt and be creative in building my personal future. Amen.

Reflecting God's Presence

Some significant events on this day

Year   Event

1899   Sigmund Freud's *The Interpretation of Dreams* is published. It took eight years to sell 600 copies.

1956   Nikita Khrushchev, leader of the USSR, sends Soviet forces into Hungary to crush the uprising that began on 23 October.

1995   Israeli Premier Yitzhak Rabin is shot and dies after attending a peace rally in Tel Aviv.

Key thought for today

A Christian is someone who shares the sufferings of God in the world.
— Dietrich Bonhoeffer

Reflection

By Patrick Jurd

Are you a disciple or an admirer?

In 1942, Clarence Jordan and his wife and another couple moved to a farm in Americus, Georgia, and called it Koinonia, which is the Greek New Testament word for 'communion' or 'community'. They started trying to do something about rural southern poverty. They practised racial equality and integration in the Deep South in the heyday of the Ku Klux Klan. They were pacifists in the middle of the Second World War. They lived communally when the Cold War with communism was gearing up, and they chose to live a very simple life during history's greatest expansion of consumer materialism. They were firebombed, shot at, vandalised, cross-burned, persecuted, prosecuted, threatened, excommunicated, boycotted and nearly driven out of Georgia.

One of the things they needed a lot of was legal help. Clarence went to his brother Robert, a lawyer, and asked him to represent Koinonia Farm. Robert said, 'Clarence, you know I can't do that. You know I'm going into politics. If I represented you, I'd lose everything. It's different for you.' Clarence said, 'Why is it different for me? You and I were baptised and joined the church on the same Sunday when we were boys. The preacher asked us both the same question, "Do you accept Jesus Christ as your Lord and Saviour?" I said, "Yes." What did you say, Robert?' Robert said, 'Clarence, I follow Jesus up to a point.' Clarence said, 'Would that point by any chance be the cross?' And Robert said, 'That's right. I follow him to the cross, but not on the cross. I am not going to get crucified.'

'Then I don't believe you are a disciple. You're an admirer of Jesus, but not a disciple of his. I think you ought to go back to the church you belong to, and tell them you're an admirer not a disciple.' Robert later was elected a state senator, and eventually he became a Justice of the Supreme Court of the State of Georgia. Clarence just went on being Clarence Jordan.

Where do you put yourself – disciple or admirer?

Prayer

God, help me not to just stand back and admire but to be in there doing. Amen.

5 NOVEMBER

Reflecting God's Presence

Some significant events on this day

Year   Event

1605   The Gunpowder Plot is foiled when Guy Fawkes is discovered under the English Houses of Parliament preparing to light a long fuse. Fawkes was later executed.

1955   The rebuilt Vienna State Opera re-opens after being destroyed in 1945 during the war.

2003   NASA announces that the *Voyager 1* space probe, launched in 1977, had travelled 13 billion kilometres, further than any other artificial object and had 'reached the end of the solar system'.

Key thought for today

Science without religion is lame, religion without science is blind.
— Albert Einstein

Reflection

By Br Bill Firman

World War II General, Omar Bradley, expressed the danger of scientific advancement in these terms:

> *We have too many people of science, too few people of God. We have grasped the mystery of the atom, and rejected the Sermon on the Mount. The world has achieved brilliance without wisdom, power without conscience.*

One problem with scientific advancement is the tendency to think that because we have discovered how to do something, we should do it. There needs to be first, however, a meeting of science and ethics.

Just because we discover how to clone a person, for example, does not mean we should do so. The field of bio-ethics is riddled with such dilemmas. Science now provides the technology for the sex of a baby to be identified before it is born. One consequence in countries of high population where there is a policy of one child per family is the practice of the selection of male children – leading to population imbalance.

Choosing the sex of one's baby, cryogenic preservation, assisting the survival and fertility of people with chromosomal or genic deficiencies, are among the modern ethical dilemmas. Science makes it possible but the moral question is still relevant: 'Should we?'

These moral questions are often loaded with emotional overtones. In earlier eras, for example, most albino people died by the age of 15. Now, with medical help, they often live on into their thirties and are quite capable of having children. But should they, given that it is highly likely the child will be albino? It has long been a dilemma of what to permit with mentally retarded people, who have identified genetic defects but who can be sexually mature and fertile. It is possible that they can have children, but should they be permitted to do so?

Unfortunately, scientific development has sometimes outstripped the development of a moral framework. Because science can do something does not mean it should be done.

Prayer

God, help me to consider honestly the difference between 'can we' and 'should we'.

Reflecting God's Presence

Some significant events on this day

Year   Event

1860   Abraham Lincoln is elected as the 16th President of the United States, the first Republican president. The anti-slavery stance of his party soon led to the secession of the southern states.

1963   Daniel Mannix, Irish-born Catholic Archbishop of Melbourne from 1912 to 1963, dies, aged 99.

1999   An Australian referendum to become a republic with a president rather than a monarchy is defeated 55 per cent against, 45 per cent for.

Key thought for today

If one of the brothers or one of the sisters is in need of clothes and has not enough food to live on, and you say to them, 'I wish you well; keep yourself warm and eat plenty', without giving them these bare necessities of life, then what good is that? Faith is like that: if good works do not go with it, it is quite dead.

— Letter of Saint James (2:15-18)

Reflection

By Br Bill Firman

'All people are equal.' Are they? Equality is one of the most overstated notions of our modern society. Yes, it is true to say all people are precious to God and all people deserve to be respected and to be loved. My whole life as a Brother is premised on the notion that one treats everyone else as a brother or sister, equally precious in the eyes of God as I am.

The starting premise of faith, however, is not that all people are equal. We are not equal in talents nor are we self-made. Our basic faith is that we are created by God and what each of us has is a gift from God – and let us be honest: some are given greater gifts and some lesser gifts.

Then there is the matter of what we do with our gifts. Some have schooled themselves to have greater knowledge and some haven't bothered so much. Some have developed their talents well and some have neglected to do so. The opinion of the well-educated person is worth more than the opinion of the person who has not researched or studied the issue. It is rarely true that 'my opinion is as good as yours' unless both persons are equally informed and equally skilled at analysing – and this is most often not the case.

How are we using our gifts? That is the proper question. Some people need clothes, food, warmth, shelter – basic requirements for living which many of us take for granted. Are we moved to help these people? Do we merely talk about doing good, or do we actually try to assist others?

Prayer

God, help me recognise my gifts so that I may use them to assist others. Amen.

Some significant events on this day

Year Event

1861 Archer wins the very first Melbourne Cup horse race.

1917 Bolshevik revolutionaries led by Vladimir Lenin seize power in Petrograd. It is called the October Revolution, since it came in October according to the Julian calendar, which was still in use in Russia at that time.

1997 Chinese engineers complete the cofferdam across the Yangtze River, diverting it to begin construction of the Three Gorges Dam, which will be the world's biggest hydroelectric power station when fully operational in 2011.

Key thought for today

That man is richest whose pleasures are cheapest.
— Henry David Thoreau

Reflection

By Hanna Dwyer

Mexico City is overcast. It is foggy, it is humid, it is busy ...

There are mothers cooking – homemade *tortilla*, *fajitas*, *quesadillas* – in the street. They are only 20 cents. It's 1.00 am. They are in the street, tired, but making sure they make enough money for the family. The food tastes so good – it's fresh, it's chilli, it's cooked with love.

Here hot water is a treat. Grandson Jadeo, 17, is hand washing the clothes in a rusted old sink. Granddaughter Meril, 17, is washing the floors, on hands and knees, a cloth with hot water and soap. Mamma Altergracias is in the kitchen cooking, up since 5.00 am making sure there is enough food for the day to feed her babes and amigos who come and go until nightfall. There's only one flame and a few odd pots and pans. She is tired.

We sit and we watch, feeling far from home. The *casa*, four walls, one bedroom, a kitchen, bathroom, seven people. Basic, damp and cold when it rains, but it is home – the door is always open and everyone is welcome. I like their home, it is held up with laughter. The other kids are in the street playing soccer. Many cannot afford education or have the guidance to endure life outside their suburb. They learn in the home and they learn on the streets, wiser than their years.

A place of simple pleasures, few commodities, yet a place of many smiles. They share the little they have, and go the end to find what they don't have for others. Our society is rich, yes, with money, in comparison, but in terms of richness these people are kings and queens. They have knowledge of their people, their country, and are rich with love and draped in jewels of happiness. Viva la Mexico!

Prayer

Mark Twain said: 'Whoever is happy will make others happy, too.' Thank you for the riches happy people share, even when they are economically poor. Amen.

Reflecting God's Presence

Some significant events on this day

Year   Event

1793   The Louvre, originally established as the royal residence of King Francis I, is opened to the public as a museum.

1895   William Röntgen discovers the radiation he calls X-rays.

1965   The first episode of the long running US series *Days of Our Lives* debuts.

1976   Birthday of Brett Lee, cricketer.

Key thought for today

We must not only give what we have; we must also give what we are.
— Letter of Saint James (2:15-18)

Reflection

By Sally Buick

You have all lived through years of being taught English. For most of you, this would not have been the case were it not compulsory. Along the way, however, you have learnt a few things. You can read and write, most of you have a capacity to put together a strong argument; you can debate, console, exclaim, exalt and entice.

You have survived Shakespeare, taught alongside Lockie Leonard; you have learnt that Greek Tragedy has a chorus and that Chaucer's tales were at times quite delicious. We have talked with you about the 'big issues' – love, death, war, family, guilt, grief, courage – and you have delighted, surprised, entertained and shocked us. These are the things that will remain with us.

The power to use language well is a gift you will never be able to repay. Your English teachers have altered your lives by making you speak in public when you were fearful, insisting that you write essay after essay to expand your vocabulary, encouraging you to write personal reflections and ensuring you can construct a rounded point of view.

These skills will enable you to be the best in an interview, to thrill your lecturers at uni, to win the great debate at the dinner table and, most importantly, to woo a friend. Remember once in a while to think fondly of those who stood before you undefeated by your repeated cries of 'but why do we have to read books?' and thank them silently for all the gifts they have given you.

My prayer for you is that, unlike Alfieri, you don't 'settle for half'; that like Stephen Blackpool you become a someone 'of perfect integrity'; that for you, unlike John and Valerie, 'love is enough', and that you know that in order to live you must be 'engaged'.

Prayer

God, help me to appreciate the gifts I have received and to use them well. Amen.

9 NOVEMBER

Reflecting God's Presence

Some significant events on this day

Year   Event

1799   Napoleon Bonaparte, just returned from Egypt, becomes French leader in a coup.
1888   Jack the Ripper kills his last known victim, Mary Jane Kelly, ending a brutal nine-week period in London.
1921   Albert Einstein is awarded the Nobel Prize for Physics.
1984   Birthday of Delta Goodrem, singer and songwriter.

Key thought for today

Holy communion is the shortest and safest way to heaven.
— Pope Saint Pius X

Reflection

By Br Bill Firman

Many young people find the celebration of the Eucharist boring. So do many adults. But I have a strong conviction that the Eucharist is indeed a special gift from the God-man that demands our participation and fidelity no matter what our preference is for a particular style of prayer and no matter how uninspiring the ritual presented in a particular Mass may be.

In the sixth chapter of St John's Gospel, Jesus is talking to his disciples about the Eucharist. He is very explicit. First he claims to have come down from heaven. Then , 'At this, the Jews began grumbling at him ...'

Jesus then claims: 'I myself am the living bread which came down from heaven and if anyone eats this bread that person will live forever ...'

The reaction of the disciples is sceptical: 'This led to a fierce argument among the Jews, some of them saying, 'How can this man give us his body to eat?'

Christ's response is to repeat the statement twice more that 'whoever eats this bread will live forever.'

Again there is scepticism: 'This is hard teaching indeed: who could accept that?' Jesus does not then soften or water down his teaching. He simply asserts again this clear imperative with the result: 'As a consequence of this, many of the disciples withdrew and no longer followed him.'

Again the reaction of Jesus is revealing. He doesn't call them back but turns to the apostles and says: 'And are you too wanting to go away?'

Peter replies: 'Lord, who else would we go to? Your words have the ring of eternal life.'

The Eucharist is so great a gift that it has always been central to Christianity, our strongest way of praying. It is both the symbol and challenge of our faith.

Prayer

Lord, your words have the ring of eternal life. Help me to be faithful to your teaching. Amen.

Reflecting God's Presence

10 NOVEMBER

Some significant events on this day

Year Event

1928 Prince Hirohito is crowned the 124th Emperor of Japan, reigning 61 years until his death in 1989.

1991 After an international boycott of 21 years, imposed in protest at apartheid, South Africa resumes test cricket.

1995 Massive avalanches near Everest cause the death of 56 people.

Key thought for today

A great war leaves the country with three armies – an army of cripples, an army of mourners, and an army of thieves.
— German Proverb

Reflection

By Br Bill Firman

My dad Jim fought in the First World War. He was brought up on a farm and could ride a horse. I guess that is why he joined the horse-drawn artillery. The soldiers, Corporal Jim included, would drag the cannon into place and it was Jim's job to sit on the front and aim at the enemy.

One fateful day during the Great War, a Turkish pilot flew overhead in one of those primitive biplanes that were modern for the day and shot Jim – with a handgun. The bullet just missed his heart. So I very nearly didn't make it into life at all! That single shot put Jim into a long recovery and out of the war. I guess I should be grateful! He didn't become a permanent member of the 'army of cripples', but the bullet remained in him until his death many years later at the age of 82.

When our family visited the Canberra War Memorial many years later, Jim showed us a cannon just like the one on which he had served. My brothers and I used to play by putting on the leather leggings Dad had worn. We also had his whip and a photograph of him as a soldier wearing jodhpurs; but that was about all. The war was the one part of his life he would never say much about. He would talk about that bullet; but not much more. I concluded the war must have been a terrible experience and its conclusion on 11 November 1918 a great relief.

At the beginning of the First World War, many young men went off on what they thought was a great adventure that would last only a few months. Few, if any, realised the mass slaughter that would be achieved by the weapons of mechanised armies. No one anticipated the horrific stalemate which would result in life in the most wretched conditions – and death – in the trenches. The 'army of mourners' created by this war was greater than ever imagined. It is salutary to remember the horror of war and to work tirelessly for lasting peace.

Prayer

Pope John Paul II said: 'Only a world that is truly human can be a world that is peaceful and strong.' Fill me, Lord, with profound respect for other human beings. Amen.

Reflecting God's Presence

11 NOVEMBER

Some significant events on this day

Year   Event

1821   Birth of Feodor Dostoevsky, considered, along with his contemporary Leo Tolstoy, as one of the greatest prose writers of Russian literature.

1880   The Australian bushranger Ned Kelly, aged only 25, is hanged at the old Melbourne Gaol, despite a petition signed by 32,000 people protesting his death sentence.

1918   World War I hostilities officially cease at the eleventh hour of the eleventh day of the eleventh month when Germany signs a treaty with the Allies in a railway carriage in France.

1975   The elected Australian Labor government, led by Gough Whitlam, is dismissed from office by the Governor General Sir John Kerr.

Key thought for today

I believe there is no one lovelier, deeper, more sympathetic and more perfect than Jesus. I say to myself that not only is there no one else like him, but that there could never be anyone like him.

— Feodor Dostoevsky

Reflection

By Br Quentin O'Halloran

In the ups and downs of life, we can sometimes feel lost and discouraged. The great Russian novelist, Feodor Dostoevsky (1821–1881), addresses this very human situation in one of his novels.

> *To be a hero for a moment, for an hour, is easier than the heroism required in everyday living. Accept life as it is, grey and monotonous, that activity for which no one praises you, that heroism which no one notices, which draws no attention to yourself. Those who bear the colourless challenge of life and still remain a human being are indeed heroes.*

Prayer

> Lord, give me the energy to live
> the challenge of my daily life.
> Don't let me be content to take a back seat
> in the work of my family.
> No job is too small.
> It's so easy to sit back and admire others.
> Don't let laziness or apathy get the better of me.
> You've given me health and talents.
> Teach me to be generous, even heroic, in using them.

Reflecting God's Presence

Some significant events on this day

Year   Event

1927   Josef Stalin becomes leader of the USSR.

1970   A cyclone creates a tidal surge that sweeps over the Bay of Bengal and East Pakistan. As many as a million people are thought to have drowned.

1990   Emperor Akihito is formally enthroned as the 125th Emperor of Japan.

Key thought for today

We should employ our passions in the service of life, not spend life in the service of our passions.
— Richard Steele

Reflection

By Jon Edgar

Neil Davis, one of Australia's best-known photojournalists, grew up in Tasmania. He was an avid and successful sportsman but, in the latter part of his teens, his interest in photography and journalism grew. He developed his talents and built his reputation in this industry, reporting from Asia. It was here that he developed a passion for the people, culture and lifestyle of this region. He became fluent in some of the many dialects from this area and was renowned for his generosity among the many underprivileged children and families. Davis reported on the Vietnam War and the situation in Cambodia during the 1960s and 70s.

Davis was the first to cover the Vietnam War from the angle of the Viet Cong. As a result of his passion to portray stories of war from all angles he was regarded with some suspicion back in his native Australia and in some circles was accused of being a communist. It would perhaps be more accurate to say that Davis was somewhat ignorant of political alliances and rather was simply trying to report to people the realities of war. He used his ability with a camera to give an unbiased and accurate account of the atrocities of war.

He went on front line patrol with the Australian, American, South Vietnamese and Viet Cong armies, but his stated preference was to travel and report with the local forces. This helped him to understand and depict the impact that war has on the societies that it is forced upon. After the Vietnam War, Davis continued to work in the area, reporting on the Khmer Rouge regime in Cambodia before being forced out of the country owing to the restrictions placed on foreigners during this time.

Neil Davis died after being caught accidentally in cross fire while reporting on an attempted political coup in Bangkok. A passionate reporter to the end, he kept his camera rolling after being shot, and the footage recorded the end of his life. Davis showed by his work that there are always two sides to every conflict and never any real winners. There are always many innocent victims. Peaceful solutions should always be sought to make sure our world becomes a safe place.

Prayer

God, give me the courage to pursue my passions in a way that reveals the truth and serves others. Amen.

Some significant events on this day

Year   Event

1916   Labor Party Prime Minister William Hughes is expelled from the Labor Party because of his support for conscription. He then formed a minority government with his supporters.

1960   African-American entertainer Sammy Davis Jr marries Swedish actress May Britt.

1985   Approximately 23,000 people are killed when the volcano Nevado del Ruiz, in Columbia, violently erupts, sending a *lahar* (volcanic mud slide) over the town of Armero.

Key thought for today

Being a star has made it possible for me to get insulted in places where the average Negro could never hope to go and get insulted.

— Sammy Davis Jr

Reflection

By Br Bill Firman

When the black song and dance comedian and entertainer Sammy Davis Jr married white woman May Britt in 1960, interracial marriage was still illegal in 31 of the US states. In the South, where the importation of slaves had been legally permitted until 1808, organisations such as the Ku Klux Klan had thrived on the myth of white superiority, and vestiges of this attitude were still reflected in the prevalent culture there. So, although a very popular entertainer, Sammy and his wife became the target of racist jokes and even death threats.

In the 1960s, racism in the USA and South Africa emerged as a major cause of unrest, civil disobedience and even riots, such as occurred in Newark and Detroit in the summer of 1967. When Pope John XXIII addressed his 1963 encyclical, *Pacem in Terris* not just to Catholics but to 'all people of good will', he argued for the total elimination of racial discrimination.

After courageous and mostly non-violent campaigns led by people such as Martin Luther King Jr, the USA abandoned segregated schools and opted for integration. South Africa, as a consequence of an effective international sports boycott and protests within the country by people such as Nelson Mandela, abandoned its apartheid policy. In Australia in the 1970s, the White Australia immigration policy was also abandoned.

I went into a hotel bar in Alice Springs with another Brother in 1976. We refused to move when they tried to re-direct us to the separate bar for 'whites'. It takes time for old prejudices to disappear totally from the mores of a society: discrimination may be outlawed but some underlying prejudice still festers. We must never be deterred from seeking peace with, and opportunity for, all people of good will. Each person is to be accepted, without prejudice, for his or her full human dignity.

Prayer

Billy Graham once said: 'Skin colour does not matter to God, for God is looking upon the heart.' Give us good heart, O Lord, in dealing with people of all races. Amen.

Reflecting God's Presence

Some significant events on this day

Year   Event

1914   The Sultan of the Ottoman Empire, recently allied with Germany, declares *jihad* (holy war) on Britain, Russia and France and enters World War I.

1922   The British Broadcasting Corporation (BBC) begins domestic radio broadcasting.

1940   Most of the English town of Coventry is destroyed by German bombing raids, which killed about 1000 people.

Key thought for today

One's work may be finished one day, but one's education never.
— Alexandre Dumas

Reflection

By Cathy Loft: This story, sometimes called 'Irish Luck', is well worth our reflection.

His name was Fleming, and he was a poor Scottish farmer. One day, out making a living for his family, he heard a cry for help coming from a nearby bog. He dropped his tools and ran. There, mired to his waist in black muck, was a terrified boy, screaming, struggling to free himself. Fleming saved the lad from what could have been a slow and terrifying death. The next day, a fancy carriage pulled up to the Scotsman's sparse surrounds An elegantly dressed nobleman stepped out and introduced himself as the father of the boy Fleming had saved.

'I want to repay you', said the nobleman. 'You saved my son's life.' 'No, I can't accept payment for what I did', the Scottish farmer replied, waving off the offer. At that moment, the farmer's own son came to the door of the family hovel.

'Is that your son?' the nobleman asked. 'Yes', the farmer replied proudly. 'I'll make you a deal. Let me provide him with the level of education my own son will enjoy. If the lad is anything like his father, he'll no doubt grow to be a man we both will be proud of.'

And that he did. Fleming's son attended the very best schools and in time, graduated from St Mary's Hospital Medical School in London, and went on to become known throughout the world as the noted Sir Alexander Fleming, the discoverer of penicillin. Years afterward, the same nobleman's son who was saved from the bog was stricken with pneumonia. What saved his life this time? Penicillin. The name of the nobleman? Lord Randolph Churchill. His son's name? Sir Winston Churchill. Someone once said: 'What goes around comes around.'

Prayer

May there always be work for your hands to do;
May your purse always hold a coin or two;
May the sun always shine on your window pane;
May a rainbow be certain to follow each rain;
May the hand of a friend always be near you;
May God fill your heart with gladness to cheer you.

14 NOVEMBER

Some significant events on this day

Year   Event

1920   Following the First World War, the first assembly of the League of Nations is held in Geneva, Switzerland.

1941   Nazi leader Heinrich Himmler officially orders the arrest and deportation to concentration camps of all homosexuals in Germany (except for a few Nazi leaders). Two years later, on the same day, he gave a similar order for gypsies

2004   Bhutan, in the Himalayas, is the first nation to ban the sale of cigarettes and tobacco. Any foreigner bringing in tobacco products can be charged with smuggling.

Key thought for today

The virtue of chastity does not mean we are insensible to the urge of concupiscence, but that we subordinate it to reason and the law of grace, by striving wholeheartedly after what is noblest in human life.
— Pope Pius XII

Reflection

By Br Bill Firman

In my choice to become a De La Salle Brother, I knew I was choosing a celibate lifestyle. Quite clearly I was opting to live as a single male, as many people who are not members of religious institutes do in life, either through circumstances or by free choice.

Most people live the first twenty or so years of their lives as single people and many the last few years when their partner dies. I guess there are people who, based on their own life experience, cannot understand how anyone can refrain from sexual activity; but many people do.

If a husband works months away from home, most men and women, I believe, would expect their partner to be celibate while the enforced separation is taking place. Cheating may be common enough, but most people would not see it as normal or correct behaviour. Most wives would be legitimately disappointed to learn that their absent husbands were 'having it off' with other women – or men! Similarly most husbands would also have a right to be disappointed by a cheating wife.

Being single or married are legitimate lifestyles. Living solo, or as part of a group of men or women, or a mixed group, in a non-sexual way, are alternative lifestyles. Sexual orientation is not even an issue since all are celibate. The community dimension or friendships fill deeper needs, rather than any expression of sexual activity. A celibate life and the practice of chastity are not really difficult for adults with confidence in their core integrity.

Prayer

Saint Augustine of Hippo said that 'Blessedness consists in the accomplishment of our desires, and in our having only regular desires.' God, grant me self-control of my desires so that I may be able to be faithful to the persons and beliefs I cherish. Amen.

Reflecting God's Presence

Some significant events on this day

Year   Event

1539   Spanish explorer Francisco Pizarro and his men defeat the Inca army at Cajamarca and capture the Inca Emperor Atahualpa.

1940   In Poland, the Warsaw Ghetto is closed off from the outside world. Over the next three years the population of the ghetto dropped from 410,000 to 70,000, as a consequence of starvation, disease and deportation to death camps.

2000   President Bill Clinton arrives in Hanoi, the first serving president to visit the unified communist nation of Vietnam.

Key thought for today

Use what talents you possess: the woods would be very silent if no birds sang there except those that sang best.
— Henry Van Dyke

Reflection

By Br Bill Firman

In the parable of the talents (Matthew, ch. 25) Jesus speaks of the master who, before going on a journey, calls together his servants and gives five talents to one, two to another and one to a third. The man with five uses the talents to produce another five; the man with two produces another two. The third digs a hole and hides the talent in the ground. So he is able to return the one talent to the master. The first two are praised, in similar terms, by the master for doing what they could with their talents but the third is condemned. The third servant is called a 'worthless servant' and thrown outside where there is 'weeping and gnashing of teeth'.

Of whom much is given, much is expected. If we have many talents then more is expected of us. Even the one talent person is expected to do something with it. It is not enough to say we have kept out of trouble. That might simply be burying our talent in the ground. Nor can we be proud that we have done more than others. If we have been given many talents are we using them for service or selfishness?

Jesus taught the Beatitudes to the crowds that flocked around him during his public life and near the end of his life he put forth a dramatic picture of the last judgement. He taught that the blessed are those who fed the hungry, gave drink to the thirsty, welcomed the stranger, clothed the naked, visited the sick and the imprisoned. The cursed are those who neglected these works of mercy and love. Where do we find this in Matthew? In the same chapter 25, immediately after the parable of the talents! Further, Jesus tells us: ' Whenever you did this for one of the least important of these brothers of mine, you did it for me!' (Matthew 25:40).

Prayer

Let me use my talents to help others. May my life be a blessing for others and an act of thanksgiving to God for the gifts God has given me. Amen.

17 November

Some significant events on this day

Year   Event

1558   Queen Mary I, known as Bloody Mary for her persecution of Protestants, dies of influenza at the age of 42. Elizabeth I followed her as queen.

1970   Electrical engineer Douglas Engelbart receives the US patent for the 'X-Y position indicator for a display system', which he nicknames a 'mouse' because its cord looks like a tail.

1989   Mass protests begin in Prague, Czechoslovakia, known as 'The Velvet Revolution'. They led to the eventual resignation of the communist government.

Key thought for today

If you tell the truth, you don't have to remember anything.
— Mark Twain

Reflection

By Br Bill Firman

We read in the Bible, in the Book of Proverbs:

The path of life is to abide by discipline, and the one who ignores discipline goes astray.

Every day a person can learn to exercise self discipline or he or she can take the easy path. Rather than taking satisfaction in a top game of rugby or netball – being part of a team effort – or in catching fish, recreation for some can become totally passive – endless TV watching, computer games and play-station, drinking and sleeping. Whatever happened to exercise?

Effort is necessary if we are to be achievers. Courage is needed to resist the temptation to give in to the apparently easier path. We develop habits of strength or habits of weakness. The choices we make, no matter how trivial, can be important in character development. Most children really do know what is the right choice to make but many are inclined to be weak. Our task, as adults, is to encourage them to be strong.

Saint Paul remarks in chapter five of his letter to the Ephesians:

Be very careful about the sort of lives you lead, like intelligent and not like senseless people.

It is sensible to exercise not only the body but also the mind and the soul. It is good practice to honour our commitments. It is imperative to learn not to be too soft on ourselves. Sometimes fishing is the better option!

If we are always giving in to ourselves in small things, we shall lack the resolve to act with discipline when confronted by major decisions. We need to acquire the strength to put principle before pleasure.

Prayer

Lord, I pray for the strength to do what I know to be right rather than simply what is easy to do. Help me not to let myself down. Amen.

Reflecting God's Presence

Some significant events on this day

Year	Event
1477	William Caxton prints the first book in England.
1820	Nathaniel Palmer, captain of US sealing ship the *Hero*, sails south looking for more hunting grounds and discovers Antarctica.
1978	In Jonestown, Guyana, 914 members of the People Temple commit mass suicide at the behest of the cult leader Jim Jones.
1991	Terry Waite returns to Britain after nearly five years as a hostage with Shi'ite Muslim terrorists in Lebanon.

Key thought for today

Fanaticism is the false fire of an overheated mind.
— William Cowper

Reflection

By Br Bill Firman

Jim Jones, a charismatic preacher, set up the Peoples Temple in San Francisco in 1965. While Jones was preaching in San Francisco, he helped many local and national campaigns and was seen as a healer with much power in the community. But there was also criticism, and in 1977, showing signs of paranoia, Jones moved his followers to a more clandestine site in Guyana, to a village hewn from the jungle, 'Jonestown'.

Away from the constraints of American soil, Jones heightened regulations on his followers and their engagement to the sect. Paranoia and complete control became keynotes of Jones' personality. He began to stage rehearsals of a mass suicide plan that he would eventually enact. These drills, called 'white nights', began with sirens going off in the middle of the night and none of the members of Jonestown would know if it was real or not. 'A mass meeting would ensue ... we would be told that the jungle was swarming with mercenaries ... we were given a small glass of red liquid to drink. We were told that the liquid contained poison and that we would die within 45 minutes. We all did as we were told' (Galanter, 1989).

In 1978, US Congressman Leo Ryan went to Jonestown to investigate supposed abuses by the People's Temple of its members. After staying for a day, Ryan tried to leave, taking four of the cult members who had decided to defect. Realising this, Jones ordered them killed, and this was done. He then decided to put his suicide plan into action. Telling his subjects that it was a 'revolutionary death', he had a large quantity of fruit punch laced with cyanide prepared. After making all 276 children at Jonestown drink the punch, all the adults did the same. In the end, after Jones apparently killed himself with a gunshot to the head, 914 people had died. The world was left to wonder how one man could establish so much power over almost one thousand people.

Prayer

James Gillis said that 'Fanatics seldom laugh. They never laugh at themselves.' God forbid that I should ever become such a fanatic that I cannot laugh at myself and the mistakes I make. Amen.

Reflecting God's Presence

19 November

Some significant events on this day

Year   Event

1863   US President Abraham Lincoln delivers the oft-quoted Gettysburg Address. Lincoln spoke for two minutes. The speaker before him, Edward Everett, spoke for two hours.

1941   In a battle off the coast of Western Australia, HMAS *Sydney* and HSK *Kormoran* sink each other with the loss of 645 Australians and 77 Germans.

1954   The first automatic toll machine is placed in service in New Jersey, USA.

Key thought for today

There are people in the world so hungry that God cannot appear to them except in the form of bread.
— Mahatma Gandhi

Reflection

By Br Gerald Barrett

During my time in Derby, WA, as principal of Holy Rosary School, I came across a rather confronting reality of life. One Friday afternoon I caught one of the Year 3 boys going through the garbage looking for scraps of food left over from lunch. I told him that if ever he was hungry I would rather he come to the Brothers' residence and get some food.

Sure enough, the next afternoon a voice resonated through the house: 'Brother Gerry, are you there?'

Recognising the voice I replied, 'Yes Clinton, I'm here.'

'Can I have some food?' It then dawned on me to ask the next question, 'How many with you?'

'Six', came back the reply.

We were in the habit of providing food to those who needed it, so rustling up some sandwiches, a cordial drink and fruit was no trouble. Sitting out on the back verandah and listening to these people and hearing some of their stories was a great way to spend a Saturday afternoon.

There is not, nor should there be, anything unusual about this story. If we are going to live the Gospel, we have to be prepared to live it in its reality. De La Salle is a wonderful example of giving to the needy – you only have to see the tremendous effort made on Mission Action Day, the fantastic collection of food items for the annual Social Justice Mass and for the St Kilda Mission. We are a generous community and we can feel proud of our achievements.

Prayer

Lord, heavenly Father, may we be reminded that your poor are with us all the time. Help us to respond generously in time and monetary means to the needs of others. We make this prayer through Christ our Lord and brother. Amen.

Reflecting God's Presence

Some significant events on this day

Year	Event
1945	Twenty-four high-ranking Nazis are put on trial in Nuremberg, Gemany, for atrocities committed during World War II
1947	Princess Elizabeth, aged 21, marries the 26-year-old Duke of Edinburgh, Philip Mountbatten. Six years later, she would become Queen of England.
1962	Satisfied that Soviet missiles had been removed from Cuba, the US lifts its blockade of Cuba.

Key thought for today

The one thing we can all agree, all faiths and ideologies, is that God is with the vulnerable and poor. God is in the slums, in the cardboard boxes where the poor play house ... God is in the silence of a mother who has infected her child with a virus that will end both their lives ... God is in the cries heard under the rubble of war ... God is in the debris of wasted opportunity and lives, and God is with us if we are with them.
— Bono, Irish musician and social activist

Reflection

By Br Bill Firman

It is natural to want certitude, but while it is comforting to have uniformity life cannot be reduced to a set of absolutes. There are many 'grey areas' in life, but there are still absolutes: the absolute priority of love of God and neighbour, the absolute demand for social justice for all, the absolute of God's willingness to forgive.

As John Deedy has written:

> *Absolutes retain their priority – probably not the rigid absolutes all Catholics once lived with, but absolutes that say, 'there are rules, there is such a thing as a norm'. Life is not merely a behavioural experience. Where sexual morality is concerned, I'm speaking of absolutes that honour chastity, integrity, sincerity, purity, within a context of love and respect. The challenge for parents is to convey a sense of these absolutes to their children. One way of doing this is by living those absolutes in their own lives.*

The Second Vatican Council ushered in an exciting, positive attitude that emphasised love more than sin. *Gaudium et Spes* was a key Council document trying to make the church a stronger force for justice and peace in the world. A stronger sense of the community dimension of the church and a greater role for a well-educated laity were very positive outcomes of Vatican II. Nothing is more important than our attitude towards others, our fellow wayfarers on life's journey. How we treat others is the real test of how Christian we are. Our students may not have absolute answers when they leave school but we hope they are equipped with the ability to think clearly, with a conscientious disposition and a set of values that will help them cope with the challenges, often unexpected, they will face on the journey ahead.

Prayer

Lord, help me to hear and respond to the cries of the vulnerable and the poor. Amen.

21 NOVEMBER

Reflecting God's Presence

Some significant events on this day

Year   Event

1783   The first successful human free flight takes place when two Frenchmen, de Rozier and Laurent, fly for 25 minutes over Paris in a balloon.

1920   In Ireland, 'Bloody Sunday' occurs when British troops, in retaliation for the shooting of several British intelligence agents in their homes that morning, open fire on a Gaelic football match at Croke Park, Dublin, killing 14 people and wounding 65.

1953   The British Museum announces that the famous Piltdown Man skull, found in Sussex in 1912 and proclaimed as the 'missing link' between humans and apes, was in fact a hoax.

1977   World Series Cricket is launched in Melbourne by Kerry Packer.

1995   The first Dayton Peace Accord is signed, bringing to an end three and a half years of fighting in Bosnia-Herzegovina.

Key thought for today

The world is charged with the grandeur of God.
— Gerard Manley Hopkins

Reflection

By Brian Long

The poetry of the Jesuit priest Gerard Manley Hopkins contains some beautiful imagery and profound meaning. Here is one example.

> *And for all this, nature is never spent;*
> *There lives the dearest freshness deep down things;*
> *And though the last lights off the black West went*
> *Oh, morning, at the brown brink eastward springs –*
> *Because the Holy Ghost over the bent*
> *World broods with warm breast and with ah! bright wings.*

Although Hopkins is primarily speaking about nature, if we change the word 'nature' to the 'human heart/spirit' it speaks to each of us of the always healing presence of the 'glory' of God.

Each of us shines like the sun. Each of us is a revelation of God's glory. There is no separateness. Each other is my sister or brother.

Prayer

Loving Father, help me to recognise that each person I meet today is my brother or sister because you are one Father of all of us. Amen.

Reflecting God's Presence

Some significant events on this day

Year	Event
1906	'SOS', meaning 'Save Our Souls', is adopted as the international distress call by the International Radio Telegraph Convention in Berlin.
1956	The 16th Olympic Games open in Melbourne – the first time they are held in the southern hemisphere.
1963	US President John F. Kennedy is assassinated in Dallas, Texas. He was pronounced dead at 1.00 pm. At 2.39 pm, Lyndon Johnson was sworn in as president.
1995	Britain's worst female serial killer, Rosemary West, is found guilty of murdering ten young women and girls, including her own daughter and stepdaughter.
1995	The first computer animated film *Toy Story* is released.

Key thought for today

All I want for Christmas is my two front teeth.
— Popular children's song from 1946

Reflection

By Br Bill Firman

Once, walking past a Cash Converters store, I was startled to see the length of the queue of people waiting to trade in their possessions for cash. A couple of days later I read an article that spoke of the ballooning credit card debt that Christmas brings. Many people overspend on Christmas and place themselves in a perilous financial position. And all this as the outcome of the season that should build hope. At the first Christmas, hope grew out of the very poor surroundings of a stable. It is fanciful to speculate whether or not Joseph would have mortgaged his carpenter's tools for better accommodation, but I fancy not. I think he knew that the love he shared with Mary was more important than fine surroundings or rich celebrations.

The wise men did bring presents eventually. There is nothing wrong in giving from the much that you have. My giving a gift is a statement that I have thought of you and care enough to want to give something to you. The size of the gift is not really significant – at least to mature adults! Christmas means the most when we recognise the full significance of its humble beginnings in a stable. Christmas brought hope to the world because of the love in the stable. The Magi and their presents came later.

Part of the role of parents is to educate children to know what is important in life. A Christmas that leads us to feel overwhelmed with hopeless debt is a sad Christmas. A good Christmas is one we can afford. The best Christmas present is helping another to find hope in the love of family and friends. We can do that on a very limited budget.

Prayer

I know I do not need to try to buy the love of my family and friends, but help me to show them in other ways that I appreciate and love them. Amen.

Reflecting God's Presence

Some significant events on this day

Year   Event

1963   The first episode of the BBC television series *Dr Who* is aired.

1971   The United Nations recognises the People's Republic of China as the sole representative of China, ousting Taiwan from the UN Security Council.

1996   Ethiopian Airlines flight 961 is hijacked by three Ethiopian men and ordered to fly to Australia. It ran out of fuel and crashed in the Indian Ocean, killing 123 of the 175 people on board.

Key thoughts for today

God is not an idea, or a definition, that we have committed to memory, God is a presence which we experience in our hearts.
— Louis Evely

People who tell me there is no God are like a six-year-old boy saying there is no such thing as passionate love – they just haven't experienced it.
— William Alfred

Reflection

By Br Bill Firman

Every boy who attends De La Salle learns the invocation 'Live Jesus in our hearts, forever'. It is an intrinsic part of the De La tradition. Also a part of that tradition is the emphasis on the presence of God. Lasallian prayer is commonly introduced by the invocation: 'Let us remember we are in the holy presence of God.' This prayer goes back 300 years to de La Salle himself who prescribed that it be used throughout the school day.

John Baptist de la Salle often spoke about the presence of God. He wrote in one of his letters:

> *You are in God's presence; that is more than enough for you ... All you need and all God wants of you is that you remain in God's presence.*

Again, in one of his meditations, he says:

> *Your sole concern ... should be the establishment of God's reign in your heart.*

De La Salle urged his teachers to be especially attentive to the presence of God in persons, knowing that if we live with an awareness of the presence of God we will have a tender regard for all other people. We will treat them with respect and friendship and we will value them as our brothers or sisters who are also loved by God. The presence of God is expressed in love. Jesus, in his farewell discourse (John 13:34), says:

> *I give you a new commandment: love one another; just as I have loved you, you must love one another. By this love you have for one another, everyone will know you are my disciples.*

Prayer

Let me recall frequently today that I am in the presence of God.

Reflecting God's Presence

Some significant events on this day

Year   Event

1642   Abel Tasman sights Tasmania from his ship, the first European to do so.

1859   *On the Origin of the Species by Means of Natural Selection* by Charles Darwin is published, outlining his theory of evolution. Since then, it has never been out of print.

1995   In a referendum, voters in the Republic of Ireland support the legalisation of divorce by a margin of just under 0.5 per cent.

Key thought for today

Faith declares what the senses do not see, but not the contrary of what they see. It is above them, not contrary to them.

— Blaise Pascal

Reflection

By St John Baptist de La Salle

Look on everything with the eyes of faith. You must never fail to do this, no matter what the reason. Viewing things with the eyes of faith will earn for you in one day more good, more interior application, closer union with God, and greater vigilance over yourself than a month of those penances and austerities to which you are attracted. Believe me, you will see its effect, though perhaps for the present you will not understand it.

The spirit of faith is a sharing in the Spirit of God who dwells in us, which leads us to regulate our conduct in all things by the sentiments and truths that faith teaches us. You should, therefore, be wholly occupied in acquiring it, so that it may be for you a shield against the fiery darts of the devil (Letters).

Acknowledge that it is, indeed, a great advantage for you that Jesus Christ ascended into heaven; it is from there that come all the gifts that should enrich and adorn your soul. In fact, it is by virtue of the power over all creatures both in heaven and on earth that Jesus Christ received this day, that he is so generous to his people.

As their head he makes them share in the life of grace, the fullness of which dwells in him, and as your mediator he presents your prayers and good works to God his Father. He himself prays for you to draw down God's mercy on you and prevent God from turning his anger on you when you offend him. For Christ's ascension is your glory, the motive of your hope, and the promise of your happiness. Lift your mind and heart heavenward, because you are destined only for heaven, should work only for heaven, and because you will not find perfect rest until you are in heaven. Beg of Christ the grace to be no longer preoccupied with anything except the things of heaven (Meditations for Sundays and Feasts).

Prayer

God, help me to aspire to a spiritual life that leads me nearer to you. Amen.

Some significant events on this day

Year	Event

1703	The worst recorded gale in the British Isles strikes the south of England, sinking 300 ships, drowning 30,000 sailors and killing 9000 people on land.

1952	*The Mousetrap* by Agatha Christie opens in London. Fifty-six years later, in 2008, it is still playing with eight performances per week, each lasting two hours 15 minutes.

1990	Following the demise of Soviet-backed communist governments, Poland holds its first free presidential elections.

Key thought for today

You cannot legislate an attitude.
— H. Rap Brown

Reflection

By Betty Rudin: I like the positive sentiments expressed and implied in the following story and prayer.

There once was a woman who woke up one morning, looked in the mirror and noticed she had only three hairs on her head. 'Well', she said, 'I think I shall braid my hair today.'

So she did and she had a wonderful day.

The next day she woke up, looked in the mirror and saw she had only two hairs on her head. 'Well', she said, 'I think I'll part my hair down the middle today.'

So she did and she had a grand day.

The next day she woke up, looked in the mirror and saw she had only one hair on her head. 'H-m-m', she said, 'I think I'm going to wear my hair in a pony tail.'

So she did and she had a fun, fun day.

The next day she woke up, looked in the mirror and noticed there wasn't a single hair on her head. 'Yea', she exclaimed, 'I don't have to fix my hair today'.

Prayer

Lord, help me to understand these sentiments:

Attitude is everything.
Be kinder than necessary for everyone you meet is fighting some kind of battle.
Live simply, love generously, care deeply, speak kindly ... leave the rest to God.
Life isn't about waiting for the storm to pass ... it's about learning to dance in the rain.

Reflecting God's Presence

Some significant events on this day

Year   Event

1922   The tomb of Tutankhamen is opened for the first time, leading to the discovery of extraordinary treasures in the Pharoah's burial chamber.

1966   The world's first tidal electricity plant is opened by President Charles de Gaulle at the Rance River estuary in Brittany, France.

1992   Queen Elizabeth II volunteers to begin paying taxes and takes most of her family off the public payroll.

Key thought for today

Help your brother's boat across and your own will reach the shore.
— Hindu proverb

Reflection

By Br Bill Firman

One of the greatest Christians of his time and winner of the 1952 Nobel Peace prize was Albert Schweitzer (1875–1965). He dedicated his early life to the study of science, music and theology and by the time he was 30 he was an accomplished organist and an authority on the life and work of Johann Sebastian Bach.

After reading a paper on the needs of medical missions in 1904, he was inspired to study medicine and became a doctor in 1913 at the age of 38. After graduation, he made the arduous journey to French Equatorial Africa where he worked among the native people establishing a hospital in the very primitive conditions.

I do not recall who it was that first told me about Albert Schweitzer but one of my teachers gave me one of Schweitzer's books, *More from the Primeval Forest,* to read when I was a student at De La Salle in Year 12. I recall that I found it difficult but struggled through it with limited comprehension.

Schweitzer wrote extensively, not only on his missionary work and music, but on theological topics such as *The Quest for the Historical Jesus* and *The Mysticism of St Paul*. One tenet of Albert Schweitzer's he stated in these terms:

> *There is no higher religion than human service. To work for the common good is the greatest creed.*

Sometimes I hear concerns expressed about falling church attendances, the irrelevance of religion and the increasing secularisation of formerly strong Christian societies, including our own. I do not play down such concerns but it is important to recognise that young people today are no less generous than any previous generation in providing human service. Maybe they are better.

Prayer

Lord, help me to see the needs of my brothers and sisters; then give me the courage to respond.

Some significant events on this day

Year	Event
1893	Women vote for the first time in a national election in New Zealand, the first nation to grant all women the right to vote.
1942	In Brisbane, tension between Australian and American servicemen leads to brawls for the second night running and the death of one soldier.
1975	Ross McWhirter, television presenter and co-founder of *The Guinness Book of Records*, is shot dead by the IRA outside his home after he offers a reward leading to the capture of IRA bombers.

Key thought for today

Little drops of water, little grains of sand,
Make the mighty ocean and the pleasant land.
So the little minutes, humble though they be,
Make the mighty ages of eternity.
   — Julia Carney

Reflection

By Margaret McPhee

Time for oneself

It is important to have time alone
because in this world of ours
we are constantly surrounded by noise,
people noise, industrial noise and traffic noise.
The human spirit needs time alone
to reflect on God's wonders, such as
the beauty of nature,
the laughter and innocence of children,
the playful nature of animals,
the beauty of the sky on a summer's day,
the crashing waves
or the mirror finish of the beach,
and the peaks of a mountain range.
Make time for yourself to renew,
recharge, revisit and revitalise
body, mind and spirit.

Prayer

Lao Tzu wrote: 'Time is a created thing. To say "I don't have time" is to say "I don't want to".' I know I can make time, take time, for myself to appreciate the beauty around me and refresh and revitalise myself – if I want to. God, help me to use the gift of time well now so that I shall be well satisfied with the life I create as time flows by. Amen.

Reflecting God's Presence

Some significant events on this date:

Year   Event

1520   The great navigator, Ferdinand Magellan, rounds the tip of South America.

1966   An Air New Zealand DC10 sight-seeing flight, TE901, crashes into the 3795 metres high Mt Erebus on Ross Island, Antartica, killing all 257 persons on board.

1989   Winner of five Olympic gold medals, the first at age 14 in 1976, gymnast Nadia Comaneci flees Romania and is granted asylum in the USA.

Key thought for today

God whispers in our pleasures but shouts in our pain.
— C. S. Lewis

Reflection

By Br Bill Firman

The courage of the explorer mariners who first sailed into uncharted oceans in ships that were relatively hard to manoeuvre, without modern communication aids or refrigeration and never knowing where they would find fresh food and water, is hard to comprehend today. They certainly knew the danger they were facing and perhaps had more deep-seated fears than we could imagine.

Aristotle had theorised that the earth was round. Columbus died with the conviction that he had proven Aristotle correct, but the real confirmation came in the expedition of Ferdinand Magellan, the captain of the first ship to sail completely around the world. Magellan, who was Portuguese, set out from Spain in 1519 with five Spanish ships. The statistics of his voyage reveal the extraordinary risks. Only one of his five ships made it back to Spain, just 12 days less than three years after their journey started. On that one ship there were only 18 sailors remaining of the 265 who set out with Magellan.

It took Magellan more than 14 months to find the frigid, stormy opening to the Pacific now known as the Strait of Magellan. What he did not count on was the immensity of the Pacific. He expected Asia to be a few hundred miles beyond the coast of South America. Instead, the expedition travelled 12,600 miles before reaching land. The fresh food and water were used up, causing scurvy, a wasting disease that results from lack of vitamin C in the diet. They were reduced to eating the leather rope guards, then sawdust and even rats. Many died. After 98 days, the fleet finally reached an island – probably Guam – in the western Pacific.

Magellan had survived 18 months at sea, but was killed in a battle in the Philippines. After his death, Captain Juan Sebastián del Cano took command of the reduced fleet and brought it to its goal, the Moluccas, where he took on a cargo of cloves. Cano made the long westward return voyage with one last ship, the *Victoria*. The cargo of cloves sold for such a high price that, despite losing four out of five vessels, the voyage earned a profit

Prayer

There is a French proverb that states: 'To a brave heart, nothing is impossible.' Grant to me, O Lord, the courage to attempt to overcome all obstacles and difficulties that I may face so that I can progress steadily on my journey to you, in the company of all those I love. Amen.

Reflecting God's Presence

Some significant events on this day

Year   Event

1781   Luke Collingwood, the commander of the slave ship, *Zong*, begins dumping 133 ill slaves overboard to claim insurance. If they died on board he could not claim the insurance but he could if they were thrown overboard while still alive 'for the safety of the ship'.

1898   The influential author and scholar, Clive Staples Lewis, is born in Belfast, Northern Ireland.

1947   The UN General Assembly passes a resolution to divide Palestine between Arab and Jewish people.

Key thought for today

There are only two kinds of people in the end: those who say to God, 'Thy will be done', and those to whom God says, in the end, 'Thy will be done.'
— C.S. Lewis

Reflection

By Eve McLellan: This passage written by C.S. Lewis is notable for its simple beauty and its conviction that it's not 'all about us!'

> *When we die and finally see God we will not say:*
> *'Lord, I could never have guessed how beautiful you are!'*
> *We will not say that.*
> *Rather, we will say:*
> *'So it was you all along!*
> *Everyone I ever loved, it was you.*
> *Everyone who ever loved me, it was you.*
> *Everything decent or fine that ever happened to me,*
> *Everything that made me reach out and try to be better-*
> *It was you – all along!'*

Prayer

C.S. Lewis also wrote: 'To love at all is to be vulnerable. Love anything, and your heart will certainly be wrung and possibly broken. If you want to make sure of keeping it intact, you must give your heart to no one, not even to an animal. Wrap it carefully round with hobbies and little luxuries; avoid all entanglements; lock it up safe in the casket or coffin of your selfishness. But in that casket – safe, dark, motionless, airless – it will change. It will not be broken; it will become unbreakable, impenetrable, irredeemable.' Lord, I do not want to be unbreakable, impenetrable, irredeemable. Help me to be open to loving in this world you have given me, especially the people in it, so that I may find you in the end. Amen

Reflecting God's Presence

Some significant events on this day

Year   Event

1609   In Padua, Italy, Galileo Galilei looks through his recently constructed telescope at the moon, and notes that it was not smooth but pitted. So began a new era of looking at the objects in the night sky.

1936   Fire destroys London's Crystal Palace, the glass and steel hall built for the 1851 International Exhibition.

1999   In Seattle, delegates at a meeting of the World Trade Organisation are surprised by major protests from the anti-globalisation movement.

Key thought for today

Live so that the preacher can tell the truth at your funeral.
— K. Beckstrom

Reflection

By Br Bill Firman

The 30th President of the United States, Calvin Coolidge (1873–1933), once invited some Vermont friends to dine at the White House. They were worried about their table manners; so they decided the best tactic was to do everything the President did. The meal passed smoothly until coffee was served and Coolidge poured his into a saucer. The guests followed suit. The he added sugar and cream. The visitors did likewise. Then Coolidge leaned over and placed his saucer on the floor for the cat. The embarrassed visitors realised that their imitation strategy had led them into an embarrassing mistake.

It is true that when we are young we learn a lot by imitating our parents and, later, our teachers, but one can't go through life just imitating others. We all have to establish our own personal direction that suits our individual talents. We also change as we pass through life. Albert Camus said:

To grow old is to pass from passion to compassion.

Young people tend to be energetic, eager and impulsive, whereas older people develop more sensitivity and stability. This is part of every life journey where attitude, values and conscience are more important pilots than imitation. I love the gentle image conjured by the French proverb:

There is no pillow so soft as a good conscience.

It is not enough to imitate others, but we can learn by watching, reflecting and choosing what we value from the behaviour we see in others, This process never ends. The young also teach the old. There is nothing like being with young people to feel some revitalisation and new hope. A good life results from living a day at a time, as well as we can. Then we can rest soundly on the soft pillow of our good conscience.

Prayer

Rabbi Elimelekh wrote: 'It is good if we can bring about that which God sings within us.' Help me to act each day true to my conscience, O God, so that you may sing within me as I journey through life and towards you.

1 DECEMBER

Reflecting God's Presence

Some significant events on this day

Year   Event

1919   Lady Nancy Astor becomes the first female member of parliament in Britain, less than a year after women in England were given the right to vote.

1955   Rosa Parks, in Montgomery, Alabama, refuses to relinquish her bus seat to a white man, sparking a bus boycott and the beginning of the US civil rights movement.

1990   English Channel Tunnel workers break through the last wall of rock to create a ground link between France and Britain.

Key thought for today

A pessimist is one who makes difficulties of his opportunities and an optimist is one who makes opportunities of his difficulties.
— Harry S. Truman

Reflection

By Kylie Busk

During the US presidential election of 1960 John F. Kennedy said, 'We stand today on the edge of a new frontier ... But the new frontier of which I speak is not a set of promises – it is a set of challenges.' As our Year 12 students leave De La Salle, they too stand on the edge of a new frontier and I hope that they can confront the challenges that life will continue to present them with.

Author Marianne Williamson expresses one of the challenges in this way :

> *Our deepest fear is not that we are inadequate. Our deepest fear is that we are powerful beyond measure. It is our light, not our darkness that most frightens us. We ask ourselves, who am I to be brilliant, gorgeous, talented, fabulous? Actually, who are you not to be? You are a child of God. Your playing small does not serve the world. There is nothing enlightened about shrinking so that other people won't feel insecure around you. We are all meant to shine, as children do. We were born to make manifest the glory of God that is within us. It's not just in some of us; it's in everyone. And as we let our own light shine, we unconsciously give other people permission to do the same. As we are liberated from our own fear, our presence automatically liberates others.*

Not everyone can be good at the same things, but everyone has the potential to be brilliant at something. Different people measure success in different ways. Judge yourself by what you know in your heart is important and be brave enough to shine in your life and therefore allow others to experience the opportunities that come from this bravery.

Prayer

Dear God, help me to appreciate those things that are special and unique about myself and others. Help me to find a way to use my skills not only to benefit my own life but also to lend a helping hand to others. Grant me the courage to be all that I can be, now and forever. Amen.

Reflecting God's Presence

2 DECEMBER

Some significant events on this day

Year	Event
1942	Italian scientist Enrico Fermi achieves the first controlled nuclear chain reaction, in a squash court at the University of Chicago.
1972	After more than two decades in opposition, the Australian Labor Party is led to an election victory by Gough Whitlam.
1995	Rogue trader Nick Leeson, who caused the collapse of Britain's oldest merchant bank Barings, is sentenced to six years and six months gaol.
2005	Australian Van Tuong Nguyen, 25, is executed in Singapore after being convicted of drug trafficking.

Key thought for today

If you make money your God, it will plague you like the devil.
— Henry Fielding

Reflection

By Br Bill Firman

Securities broker Nick Leeson lost 850 million pounds ($1.4 billion) by speculating on the Singapore international monetary exchange, using futures contracts. He caused the collapse of Britain's oldest merchant bank, Barings, and said later: 'I knew I had lost millions of pounds, but I didn't know how much. I was too frightened to find out. The numbers scared me to death.' Many people lost huge sums of money and many their jobs – brought about by the modern technology that underpins financial trading. Many people unjustly become the victims of mismanagement on this scale when major companies collapse. Michel Quoist wrote:

> *Money is frightening. It can serve or destroy us.*

We do need some money. The trouble starts, however, when need becomes greed. Too many people succumb to the pursuit of more money no matter what effect that pursuit has on others. Billy Graham argued:

> *If a person gets his attitude toward money straight, it will help straighten out almost every other area in life.*

Roman philosopher Seneca commented long ago that 'Money has never made anyone rich', and Henrik Ibsen offers some sound cautions:

> *Money can buy the husk of many things, but not the kernel. It brings you food, but not appetite; medicine, but not health; acquaintances, but not friends; servants, but not faithfulness; days of joy, but not peace and happiness.*

I admire John Baptist de La Salle who gave all his money away. I also admire the wisdom of Bill Gates and Warren Buffet who are putting so much of their vast wealth into long-term foundations that will finance improvements for other people. Ultimately, it is well to recall, as Tertullian stated:

> *Nothing that is God's is obtainable with money.*

Prayer

John Wesley said: 'Make all you can, save all you can, give all you can.' Never let me forget the last part.

Reflecting God's Presence

Some significant events on this day

Year   Event

1854   In an event claimed by some to be the birth of Australian democracy, more than 20 goldminers at Ballarat are killed by state troopers in an uprising over mining licences known as the Eureka Stockade.

1967   At Groote Schuur Hospital in Cape Town, South Africa, a transplant team headed by Dr Christiaan Barnard carries out the first successful human heart transplant on 53-year-old Louis Washkansky.

1984   A poisonous leak from a Union Carbide pesticides plant in Bhopal, India, kills more than 3800 people and injures more than 150,000 others (some 6000 of whom would later die from their injuries) in one of the worst industrial disasters in history.

Key thought for today

Mishaps are like knives that either serve us or cut us, as we grasp them by the blade or the handle.
— James Russell Lowell

Reflection

By Br Denis Loft

One of the most memorable lads I ever taught was Simon. Simon was born in a remote Sepik village in Papua New Guinea. He had neither legs nor arms.

His family were subsistence farmers, who fished and hunted daily and relied on sago crops for their existence. Unlike his brothers and sisters, Simon was not offered any education. His situation was pointed out to Cheshire Homes, a group founded by Leonard Cheshire, a famous English pilot of World War II. After being an official observer of the nuclear bombing of Nagasaki, he dedicated the rest of his life to supporting disabled people. Simon began primary school at the age of 18. When I met him he was doing secondary studies at Hohola in Port Moresby. He was 23 years old and weighed 30 kilograms. He was the most popular young man at the school. He knew everyone's names, had a great collection of stories and loved drama. Students vied to push him around in his wheelchair or, when that was broken, in a wheelbarrow. In drama, he played roles such as a baby in a pram, and once as the head of John the Baptist, presented on a plate! Simon learned to type at 17 words per minute, using a pencil held between his chin and shoulder. On leaving school, Simon got a job with a security company, managing their radio call centre.

Had it not been for the atrocities of the war, Leonard Cheshire may never have founded his service, and people like Simon may have remained neglected for their entire lives. It always amazes me that even from the worst situations good seems to arise. I am reminded of the psalmist who claims: 'God's ways are not our ways.'

Prayer

May God be a part of my journey through life. May I see God in those who appear less fortunate than me. May I appreciate my blessings and use them appropriately. May I search for the good and turn from evil. Amen.

Reflecting God's Presence

Some significant events on this day

Year Event

1154 The first and only Englishman to have headed the Roman Catholic Church, Cardinal Nicholas Breakspear, is elected Pope Adrian IV.

1872 The brigantine *Mary Celeste* is found drifting west of Gibraltar with no one on board. What happened to its passengers and crew is still a mystery.

1991 After 64 years of operation, the American airline Pan Am, burdened by massive debts, ceases service.

Key thought for today

The man who cannot wonder is but a pair of spectacles behind which there is no eye.
— Thomas Carlyle

Reflection

By Br Bill Firman

Many times over the years, I have watched the pelicans, at Harrington on the NSW coast, sitting on top of the light poles or waiting on the rocks for the scraps thrown by the fishermen cleaning their fish. Pelicans are large, heavy birds and have always seemed to me to be ungainly. They fly at low level by flapping their large wings. Today, however, was different!

I watched six pelicans in the air, soaring. With wings outstretched, they were riding the strong wind, facing into it and rising on the unseen currents. They would fly, facing into the wind, remaining stationary overhead for a brief time, and then let themselves be taken downwind for hundreds of metres, only to return effortlessly half a minute later to take up station again over the headland.

Only once did I see a pelican, flying low, flap its wings. Like kites without strings, they surfed the currents with outstretched wings – living, natural hang-gliders, using the air to move as they pleased.

They were not fishing. Most of their flying was over land and none of them dived for fish. Neither were they going anywhere. It seemed to me they were flying for fun, for the exhilaration of being carried by the wind rather than having to flap their way through it. These large birds needed a strong wind: this was their day and they were seizing it.

We all need the occasional soaring moment. Most of our time will be spent in unspectacular routine. We may even be misjudged from afar as 'heavy' or 'ungainly'. But when conditions suit and opportunity presents we must grasp it and be the best we can possibly be. And be refreshed by those moments.

Prayer

I wished I had my camera, but as I wished I knew that my own sense of wonder could keep this image true. Thank you, God, for the wonder of your creation. Amen.

Some significant events on this day

Year	Event
1924	Percy Christmas opens Australia's first Woolworths store in Sydney's Imperial Arcade.
1933	America officially repeals its 13-year-old prohibition laws forbidding the making and selling of alcohol.
1952	A dense fog shrouds London for five days, causing an estimated 12,000 deaths from respiratory illness.

Key thought for today

Science cannot resolve moral conflicts, but it can help to more accurately frame the debates about those conflicts.

— Heinz R. Pagels

Reflection

By Br Bill Firman

When I was a boy, there were still vestiges of the attitude that the illegitimacy of a child somehow made that person inferior or unacceptable. I remember getting a holiday job on a building site while still a boy at school, and working with a rigger who had a cleft palate. He said: 'You can call me anything but don't call me a bastard'. There is no doubt that the stigma of illegitimacy has been correctly removed during my life time. All persons are entitled to full respect and love, no matter the circumstances of their birth. But I also have no doubt that something is out of balance when some kids proclaim loudly that they are 'bisexual', meaning they can 'make it' with either sex. They are declaring to be neither heterosexual nor homosexual but just happy to have sex with anyone. Some magazines have promoted this as 'chic'. Frankly, it degrades the gift of sexuality.

If the intimacy of the sexual relationship is being deprived of its place as the deepest act of physical communication with a person one loves and is being left as just an activity we do with anyone for pleasure, it is being devalued from a profound expression of love to nothing more than mutual masturbation.

Professor Kay Wellings in a British government-sponsored report has said:

> *In the 1950s an average man first had sex at 20 and a woman at 21. Now the average age for both sexes is 16. In the 1950s fewer than one in 100 girls had sex before the legal age of consent. Now one in four had sex before 15. Four in 10 women born in the 1930s were married before they had sex. By the 1990s, fewer than one in 100 women had sex for the first time with a man to whom they were engaged or married.*

The report, however, made the point that, unlike most men, women who have sex at a young age tend to regret it in later life. Women, especially with the wisdom of hindsight, often feel exploited – used and discarded. Professor Wellings said: 'Women are twice as likely as men to regret their first experience of intercourse and three times as likely to report being the less willing partner.'

Prayer

Help me to be honest in relationships and not just use and abuse for my own pleasure. Amen.

Reflecting God's Presence

Some significant events on this day

Year Event

1768 The first volume of the *Encyclopaedia Britannica* is published in Edinburgh, Scotland.
1921 The Anglo-Irish Treaty is signed, creating an independent Irish Free State, while the six north-eastern counties of Ireland remain part of the UK.
2001 New Zealand yachtsman and environmentalist Sir Peter Blake is murdered by pirates on the Amazon River in Brazil.

Key thought for today

Neither you nor the world knows what you can do until you have tried.
— Ralph Waldo Emerson

Reflection

By Patrick Jurd: I came across this tale that I would like to share with you.

Once upon a time a group of people lived in a cave, way under the earth. It was very dark in the cave, but they had a little lamp which gave them some light. This light cast their shadows on the wall of the cave, and they sat for hours amused by the movement of their shadows.

In this cave, there was one who wondered about the possibility of life outside the cave. One day, he came to a decision. He would explore – see if there were other ways of spending his days. He began to tunnel, and one day he surfaced. He saw for the very first time the sun and the sky, trees, flowers, birds, animals. He stood amazed, gazing in wonder. 'I must go back at once and tell the others', he decided.

He made his way back through the dark tunnel, until he came to the cave where his friends were sitting gazing at their shadows on the wall. 'Come out!' he cried. 'Come out into the light! Leave this dark half-light. You've never seen anything like it!' But the others sat happily in the dimly lit darkness. 'He's crazy', they said. 'Of course, he always was a bit different', and they shook their heads knowingly at one another. But when he continued to disturb them they grew angry. 'Go away', they shouted. 'Stop bothering us.'

'How can I stop?' he asked himself. 'I can no longer live the half-awake life of a slave. I have seen the real, the truth. I must leave here. But where am I going? What am I going to? ... I'm not sure ... All I know is that I must go.' So he left the cave, his companions, his life, and went forward to meet the claims of the truth.

Prayer

Give me the courage to move out of my comfort zone and to take bold steps that will set me on a challenging life journey. Extend me beyond my twilight area of security to new levels of vision and conviction. Help me to be an honest seeker of truth.

Some significant events on this day

Year   Event

1941   Japanese bombers launch a surprise attack at Pearl Harbour, killing 2400 Americans.

1975   Following Portugal's withdrawal, Indonesian troops invade East Timor. They remained there until 1999.

1988   A massive earthquake in the Soviet republic of Armenia kills an estimated 55,000 people.

Key thought for today

And the lonely voice of youth cries: 'What is truth?'
— Johnny Cash

Reflection

By Br Bill Firman

There are some people who like to think that the Bible gives us absolute truth in every aspect. They want absolute certainty, but life isn't like that. God gave us a universe in which we are frequently discovering new wonders – especially as science delivers better tools – and which we are seeking to understand better. In fact, God made a world which is constantly changing and evolving, not one which is static and immutable.

The church was once so certain that the earth was at the centre of the universe that Galileo was branded a heretic and made to recant his heliocentric theory because his wisdom did not match the conventional wisdom of the day. In fact Galileo was also wrong – the universe is not heliocentric – but he was nearer the truth than the geocentric position espoused by the church of his day.

Some people cling to certainty and some, especially in positions of power, can tend to assert a dogmatic claim, at times an almost arrogant claim, to possess the truth. There are some clear truths that have their source in the Bible and the teaching of Jesus, but they are rather broad and based on what we know are the qualities of God: God is the creator, God is good, God is the truth, God loves us.

But what about humankind? We don't even know if we are unique or whether God has created other intelligent species. We know our knowledge is imperfect, we know we are called to love God, but we can be very confused about how to do that. We can be too certain, too judgemental, too self-righteous. We are, then, subjective seekers of the truth, not possessors of objective truth. Bishop Geoffrey Robinson has this to say:

> *It is possible to move beyond a subjective understanding of goodness to a more objective understanding of what God's goodness asks of us, but it involves a serious and never-ending search, both for individuals and for the whole human race. We should spend our whole life in this search, while also constantly making decisions and acting on the basis of our present and inadequate understanding of that goodness.*

Prayer

Remind me, Lord, that I am not God, but that I must seek to understand what God's goodness is asking of me and how to use the gifts God has given to me.

Reflecting God's Presence

Some significant events on this day

Year	Event
	The feast day, adopted in the 7th century, of the Immaculate Conception of Mary, the Mother of God, conceived in her mother St Anne without stain of sin.
1941	The US declares war on Japan, the day after the Japanese bombing of Pearl Harbour.
1980	John Lennon is shot dead in New York by 25-year-old Mark Chapman.
1987	The first arms reduction agreement between the two superpowers is signed by Soviet leader Mikhail Gorbachev and US president Ronald Regan.
1987	Frank Vitkovic, aged 22, fatally shoots eight people in the Australia Post building, Queen Street, Melbourne, before leaping to his death from the 11th floor.

Key thoughts for today

A yawn is a silent shout.
— G.K. Chesterton

Faith is not just something you have; it's something you do.
— Barack Obama

Reflection

By Hilary Hayes, old Collegian

Early in my time at De La Salle, on 19 March 1937, Pope Pius XII commented

> *There are still too many Catholics who are Catholic hardly more than in name. There are still too many who fulfil more or less faithfully the essential obligations of the religion they boast of possessing but have no desire of knowing it better, of deepening their inward convictions.*

Seventy years later, things have surely not improved in many cases. Faithfulness to 'essential obligations' has greatly lessened, numerous men and women no longer boast of professing the faith and grow further away, so that more than a generation lack any regular attachment to the faith. Whatever impression might be gained from occasions such as World Youth Day, or others designed to rally enthusiasm for religious issues, we are now in the midst of a crisis of faith, and that can lead to a crisis in many aspects of our lives.

In the final analysis, it comes down to individual effort and application if the present problems are to be solved. I believe that we are here to fulfil an eternal destiny, to achieve personal holiness, whatever vocation we follow. We must listen to the God who loves us and take steps to grow in the knowledge of the faith, not only for ourselves but for the generations to follow.

Prayer

Lord, increase our faith, support us in our needs and give us the grace to know you better day by day.

Some significant events on this day

Year   Event

1758   Matthew Flinders and George Bass confirm that Van Diemen's Land (Tasmania) is separated from Australia.

1929   Birthday of Bob Hawke, later to become Australian prime minister.

1992   Prince Charles and Princess Diana announce their plans to separate.

2002   America's second largest air carrier, United Airlines, after losing $4 billion over the previous two years, files for Chapter Eleven Bankruptcy.

Key thought for today

It is not because things are difficult that we do not dare; it is because we do not dare that thinga are difficult.

— Seneca

Reflection

By Brian Long

In one of the stories in the New Testament, Jesus calls Peter to leave his boat and walk across the water to him (Matthew 14:22-34). This is how I imagine Peter might recall the scene:

Jesus had spoken these words: 'Peter, come to me.'

I had stepped out of my boat before, always to feel the lumpy pebbles and swirling mud on my bare feet. This time nothing, only water. The wind tore at me. Waves snatched at legs. I felt fearful water, deep sea, the deepest fear of all fishermen – the unknown depths tugging at me, dragging my heart, my soul into blackness. My heart closed, and like lead I began to sink. I would die. I reached out in my terror, eyes pleading, crying out to my Lord. Arms imploring into cold, scalding rain and roaring wind, I called in an agony of despair, 'Lord, save me. I'm drowning.'

At once Jesus stretched out his hand and saved me.

I was lifted up. He held me tight.

He looked at me. He had a way of looking at me when I had acted out of fear or weakness of heart. He simply looked and loved and knew. He said gently,

'Peter, my beloved, you need not have been afraid. I am with you. Would I let you drown? Would I let the waters overwhelm you? I called you to me. You are mine. I will never let you go. My hand is always outstretched to save. Do not fear. I love you.'

Prayer

Jesus, remind me when I am afraid that all I have to do is stretch out my arms and call to you. You will never fail to answer me, and all will be well. Amen.

Reflecting God's Presence

Some significant events on this day

Year   Event

1868   The first traffic lights, comprising red and green gas lamps and semaphore arms, are installed near London's Houses of Parliament.

1901   The inaugural Nobel Prizes are awarded.

1902   In Egypt, the Aswan Dam on the Nile River, 40 metres high and two kilometres long, is completed.

1948   The United Nations General Assembly, meeting in Paris, adopts and proclaims the Universal Declaration of Human Rights. The anniversary of this event is marked each year as International Human Rights Day.

1996   President Nelson Mandela signs a new democratic constitution for South Africa.

Key thought for today

To be a human being is, precisely, to be responsible.
— Antoine de Saint-Exupéry

Reflection

By Br Bill Firman

On submitting the Declaration of Human Rights in 1948, just over three years after the end of World War II, Eleanor Roosevelt said: 'We stand today at the threshold of a great event in the life of the United Nations and in the life of mankind.' The Declaration was a clear expression of people's rights and responsibilities, but they continue to be ignored by oppressive regimes around the globe with appalling consequences for innocent people.

In 1963, the pope who in my life time has inspired me more than any other, John XXIII, published the great Catholic document on human rights, *Pacem in Terris.* In this encyclical, he says:

> *'It is generally accepted today that the common good is best safeguarded when personal rights and duties are guaranteed. The chief concern of civil authorities must therefore be to ensure that these rights are recognised, respected, coordinated, defended and promoted, and that all people are enabled to perform their duties more easily. To safeguard the inviolable rights of human persons, and to facilitate the performance of their duties, is the principal duty of every public authority.*
>
> *Thus any government which refused to recognise human rights or acted in violation of them, would not only fail in its duty; its decrees would be wholly lacking in binding force. One of the principal duties of any government, moreover, is the suitable and adequate superintendence and coordination of people's respective rights in society.*
>
> *This must be done in such a way that the exercise of their rights by certain citizens does not obstruct other citizens in the exercise of theirs; that individuals, standing upon their own rights, do not impede others in the performance of their duties; and that the rights of all be effectively safeguarded and completely restored if they have been violated.*

All people share the common responsibility to respect the rights of others.

Prayer

May a profound respect for the rights of others be a key part of my personality. Amen.

Some significant events on this day

Year   Event

1936   King Edward VIII abdicates the throne of England to marry American divorcee Wallis Simpson.

1941   Germany and Italy declare war on the USA, following President Roosevelt's announcement, after the Pearl Harbour attack, that the USA was at war with Japan.

2005   Mob violence, directed at people of Middle Eastern origin, erupts at Cronulla Beach in Sydney after two local lifeguards were bashed a week earlier.

Key thought for today

Pay no attention to what the critics say; no statue has ever been erected to a critic.
— Jean Sibelius

Reflection

By Kerry Martin

> *The mass media play a crucial role in defining the problems and issues of public concern. They are the main channels of public discourse in our segregated society' (Stuart Hall).*
>
> *'The question is whether privileged elites should dominate mass communication, and should use this power as they tell us they must – to impose necessary illusions, to manipulate and deceive the stupid majority and remove them from the public arena. The question in brief is whether democracy and freedom are values to be preserved or threats to be avoided. In this possibly terminal phase of human existence, democracy and freedom are more than values to be treasured, they may well be essential to survival (Noam Chomsky).*

At university, I studied the work of both Noam Chomsky and Stuart Hall. Along with other influential media and cultural theorists, they are concerned about the power of the media. Teachers are aware of the power of the media and work to make students aware of this. Media Studies students at De La Salle develop a media literacy which enables them to decipher media messages to discern truth from non-truth.

As parents, we are concerned about the media's influence on our children, and, while most of us agree that there is some anecdotal evidence of influence, there is, to date, no empirical evidence to prove that the media has a negative influence on individuals. The media, as rock'n'roll was once, are sometimes blamed for society's troubles. For example, after the horrific Columbine High School massacre in the United States, the video game *Doom* was blamed for the actions of the perpetrators. However this viewpoint was put forward as a smokescreen to hide the real problems underpinning American society at the time. It is essential, therefore, that as educators and parents we remain open to an array of viewpoints and arguments in trying to understand young people.

Prayer

Help me never to lack courage and character in the knowledge that 'Courage is not the absence of fear, but rather the judgement that something else is more important than fear' (Ambrose Redmoon).

Reflecting God's Presence

Some significant events on this day

Year   Event

1800   Washington, DC, becomes the capital of the United States, replacing the interim capital Philadelphia.

1889   The poet Robert Browning dies.

1901   Guglielmo Marconi receives the first transatlantic radio signal in Newfoundland, USA, using a 120 metre high antenna. It was later discovered that the powerful signal, sent from Cornwall in England, must have bounced off the ionosphere twice to traverse the distance.

1939   Production begins in the DuPont plant in Delaware, USA, of nylon, a new synthetic fibre invented by Wallace Carothers.

Key thought for today

I thirst for truth, but shall not reach it till I reach the source.
   — Robert Browning

Reflection

By Br Bill Firman

Henry Ward Beecher asserted that:

Theology is but our ideas of truth classified and arranged.

His words are based on the understanding that God is the eternal truth and we are seekers after truth. St Paul urged us to live by the truth (Ephesians 4:11) and the poet John Dryden said:

Truth is the foundation of all knowledge and the cement of all societies.

The courageous, Russian, dissident author, Alexander Solzhenitsyn, who died in August 2008, aged 89, was a fearless advocate of telling the truth. He asserted that

No one can bar the road to truth, and to advance its cause I am ready to accept even death.

Unfortunately, truth seems to have been somewhat devalued in modern society and there are abundant examples of prominent people failing to be truthful. I am sure Bill Clinton must have come to regret his vehement lies about his relationship with Monica Lewinsky. Ted Kennedy lost any chance of becoming president when he lied about the death of Mary-Jo Kopechne. The lies told by Collingwood footballers Heath Shaw and Alan Didak over a drink-driving accident greatly compounded a situation where disclosure of the truth would have led to a better outcome. Truth should be a high priority value in our society. People will always make mistakes. We all share human weakness and are prepared to forgive and forget mistakes such as the poor judgement of those who drink and drive; but we are not so forgiving when we are lied to. We lose our respect for people who 'play with the truth', that is, who lie outright or who amend the actual circumstances. Truth is a value to be cherished.

Prayer

Help me adhere to the value expressed in the Turkish proverb: 'Those who speak the truth are always at ease.'

Reflecting God's Presence

Some significant events on this day

Year   Event

1577   Francis Drake sets sail from England on a voyage around the world that lasted almost three years.

1642   The Dutch explorer Abel Tasman sights the islands now called New Zealand, the first European to do so.

1937   Nanking, then capital of China, falls to the Japanese. They killed 300,000 people over the next six weeks and reduced the city to ruins.

Key thought for today

Blessed is the influence of one true, loving soul on another.
— George Eliot

Reflection

By Br Bill Firman

Former US President Jimmy Carter, had this to say about his choice in life:

> *I have one life and one chance to make it count for something ... I'm free to choose what that something is, and the something I've chosen is my faith. Now, my faith goes beyond theology and religion and requires considerable work and effort. My faith demands – this is not optional – my faith demands that I do whatever I can, whenever I can, for as long as I can, with whatever I have, to try to make a difference.*

Choosing to do whatever one can to make a difference is a fine choice indeed, and if we can hand that gift of choice to another who has lost it, we have achieved something great. If we live our own lives well, we give new hope to others.

If we help others to overcome disadvantage and transform futility into direction and purpose, we are sharing with them a great gift indeed. Extending a helping hand to others is the practical expression of loving God in a very effective way. I am sure, in the eyes of God, it makes up for any number of personal weaknesses.

If we become, metaphorically, a brother or sister to those who have no one walking beside them, we are continuing to grow and are really making our lives count. We are doing what our God asks of us. We may not be 'religious' in a formal or pious sense but we are religious in the way we live.

It is not enough to say, as the Gaoler did, in Robert Bolt's play *A Man For All Seasons*: 'You must understand my position, sir. I'm a plain, honest man and I just want to keep out of trouble.'

They were all plain, honest wayfarers who passed the injured man by, in the parable, until the Good Samaritan came along! Our faith demands we reach out to help others.

Prayer

Robert Hugh Benson once wrote that 'no man can be a friend of Jesus Christ who is not a friend of his neighbour'. May I help those who are my neighbours and grow closer to God.

Reflecting God's Presence

Some significant events on this day

Year   Event

1900   In an event marking the birth of Quantum Physics, Max Planck presents a paper to the German Physical Society, proposing that energy exists in discrete packets which he called 'quanta'.

1911   Norwegian explorer Roald Amundsen and his team arrive at the South Pole, 35 days before the British party led by Captain Robert Scott.

1918   In Britain, women are permitted to vote in a general election for the first time.

1994   The Wollemi Pine, a relic species from the dinosaur age, is found growing in the Blue Mountains in NSW.

Key thought for today

Being a Christian is more than just an instantaneous conversion – it is a daily process whereby you grow to be more and more like Christ.
   — Billy Graham

Reflection

By Phil Ryan

Not only are we to receive Christ in others as guest; we are to *be* Christ to others. This is the basis of Christian hospitality

At a daily level this means we are attentive and listening. We are ready to listen with our mind and our heart and to accept people as they are. Rather than focusing on their faults, as we do at times, we can practise hospitality by seeing the good in other people, accepting them just as Christ has accepted us. St Augustine said, 'Have Christian eyes.'

We can do what Henri Nouwen suggests when living out hospitality. He describes hospitality as a space around us that we create for others into which they can come, be themselves, and discover who they are.

When we allow people to come into our space, we need to prepare ourselves to be people of peace through prayer and by being attentive to God's love and presence in our own lives. If we are people of peace through prayer and self acceptance, we can allow others to be comfortable and experience God's abundant love through attending and listening.

Prayer

My prayer is to ask God to help us to see everyone through 'Christian eyes', to see everyone as a moment, not of interruption or annoyance but of Christ's presence. Let us pray to be open to Christ in that person while we are in a moment of attending and listening.

Some significant events on this day

Year   Event

1978   US President Jimmy Carter reverses the former government's stance, announcing that the US would recognise Communist China and sever ties with Taiwan.

1999   Two weeks of unrelenting rain in coastal Venezuela causes floods and mud slides resulting in 30,000 deaths and 100,000 homeless people.

2005   Ten million Iraqis take part in the first democratic election since the defeat of the Saddam Hussein regime.

Key thought for today

O Lord, I leave my past to your mercy, my present to your love, and my future to your providence.
— Padre Pio

Reflection

By Br Bill Firman

Faith is a personal decision. Jesus was incredibly respectful of people and always left room for our doubts and difficulties. It is the human condition to have doubts and difficulties. We are not all-knowing like God. As Thoreau has said:

Faith keeps many doubts in her pay. If I could not doubt, I should not believe.

It is natural to want certitude and unassailable convictions. I suspect that fundamentalists – those generally devout Christians who read literal truth into every statement of the Bible – are seeking too much certitude. Father Henry Fehren wrote:

Fundamentalists would stop the pilgrim church dead in its tracks.

Fundamentalists seek to impose a specificity of detail on scripture that was never intended either by the human authors or by God. Sometimes the scripture is not totally clear, leading the poet William Blake to say:

Both read the Bible day and night.
But thou read'st black where I read white.

The faithful man or woman is not the person who adheres rigidly to a black or white position but rather the honest seeker after truth, the person who makes a path through the grey, searching for God in the midst of uncertainty and even some confusion. The faithful man or woman suffers the same anguish as the man in the gospels who prayed:

Lord, I do believe; help Thou my unbelief.

Prayer

St Ignatius of Antioch said: 'Faith is the beginning and the end is love, and God is the two of them brought into unity.' Lord, help me to find you in faith and love. Amen.

Reflecting God's Presence

Some significant events on this day

Year   Event

1653   Following the execution of Charles I, Oliver Cromwell is declared Lord Protector of England.

1773   In an action, since labelled the Boston Tea Party, US colonists disguised as Mohawk Indians fling a cargo of tea into the Boston Harbour in protest at British taxes and trade restrictions.

1997   An episode of *Pokemon* on Japanese television results in 685 children suffering epileptic seizures. The particular episode is no longer broadcast anywhere in the world.

Key thought for today

An atheist is a man who believes himself an accident.
— Francis Thompson

Reflection

By Br Bill Firman

In the First World countries that were once known as Christian countries there has been a rise of secularism, with diminishing numbers attending mainstream churches and fewer vocations to the priesthood or religious congregations. The spiritual is increasingly subjugated to the material and God is rapidly removed from people's lives. 'I never left the church', said one person, 'I just drifted away.' Jesuit Tom O'Donovan writes that the removal of God results in two kinds of denial of God which one could call 'atheisms', not in the narrow, technical sense of a formal rejection of God but in the broad sense that God simply plays no part in our lives.

The first type of modern atheism O'Donovan calls the 'Atheism of Distraction'. This describes people who are too busy to have any time for God, people whose way of life affirms that religion might be okay, even good for the kids, but I don't have any time to worry about things like that. The second type O'Donovan calls the 'Atheism of Materialism'. This describes a group of self-satisfied people who believe they have all they need in the things they possess. When a young Danish woman was asked in a television interview whether or not her family went to church, she replied in words that sum up the atheism of materialism: 'We don't go to church. We have everything we want. We don't need God.'

In similar vein, George Bernard Shaw's character Major Barbara proclaims:

> *I am a millionaire. That is my religion.*

Unless we have learned to foster the love of God in our lives, unless we keep our spiritual ideals in sight, we can easily succumb to indifferentism and we shall be part of the atheism of distraction – I don't have time for God – or the atheism of materialism – I have everything I want, I don't need God. Perhaps this is part of what Jesus meant when he spoke of how hard it is for a rich man to enter the kingdom of heaven.

Prayer

Meha Baba said: 'The finding of God is the coming to one's own self.' Help me find God and recognise who I am.

Some significant events on this day

Year	Event
1843	*A Christmas Carol* by Charles Dickens is published, earning wide acclaim.
1903	Brothers Orville and Wilbur Wright make the first successful flight in a heavier-than-air machine at Kitty Hawk in North Carolina, USA.
1907	The outstanding Scottish scientist Sir William Thompson, most often referred to as Lord Kelvin, dies at the age of 82.
1967	The Australian Prime Minister Harold Holt disappears while swimming off Cheviot Beach near Portsea, Victoria. His body was never recovered.
1983	Six people are killed when an IRA car bomb explodes outside Harrods department store in London.

Key thought for today

No one is useless in this world who lightens the burden of another.
— Charles Dickens

Reflection

By Br Quentin O'Halloran

Consistency in little things

The notable Scottish scientist Lord Kelvin regularly used the following experiment when commencing his Physics course with first year university students.

From the lecture theatre ceiling, he would suspend a 50-kilogram lump of iron. He invited his students to take paper pellets from a basket on his desk and bombard the metal. At first, nothing much happened, to the amusement of the students. Then, gradually, the iron mass began to shake, move, swing and then swing wildly. The movement continued as long as the pellets were thrown. The iron came to a standstill once the pellet throwers ceased their fun.

Lord Kelvin would then encourage his budding physicists to reflect on the importance of small things in nature and life and the great power that can be wielded by consistency.

Prayer

Lord, help me to face each new day
as a gift from you.
May I be faithful in my everyday tasks
and realise that fidelity is a force of good.
Help me to look beyond the daily grind
to appreciate the wonders of nature
and of the human body, mind and spirit.

Reflecting God's Presence

Some significant events on this day

Year   Event

1915   ANZAC forces complete their retreat from Gallipoli without a casualty. The rest of the campaign cost 10,000 Australian and New Zealand lives.

1916   The Battle of Verdun, the longest engagement of World War I, ends. More than 500,000 French and German troops were killed and a similar number wounded.

1938   German chemist Otto Hahn bombards uranium with neutrons, resulting in nuclear fission. Hahn was the first person to split the atom.

Key thought for today

There is but one thing in the world worth pursuing – the knowledge of God.
— Robert Hugh Benson

Reflection

By Br Bill Firman

Our understanding of the universe has improved dramatically since space probes and extra-terrestrial telescopes, such as Hubble, have been designed and implemented. God is the creator of a universe far grander than ever before known or imagined. The limitations to our understanding of it come from our own finite intellectual and emotional capacity. We are learning more, but it is a fallacy to think that science can determine all the answers. Science is good at posing more and more questions. Every answer seems to generate ever more complex questions.

The most comfortable scientific hypothesis would be, in fact, that nothing exists and all this talk of the cosmos – and of the nature of matter – is just a giant fairytale or illusion. But with Descartes we respond: '*Cogito ergo sum.*' We know we are here because we are thinking about it.

The universe is truly awe-inspiring. The fact that God's creation is now known to be so vast reflects that God is as infinite and ubiquitous as we were brought up to believe. We will almost certainly never visit most of this universe and it is a continuing struggle to come to terms with what we can learn of it.

Nor will we ever understand everything about our faith in the loving God who made us, the awesome God who is the source and sustainer of all that is.

There is a Welsh proverb that states:

There are three things that only God knows: the beginning of things, the cause of things, and the end of things.

God is truth. We are seekers after the truth. It will be an endless search.

Prayer

Lord, 'if I climb to the highest heavens you are there'. Help me to seek to know you, to love you and to be faithful to your biblical and scientific revelation. Amen.

Reflecting God's Presence

Some significant events on this day

Year   Event

1986   Soviet leader Mikhail Gobachev releases dissident Andrei Sakharov and his activist wife Yelena Bonner from internment.

1989   US President George Bush sends US troops into Panama to overthrow Manuel Noriega's regime.

2003   Colonel Gaddafi, leader of Libya, makes a surprising pledge to destroy his country's arsenal of weapons of mass destruction.

Key thought for today

Power is the ultimate aphrodisiac.
— Henry Kissinger

Reflection

By Br Bill Firman

The founder of modern psychology, Sigmund Freud, suggested that people are motivated by an innate or instinctive search for pleasure. Freud suggested we have a sex (pleasure-seeking) drive and an aggression drive but most of his work was spent focusing on the former. Freud suggested that people act to satisfy their instinctive drive for pleasure. A disciple of Freud, Alfred Adler, was, like Freud, born in Vienna and had a medical degree. In 1902 he was invited by Freud to join his psychoanalytic circle. By 1911, however, theoretical differences between Freud and Adler had developed to the extent that Adler resigned. Whereas Freud had suggested that a person's main motivation came from an innate drive for pleasure, Adler maintained that people were more motivated by a search for power or superiority over others. Adler saw people as social beings and put less emphasis on the interior drives of the person and more on social interaction with other people.

It seems to me that young people are often motivated very much in their behaviour by a search for pleasure. They tend to make the equation that happiness is the same as pleasure and go to a frenetic round of parties, raves and the like in the pursuit of nights of pleasure. As people become older, pleasure-seeking becomes a less satisfying pastime. Much of what people do in their thirties and forties is career orientated and perhaps motivated by the seeking of power or superiority. It is not uncommon to meet a person who is prepared to put all things at risk for the sake of his or her career or status. This age group does less partying and puts more into career advancement and setting up home and family.

'Home and family' suggests there might be more to motivation than pleasure and power. The third Viennese school of psychotherapy was led by Dr Viktor Frankl, who proposed that what people are really searching for in life is meaning and he concluded that this meaning is most commonly found in love. Happiness in life is found through giving and loving.

Prayer

May I come to understand that pleasure and power are ultimately transitory and that real happiness comes from a meaningful life, loving others and helping where I can. Amen.

Reflecting God's Presence

Some significant events on this day

Year   Event

1894   The birthday of Sir Robert Menzies, Australia's longest-serving prime minister.

1987   The Philippines ferry *Dona Paz* sinks after a collision with an oil tanker, causing the deaths of more than 4300 people.

1991   After defeating Bob Hawke in a party-room ballot, Paul Keating is sworn in as prime minister of Australia.

Key thought for today

I do not want merely to possess a faith; I want a faith that possesses me.
— Charles Kingsley

Reflection

By Br Bill Firman

Dr Tracey Roland, a convert from Anglicanism to Catholicism, wrote:

> *I think that people who leave the church are not leaving the church because they are rejecting the teachings of John Paul II or Pope Benedict. Most of them leave because they go to Catholic schools and they think that the kind of warm secular humanism with Christian gloss that they get in Catholic schools is in fact the Catholic faith and it hasn't captured their imagination, their love or their intellect, so they are walking away from something that they do not know. It's not like a love affair where you reject a person you have learnt to love and know. They've never been in love with the church. They've never known it.*

For those of us who run Catholic schools, this is a major concern. Are we leading our communities beyond a warm secular humanism to a more profound understanding of the Catholic faith? Yes, good pastoral care, a compassionate and caring environment and a strong sense of community are important, but seeking God and possessing religious faith is more than that. In recent years, the stronger emphasis on social justice – helping others because we believe every person is deserving of love and therefore important enough to deserve help – is an excellent development. But unless there is some accurate knowledge of the revelation handed on through scripture and the scholarship and traditions of the church down the ages, there is every possibility we will drift away from a church we have never really known.

The challenge for those leaving school is to explore a theological basis for decision-making. When someone can explain the principal mysteries of the Incarnation and the Holy Trinity, as revealed through scripture and tradition, I can accept that he or she may then be in a position to decide to leave the church conscientiously. A profound religious thinker such as C.S. Lewis tried to turn atheist but couldn't make that step and maintain personal intellectual integrity. Most people do not act with such honesty and conviction but simply drift into a comfortable, secular humanism capable of expedient rationalisation to suit whatever they want to do.

Prayer

God, grant me to be genuine in seeking to understand the real basis of religious belief rather than just drift away from an inadequate childhood understanding.

Some significant events on this day

The summer solstice, the longest day of the year in the southern hemisphere.

Year	Event
1620	Pilgrims on the *Mayflower* land at Plymouth, Massachusetts, where they established one of America's earliest successful colonies.
1940	The death of American author F. Scott Fitzgerald.
1948	With the signing of the Republic of Ireland Act, enforced on 18 April 1949, the state of Eire becomes a republic and leaves the British Commonwealth.
1958	General Charles de Gaulle is elected in France by a wide margin to become the first president of France's Fifth Republic.

Key thought for today

Either you think, or else others have to think for you and take power from you, pervert and discipline your natural tastes, civilise and sterilise you.
— F. Scott Fitzgerald

Reflection

By Tom McIlroy

Ask young men their favourite book and one of the most frequent answers is *The Great Gatsby* by F. Scott Fitzgerald. Fitzgerald's life was a sad one, plagued by alcoholism and the mental illness that haunted his wife Zelda, but his wisdom in his 1925 masterpiece has helped form the minds of students for decades. The book begins with the protagonist, Nick Carraway:

> 'In my younger and more vulnerable years', he explains, 'my father gave me some advice that I've been turning over in my head ever since. "Whenever you feel like criticising anyone ... just remember that all the people in this world haven't had the advantages that you've had".'

This wise yet simple lesson is often read by young men and women just as they are on the verge of learning for themselves the realities of growing up – as they begin to recognise the loss of some of the innocence that is a requisite of being young. Slowly we see things that were invisible before. Our eyes and ears are open to events in our families, difficulties between friends and colleagues, and eventually we learn of the hardship and pain that greet us all at some point or other. Equally, we discover the wonders of independence and love and understanding of others. We see our parents as the most accessible heroes and our friends as the truest companions. Importantly, we begin to see ourselves free of some of the self-consciousness that has visited us every day in our youth.

Prayer

F. Scott Fitzgerald advised: 'Never confuse a single defeat with a final defeat.' Let us always have the courage to pick ourselves up and to try again. Help us, Lord, to remember you are with us in good times and bad, and that you watch over us and protect us. We pray that we can be there for friends and loved ones. Amen.

Reflecting God's Presence

Some significant events on this day

Year   Event

1938   The coelacanth, a fish species considered to have been extinct for 70 million years, is discovered in the Indian Ocean.

1988   Brazilian environmental campaigner Chico Mendes is shot dead by the son of a cattle rancher.

1993   The Australian federal government, led by Prime Minister Paul Keating, passes the Native Title Act recognising the traditional rights and interests of Aboriginal and Torres Strait Islanders.

Key thought for today

If you miss your moment, you spend the rest of your life paying for it.
— Mikhail Gorbachev

Reflection

By Br Bill Firman

Billy Graham used to say:

> *Most of us follow our conscience as we follow a wheel barrow. We push it in front of us in the direction we want to go.*

It is amazing how flexible our consciences can become if we have a particular action we want to justify! The opinion of a child is generally not as good as the opinion of his or her parent. The child lacks experience and knowledge. The opinion of a student is not as good as that of the teacher – until the student matches the teacher in scholarship and understanding.

If a leader decrees that something is right or wrong, one can assume that they have taken advice from experts and have studied the issue. Yes, we retain the right to follow our conscience and make our own decisions – but only if we have taken the trouble to look seriously at the issues. We must have an 'informed conscience' not just a funny interior feeling! Understanding obligation is part of the process of forming our conscience. But are we not still free to do as we like? It depends on what one means by 'freedom'. Charles Kingsley said:

> *There are two freedoms – the false, where we are free to do what we like; the true, where we are free to do what we ought.*

In life, we seek the truth of knowing what we ought to do as a creature of God. It is then our free choice to live up to what we know is right, or not. We become integral people by choosing to do what we know to be right, not what we like – unless it is the same thing. It was Eddie Cantor who wryly remarked:

> *A sleeping pill will never take the place of a clear conscience.*

People who develop a clear set of values and live conscientiously in accord with those values are integral people. They are just and honest people. You can't achieve that by taking a pill.

Prayer

Lord, I am free to be a person of principle and values. Help me to be one, so that I may live comfortably with myself. Amen.

Some significant events on this day

Year Event

1888 Dutch painter Vincent Van Gogh slices off part of his ear following an argument with fellow artist Paul Gauguin.

1947 A new era in electronics is ushered in with the development by Bell laboratories of the transistor.

1986 The *Voyager* aircraft, piloted by Americans Dick Rutan and Jeana Yeager, completes the first non-stop flight around the globe on one load of fuel.

Key thought for today

Know how sublime a thing it is to suffer and be strong.
— H. W. Longfellow

Reflection

By St John Baptist de La Salle

Jesus Christ predicted to his apostles the persecutions they would have to suffer. The reason the world maltreats and insults the disciples of Jesus is because this world has not known him nor his Father who sent him. Indeed worldly people, as a rule, have no love except for people like themselves, that is for those who enjoy nothing but what caters to their senses. They have only a very imperfect knowledge of God, as they do not think about him, never speak about him, do not willingly hear about him, and scarcely ever pray to him!

At times you may have to teach children who do not know God because they have been brought up by parents who do not know God themselves. Strive to know God so well through reading and prayer that you may be able to make him known to others, and make him loved by all those to whom you have made him known (Meditations for Sundays and Feasts).

The honour we pay to the Cross of Christ should not be limited to showing it respect and veneration. Rather, we must love it with all the affection of our hearts and desire to die attached to it. Because we have been freed from sin by means of it, we must not doubt that if we love the cross in union with Jesus Christ all the miseries of this life will become pleasant and agreeable to us. In this way we will be truly happy, having found our paradise in this world.

As Minucius Felix so well says, although Jesus Christ requires that we adore his holy cross, yet that is not what he asks the most; it is that we drink cheerfully of his sacred chalice if we desire to be his friend and to have a place with him in his kingdom. Let us then place all our glory in bearing in our bodies the sacred wounds of the suffering Jesus. When you have some trouble, unite yourself to Jesus suffering and this will soothe your pains (Meditations for Sundays and Feasts).

Prayer

Lord, help me to accept that what is annoying, upsetting or uncomfortable, can make me stronger. Amen.

Reflecting God's Presence

24 DECEMBER

Some significant events on this day

Year   Event

1851   Thirty-five thousand volumes, including most of Thomas Jefferson's personal collection, are destroyed when fire rages through the Library of Congress in Washington, DC.

1865   The Ku Klux Klan is established in Tennessee by six confederate veterans of the American Civil War.

1968   *Apollo 8* carries the first humans to orbit the moon to within 110 kilometres of its surface.

Key thought for today

The light shone in the darkness and the darkness did not overcome it.
— Saint John's Gospel 1:5

Reflection

By Br Bill Firman

The original lyrics of the Tyrolean folk song *Silent Night* (in German, *Stille Nacht*) were written in German by Pastor Joseph Mohr of the Church of St Nicholas in Oberndorf, Austria, in 1816. The music was added two years later by Franz Gruber, the choir master. The popularity of the song spread and it became a well-known Christmas carol translated into many other languages.

The First World War began on 1 August 1914, when Germany declared war on Russia – the Eastern Front – and two days later Germany declared war on France – the Western Front. The troops heading off to war were told they would be home by Christmas!

By mid-September, trenches were appearing and both sides dug in not very far apart. On Christmas eve at Ypres in Belgium, German troops on one side and British on the other, began singing *Silent Night* in their own languages. Eventually, soldiers emerged from their trenches and met in no man's land, setting up a Christmas tree and exchanging gifts such as cigars, jam and whisky. This was a moment of Christmas peace when human spirits rose above the dreadful conflict. No shots were fired. Emulation of the truce spread to the Eastern Front, and there were also examples of Christmas truces in later conflicts such as World War II.

Alfred Anderson, last survivor of the original Christmas Truce, died in 2005, aged 109. The truce has been depicted in three movies: Richard Attenborough's *Oh What a Lovely War* (1969), *Snoopy and The Red Baron* (1999) and *Joyeux Noel* (2005).

In modern society, those who decide to send troops to war are not the same people who fight the battles. Peace in the hearts of individuals can sometimes rise above the hideous conflict in which they are embroiled. Soldiers on both sides have much in common as human beings; they are not simple statistics.

Prayer

The proverb wisely says: 'It is better to light a candle than to curse the darkness.' Let me light a few candles, as did the brave men of that Christmas truce.

Some significant events on this day

Year   Event

Celebration of the birth of Jesus Christ

1926   Prince Hirohito becomes the 124th Emperor of Japan. He reigned until his death in 1989, the longest serving emperor in Japanese history.

1974   Cyclone Tracy kills 63 people in Darwin, injuring hundreds and destroying 90 per cent of the city's buildings.

1991   Mikhail Gorbachev resigns as president, bringing the final chapter of the USSR to a close. He had been named *Time* magazine's 'Man of the Decade' in 1989 and won the Nobel Peace Prize in 1990 for his role in ending the Cold War.

Key thought for today

We make a living by what we get but we make a life by what we give.
— Sir Winston Churchill

Reflection

By Br Bill Firman

There is something magical about Christmas, a time when busy society eventually stops to put commerce aside and family first. Although one cannot deny there is an intense period of commercial trading leading up to Christmas, Christmas is a time when we unite with family and friends and recall what is most important.

The nineteenth century essayist and poet Washington Irving once wrote:

Christmas!'Tis the season for kindling the fire of hospitality in the hall, the genial fire of charity in the heart.

I like that expression, 'the genial fire of charity in the heart'. It captures, with poetic imagery, the essence of the Gospel beatitude that it is more blessed to give than receive. Our hearts are warmed when we reach out to others in need. W.C. Jones, of whom I know little but who is sometimes quoted on Christmas cards, accurately describes the special character of Christmas giving in these terms:

The joy of brightening other lives, bearing with each other's burdens, easing each other's loads and supplanting empty hearts and lives with generous gifts becomes for us the magic of Christmas.

Of course, the spirit of giving and caring should apply all year round. There is no greater gift to a hungry person than to appease that hunger. There is no greater gift to a cold and homeless person than the gift of shelter. There is no greater gift to the unemployed than the dignity that comes with a job and the capacity to earn a living. There is no greater gift to a child than security and love.

Christmas, nonetheless, is a special time for giving to those whom we love but whom we often take for granted.

Prayer

May I forget any grievances and ensure 'the genial fire of charity' burns strongly in my heart towards everyone I meet today.

Reflecting God's Presence

Some significant events on this day

Year   Event

1943   The German battleship *Scharnhorst* is sunk. Only 36 survived from a crew of 2000.

1982   Rather than the usual nomination of a 'Man of the Year', *Time* magazine names a 'Machine of the Year' – the computer, .

2004   A tsunami kills 250,000 people in 11 countries bordering the Indian Ocean.

Key thought for today

Love is the one thing that cannot hurt your neighbour; that is why it is the answer to every one of the commandments.

— Romans 13:10

Reflection

By Br Bill Firman

More than two hundred thousand people died in very few minutes when a terrifying tsunami struck Asian countries on Boxing Day, 2004. A deep tectonic movement in the Indian Ocean had unleashed awesome destruction on many surrounding countries.

In among the wholesale devastation and loss of life, there were stories of heroic survival and courage. No doubt the survivors – and those gallant people who went to their aid – now have to live with nightmarish memories.

We cannot imagine how anyone might cope with searching for, discovering and identifying decomposing bodies in the weeks and months that followed. Yet people had to carry out this gruesome task – ordinary people finding extraordinary, heroic strength in a time of need.

There were some positive outcomes. Political and religious differences suddenly assumed less significance. People helped others simply because they were fellow human beings needing help. The brotherhood and sisterhood of humankind evoked deep compassion and washed away superficial bigotry.

Some high profile people with substantial resources made commendably large donations but it was the incredible number of people who contributed that was quite overwhelming. The totals raised by relief appeals far exceeded the expectations of most of us – and our prime minister enjoyed popular support in pledging a billion dollars in aid. It felt good to be Australian.

Prayer

'How happy are the poor in spirit; theirs is the kingdom of heaven ...
Happy those who mourn; they shall be comforted ...
Happy the merciful; they shall have mercy shown them ...
Happy the pure of heart; they shall see God.'

27 DECEMBER

Reflecting God's Presence

Some significant events on this day

Year   Event

1949   Indonesia gains independence from the Netherlands, ending Dutch colonial rule.

1979   Soviet troops invade Afghanistan to support the embattled Marxist government.

1985   American naturalist Dian Fossey is found murdered at a gorilla research station in Rwanda. Her work was made known by her book and the film based on it, *Gorillas in the Mist*.

Key thought for today

What children expect from grownups is not to be 'understood', but only to be loved, even though this love may be expressed clumsily or in sternness. Intimacy does not exist between generations – only trust.
— Carl Zucker

Reflection

By Br Bill Firman: Here is an extract from *Celtic Meditations* by Edward J. Farrell. It is well worth thinking about as we enjoy Christmas with children.

We are already beyond childhood when we begin to recognise children, yet we never let go of our lost childhood. Every year of our childhood remains within us and our delight with little children is in having them discover the little child in us.

Children are little people and we are continually amazed at their various sizes, shapes, forms. Some people are bird watchers; but all people are child watchers. Children give birth to adults time and again. How a child can lead us, free us, unite us! How much peace, joy, hope a child can bring to a street, a room, a bus, a plane.

To walk with a child is to learn how to walk all over again. It is to see with new eyes, to hear with new ears, to touch with new hands. Children are the first blessing uttered by God in creation. And every child is a promise, a guarantee that God has not yet given up on the world.

The world of a child is today, the immediate environment – what I see, touch, smell, taste. Knowledge, the history of good and evil have not yet appeared. There exists unlimited possibility for goodness or its opposite. It is the age of un-premeditation; everything is total experience. Reflection, understanding are but beginning.

What would our life be like without little children? What would happen to us without Christmas? Jesus was a baby! He has lived every year of our childhood. How central is his theme: 'Unless you become like little children ...' 'A little child shall lead them', says the prophet Isaiah. The more we discover the Father, Abba, the more we can become little children.

Prayer

Eleanor Farjeon said that 'the events of childhood do not pass but repeat themselves like seasons of the year'. So let us rejoice and give thanks for the joy of children at Christmas each year.

Reflecting God's Presence

Some significant events on this day

Year Event

1065 London's Westminster Abbey is consecrated.

1895 The first genuine motion picture is screened by French brothers Louis and Auguste Lumière, using their new invention, the cinématographe.

1989 Eleven people are killed in an earthquake in Newcastle, NSW.

1998 In a Sydney to Hobart yacht race, wild seas lead to six drownings off the NSW south coast; 115 boats started and only 44 finished,

Key thought for today

The glory of friendship is not the outstretched hand, nor the kindly smile, nor the joy of companionship: it is the spiritual inspiration that comes to one when he discovers that someone else believes in him and is prepared to trust him with his friendship.
— Ralph Waldo Emerson

Reflection

By Bryan Smith and Felicity MacDonald

Growing in acceptance

Strangers move in down the street. Alien. Different. Impoverished refugees. Culturally different, physically different. Tall and lanky, coal-black skin, electric-coloured clothes. Don't speak English. Suspicion and mistrust. A gulf between us and them.

Then, one hot summer's day, you notice your kids have become embroiled with them in a game of hide and seek. You spy them in the back yard, shooting hoops at the basketball ring. Then they're at the back door, lining up for a glass of cordial. A knock on the door and their mum is looking for them. Your wife invites her in. A broken English conversation over cups of tea. Soon, driving lessons, sharing food and informal English classes are happening. You're invited over for a meal or a celebration.

Gradually, they are not strangers at all, but new-found friends.

Prayer

Shirley MacLaine said that 'Fear makes strangers of people who would be friends.' Help me overcome my fear of strangers, especially those who are obviously very different in appearance from me. Help me understand their fear of me. Help us together to be friends. Amen.

Reflecting God's Presence

Some significant events on this day

Year   Event

1972   After their rescue, the survivors of a plane crash in the Andes admit to eating the bodies of fellow passengers to stay alive.

1997   To prevent the spread of avian (bird) flu to humans, the Hong Kong government orders the culling of all chickens – an estimated 1.2 million.

1998   Khmer Rouge leaders publicly apologise for the 'killing fields' slaughter of the 1970s, in which an estimated 1.7 million Cambodians were killed.

Key thought for today

Hold fast to simplicity of heart and innocence. Yes, be as infants who do not know the wickedness that destroys people's lives.

— The Shepherd of Hermas

Reflection

By Br Bill Firman

Holiness consists in being yourself. For the adult, it is to be an adult; for the child, it is to be a child. It takes time to grow up. Childhood is a time of wondrous excitement. Yes, the aim is for a child to become a responsible adult eventually, but there is no virtue in trying to accelerate that process and thereby deprive the child of the opportunity to experience a full and comprehensive childhood.

In a newspaper column, researcher Hugh Mackay describes 'Accelerated Child' (AC) syndrome as:

> ... reflecting the curious desire of parents ... to hasten their children's development towards adulthood by encouraging them to act like mini-adults. The 'training bra' for pre-pubescent girls was an early sign of the AC syndrome. Now you can find parents who willingly serve young children drinks that simulate adult cocktails and who buy their daughters clothes, shoes, cosmetics, dolls and music designed to create the illusion of a precocious, premature sexuality ... The likely consequence of accelerated childhood is degenerated childhood. If we wrap our kids in the cloak of adolescence before they are emotionally ready to wear it, they are bound to be corrupted ... There are parents who phone each other to work out ways of saying a collective 'no' to pressures they regard as destructive of their children's innocence and natural development. But others seem cheerfully complicit in the process of tarnishing the innocence of their own offspring.

I believe parents should encourage kids to enjoy kids' activities that are not 'sophisticated'. The best way is for parents to give their kids time and to join in the kids' activities whenever they can – even hide and seek. We should make it plain in all we say and do that childhood is there to be enjoyed fully while we are young enough. There is plenty of time later to be an adult.

Prayer

May we cherish the gift of childhood and encourage children to enjoy being children to the full. Childish things are good for children. Time enough to be adults later.

Reflecting God's Presence

Some significant events on this day

Year	Event
1903	When Chicago's recently opened Iroquois Theatre goes up in flames, some 600 people perish.
1922	The Union of Soviet Socialist Republics (USSR) is formally established.
1924	Astronomer Edwin Hubble reveals there are galaxies beyond the Milky Way.
1999	Former Beatle George Harrison is stabbed several times in the chest but recovers. He lived two more years before dying from lung cancer.

Key thoughts for today

The gem cannot be polished without friction, nor humanity perfected without trials.
— Confucius

Reflection

By Br Bill Firman

Scientists cannot create life but they do play at the edges of life. Could it ever reach the stage that a top sportsman sells his sperm, or a sportswoman an ovum, for the purpose of breeding a super-athlete? It could become possible, but it should never be permitted. Even in the thoroughbred racehorse industry there are strict rules on artificial breeding in order to avoid the devaluing of stock. Cloning horses is forbidden. Cloning humans would be debasing the human personality.

I believe strongly in the principle that only God gives life and only God can take it away. While it is legitimate to use medicine and our knowledge of science to assist the preservation of life, it is not legitimate for one person to decide to take life away from another. Euthanasia cannot be justified. Nor can suicide, although those who take their own lives may be so depressed as to be unable to think clearly and therefore have diminished personal responsibility.

Stephen Hawking, diagnosed in 1962 with Lou Gehrig's disease, was told by doctors he had two or three years to live. He could have been a candidate for euthanasia if he had been less optimistic. He has now lived more than forty years since that diagnosis. Jane Hawking, Stephen's wife and a Christian, said in 1986:

> *Without my faith in God, I wouldn't have been able to live in this situation [the deteriorating health of her husband]. I would not have been able to marry Stephen in the first place because I wouldn't have had the optimism to carry me through and I wouldn't have been able to carry on with it.*

Stephen Hawking is one of our modern-day gems, a brilliant, polished thinker who has not let the frailty of his existence diminish his achievements. Maybe his physical limitations have even spurred him on to become the person many would call the greatest living scientist today.

Prayer

Lord, we thank you for the inspiration of people like Stephen Hawking and his wife. What have I to complain about? What excuse do I have for not achieving?

Some significant events on this day

Year   Event

1933   Charles Darrow patents the board game *Monopoly* in the USA. A London version of the game was launched the following year.

1948   Death of racing-car driver Malcolm Campbell, father of Donald Campbell.

1964   Englishman Donald Campbell sets a world water speed record of 441.71 km/hr in *Bluebird* in Perth, WA, becoming the first man to hold world land and water speed records in the same year.

1999   Boris Yeltsin resigns as Russian president, handing over power to Vladimir Putin as acting president.

1999   The United States, who built the Panama Canal, opened in 1914, finally transfers control to Panama.

Key thought for today

The future belongs to those who give the next generation reason for hope.
— Teilhard de Chardin

Reflection

By Br Quentin O'Halloran: I offer this farewell message to Year 12 students.

> *And when time has blazed a path beyond*
> *the horizon, to see day surrender to night,*
> *I will hold your memories close to myself.*
> *When I travel to the edge of heaven,*
> *I will remember our being together.*
> *When my heart yearns for the voices of friends,*
> *for the laughter and tears,*
> *then I will turn to your echoes.*
> *But, for now, it is over,*
> *and I can only promise never to forget.*

Prayer

> *Look to this day!*
> *For it is life,*
> *the very life of life.*
> *In its brief course*
> *lie all the verities*
> *and realities of your existence:*
> *the bliss of growth;*
> *the glory of action;*
> *the splendour of achievement.*
> *For yesterday is but a dream,*
> *and tomorrow is only a vision.*
> *But today, well lived,*
> *makes every yesterday*
> *a dream of happiness,*
> *and every tomorrow*
> *a vision of hope.*

(attributed to the ancient Sanskrit poet, Kalidasa)

☆ ☆ ☆ ☆ ☆ ☆ ── *Mirabile dictu* ── ☆ ☆ ☆ ☆ ☆ ☆

Mirabile dictu

Mirabile dictu

☆ ☆ ☆ ☆ ☆ ☆ —— *Mirabile dictu* —— ☆ ☆ ☆ ☆ ☆

☆ ☆ ☆ ☆ ☆ ☆ —— *Mirabile dictu* —— ☆ ☆ ☆ ☆ ☆ ☆

www.ingramcontent.com/pod-product-compliance
Lightning Source LLC
Chambersburg PA
CBHW081227080526
44587CB00022B/3846